NATIONAL TELEVISION V[I]OLENCE STUDY

3

University of California, Santa Barbara
University of North Carolina, Chapel Hill
University of Texas, Austin
University of Wisconsin, Madison

Edited by
Center for Communication and Social Policy,
University of California, Santa Barbara

SAGE Publications
International Educational and Professional Publisher
Thousand Oaks   London   New Delhi

For information:

 SAGE Publications, Inc.
2455 Teller Road
Thousand Oaks, California 91320
E-mail: order@sagepub.com

SAGE Publications Ltd.
6 Bonhill Street
London EC2A 4PU
United Kingdom

SAGE Publications India Pvt. Ltd.
M-32 Market
Greater Kailash I
New Delhi 110 048 India

Printed in the United States of America

Library of Congress Cataloging-in-Publication Data

Volume I   ISBN 0-7619-0801-3 (cloth)
              ISBN 0-7619-0802-1 (paper)

Volume II   ISBN 0-7619-1087-5 (cloth)
              ISBN 0-7619-1088-3 (paper)

Volume III   ISBN 0-7619-1653-9 (cloth)
              ISBN 0-7619-1654-7 (paper)

98 99 00 01 02 03 04 7 6 5 4 3 2 1

Acquiring Editor: Margaret Seawell
Production Editor: Sherrise M. Purdum
Keylining: Christina M. Hill
Cover Designer: Ravi Balasuriya
Print Buyer: Anna Chin

CONTENTS

ACKNOWLEDGMENTS xii

INTRODUCTION 1

Joel Federman

Project Overview 1
Learning Aggression in the Television Environment 2
Report Goals 3

PART I VIOLENCE IN TELEVISION PROGRAMMING OVERALL:
UNIVERSITY OF CALIFORNIA, SANTA BARBARA STUDY 5

Stacy L. Smith, Dr. Barbara J. Wilson, Dr. Dale Kunkel, Dr. Dan Linz,
Dr. W. James Potter, Carolyn M. Colvin, and Dr. Edward Donnerstein

SUMMARY 7

BACKGROUND AND OVERVIEW OF THE STUDY 8
    Foundations Underlying the Research 10
    The Importance of Context 11
    Nature of Perpetrator 14
        Nature of Target 14
        Reason for Violence 14
        Presence of Weapons 15
        Extent and Graphicness of Violence 15
        Realism of Violence 16
        Rewards and Punishments 17
        Consequences of Violence 17
        Humor 18
        Developmental Differences in the Processing of Television Content 19
        Summary: Contextual Patterns 19
    Overview of the Content Analysis Framework 20
        Definition of Violence 20
        Units of Analysis 21
        Measures 22
        Coding of Content 22
        Sample 22
    Conclusion 23

DESCRIPTION OF METHODS..25

Sample of Programs 25
    Basic Parameters of the Sample 25
    Obtaining a Representative Sample of the Program Population.................... 26
    Summary Description of the Sample 28
Content Measures 30
    Definition of Violence 30
    Units of Analysis 30
    Contextual Measures 32
Coding and Reliability 37
    Checking the Quality of Data 38
    Check for Fatigue in Coder Performance 42
    Summary of Reliability 42
Three-Year Assessment of the Methods 47
    The Sample 47
    Checking the Quality of Data 51
    Reliability 51
    Summary of Methods 52

RESULTS: YEAR THREE DATA 56

The Presence of Violence: Prevalence, Saturation, and Rate 58
    Prevalence... 58
    Saturation... 60
    Rate 62
    Prevalence of Programming With an Anti-Violence Theme 62
    Adjusted Presence 62
    Summary of Presence 63
Context: The Meaning of the Violence 63
    Nature of the Perpetrator 64
    Summary of Perpetrators.. 69
    Nature of the Target 70
    Summary of Targets.. 74
    Reasons for Violence 75
    Justification.. 76
    Means/Presence of Weapons 76
    Extent of Violence 78
    Graphicness of Violence.. 80
    Realism 83
    Rewards and Punishments.. 87
    Consequences of Violence.. 90
    Humor 97
    Sexual Violence 98
    Programming with an Anti-Violence Theme 99

Drama Series..99
Comedy Series...101
Reality Programming 101
Movies 102
Children's Programming 103
Music Video 103
Analysis of Prime-time Programming 104
Summary of Results 107
Presence of Violence 107
Saturation of Violence 107
Rate of Violence 107
Protection from Violence...108
Context or Nature of Violent Portrayals 108

ASSESSING CHANGE IN TELEVISION VIOLENCE....................................**110**
Thresholds for Detecting Change 110
Statistical Significance 111
Practical Differences 112
The Pattern of Differences 112
Measurement Error for the Contextual Variables 113
Prevalence Levels for Violent Programming 114
Overall Prevalence...114
Prevalence by Channel and Genre 115
Three-Year Comparison of Demographics and Attributes
of Perpetrators and Targets 117
Assessing Change on the Major Contextual Variables in
Television Programming Overall 119
Assessing Change on the Major Contextual Variables by
Channel Type and Genre 122
Changes by Channel Type 122
Changes by Program Genre 123
Prime-time Analysis 123
Prevalence of Violence 123
Major Contextual Variables...124
Summary of Prime-time Analyses 126
Conclusions About Change in the Prevalence and
Contextual Patterns of Violent Portrayals 126

**HIGH-RISK PORTRAYALS THAT ENCOURAGE LEARNING
OF AGGRESSION** **128**
Composite for Learning: Definitional Issues....................................129
Unit of Analysis: Violent Interactions Rather Than Programs..........131
The Need for Two Composites: Developmental Considerations 132

Filters for High Risk... 133
Results.. 135
    High Risk for Young Children... 135
    High Risk for Older Children & Adolescents........................ 145
    Change in High-Risk Patterns Since 1995-96 154
Examples of High-Risk Violent Interactions 158
Summary.. 161

DISCUSSION **164**
    What Does Violence on Television Look Like? 164
    Has Violence on Television Changed Over the Past Three Years?...... 166
    How Is Violence Presented Across Different Types of Channels?...... 169
    How Is Violence Presented Across Different Types of Program Genres? 172
    What Portrayals Pose a High Risk for Children's Learning of Aggression?....... 175
    Recommendations 176
        For the Television Industry 176
        For Public Policy-makers 180
        For Parents 182
        For the Academic Community 184
        Final Thoughts... 186

REFERENCES **188**

APPENDIX 1: NATIONAL TELEVISION VIOLENCE STUDY
SAMPLE OF PROGRAMS FOR CONTENT ANALYSIS 1996–1997 ....**195**
    National Television Violence Study Sample of Programs for
        Content Analysis: Sample of Programs for Content Analysis........................ 196
    Legend for Scheduling Grid... 196

PART II. TELEVISION VIOLENCE IN
"REALITY" (NON-FICTIONAL) PROGRAMMING:
UNIVERSITY OF TEXAS AT AUSTIN STUDY 221

Dr. Charles Whitney, Dr. Ellen Wartella, Dr. Dominic Lasorsa,
Dr. Wayne Danielson, Adriana Olivarez, Nancy Jennings, Rafael Lopez

SUMMARY...**223**

INTRODUCTION..**224**
    Reality Programming Defined 224

MEASURING VIOLENCE IN REALITY PROGRAMS **226**
    Violence Defined 226

Levels of Analysis 226

SAMPLING 229

METHODS..230

RELIABILITY 230

RESULTS 235
Description of Sampled Programs 235
Presence of Violence in Reality Programs............................. 239
Contextual Factors in Violent Portrayals 246
Additional Context Features in Reality Program Visual Violence...................... 252
Context Features in Reality Program Talk About Violence............................... 253
Characters Involved in Violence 254

VIOLENCE IN REALITY GENRES.....................................257
Police Shows.. 257
Entertainment Non-News 258
Entertainment News and Review 258
Documentaries 259
News and Public Affairs 259
Tabloid News 260
Talk Shows... 260

SUMMARY, CONCLUSIONS & RECOMMENDATIONS 261

REFERENCES 264

APPENDIX 1: Reality Shows in the 1996-1997 Sample 265

APPENDIX 2: Tables and Figures 270

**PART III. RATINGS AND ADVISORIES
FOR TELEVISION PROGRAMMING:
UNIVERSITY OF WISCONSIN–MADISON STUDY** 285

Dr. Joanne Cantor, Amy Nathanson

SUMMARY 287

INTRODUCTION 288

THE USE OF "TV PARENTAL GUIDELINES" IN THE COMPOSITE WEEK OF TELEVISION **289**
    Implementation of the New Ratings System 290
    Distribution of Rating Levels 293
        Distribution of Rating Levels Within Genres 294
        Distribution of Rating Levels Within Channels......................... 297
    The Use of TV Parental Guidelines in Programs With vs. Without Violence 302
    Distribution of TV Parental Guidelines Across Dayparts 303

USE OF ADVISORIES, RATINGS, AND CONTENT CODES IN THE COMPOSITE WEEK OF TELEVISION **305**
    Use of Advisories in the Sample 305
        Presence of Oral and Written Advisories................................. 305
        Text of Advisories... 306
    Use of MPAA Ratings and Content Codes in the Sample 308
        MPAA Ratings.. 308
        Content Codes 310
        Relationship Between MPAA Ratings and Content Codes.......... 312
    Scheduling of Advisories, Ratings, and Codes................................... 315

DISCUSSION OF FINDINGS AND IMPLICATIONS **317**
    Findings of the Content Analysis... 317
        The Use of the TV Parental Guidelines 317
        Use of Advisories, MPAA Ratings, and Content Codes
        in the Sample of Programs 318
    Implications 319

REFERENCES **321**

PART IV. TESTING THE EFFECTIVENESS OF PUBLIC SERVICE ANNOUNCEMENTS THAT DEPICT IMMEDIATE PHYSICAL CONSEQUENCES OF HANDGUN VIOLENCE: UNIVERSITY OF NORTH CAROLINA, CHAPEL HILL STUDY **323**

Jay M. Bernhardt, Dr. Jane Brown, Shelley Golden

SUMMARY **325**

INTRODUCTION **326**
    Health Communication Campaigns 327
    Public Service Announcements... 327
    Study Objectives... 328

THEORETICAL PERSPECTIVES 329
    Social Cognitive Theory of Violence.. 329
        Outcome Expectations... 329
    Violence Prevention Theory.. 330
        Consequence severity 330
    Observer Characteristics 331
        Experience With Violence 331
        Exposure to Violence.. 331
    Intervention Model 331

PSA DEVELOPMENT 333
    Background.. 333
    PSA Content 333

METHODS...336
    Study Participants... 336
    Procedure 338
        Theater Testing 338
        Pretest 338
        Randomization.. 338
        Experiment.. 339
        Posttest 339
        Secondary Exposure and Follow-up Measures...................... 339
    Study Variables and Measures... 339
        Cognitive Outcome Variables 339
        Individual Characteristics 340
        PSA Perception Variables 340
        Foils 341

RESULTS AND DISCUSSION 343
        Background... 343
        Violence Exposure and Experience 343
        Group Equivalence 344
        Recall 344
        Outcome Expectations... 344
        Message Processing 345
        PSA Comparisons 346

FINAL RECOMMENDATIONS 349
    Making PSAs More Effective 349
    Target Audience Composition... 350
        Findings From the NTVS 350
        Recommendation.. 350

Public Service Announcement Format 351
    Findings From the NTVS 351
    Recommendation 351
Writing Public Service Announcement Messages 351
    Findings From the NTVS 351
    Recommendation 351
Taking Credit 353
    Findings From the NTVS 353
    Recommendation 353
Television and Violence Prevention 353

REFERENCES **354**

ACKNOWLEDGMENTS

Center for Communication and Social Policy
University of California, Santa Barbara

We wish to express our heartfelt gratitude for the friendship and support of the research teams from the Universities of California, Texas, North Carolina and Wisconsin, and to acknowledge the enormous personal and intellectual commitment they have made to this study. Their cooperation, integrity, persistence and skill has made the coordination of this project a pleasure.

In addition, our deep appreciation goes to the members of the National Television Violence Study Council, representing leadership in the legal, medical, public health, entertainment, academic and public advocacy professions. The Council's oversight and review of the research process has been invaluable, providing insight into the issue of television violence from a wide diversity of intelligently articulated and well-informed perspectives. Year 3 Council members were: Trina Menden Anglin, M.D., Ph.D. (Society for Adolescent Medicine), Decker Anstrom (National Cable Television Association, ex-officio), Char Beales (Cable & Telecommunications: A Marketing Society), Darlene Chavez (National Education Association), Belva Davis (American Federation of Television and Radio Artists), Carl Feinstein, M.D. (American Psychiatric Association), Charles FitzSimons (Producers Guild of America), Carl Gottlieb (Writers Guild of America, West), Felice Levine, Ph.D. (American Sociological Association), Ann Marcus (Caucus for Producers, Writers and Directors), Virginia Markell (National Parent Teachers Association), Robert McAfee, M.D. (American Medical Association), E. Michael McCann (American Bar Association), Gene Reynolds (Directors Guild of America), Donald F. Roberts, Ph.D. (International Communication Association), Donald Shifrin, M.D. (American Academy of Pediatrics), Barbara Staggers, M.D., M.P.H. (National Children's Hospital Association), and Brian L. Wilcox, Ph.D. (American Psychological Association).

We also very much want to thank the staff of the Institute for Social, Behavioral, and Economic Research (ISBER) for their tireless efforts in helping to administer this project. Special thanks go to ISBER Director Richard Appelbaum, Assistant Director Barbara Harthorn, Management Services Officer Tim Schmidt, Contract and Grants Accounts Manager Jerrel Sorensen, and Administrative Assistants Jan Holtzclaw, Jan Jacobson, and Rosanna Brokaw.

We also wish to acknowledge the contributions of the employees of Mediascope--including Bill Boyd, Stephanie Carbone, Maisha Closson, Linda Evans, Marcy Kelly, David Stoll, Elena Sweet and Vickie Valice--who coordinated the National Television Violence Study from its inception through the release of the Year 1 Annual Report and the taping of the Year 2 content analysis sample.

We are, of course, deeply grateful to the National Cable Television Association (NCTA), and particularly its President, Decker Anstrom, for providing funding for the study. Special appreciation is due to Jill Luckett, NCTA Vice President for Program Network Policy, for her cooperation, good humor, and finely developed communication skills.

We express much gratitude to former U.S. Senator Paul Simon, long the leading national voice on the issue of television violence, whose encouragement to the television industry to sponsor an independent assessment of TV violence resulted in the creation of this study.

Finally, on behalf of everyone involved in the National Television Violence Study, we note our regret that Tony Cox, former Showtime President and longtime proponent of this project, is no longer here to share its completion with us. His vision and leadership in helping the television industry address the issue of violence was extraordinary and is greatly missed.

Department of Communication
University of California, Santa Barbara

This year's report brings to a close a journey that began four long years ago, counting the year of planning and design that preceded three years of data collection and analysis. Reaching the end of this road has required countless steps, some huge and some small, some conceptual and others logistical, but certainly all essential to the ultimate success of this project. The authors alone could never have completed this study without the extraordinary contributions of many individuals whom we wish to recognize here. Like us, each one of these people has shared our enthusiasm and drive to generate the highest quality of research about an issue that touches the lives of virtually every American, as well as most people world-wide.

Special appreciation goes to the Center for Communication and Social Policy staff, including Co-Director Joel Federman, Program Associate Heather Hinman-Espey, and Student Assistants Melissa York and Julie Siebold. We are grateful for wise advice and counsel concerning meeting facilitation from our UCSB colleague Dr. John Lammers. We also wish to thank Faye Nennig, who has handled a tremendous load of administrative tasks for the study from the very outset, and others at UCSB who have helped us maneuver through a maze of details, rules, regulations, and requirements, including ISBER staff Rich Appelbaum, Tim Schmidt, Jan Jacobson, Jan Holtzclaw, Jerrel Sorenson, Barbara Herr Harthorn, and Vice-Chancellor for Research France Cordova.

We extend our deep gratitude to all of the members of our outstanding national advisory board; to our colleagues at the other research sites; and to Decker Anstrom and Jill Luckett at the NCTA, who made good on their promise to keep our content analysis of television violence totally independent and free from any attempts at industry influence.

Finally, we thank our project support staff, all of whom have worked tirelessly. Charles Mullin lost more sleep than he ever dreamed he could possibly do without while coordinating and managing the taping of several thousand programs, all meticulously selected like tiny pieces of a giant jig-saw puzzle. Emma Rollin adeptly supervised the laboratory work of more than 50 undergraduate coders who had the painstaking task of analyzing all of the programs taped. Nancy Woo directed our data input and analysis, and must stand without peer in that domain given that we produced more than 17,000 cases in the past year with over 40 variables per case. Our multiple levels of analysis no doubt required multiple levels of both patience and computer expertise on Nancy's part.

Working with each of these three individuals were many undergraduate tapers, coders, and data entry staff who all contributed significant efforts to the project. There were many specialized tasks to be handled and these were performed expertly by all of the individuals who are listed below by their relevant category. We are deeply grateful for the long, hard, and careful efforts from each and every one of them. Without their contributions, there would be no report at all.

Coders

Anderson, Scott	Giamona, Maya	Nelson, Akane
Ausanne, Alisa	Giang, Becca	Nelson, Greta
*Bennett, Carolyn	*Goodhue, Liz	*Nelson, Ingrid
Bernstein, Malinda	Haynes, Lesley	*Odgers, Brandie
Branson, Christina	*Holman, Joy	*Padilla, Steven
Brodkin, Jill	*Ishibashi, Chris	Reeder, Megan
Cargill, J.D.	Ivey, Christina	Robertson, Michele
Carper, Scott	Jaenichen, Sonja	Ryan, Lynn
Champion, Katherine	Keating, Kathleen	Samuelson, Ryan
Cheng, Denise	*Kochly, Sarah	Schaffzin, Loren
Derry, Amanda	Kono, Beth	Schneider, Cassandra
*Dwyer, Erin	Krenn, Rob	Sindorf, Shannon
Dyer, Kathleen	Kuper, Samantha	Strasna, Lenka
Eachus, Suzy	*Lindstrom, Brett	Sugimoto, Nicole
Egizi, Laura	Luini, Christina	Walker, Jeremy
*Elayda, Kym	Lum, Mia	Walton, Bradford
Ferris, Amy	McCorduck, Kelly	Wohlken, Bill
Gervase, Jennifer	Nachenberg, Jamie	Woo, Lisa

Tapers

Arata, Anthony	LaChapelle, Brian
Carillo, Hector	Schaiman, Michael
Chen, Ted	Slater, Dylan
Hansen, Julie	Tees, Brian
Kennedy, Adam	Wu, Michael

Reliability

*Fraser, Mandy
Hoffman, Amy
*Rhoades, Jenny

Data Entry

Erica Biely	Michelle Lopez	Juliana Siebold
Slade Giles	Christin Lyons	*Nancy Woo
Norma Hernandez	Ashley Lyman	
Josh Krom	Jennifer Rattan	

* lab supervisor

University of Texas, Austin

The University of Texas at Austin would like to thank the following for their assistance on Year 3 of the study;

From the office staff of the UT-Austin College of Communication: Jackie Srnensky, Janice Daman, Pat Wilson, and most especially Anne Reed.

Julie Lane, who served as a graduate research assistant in the fall of 1996; Pamela Rivero, our coding supervisor; and data entry specialist Thuyet Truong.

We are also grateful to our coders: Sherry Bradford, Lorraine Brandt, Robert Branum, Ryan Craig, Sheila de la Cruz, Henry Elliott, Veronica Garcia, David Gutierrez, Jason Haugen, Amy Herrup, Debbie Hsu, Rona Anais Mattocks, Jay Miller, Eloy Perez, Diane Quest, Arlene Rivero, Alex Ruenes, ReseAnne Sims, Hanna Sliz, Ian Tennant, and Brad Wilson.

University of Wisconsin, Madison

We would like to express our gratitude to Linda Henzl for all her hard work and secretarial support, and especially for her creative contributions to the graphic display of data. We also thank Debbie Hanson for patiently and efficiently managing the accounting on this project, including keeping track of personnel and purchasing. Thanks are also due to Eugenia Peck for her participation in the coding of advisories. Finally, we again thank the dozens of others who made enormous contributions to this research in the first and second years of the study.

University of North Carolina, Chapel Hill

Our deepest gratitude goes to the people who enabled us to implement our study with North Carolina middle school students. We particularly thank Rebecca Banks, Mike Vidala, Charles Clinton, Celeste Bass, and all of the wonderful students and staff in the "Support Our Students" program.

We also thank the excellent research assistants who made this study possible: Jean Breny Bontempi, Heather Britt, Kari Hartwig, Lorna Haughton, Stacey Hoffman, Sarah Keller, Kelly Ladin, Greg Makris, Olivia Silber, Alisa Simon, and Angely Sy. Very special thanks go out to Alan Muriera for his instrumental and tireless work all year long, both in the field and in the lab; and to Sheryl Ball for her invaluable advice, support, and keen data entry skills.

Tremendous thanks go out to Michelle Taylor from the UNC-CH School of Journalism and Mass Communication for meticulously managing the finances and purchasing for this project; to Richard Simpson, Bruce Curran, and Andew Brawn for creating the wonderful public service announcements; to Brian Cheuvront, Chris Jackson, Mike Symons, and especially Jim Sorenson for their substantial scientific insights; and to everyone at the UNC Health Communications Research Laboratory, who make doing health communications research a pleasure.

Finally, we would like to thank our colleagues from the other participating universities and members of the NTVS Council for their advice and support, and Joel Federman, Co-Director of the Center for Communication and Social Policy at UC-Santa Barbara, for three years of dedication, patience, and friendship.

INTRODUCTION

Joel Federman
Center for Communication and Social Policy
University of California, Santa Barbara

This volume is the final report of the National Television Violence Study. The report represents the efforts of more than 300 people, involving the videotaping of nearly 10,000 hours of television programming for analysis over a three year period, and the participation of more than 1,600 individuals as study participants in five separate behavioral experiments. The project is a landmark in the history of television research in that its content-based findings are based on the first truly representative sample of the television landscape collected over the course of each year on 23 broadcast, cable and independent channels.

Project Overview

Violence on television has been the subject of national debate for decades. In the last few years, public concern over this issue has intensified in response to overwhelming scientific evidence that TV violence has harmful effects on society. Due to this public concern, policy makers have called on the entertainment industry to more closely examine the way in which violence is shown on television. The National Television Violence Study (NTVS) came into being in this historic context.

Initiated in 1994, the National Television Violence Study is a three-year effort to assess violence on television. The project is funded by the National Cable Television Association (NCTA). The National Television Violence Study involves the efforts of media researchers at four universities, an oversight Council of representatives from national policy organizations, and project administration and coordination. The project is the largest scientific study of television violence ever undertaken.

Researchers at the University of California, Santa Barbara, assess violence in entertainment programming, such as drama, comedy, movies, children's shows, and music videos. Researchers at the University of Texas, Austin, examine violence in a particular type of programming—reality-based shows, such as tabloid news, talk shows, police shows, and documentaries. Researchers at the University of Wisconsin, Madison, study violence ratings and advisories used on television, including their impact on the viewing decisions of parents and children. Researchers at the University of North Carolina, Chapel Hill, examine the effectiveness of anti-violence public service announcements produced by the television industry.

The project also involves the efforts of an oversight Council, whose role is to safeguard the integrity and independence of the study, provide advice and counsel to the researchers, ensure the scientific validity of the study, and identify implications from the findings. The Council is comprised of representatives from 17 national organizations that are concerned with the impact of television on society. These organizations represent the fields of education, medicine, law, violence prevention, psychology, and communication. In addition, one third of the Council members represent the entertainment industry.

The administration and coordination of the study is conducted by the Center for Communication and Social Policy at the University of California, Santa Barbara. This responsibility includes managing the videotaping of more than 3,000 programs each year for the content analysis, convening the NTVS Council, coordinating the research efforts among the four university sites, and releasing the study's report and findings. The initial phases of this project, including the taping of the Year 2 sample, were coordinated and administered by Mediascope, a nonprofit organization, before moving to UCSB in June 1996.

In very many ways, the study as a whole has been a collaborative effort. Though their studies were conducted separately, the researchers from the four universities met together frequently, particularly during the design phase of the project. In addition, the Council and researchers met together a total of six times during the course of the study, reviewing and vetting its design, results and recommendations.

Learning Aggression in the Television Environment

Prior to this study, it had already been well-established that television influences many kinds of attitudes and behaviors by modeling them as appropriate and/or desirable. A highly successful multi-billion dollar advertising industry is built on that premise. More specifically, violence on television has been shown in hundreds of studies to have an influence on aggressive behavior. Over the past 20 years, numerous respected academic and public health organizations and agencies-- including the American Psychological Association, the American Medical Association, the Surgeon General's Advisory Committee on Television and Behavior, and the National Institute of Mental Health--have reviewed the existing body of evidence in this area and have unanimously affirmed the validity of that conclusion. Three main effects of viewing televised violence have been noted in the literature: learning aggressive attitudes and behaviors, desensitization to violence, and increased fear of becoming victimized by violence.

Scientific evidence has also established that the portrayal of violence on television need not lead to the reinforcement of aggressive attitudes and behaviors. If the consequences of violence are demonstrated, if violence is shown to be regretted or punished, if its perpetrators are not glamorized, if the act of violence is not seen as justifiable, if in general violence is shown in a negative light, then the portrayal of violence may not create undesirable consequences. But, if violence is glamorized, sanitized or made to seem routine, then the message is communicated that it is acceptable, perhaps even desirable. Television can be a powerful influence on social mores concerning violence and aggression, for good or for ill.

The crucial question then becomes: in which of these ways does television currently portray violence? Does television today encourage or discourage the learning of aggression? That is a central question addressed by the National Television Violence Study. The study shows conclusively that, across all genres and channels of television, when violence is portrayed, its likely effect is to contribute to the learning of aggression. Further, despite all the public attention given to the issue, there has been no change in the way TV portrays violence during the three years of the study. Given the findings of this study that more than 60 percent of all TV shows contain some violence, and that such programs are likely to contain elements that encourage aggressive attitudes and behaviors, at least two conclusions can be drawn: for children and young adolescents, viewing television increases the risk of learning aggressive attitudes and behaviors; and for adults as well as children, viewing television carries with it the risk of becoming desensitized to violence, both on television and in the real-world.

The study does not exaggerate the importance of televised violence among the myriad contributors to violence in society. It recognizes that the causes of violence are manifold, and include biological and psychological factors as well as broader social and cultural ones. It also recognizes that televised violence does not have a uniform effect on viewers. The relationship between viewing violence and subsequent behavior depends both on the nature of the depiction and the makeup of the audience. In some cases, the same portrayal of violence may have different effects on different audiences. For example, graphically portrayed violence may elicit fear in some viewers and aggression in others. Peer influences, family role models, social and economic status, educational level and the availability of weapons can each significantly alter the likelihood of a particular reaction to viewing violence on television.

One of the most notable findings of this report is the relative lack of change in the portrayal of violence over three years. However, this finding does not necessarily mean that no efforts were made within the television industry to address the problem of violence. It may be that many well-intentioned production companies or television networks made efforts to limit or alter the nature of violent portrayals during the three-year study period. Any such efforts are certainly laudable, but the study shows they were not cumulatively sufficient to significantly alter the television environment overall.

The study reaches the conclusion that efforts by the television industry to alleviate or reverse the negative effects of violence in its programming must be undertaken with great care. As the study's analysis of ratings and advisories shows, sometimes such efforts can have the opposite effect for which they are intended, such as attracting some younger viewers to programs that glamorize or trivialize violence. Likewise, the study indicates that funds and energies devoted to the production of anti-violence public service messages may be ill-spent when they are not designed to target the most appropriate audiences or their images are not crafted to reinforce their message.

Report Goals

The following report was conducted with the goal of encouraging more responsible television programming and viewing. It does not, however, argue for government to censor television, or to otherwise legislate television content. In the context of a free society, it simply calls on the creators and viewers of television to reconsider their programming and viewing habits in light of the overwhelming evidence of the harmful effects of violence as it is currently portrayed on television.

Public concern about violence in the media, particularly television, has become highly politicized. The television industry has become a focal point for attention in the national attempt to redress the enormous social and personal costs of violence. It is hoped that the National Television Violence Study will contribute to a larger national dialogue about the causes and prevention of violence that places television violence in its broader context among many other factors contributing to violence in society, including gangs, the availability of guns, poverty and racism. Although it would be an error in judgment to place the burden of blame for violence on a single social institution, the study concludes that the effect of thousands of messages conveyed through the most powerful medium of mass communication cannot be underestimated.

PART 1

VIOLENCE IN TELEVISION PROGRAMMING OVERALL: UNIVERSITY OF CALIFORNIA, SANTA BARBARA STUDY

Stacy L. Smith
Dr. Barbara J. Wilson
Dr. Dale Kunkel
Dr. Dan Linz
Dr. W. James Potter
Carolyn M. Colvin
Dr. Edward Donnerstein

SUMMARY

This study examines the nature and extent of violence presented during the 1996-97 television season. It also compares findings from this period with the levels reported during the previous two seasons (1994-95, 1995-96), yielding a three-year longitudinal analysis. Our research examines most of the complete range of sources of television content, including the broadcast networks; independent broadcasters; public broadcasting; basic cable; and premium cable. Besides comparing findings across channel type, we also assess variability in violence across different program types or genres, including children's programming. In sum, the study has analyzed over 50,000 violent interactions that were observed in a total of roughly 10,000 hours of television programming across the three years examined.

There are a number of key assumptions underlying this report, all of which are grounded in the extensive base of previous research documenting the effects of viewing media violence. First, our review of the scientific literature leads to the conclusion that television violence contributes to anti-social effects on viewers. Second, there are three primary types of effects from viewing televised violence: (1) learning of aggressive attitudes and behaviors; (2) desensitization to violence; and, (3) fear of being victimized by violence. Finally, not all violence poses the same degree of risk of these harmful effects. The context in which violence occurs may vary in many important ways, and those differences can hold crucial implications for their impact on viewers. Some aspects of violent depictions may increase the risk of a negative effect, whereas others may decrease that risk. Thus, it is essential to evaluate the contextual features of any violent portrayal in order to best predict its likely impact on the audience.

Over the 1996-97 television season, our findings show (1) that the majority of programs (61%) contain violence and (2) that most violent portrayals on television reflect a pattern of context features that heightens their risk of harmful effects. For example, most violent incidents are sanitized; that is, they show no pain for victims, unrealistically mild degrees of harm, and/or no long-term negative consequences. In addition, violence on television is often glamorized; more than one of three violent incidents involve attractive perpetrators who are likely role models for children. On the positive side, relatively few violent incidents (14%) show explicit blood/gore. A final concern raised by the study involves the finding that many children's cartoons contain violent portrayals that pose particular risk for young children's learning of aggression.

Across the past three television seasons, our data show that neither the context nor overall amount of violence has changed to any meaningful extent. Across a wide range of individual context measures, we found remarkable consistency over time. Many of our measures of violence held so stable that they changed no more than a single percentage point across each year's sample of 3000+ hours of programs. With very few exceptions, the overall profile of violence presented on television in 1996-97 looks nearly identical to that in 1994-95.

The study concludes that violence on television remains an important social problem. Recommendations are offered for the television industry, public policy-makers, and parents to consider when confronting the concerns about televised violence.

Chapter 1

BACKGROUND AND
OVERVIEW OF THE STUDY

The central element of the NTVS project is the content analysis study examining the nature and extent of violence presented across the overall television landscape. That work has been pursued over a three-year period by the UCSB research team, studying the programming delivered during the 1994-95, 1995-96, and 1996-97 television seasons. This document represents the third and final annual report for the project initially commissioned in 1994 by the National Cable Television Association.

At the outset, our content-based research had two primary goals: (1) to identify the contextual features associated with violent depictions that most significantly increase the risk of a harmful effect on the audience; and (2) to examine their presence in violent portrayals over time, determining whether or not any meaningful changes or improvements have occurred across the three years of the study.

Our first goal was realized in year one of the project. We reviewed the entire body of existing scientific knowledge regarding the impact of televised violence. Drawing conclusions as warranted from this evidence, we devised an elaborate framework for evaluating the important contextual features associated with violent depictions. These measures formed the basis for our first year report examining television programming during the 1994-95 season.

In the study's second year, we began to address the second of our two goals. Our second annual report not only presented the content-based findings for the 1995-96 television season, but also compared our new observations to the indicators we had obtained the year before. In the process, we began to engage the issue of change but of course were tentative in drawing any conclusions on the basis of comparisons across only two points in time.

This year, our report completes our initial agenda by providing a third year of data that now allow us to confidently address the question of whether any meaningful changes have occurred since 1994 in the presentation of violence on television. This final report for the project contains two primary foci. First, as we have done in each of the previous years, we present an analysis of the patterns observed in the presentation of violent material *throughout the past year*, both on television overall as well as within particular genres of programming (e.g., dramas, movies, situation comedies) and on different types of channels (e.g., broadcast network, basic cable, premium cable). As a part of this description, we include our "High-Risk" analysis, which identifies portrayals that pose a particular risk of harm for children's learning of aggression. Second, and of arguably greater import, we provide an *analysis of change over time* in the presentation of violence, spanning the complete three-year period from fall, 1994 to spring, 1997.

While the first of these two elements represents an important "snapshot" at a given point in time of the levels and types of violent portrayals, it is the second aspect -- the analysis of change over time -- that provides the most valuable finding of this entire study. By comparing the patterns of violence in the first year to the patterns observed now in the third year of the project, our data will identify the direction in which the television industry seems to be moving in its approach to presenting violent material.

There are many patterns of change in our world that occur so slowly and subtlety that they go undetected by most observers. In meteorology, for example, global warming will not be perceptible even in a rigorous study if the analysis spans only a limited amount of time; data must be gathered over an extended period to make sense of the gradual shifts that are occurring in the world's climate. The television world too may experience ebbs and flows in its programming strategies and practices that escape obvious or immediate notice. Such changes in content patterns, if they occur at all, will be most readily identified by a precise scientific study that holds its content measures stable over time and examines a large, representative sample of programming across several years -- which is precisely the formula employed by the NTVS project. From the outset, our content analysis study was designed to assess the extent to which the television industry was fulfilling its publicly stated goal of reducing harmful depictions of violence. Now, three years hence, this report provides our answer to that question.

It is important to bear in mind that in the realm of TV violence, as with the issue of global warming, modest shifts in the phenomena being measured may hold substantial implications in terms of impact or effects. Most of the harmful effects associated with watching TV violence are a function of viewers' cumulative exposure to a large number of violent portrayals over time. If even a 10% reduction occurred in the amount of violence that posed a risk of psychological harm, this could translate into millions of Americans seeing hundreds if not thousands of fewer instances of violence each year. From a collective perspective, this would seem to reflect a significant reduction in the risks to society that are posed by televised violence, while obviously not fully ameliorating the problem. Our analysis of change over time will indicate how the presence of violence has varied over the past three years, if at all, and what the current levels of violence on television suggest in terms of the risk of harmful effects they pose to the audience, and in particular to child viewers.

In the remainder of this chapter, we offer several sections that serve as useful background for readers unfamiliar with the ongoing study and its methodology. First, we present three fundamental premises that underlie our approach to the topic of television violence. Next, we offer a summary of previous research that has established the risks that are posed by viewing televised violence, focusing specifically upon the contextual features that tend to either diminish or enhance the risk of harmful effects. This evidence was pivotal in helping us shape the content-based measures that we initially designed to examine each year's sample of television programming. Finally, we provide a brief overview of the methods we employed in performing our content analysis research, including our definition of violence, the units of analysis that were used for our measures, and the sampling design.

Some readers, particularly those in the scientific community, may wish to gain further information about the rationale underlying the creation of our measures. In our first year report, we specified in elaborate detail the nature of the content measures we devised, as well as the theoretical and empirical evidence that establishes their importance. Rather than reiterate all of that information in the present volume, we have chosen to summarize only its most salient aspects, and to refer the interested reader to the project's first year report (Wilson et al., 1997) for more complete information.

Foundations Underlying the Research

At the outset of this project, we conducted an exhaustive review of the complete body of scientific knowledge assessing the effects of televised violence on the audience. After reviewing all of the existing evidence, we reached the following conclusions, which represent the key assumptions underlying this report.

Premise #1: **Television violence contributes to anti-social effects on viewers.**

This position is supported by an overwhelming number of studies that reflect a wide range of methodological approaches. While not every finding indicates harmful effects, a clear pattern of negative outcomes has emerged overall from viewing televised violence. Our conclusion that violence on television contributes to anti-social effects on viewers is hardly novel. That same conclusion has already been reached by virtually every major investigation into the topic. Groups or agencies such as the American Psychological Association, American Medical Association, National Academy of Science, National Institute of Mental Health, and the U.S. Surgeon General have all concurred that viewing violence is an important factor in contributing to real world violence and aggression.

Premise #2: **There are three primary types of effects from viewing televised violence:**

a) learning of aggressive behaviors and attitudes;
b) desensitization to violence;
c) fear of being victimized by violence.

Although the public increasingly understands that television violence contributes to aggressive behavior, it is less widely known that there are other anti-social effects from viewing violent portrayals. There is strong empirical evidence that repeated exposure to violence can cause viewers to become more callous, or desensitized, to the harmfulness of violent behavior. In addition, long-term exposure to violent portrayals also may contribute to unrealistic fears about the likelihood of being targeted by a violent assailant. Although each of these three types of effects pose somewhat different types of issues, they all raise concerns that warrant the attention of parents, policy-makers, and the television industry.

Premise #3: **Not all violence poses the same degree of risk of these harmful effects.**

Although it is well established by scientific research that exposure to televised violence contributes to a range of anti-social or harmful effects on many viewers, the effects from viewing violence are not uniform across the full range of examples of violent depictions.

Obviously, there is a vast array of approaches to presenting violent material. In terms of its visual presentation, the violence may occur on-screen and be shown graphically, or it may occur off-screen but be clearly implied. Violent acts may be shown close-up or at a distance. There are also differences in scripting of characters who commit violence and their reasons for doing so. And there are differences in the depiction of the results of violence, including both the pain and suffering of victims as well as the outcomes for the perpetrator. Simply put, not all portrayals of violence are the same. Their context may vary in many important ways, and those differences can hold crucial implications for their impact on the audience. Some aspects of violent depictions may increase the risk of a negative effect, while others may decrease that risk. It is essential to evaluate the contextual features of any violent portrayal in order to fully appreciate its likely impact on the audience.

With these assumptions as our foundation, we began the study by devising an analytical framework that assesses important contextual features associated with violent portrayals, as indicated in the sections below.

The Importance of Context

The research literature over the last three decades has been highly consistent in its findings in three major areas of effects of exposure to media violence. First, there is increased violence toward others due primarily to the effect of *learning and imitation*. Second, there is increased callousness toward violence among others, which has commonly been labeled the *desensitization* effect. And third, there is increased *fearfulness* about becoming a victim of violence, often referred to as the "mean world syndrome" by Gerbner and his colleagues. Collectively, this evidence represents the scientific basis for concern about the effects of televised violence on the audience.

The research that documents these different types of effects shows clearly that different types of violent depictions are capable of producing different effects. Not all violent portrayals are equal with regard to the risk they might pose, whether for a particular type of effect or for any harmful influence at all. In this section, we turn to a more specific task -- that of identifying the specific contextual features that heighten the probability that a given depiction of violence will generate one of these three types of effects.

Consider, for example, a documentary about gangs that contains scenes of violence in order to inform audiences about this societal problem. The overall message about violence in such a program is likely to be quite different from that of an action-adventure movie featuring a violent hero. The documentary actually may discourage aggression whereas the action-adventure movie may seem to glamorize it. A comparison of a film like *Schindler's List* about the Holocaust with a film like *The Terminator* illustrates this difference.

Such a contrast underscores the importance of considering the context within which violence is portrayed. Indeed, the television industry itself has long recognized that violence can have different meanings depending upon how it is presented within a program. Standards and practices guidelines at the broadcast networks warn against showing "callousness or indifference to suffering," "scenes where children are victims," and "portrayals of the use of weapons or implements readily accessible" to children (Network Television Association, 1992). Most of these programming guidelines focus on contextual cues and the different ways that violence can be portrayed.

The significance of context is highlighted not only by television industry guidelines, but also by academic research. Several major reviews of social science research demonstrate that certain depictions are more likely than others to pose risks for viewers (Comstock & Paik, 1991; Gunter, 1994; Wilson, Linz, & Randall, 1990). For example, Comstock and Paik (1991) examined much of the experimental literature and concluded that three dimensions of a portrayal are important in predicting whether a program is likely to facilitate aggression among viewers: 1) how efficacious or successful the violence is; 2) how normative or justified the violence appears; and 3) how pertinent the violence is to the viewer.

Prior to developing our content coding scheme for this project, we conducted our own careful and exhaustive search of the social science research. The most immediate outcome of that effort, an update of previous reviews of the social science research literature in this realm, is found in our first year report (Wilson et al., 1997). The more unique by-product of that review, however, is the framework we produced for summarizing the contextual factors that influence audience reactions to violent portrayals.

Specifically, we identified nine contextual factors: 1) the nature of the perpetrator; 2) the nature of the target; 3) the reason for the violence; 4) the presence of weapons; 5) the extent and graphicness of the violence; 6) the degree of realism of the violence; 7) whether the violence is rewarded or punished; 8) the consequences of violence; and 9) whether humor is involved in violence. The research findings regarding each factor are briefly reviewed below, with an indication of whether a given contextual feature affects learning of aggression, desensitization, and/or fear, and if so, how. Although some of the factors increase the probability that a violent portrayal will pose risks to viewers, other factors decrease that probability. A summary of these relationships is presented in Table 1.

In the discussion below, we will focus on what we know about each factor rather than what we do not know. Consequently, if fear and/or desensitization are not mentioned in the discussion of a particular factor, then it can be assumed that there is no controlled research relevant to this potential outcome, as indicated in Table 1.

Table 1

**Predicted Impact of Contextual Factors
on Three Outcomes of Exposure to Media Violence**

Outcomes of Media Violence

Contextual Factors	Learning Aggression	Fear	Desensitization
Attractive Perpetrator	Δ		
Attractive Target		Δ	
Justified Violence	Δ		
Unjustified Violence	▼	Δ	
Presence of Weapons	Δ		
Extensive/Graphic Violence	Δ	Δ	Δ
Realistic Violence	Δ	Δ	
Rewards	Δ	Δ	
Punishments	▼	▼	
Pain/Harm Cues	▼		
Humor	Δ		Δ

Note. Predicted effects are based on review of social science research on contextual features of violence. Blank spaces indicate that there is inadequate research to make a prediction.

Δ = likely to *increase* the outcome
▼ = likely to *decrease* the outcome

Nature of Perpetrator

When a violent event occurs in a program, typically there is a character or group of characters who can be identified as the perpetrator. The meaning of the violence is closely connected to the characteristics of the perpetrator. For example, viewers are likely to interpret a gunshot from the star of a popular police series differently than a gunshot from a criminal.

Character evaluations have important implications for how a viewer ultimately will respond to a particular portrayal. Research indicates that both children and adults are more likely to attend to and learn from models who are perceived as attractive (Bandura, 1986, 1994). Thus, a perpetrator of violence who is attractive or engaging is likely to be a more potent role model for viewers than is a neutral or unattractive character.

What types of characters are perceived as attractive in entertainment programs? Studies suggest that viewers assign more positive ratings to characters who act pro-socially (e.g., benevolent, heroic) than to characters who are cruel (Hoffner & Cantor, 1985; Zillmann & Cantor, 1977). Moreover, children as young as four years of age can distinguish between prototypically good and bad characters in a television program (Berndt & Berndt, 1975; Liss, Reinhardt, & Fredricksen, 1983).

Nature of Target

Just as the nature of the perpetrator is an important contextual feature of violence, so is the nature of the target. Once again, viewers are more likely to react strongly to a target who is perceived as likeable or attractive. Consider a scene in which a likeable star of a detective series is about to be shot. Exchanging the popular detective with a malicious criminal illustrates the importance of the target in terms of audience reactions.

Interestingly, the nature of the target is most likely to influence audience fear rather than learning. Research indicates that viewers feel concern for characters who are perceived as attractive and often share such characters' emotional experiences (Zillmann, 1980, 1991). This type of empathic responding has been found with characters who are benevolent or heroic (Comisky & Bryant, 1982; Zillmann & Cantor, 1977), as well as characters who are perceived to be similar to the viewer (Feshbach & Roe, 1968; Tannenbaum & Gaer, 1965). Thus, a well-liked character can encourage audience involvement. When such a character is threatened or attacked in a violent scene, viewers are likely to experience increased anxiety and fear.

Reason for Violence

How we interpret an act of violence is dependent to a great extent on a character's motives or reasons for engaging in such behavior (Gunter, 1985; Hoffner & Cantor, 1991). For example, a father may shoot someone who is trying to kidnap his child. Certain motives such as self-defense and defense of a loved one seem justified, and viewers may even cheer when a character kills the kidnapper. In contrast, a character who shoots a bank teller for not getting the money out of a drawer fast enough is likely to be judged as malicious and not receive much sympathy from a viewer.

Research establishes that television violence that is motivated by protection or retaliation, to the extent that it appears to be justified, facilitates viewer aggression (Berkowitz & Geen, 1967; Berkowitz & Powers, 1979; Berkowitz & Rawlings, 1963; Geen & Stonner, 1973, 1974; Hoyt, 1970). Researchers have speculated that when violence is portrayed as morally proper or somehow beneficial, it lowers a viewer's inhibitions against aggression (Jo & Berkowitz, 1994). The prototypical "justified" scenario is the hero who employs violence to protect society against villainous characters. In contrast, violence that is undeserved or purely malicious should decrease the risk of audience imitation or learning of aggression.

Presence of Weapons

A variety of methods and tools can be used to enact violence against a target on television. A perpetrator can use natural means such as punching with a fist or slapping with a hand. Alternatively, a perpetrator can use a weapon like a gun or a knife or a more unconventional tool like a frying pan or a chain saw. Berkowitz (1984, 1990) has argued that certain visual cues in a film can activate or "prime" aggressive thoughts and behaviors in a viewer, and that weapons can function as such cues.

In support of this idea, a meta-analysis of 56 published experiments found that the presence of weapons, either pictorially or in the natural environment, significantly enhanced aggression among angered as well as non-angered subjects (Carlson, Marcus-Newhall, & Miller, 1990). According to Berkowitz (1990) and others (e.g., Leyens & Parke, 1974), weapons like guns and knives are more likely than unconventional means to instigate or prime aggression in viewers because such devices are commonly associated with previous violent events stored in memory. Thus, a television portrayal that features traditional weapons poses the greatest risk for the so-called "weapons effect" on audiences.

Extent and Graphicness of Violence

Television programs and especially movies vary widely in the extent and graphicness of the violence they contain. A violent interaction between a perpetrator and a target can last only a few seconds and be shot from a distance or it can persist for several minutes and involve many close-ups on the action. The media industry recognizes this difference when it provides ratings and advisories for certain programs largely on the basis of such considerations.

Research suggests that audiences can be influenced by the extent and explicitness of violent portrayals. Most attention has been devoted to the impact of extensive or repeated violence on viewer desensitization. For example, several early studies on adults showed that physiological arousal to prolonged scenes of brutality steadily declines over time during exposure to a 17-minute film (Lazarus & Alfert, 1964;

15

Lazarus, Speisman, Mordkoff, & Davison, 1962; Speisman, Lazarus, Mordkoff, & Davison, 1964). Even children have been shown to exhibit such physiological desensitization over time during exposure to a violent film, with the decrement being strongest for those who were heavy viewers of TV violence (Cline, Croft, & Courrier, 1973).

More recently, studies have confirmed that exposure to extensive graphic violence, either within a single program or across several programs, produces decreased arousal and sensitivity to violence (Linz, Donnerstein, & Penrod, 1988; Mullin & Linz, 1995). This is the desensitization effect.

Does extensive or repeated violence influence the other two effects of concern, the learning of aggression and fear? Huesmann and his colleagues have conducted several longitudinal surveys demonstrating that the more TV violence children watch in a given year, the more likely they are to behave aggressively in subsequent years (Huesmann, 1986; Huesmann, Eron, Lefkowitz, & Walder, 1984). Furthermore, these findings fit perfectly with relevant theory that predicts heavy exposure to a variety of violent models and behaviors on television will foster the development of well-established scripts and routines for responding aggressively.

The impact of extensive and graphic violence on fear, however, is less obvious. One could argue that prolonged exposure to explicit scenes of violence will enhance fright reactions among viewers. Alternatively, if the images are constant and repeated within a program, a viewer could become desensitized and feel *less* upset over time. An experiment by Ogles and Hoffner (1987) suggests that extensive exposure to violence promotes rather than diminishes fear. Male undergraduates were randomly assigned to view five slasher films (e.g., *Toolbox Murders*, *Maniac*) over a two-week period or two slasher films within a one-week period. Subjects in the extended exposure condition perceived significantly more crime in the real world and felt personally more vulnerable to it, and these perceptions correlated with feelings of fear. These findings taken together with the research reviewed earlier on cultivation effects indicate that viewing extensive violence is likely to be frightening.

Realism of Violence

Numerous studies indicate that realistic portrayals of violence can pose more risks for viewers than unrealistic ones. For example, Berkowitz and Alioto (1973) found that exposure to a war film led to more aggression among adult males when it was described as a documentary than when it was labeled a Hollywood production. Subsequent studies found that a film of a campus fistfight that was introduced as something that actually happened led to greater aggression among college-aged males than did the same fight when it was described as staged (Geen, 1975; Thomas & Tell, 1974).

Not only adults but children too seem to respond to the realism of violence. In an experiment by Feshbach (1972), 9- to 11-year-old children were exposed to the same campus riot footage that was described either as part of a news story or as a Hollywood film. Children who perceived the content to be more realistic subsequently behaved more aggressively. Atkin (1983) obtained similar results when 10- to 13-year-olds viewed the same violent scene presented within an actual newscast, as compared to viewing the scene within a movie promo.

The realism of a portrayal can also enhance viewers' fear reactions to violence (Geen, 1975; Geen & Rakosky, 1973; Lazarus, Opton, Nomikos, & Rankin, 1965). Studies have demonstrated that adults are far more emotionally aroused by violent scenes that are perceived to have actually happened than if the same scenes are believed to be fictional.

To summarize, research suggests that more realistic portrayals of violence can foster the learning of aggressive attitudes and behaviors among children as well as adults. Realistic depictions of brutality also can elevate viewers' fear responses. Based on this contextual factor, one might expect that cartoon or fantasy violence on television is relatively harmless. After all, such depictions obviously are not very authentic. However, research with very young children cautions against such a conclusion. In fact, what seems unrealistic to mature viewers may appear to be quite real to a younger child. We will turn our focus shortly to the topic of developmental differences in how children understand television. Some of our contextual factors take on special consideration when the audience is composed primarily of younger children.

Rewards and Punishments

A critical feature of any violent portrayal concerns whether the aggressive behavior is reinforced or rewarded. In general, rewarded violence or violence that is not overtly punished fosters the learning of aggressive attitudes and behavior among viewers. In contrast, portrayals of punished violence can serve to inhibit or reduce the learning of aggression. These conclusions are established by a strong base of direct empirical evidence (e.g., Bandura, 1965, 1986; Bandura, Ross, & Ross, 1961,1963) as well as meta-analyses (Paik & Comstock, 1994).

Can such reinforcements affect other audience responses besides aggression? One experimental study mentioned previously examined the impact of rewards and punishments on fear. Bryant, Carveth, and Brown (1981) exposed adults to six weeks of action-adventure programs that depicted either just endings in which violence was punished or unjust endings where violence went unpunished. Subjects who viewed unpunished violence were significantly more anxious and pessimistic about the consequences of real-life violence than were those who saw the just endings. Thus, rewards and punishments can influence fear reactions as well as the learning of aggression.

Consequences of Violence

Another important contextual feature of media violence concerns whether the consequences of aggressive actions are depicted. Several studies suggest that viewers interpret violent scenes with observable harm and pain as more serious and more violent than scenes showing no such consequences (Gunter, 1983, 1985).

Cries of pain and other signs of suffering can affect not only interpretations but also imitation of aggression. Numerous experiments have found that adults who are exposed to overt, intense pain cues from a victim subsequently behave less aggressively than do those who see no such pain cues (Baron, 1971a, 1971b; Gorenson, 1969; Sanders & Baron, 1975; Schmutte & Taylor, 1980). The assumption is that pain cues inhibit aggression by eliciting sympathy and reminding the viewer of social norms against violence. Children also have been shown to be influenced by the consequences of violence. In one experiment, boys who viewed a violent film clip that showed explicit injuries and blood subsequently were less aggressive than were those who saw a violent clip with no such consequences (Wotring & Greenberg, 1973). Overall, the explicit depiction of pain and harm in violent portrayals is likely to inhibit the learning of aggressive attitudes and behaviors.

Humor

Portrayals of violence on television often are cast in a humorous light. Slapstick shows like *The Three Stooges* and cartoons such as *The Road Runner* are examples in which almost every act of violence has a comical tone to it. But even dramatic action-adventure programs can contextualize violence with humor. For example, *Dirty Harry* challenged criminals to shoot first by saying "Go ahead ... make my day."

What impact does the addition of humor to a violent scene have on the viewer? Of all the contextual variables that have been examined, we know the least about humor. For one thing, there are many types of humor that can be used in a portrayal. A perpetrator could crack a joke while harming someone, the violent act itself can be shown as farcical, or the target could over-react with pain to a slight injury. Moreover, humor can come in a variety of forms such as sarcasm, a witty remark, a nonverbal gesture, or a funny story. To further complicate the situation, an entire program can be funny or humor can be restricted to violent scenes. Unfortunately, there is no systematic research to date that examines all these various manifestations of humor.

Mueller and Donnerstein (1977) found that exposure to highly arousing jokes on an audiotape produced significantly more aggressive behavior among angered subjects than did exposure to milder jokes. A subsequent study revealed similar effects for a humorous movie clip (Mueller & Donnerstein, 1983). Although some forms of mild humor are capable of reducing aggression by distracting or creating a positive mood (Berger, 1988; Zillmann & Bryant, 1991), other more intense forms of humor can instigate aggression because they are arousing. Two additional experiments (Baron, 1978; Berkowitz, 1970) support this perspective.

Overall, we draw the conclusion that the presence of humor will generally contribute to the learning of aggression. However, we should underscore that our conclusion about this facilitative effect is tentative until more systematic research on the impact of a violent scene with and without different forms of humor is undertaken.

Some research on audience perceptions of violence suggests that humor also may foster desensitization. Gunter (1985) and Sander (1995) have found that adults actually perceive violent scenes that contain humor to be less aggressive and less brutal than are similar scenes without comedic tones. Thus, we tentatively conclude that humor can trivialize violence and its consequences, though clearly further research is needed.

Developmental Differences in the Processing of Television Content

The preceding discussion establishes that both children and adults are influenced by the nine context factors indicated above. Moreover, each factor affects children and adults in the same basic direction. For example, rewarded violence *increases* the risk for learning of aggression regardless of the age of the viewer, whereas punished violence *decreases* that risk. Nevertheless, some unique concerns regarding the viewer's interpretation of context come into play when considering very young age groups.

Because of inherent limitations in young children's information-processing capabilities, younger children may understand and therefore respond to two context factors in somewhat different ways than will older children and adults. Younger viewers are more likely to perceive fantasy and animated violence as realistic, thus increasing the risk of imitation and fear when this age group is exposed to such content. They also are less able to link scenes together that are temporally separated. Thus, punishments may not serve as effective inhibitors of imitation and aggression unless such restraints are depicted in the same scene or immediately adjacent to the violence. These special contingencies will be of interest when we consider the 2- to 6-year-old audience and when we examine children's programming in particular.

Summary: Contextual Patterns

The research reviewed above establishes clearly that certain depictions of television violence pose more of a risk for viewers than do others. Specifically, nine different contextual cues or message factors have been documented as important influences on audience reactions. Because the experimental studies to date have only tested these context factors in isolation from one another, we have no solid information about which factors may be most critical or how such factors might interact with one another. For example, it might be that pain and harm cues are more influential when shown within a realistic portrayal of violence than in the context of a fantasy program.

Until more detailed analyses are conducted, we must assume that each factor is somehow important to the overall risk associated with a given portrayal. In that case, a violent program that contains several contextually-based risk factors presumably is more problematic than a portrayal featuring only one.

The context factors can be examined collectively to reveal certain patterns of portrayals in a program that would affect the potential risk for the audience. A careful review of Table 1 reveals such patterns. For example, a portrayal that poses the greatest risk for the learning of aggression would feature an attractive perpetrator who is motivated by morally proper reasons; who engages in repeated violence that seems realistic, is rewarded, and employs conventional weapons; and whose violent actions produce no visible harm or pain and are accompanied by humor. In contrast, a portrayal that poses the least risk of learning aggression would feature an unattractive perpetrator who is motivated by greed or hatred, who commits violence that produces strong negative consequences for the victims, and who is ultimately punished for this aggression.

Somewhat different risk patterns exist for the other outcomes of concern, desensitization and fear. A portrayal that poses the greatest risk for desensitization would contain violence that is repeated or extensive and that is depicted as humorous. A portrayal that poses the greatest risk for audience fear would feature violence aimed at an attractive or likeable target, that seems unjustified, that is extensive and realistic, and that goes unpunished.

Having established the relationship between the contextual features described above and the three primary types of harmful effects of viewing televised violence, we turn now to providing an overview of the methods we have employed to measure violent portrayals using scientific content analysis techniques. In the following section, we introduce the basic elements of the study, including our definition of violence, units of analysis (a scientific term that indicates how we count things), and the strategy for selecting the television programming we examine.

Overview of the Content Analysis Framework

The goal of our project is to distinguish portrayals of violence most likely to contribute to effects generally considered as anti-social or harmful from portrayals that may be less problematic, if not in some cases even beneficial. To accomplish our goal, we have devised a content analysis framework that we believe is uniquely sensitive to the context in which depictions of televised violence occur. Before examining those contextual features, however, we must first determine whether or not a given program contains any violence.

Definition of Violence

The most critical aspect for any study of television violence is the definition that is employed to identify acts classified as "violent." Our fundamental definition of violence places emphasis on three key elements: intention to harm, the physical nature of harm, and the involvement of animate beings.

Violence is defined as any overt depiction of a credible threat of physical force or the actual use of such force intended to physically harm an animate being or group of beings. Violence also includes certain depictions of physically harmful consequences against an animate being/s that result from unseen violent means.

Thus, our study identifies three primary types of violent depictions: credible threats, behavioral acts, and harmful consequences of unseen violence.

This definition insures that depictions classified as "violent" represent actual physical aggression directed against living beings. Such physical action lies at the heart of any conception of violence, and limiting our definition to this type of portrayal (as opposed to including, for example, verbal aggression that might cause emotional harm) renders it a conservative measure of violence on television.

Units of Analysis

In order to capture thorough information about the context of each violent act, it is essential that acts not be viewed in isolation; rather, each act should be considered as part of an ongoing exchange between characters, and each exchange must also be situated within the larger setting of the program as a whole. The richest meaning of any portrayal is found in larger units or chunks, rather than in individual acts. We plan to tap into these larger units of meaning through several different and novel techniques.

First, although we count as violence any act which fits the definition indicated above, we classify acts collectively as part of a larger, superordinate unit of analysis known as a *violent incident*. A violent incident involves an interaction between a perpetrator (P), an act (A), and a target (T), yielding the convenient acronym PAT as the label for this summary unit. We track and report collectively all violence within the same PAT framework, and refer to this as the *PAT level* of analysis. For each PAT incident, we ascertain an array of contextual information particular to that exchange that helps us to estimate the likely impact of the depiction.

Second, we gather and report additional descriptive information about the context of violent depictions at the *scene level*. A violent scene encompasses an interrelated series of violent incidents that occur without a meaningful break in the flow of actual or imminent violence. Analysis at this level affords the opportunity to examine combinations of contextual features that together comprise the patterns most frequently used in the presentation of violence.

Finally, we also examine violent content at the *program level*. It is important to consider the larger meaning or message that is conveyed by a program, and to do so accurately requires assessment at this level. Some critics have argued that previous studies have failed to differentiate the violence in an artistic or historical program from the violence contained in an entertaining action-adventure program. Both types of programs may contain numerous acts of violence when the focus is at the micro-level of analysis. However, the overall narrative of an historical or educational program may be to condemn the evilness of violence, whereas the action-adventure show may seem to glorify violence. For example, the broadcast network program *Kids Killing Kids* first presents situations resulting in youth violence, but then replays each scene a second time, illustrating non-violent alternatives to conflict resolution. An analysis of content of *Kids Killing Kids* at the micro-level would reveal that it ranks very high in terms of frequency of violent acts. Yet the overall message of the program, when viewed at the program level, is an anti-violence one.

By analyzing violence at all three of these levels -- the incident or PAT level, the scene level, and the program level -- we hope to provide the most rich and meaningful data regarding the nature and extent of violent portrayals yet presented by the scientific community. These units of analysis represent a novel framework devised specifically for this project. Both this overall framework for analysis as well as the individual context measures that are assessed at each of the appropriate levels were refined over roughly a six-month period during which the principal investigators evaluated their validity and reliability. The measures that have survived this process are theoretically grounded, consistent with all existing scientific research assessing the effects of televised violence, and as we will demonstrate, can be applied consistently by different coders who are assigned to evaluate television program content.

Measures

The preceding section addressing "The Importance of Context" has foregrounded the areas in which we have crafted measures that are used to describe the most important aspects of violent depictions. These measures include assessment of the type of violent depiction (credible threats, behavioral acts and harmful consequences); the means by which violence is accomplished (e.g., type of weapon); the extent and graphicness of the violent portrayal; characteristics of the perpetrator and target; the reason for the violence; the consequences of the violence (e.g., pain, harm); the rewards or punishments associated with violence; the degree of realism of the violence; and the use of humor in depictions of violence. In addition, a judgment regarding the overall narrative purpose of each program is applied to help further contextualize any violent depictions. Details regarding the range of values for each measure and the procedures for judging specific content are included in the first year report (see Wilson et al., 1997).

Coding of Content

Each program included in the sample was evaluated by one of 56 undergraduate research assistants who were trained as coders. Prior to the beginning of the coding process in which judgments are recorded for each of the content measures included in the overall study, coders received approximately 40 hours of classroom training and 20 hours of laboratory practice in recording their observations properly. Only coders who demonstrated strong proficiency with our measures at the completion of training were allowed to continue with the project.

Once the actual process of evaluating videotapes began, taped programs were assigned randomly to coders for evaluation. They performed their work in small, individual rooms in a laboratory at UCSB. The consistency of judgments across coders was monitored on a bi-weekly basis throughout all periods of data collection, and the results of these reliability tests are reported in Chapter 2 of this report. This monitoring insured that the quality of the judgments that were recorded for each tape was consistently high.

Sample

There are two major features that set our sample apart from other content analyses. First, it is significantly larger than most previous studies of television violence. The typical sample size in the studies cited previously in this chapter is in the range of

80-120 hours. In contrast, this project sampled approximately 2700 hours of material each year. The sample includes programming from 6 a.m. until 11 p.m. across a total of 23 different channels (affiliates of the four leading commercial broadcast networks; a public broadcasting affiliate; three independent commercial broadcast stations, 12 basic cable channels, and three premium cable channels).

Second, rather than sampling intact days or weeks of programming, we selected each individual *program* randomly from a population of all programs appearing from October 1996 to June 1997. Therefore, our sample technically involves literally thousands of sampling units (programs) rather than the more traditional seven units (days). When a sample relies on large units like entire days or weeks, there is a greater risk of an anomalous event occurring (e.g., a breaking news story) that could make that block of programming unrepresentative. In contrast, an anomalous event occurring in one of several thousand units would have much less impact on the overall representativeness of the sample.

Our videotaped sample includes all forms of programming on television. However, we did not analyze all shows for violence. Excluded were the genres of religious programming, game shows, instructional shows, home shopping, sports, and newscasts. Consequently, the cable program services CNN and ESPN were excluded entirely from the study. All of these exclusions were stipulated as part of the research contract with the study's funder, the National Cable Television Association.

Conclusion

This chapter has presented a brief review of the conceptual underpinnings of the current study, as well as an overview of key aspects in the design of our research. We believe our methodological approach to the topic offers several unique advantages. These assets are a function of our clear, precise, and conservative definition of violence, as well as innovations in the areas of units of analyses, sampling, reliability, and the consideration of context.

Our definition of violence clearly identifies only those acts that raise valid concerns for negative effects on the audience. As for units of analyses, we provide for a simultaneous, multiple level (PAT, scene, and program) examination. Our sample of programs is far more broad than any other scientific content analysis study. Our reliability design is particularly sophisticated because of our use of so many coders and the elaborate nature of our measures. And finally, our focus on contextual variables is grounded strongly in the effects literature, so we can be confident of the importance of the content attributes we have selected for study.

In the following chapter, we provide greater detail about our research methods and measures before turning to our content analysis findings. In Chapter 3, we report the data for programs sampled during the 1996-97 television season. In Chapter 4, we assess the change that has occurred over the full three years of the study in our measures of violent portrayals. And in Chapter 5, we devote attention to portrayals that can be categorized as "high-risk" for increasing children's learning of aggression.

Finally, after reporting our overall findings, we summarize and interpret their meaning in Chapter 6, and conclude our report by offering recommendations to the television industry, policy-makers, parents, as well as to our colleagues in the academic community.

Chapter 2

DESCRIPTION OF METHODS

In this chapter, we explicate the methods employed in the present research. We begin with information about the sample, then turn to the content measures and a review of the coding and reliability of our data. Finally, we report on the sample, coding and reliability of our data for the three years of the project in an overall assessment of the methods employed in this study.

Sample of Programs

Basic Parameters of the Sample

The sampling frame for the present investigation is defined by four parameters: channels, program types, sampling times (i.e., times of day), and sampling periods (i.e., times of year).

Channel. A total of 23 channels (see Table 2) are included in the sample. The channels include stations representing the commercial broadcast networks, commercial broadcast independents, the public broadcasting network, as well as basic cable and premium cable program services. All monitoring for each channel was conducted in the Los Angeles market. For the commercial broadcast networks, their Los Angeles affiliates were sampled. These include KABC, KCBS, KTTV for Fox, and KNBC. We did not differentiate between material aired on these stations that originated from the network as opposed to non-network material presented at the discretion of the local affiliate.

Program type. Religious programs, game shows, "infomercials" or home shopping material, instructional programs, sports, and news (see Whitney et al., 1997 for definition of news) were excluded from analysis in the study. To maintain the integrity of the sample design and its representativeness of the overall television environment, these programs were included in the sample grid whenever they were selected by the random draw that created our composite week of programming (that process is detailed below). However, none of these program types were examined for violence.

Time of day. All programs listed in *TV Guide* from 6:00 a.m. until 10:59 p.m. were eligible for inclusion in the sample, a total of 17 hours per day.

Sampling period. A set of 21 weeks beginning October 5th, 1996 and ending June 6, 1997 was chosen as the sampling period for the third year of the study (Table 3). The time periods around certain holidays (Thanksgiving, Christmas, and Easter) were excluded from the sampling frame. Holiday specials and non-regular programming presumed to be highly variable from year to year were therefore eliminated. Summer weeks were not included in the sample period in order to avoid the over-inclusion of programs due to repeated scheduling.

Table 2
List of Channels in Sample

Broadcast Networks	Independent Broadcast	Public Broadcast	Basic Cable	Premium Cable
ABC	KCAL	KCET	A&E	Cinemax
CBS	KCOP		AMC	HBO
Fox	KTLA		BET	Showtime
NBC			Cartoon Network	
			Disney	
			Family Channel	
			Lifetime	
			MTV	
			Nickelodeon	
			TNT	
			USA	
			VH-1	

Obtaining a Representative Sample of the Program Population

Rather than being selected on the basis of convenience as in most other content analysis studies, the programs chosen in the present study were selected with a modified version of the equal probability of selection method (EPSEM). With this method of selection every program has an equal chance, or opportunity, to appear in the sample. This method insures that a subset of the population of television programs obtained for analysis is *representative* of the entire population of programs.

The strength of the method employed in this study is that the sample is representative because every program has an approximately equal chance of being included. This method of selection offers an additional benefit. Because each show is chosen randomly, each program can be said to be "independent" of every other program in the sample. This independence among sampling units permits us to make the strongest possible statistical comparisons between groups of programs that might be distinguished by time-of-day or type of channel, for example.

Program selection. Two half-hour time slots (defined by hour of day and day of week) were randomly selected for each channel during each week that the sampling occurred. Once a time slot was selected, the *TV Guide* was consulted and the program corresponding to that time slot was entered into a scheduling grid several days before the target week of programming began. Programs were retained in the sample in their entirety regardless of the number of time slots they occupied. For example, if the time slot 1:30 p.m., Tuesday was randomly selected and an hour long program which began

Table 3

Year 3 Sample Weeks

Week Number	Dates
1	October 5-October 11, 1996
2	October 12-October 18
3	October 19-October 25
4	October 26-November 1
5	November 2-November 8
6	November 30-December 6
7	January 11-January 17, 1997
8	January 18-January 24
9	January 25-January 31
10	February 1-February 7
11	February 8-February 14
12	March 1-March 7
13	March 8-March 15
14	March 16-March 21
15	April 19-April 25
16	April 26-May 2
17	May 3-May 9
18	May 10-May 16
19	May 17-May 23
20	May 24-May 30
21	May 31-June 6

at 1:00 p.m. was identified in the *TV Guide*, that program was selected for inclusion in the sample and permitted to occupy two half-hour time slots (1:00 p.m. - 2:00 p.m.).

Programs exceeding the 6:00 a.m.-11:00 p.m. time-of-day frame. Programs that began before 6:00 a.m. or continued beyond 11:00 p.m. were taped in their entirety whenever they were selected by the sampling process. For example, a program that was selected for sampling for the 10:00 p.m block that ran 90 minutes would be included even though its final half-hour aired after 11:00 p.m.

Preemptions. Only scheduled programming was included in the sample. Programs that were preempted by news bulletins or special reports that exceeded five minutes in length per half-hour of programming were excluded from the sample.

Program overlap. Sampling by half-hour unit resulted in some program overlap due to the availability of half-hour time slots which were "sandwiched" between programs already in the sample. These programs were taped in their entirety and included in the sample. Table 4 lists the number and percentage of program overlap by channel. Premium channels, with a high proportion of movie programming, accounted for the highest overlap. Overall, 15% of the programs included in the sample overlap with other programs.

Summary Description of the Sample

A composite week of programming. The sampling procedure described above resulted in a seven-day composite week of programming. Virtually all shows in the regular program schedule for each channel appear in the final composite week.

Total program count and error rate. The taped sample includes a total of 3,212 programs. A complete grid of all programs selected for inclusion in the sample appears in Appendix 1. A total of 159 programs (5%) were removed from the sample due to taping errors or other technical problems. Table 4 includes a breakdown of missing program blocks by individual channel.

Sample exclusions. Of the total 3,212 programs, 462 (14%) are religious programs, game shows, sports, "infomercials", instructional shows and breaking news, and thus were not included in the coding analyses.

Table 4

Breakdown of Programs and Exclusions in Sample

Channel	Number of Programs	Not Coded	% Not Coded	Taping Errors	% Taping Errors	Program Overlap	% Overlap
ABC	148	58	39%	2	1%	12	8%
CBS	138	42	30%	7	5%	10	7%
NBC	135	45	33%	7	5%	15	11%
FOX	189	29	15%	6	3%	8	4%
PBS	178	16	9%	4	2%	8	4%
KCAL	156	39	25%	4	3%	8	5%
KCOP	136	24	18%	7	5%	2	1%
KTLA	155	28	18%	7	5%	6	4%
A&E	107	4	4%	2	2%	3	3%
AMC	85	0	0%	0	0%	71	84%
BET	107	19	18%	11	10%	14	13%
CAR	211	0	0%	9	4%	2	1%
DIS	174	0	0%	2	1%	13	7%
FAM	124	41	33%	5	4%	12	10%
LIF	148	62	42%	4	3%	22	15%
MTV	156	14	9%	8	5%	13	8%
NIK	225	0	0%	8	4%	2	1%
TNT	100	2	2%	2	2%	21	21%
USA	147	35	24%	13	9%	36	24%
VH-1	138	4	3%	37	26%	16	11%
HBO	83	0	0%	6	7%	48	58%
MAX	82	0	0%	6	7%	67	82%
SHO	90	0	0%	2	2%	71	79%
Total	3,212	462	14%	159	5%	477	15%

Content Measures

In this section, we provide an overview of the measures that are applied in our analysis of the content we have sampled. We deal with three main topics: defining violence, units of analysis, and contextual measures. A more detailed and comprehensive account of these measures is included in Volume 1 of the National Television Violence Study report (Wilson et al., 1997). The study's first year report also includes as an appendix of the complete coding guide that is used as the basis for judging all content for the study.

Definition of Violence

Our fundamental definition of violence places emphasis on a number of elements, including intention to harm, the physical nature of harm, and the involvement of animate beings. We use the following definition of violence in this study:

> Violence is defined as any overt depiction of a credible threat of physical force or the actual use of such force intended to physically harm an animate being or group of beings. Violence also includes certain depictions of physically harmful consequences against an animate being/s that result from unseen violent means.

Thus, there are three primary types of violent depictions: credible threats, behavioral acts and harmful consequences.

Three forms of violence. A violent action is any depiction that qualifies as violence according to our basic definition. We have classified violent actions into three primary types: credible threats of violence, behavioral acts, and depictions of harmful consequences of violence.

First, a credible threat is an overt behavior which threatens the use of violence. The behavior may be either verbal or nonverbal. A credible threat occurs when a perpetrator evidences a serious intent to harm a target by either directly communicating the threat verbally or by displaying violent means in a threatening manner. Second, a behavioral act is an overt action using violent physical force against another animate being. These types of acts may employ weapons, ordinary objects, or the perpetrator's own natural means. Third, harmful consequences are depictions of the victims of violence when the violence is clearly implied but not portrayed overtly as it occurs. Depictions of harmful consequences are coded only when a program does not include any portion of the violent act, but rather depicts only its physical aftermath.

Units of Analysis

The judgments and observations we have recorded for each instance of violence are organized into three distinct levels, or units of analysis. These three levels include: (1) the violent interaction, or PAT level; (2) the scene level; and (3) the program level. The PAT level is the most microscopic of the three.

PAT level. All violent incidents can be said to represent an interaction between a perpetrator (P) who performs a type of act (A) directed at a target (T). For example, a hijacker with a bomb strapped to his back who threatens a planeload of passengers would be categorized at the PAT level in the following manner: P = hijacker, A = credible threat, T = passengers on the plane. A CIA agent who shoots a handgun at a group of terrorists would be unitized as: P = CIA agent, A = behavioral act, T = terrorists. When a violent action occurs, it is coded first as a PAT case or observation. The information recorded for that case encompasses all of the violent actions directed by a particular perpetrator at a particular target within the same scene, so long as the type of act remains the same.

Scene level. The second and intermediate level of analysis is called a scene. A violent scene is defined as a related series of violent behaviors, actions, or depictions of harmful consequences of violence that occur without a significant break in the flow of actual or imminent violence. In other words, the actions maintain a narrative flow in which a sequence of actions are connected or related to one another. Therefore, violent scenes typically occur in the same general setting among the same characters or types of characters. One or many PAT interactions may occur within a given scene.

A violent scene begins whenever any action that fulfills the definition of violence is observed. A scene ends whenever a significant break or pause transpires in the ongoing violence. A significant break occurs when the imminent threat of violence ceases to exist or when there is an interruption in the time, place, or setting that would reflect what is commonly referred to as a scene change. Again, specific operational rules have been crafted to facilitate consistency in judgments across coders.

Program level. The macro-ordinate unit of analysis is an entire program. While it is important to evaluate violent interactions at both the PAT and scene level in order to capture vital contextual differences between different interactions, it is also important to evaluate content at the broader level of overall themes or messages represented in a show. We believe the judgments at this level very nearly approximate some of the overall messages that average adult viewers would obtain after watching an entire program.

Most programs consist of one thematic story or unfolding narrative whose beginning, middle, and end is presented across a scheduled block of time. These programs typically begin and end their time slots with production credits and/or conventions (e.g. teasers, previews, "promos"). Examples of these types of programs are situation comedies, dramas, daytime soap operas, and movies.

Some other types of programs, however, feature two or more self-contained stories whose unfolding narratives are each presented independently of one another. Each of these segments represents only a portion of the overall time devoted to a scheduled program, yet each is an independent "story." The plotline, characters, and/or geographical locations in each segment tend to vary from one story to the next. A good example of this would be a magazine format show such as the long-running Sunday night program *60 Minutes*. We refer to such content as a *segmented program*.

Segmented programs also typically begin and end their time slots with standard production credits and/or conventions (e.g. teasers, previews, "promos"). However, each independent story nested within the program is introduced and separated in some way from other stories by some form of productions credits and/or conventions. For example, a narrator or program host might introduce each segment. Examples of these types of programs are music videos, news magazines, certain reality-based programs, and some cartoon shows. For material classified as a segmented program, the program level variables are assessed for each segment within that particular program in order to capture the differences which may exist between discrete narrative segments in a program.

Contextual Measures

In order to measure the contextual factors presented in Chapter 1, two types of variables were created: event-based and character-based variables. In the section that follows, each event-based contextual measure will be defined and explicated at the level of analysis in which it was assessed. Then, each of the character-based contextual variables designed to capture the qualities of the perpetrators and targets involved in violence will be conceptually and operationally defined.

PAT level context variables. The first contextual factor assessed at the PAT level was the perpetrator's primary *reason* or motive for engaging in violence. This variable was assessed at the most micro-level of analysis because a perpetrator's reason for acting violently may vary as a function of the target s/he is confronting. There were six possible values for this measure: protection of life, retaliation, anger, personal gain, mental instability, and other. In year one we developed a justification variable by collapsing the above reasons into "justified" and "unjustified" violence.

In the second year of coding we added a new variable which we labeled *justification*, which more globally captured the nature of this concept. By definition justified violence is defined as those aggressive acts and or threats that are portrayed as "morally correct," "right," or "just" given the circumstances in the unfolding narrative. Each interaction was coded as justified, unjustified, or mixed.

The third contextual variable assessed the *means* used in each violent interaction. Means were defined as any object, weapon or device that perpetrators use to threaten and/or harm targets. There were six categories of means: natural means (using a character's normal physical capabilities such as striking with a fist), unconventional weapons (striking with a chair or bottle), conventional weapons non-firearms (police baton, knife), handheld firearms (gun, pistol), heavy weaponry (submarines, tanks) and bombs (timer, remote, hand grenades). For any given violent interaction, each different type of means used by a perpetrator against a particular target was captured.

In addition to assessing the type(s), the *extent* of each means used was also recorded. Extent was measured within each means category for a given interaction. There were five values for the extent variable: one (single example of act), some (between two and nine examples of the act), many (between 10 and 20 examples of the act), and extreme (over 20 examples of the act).

The next three contextual factors measured the immediate consequences of each violent interaction. Consequences refers to the amount of physical harm and pain that a target incurs as a result of violence. For each violent interaction, both depicted harm and likely harm were assessed. Subsequent comparison of these two measures allows us to draw inferences about the degree of realistic harm associated with specific portrayals.

The evaluation of *depicted harm* was based on two specific factors: the amount of physical injury done to a target's body, and the target's ability to function after experiencing violence. In some cases of unrealistic depictions, such as in cartoons, these two elements are often in conflict. That is, a character may be flattened like a pancake by a steamroller, but then pop right up and walk away unfazed. In such cases, the depicted harm would be judged as minimal because the target continued to function seemingly without harm even though suffering temporary disfiguration of the body. There were four possible values for depicted harm: none, mild, moderate, or extreme.

A complementary measure of *likely harm* assessed the level of physical injury and incapacitation that would occur if the same violent means were targeted toward a human in real life. To judge this, an inference had to be drawn about the potential seriousness of the means used. The values for likely harm were the same as for depicted harm.

In addition to depicted and likely harm, the amount of *depicted pain* a target experienced as a result of violence was assessed. Conceptually, pain was defined as the audible (i.e., screams, moans, yells, gasps) or visible (i.e., facial expressions, physical reactions such as clutching of a wound/injury) expression of physical suffering that occurred as a result of violence. There were four possible values for pain: none, mild, moderate, and extreme. The measure was not applied in cases where there was no opportunity to observe a target's pain or suffering either during or immediately after experiencing violence.

Finally, violent behaviors were assessed for instances of *sexual assault*. Sexual assault was defined as violence that occurred in conjunction with intimate physical contact involving sexual and/or erotic overtones; or other erotic touching or physical contact intended to arouse or sexually gratify the perpetrator against a target's will. If any of these elements were present either immediately before, during or after a violent act, then the act was coded as including sexual assault.

Scene level context variables. At the scene level, several event-based contextual variables were assessed. These variables were judged after the coder had viewed the entire scene *and* the one that immediately followed it. If a violent scene was followed by a commercial break, by definition, no subsequent scene existed and the coder was instructed to simply assess the following variables at the end of the scene. The primary value of the scene level measures is that they allow us to analyze the presentation of violence as it is likely to be understood by young children. Young viewers are not skilled at linking relations among scenes that are temporally distant in adult-oriented programs; instead they tend to understand the scenes as a series of discrete events. Thus, it is important to consider the depiction of violence at the scene level in assessing the likely impact of violent depictions on young children in the audience.

The first contextual factor at the scene level assessed the *rewards* that were associated with a perpetrator's violent action. A reward was defined as any verbal or nonverbal reinforcement that was given to or taken by a perpetrator for acting violently. The presence or absence of three types of rewards were assessed at this level: self praise, praise from others, or material rewards.

Similarly, *punishments* associated with violent actions were also measured at the scene level. Conceptually, a punishment was defined as any verbal or nonverbal sign of disapproval or disappointment that was expressed towards a perpetrator for acting violently. The presence or absence of four specific types of punishments were assessed at the scene level: self condemnation, condemnation from others, nonviolent condemnation, and violent condemnation.

The next contextual factor assessed at the scene level was *graphicness*. Three types of graphicness were assessed. The first factor assessed the explicitness of the violent behavioral act and the second measured the explicitness of the means-to-target impact. Explicitness was defined as the focus, concentration or level of detail with which violence was presented. The camera focus for each of these variables was coded as either shown up-close, shown long-shot, or not shown at all.

In addition to explicitness, the amount of *blood and gore* displayed within each scene was also measured. This variable evaluated the degree or quantity of blood, gore, and/or dismemberment that was depicted within a violent scene. There were four levels of graphicness: none, mild, moderate and extreme.

The last contextual factor assessed at this level was *humor*. Humor was defined as the use of speech, actions and/or behaviors that a character engaged in that were intended to amuse either the self, another character or characters, and/or the viewer. Humor, regardless of type, was simply coded as present or absent within each violent scene.

Program level context variables. At the program level, several global or macro-level contextual variables were measured. These variables were ascertained by the coder only at the end of each program viewed. The first variable was designed to assess the program's purpose for including violence within its unfolding narrative. More specifically, this variable measured whether or not the program contained an *anti-violence theme*.

A program was judged to possess an anti-violence theme if it illustrated that using violence is morally and/or socially wrong. Operationally, an anti-violence theme was coded as present if any of the following conditions were met within the context of the unfolding narrative: 1) alternatives to violent actions were presented and/or discussed throughout the program; 2) main characters repeatedly discussed the negative consequences of violence; 3) the physical pain and emotional suffering that results from violence were clearly emphasized; or 4) punishments for violence clearly and consistently outweighed rewards. If a program did not fit one of these criteria, then it was coded as having no anti-violence theme.

The next two contextual variables assessed the degree of realism surrounding the presentation of violence and its negative effects. The purpose of these program level contextual variables was to identify and discriminate those programs that present violence in a realistic context from those that present violence in a fantastic context.

Operationally, each program was evaluated for its *level of realism*. The coder assessed whether the content represented: 1) actual reality (i.e., programs that show footage of actual, real life events); 2) re-creation of reality (i.e., reenacted events that are presented similarly to how they actually occurred); 3) fiction (i.e., creative constructions that are not based upon actual events, but depict actions and events that could possibly occur; and 4) fantasy (i.e., programs containing characters that could not possibly exist or events that could not possible happen in the real world as we know it).

The second measure of realism assessed the *presentational style* of each program. This variable indicates whether a program was presented via animation, live action, or a mix of both formats.

Although research evidence indicates that more realistic portrayals of violence put most viewers at a greater risk in terms of learning aggressive acts, research also suggests that realistically depicting the negative consequences that result from engaging in violence inhibits viewers from learning and/or modeling aggressive actions. In an effort to assess how each program presented the long-term pain and suffering that results from violence, the next contextual factor, *harm/pain* was assessed at the end of each program viewed. This program level variable was defined much more broadly to include not only physical harm, but also emotional, financial, and psychological suffering that is experienced as a result of violence.

Those programs that presented harm/pain as a result of violence in the same scene or in the immediately adjacent scene were coded as presenting the consequences of violence in a "short-term" fashion. Those programs that depicted harm/pain later in the program were coded as presenting the consequences of violence in a "long-term/ extended" fashion. Those programs that did not present any harm/pain within the context of the plot, were coded as presenting "no harm" as a result of violence.

The next program level contextual factor assessed the overall *pattern of punishments* that were delivered to all good, bad, and both good and bad (defined below) characters involved in violence. The focus of this variable was to ascertain the patterns with which different types of characters (i.e., all of the good characters or all of the bad characters) received punishment for acting violently in a program. All good, bad, and both good and bad (blended) characters that engaged in violence were coded as being punished in one of the following patterns: punished throughout an entire program, punished at the end only, never or rarely punished, or not punished by any one of the above patterns.

Character context variables. In addition to assessing the nature and consequences surrounding violent acts, several character-based context variables were crafted in an effort to gain rich, descriptive data about the perpetrators and targets involved in violence. All characters, whether they instigated violence or received it, were coded for both demographic and attributive qualities. In terms of demographics, a character was assessed for its *type* (i.e., human, animal, supernatural creature, anthropomorphized animal, anthropomorphized supernatural being), *form* (single, multiple, implied), *size* if a multiple unit (i.e., 2; 3-9; 10-99; 100-999; 1000 or more), *sex* (i.e., male, female, can't tell), *age* (i.e., child, teen, adult, elderly, can't tell) and *apparent ethnicity* (i.e., white, hispanic, black, native american, asian/pacific islander, or middle eastern).

In addition to these demographic data, characters were assessed in terms of specific attributive qualities. The following contextual features were crafted in an effort to measure the *attractiveness* of the characters who engaged in violence. First, a character's "goodness" or "badness" was evaluated. Good characters were defined as those who acted benevolently, helped others, and/or were motivated to consider the needs of others before themselves. Bad characters, on the other hand, were those who acted primarily in their own self-interest, accommodated their own needs, and had very little regard for others. Those characters who were both good and bad were those that displayed a balance of both characteristics in a program. Characters were coded as "neutral" if they were either: (1) not featured long enough to ascertain their orientation towards others; or (2) their orientation could not be determined from the context of the plot.

Each character was also assessed for *hero status*. As indicated in the literature review, heroes are characters that children and adults are most likely to identify with and potentially imitate. In order to clearly differentiate heroes from good characters, we crafted a very narrow definition of this variable. A character was only coded as a hero if he/she/it met all of the following criteria: 1) appeared as one of the primary characters in the program's plot-line; 2) the character's role in the program was to protect others from becoming victims of violence; and 3) the character engaged in helping of other characters above and beyond the call of duty. All characters who did not meet this definition were coded as a "non-hero."

In year two of the study, we added three new character variables: primary character, government authority or law status, and overall pattern of punishment for *each* violent perpetrator. *Primary characters* are defined as those who are central and crucial to the plot. In order to be coded as primary, a character must meet all of the following criteria: (1) be someone for whom the story would be substantially different if the character was omitted; (2) have a speaking part; and (3) appear in more than one scene. Characters were coded as either primary or not.

Characters with *governmental authority* or law status were defined as any character who is employed full-time by a standard governmental body with the purpose of maintaining the peace of society and or safety of its citizens. Police and soldiers are the most common examples. Each character involved in violence was coded as either a governmental figure or not. For those characters who have governmental status, they were further coded as either military or non-military status.

And finally, we assessed the *pattern of punishment for each individual character* who perpetrated violence. Similar to the pattern of punishment for all good, bad and blended characters defined above, the variable assessed the pattern of negative reinforcements delivered to each perpetrator in a program for his/her/its violent behavior. At the end of each program, the pattern of punishment for each character was coded as either punished throughout, punished at the end only, never/rarely punished, or none of the above.

Coding and Reliability

The coding of data for this project was performed by 56 undergraduate students at the University of California, Santa Barbara. Individuals were recruited in the Department of Communication, and screened to obtain those with the strongest academic records. To perform coding work, individuals had to master all aspects of our codebook, which explicates all of our variables and measures in detail at both the conceptual and operational levels. This training was accomplished through a number of complementary processes. We began with approximately 40 hours of classroom instruction. Then we added approximately 20 hours of lab time where coders practiced applying our measures to different types of violent television content. Feedback on these practice sessions was provided individually, in small groups, and to the entire class of coders as appropriate to the training task.

Our testing for the reliability of coders was conducted in two phases. In the first phase, we monitored the decision-making of the coders in order to determine when they were fully trained and able to begin coding of actual data to be used in the analyses. Here the focus was on the coders themselves and their aptitude in internalizing all the coding rules. The second phase consisted of two different prongs. The first was an examination of the patterns in the coded data themselves so as to determine the degree of reliability, and hence the quality, of the data. For this analysis, we shifted the focus from individual coders to individual decision points in the process of coding. The second prong involved an assessment focused again on the coders' performance so as to spot fatigue or other problems that might diminish the quality of the data. Both of these different aspects of the second phase were conducted concurrently throughout the duration of the coding process. The same raw data were employed for both of the prongs, but they were analyzed in different ways.

Once training was complete, the actual data coding process was conducted by randomly assigning programs to individual coders. Coders viewed each show alone in a video lab and could watch the entire program or any segment of it as many times as necessary to ascertain the required coding judgments. Data for each program were obtained from the observations of a single coder. For this reason, it is essential to demonstrate that the coding process maintained a strong and consistent level of performance over time in order to insure the quality of the data. The next section describes how we monitored the reliability in coding of the data upon which the findings of this study are based.

Checking the Quality of Data

Procedure. The coding process required roughly 20 weeks (not counting holidays and break periods) to complete. During each week when coding was conducted, half of the active coders independently evaluated the same program. Their coding judgments were then compared for reliability assessment purposes. Thus, the decision-making of each coder was checked once during each two-week period.

The programs selected for reliability assessments were randomly chosen within each genre. All genres were examined at least twice. Two examples of each genre were tested in back-to-back weeks so that each coder's performance would be evaluated across the complete range of program content. Table 5 presents the list of randomly selected programs used for the reliability tests.

Conceptualization of reliability. Because the coding scheme developed in this project is very complex, coders had to make many different types of decisions when examining a show. It is best to categorize these decisions as existing at two distinct levels. The first level focuses on unitizing, that is, the identification of PATs and scenes. The second level is concerned with the degree of consistency among coders in choosing the same value for our 41 variables once the unitizing boundaries are established. Below, we explain the purpose and procedures for evaluating reliability at both of these levels.

Unitizing. This is a critical part of the coding process. In this study, unitizing refers to the process of identifying each PAT and each scene. If coders agree at the beginning and ending point of each PAT and each scene, then they are consistently identifying our units of analysis. The fundamental building block of the coding scheme is the PAT -- a single interaction involving violence. Every time a coder perceived an act of violence, s/he created a line of data that included the string of values on the variables that had to be coded at this level. In evaluating the unitizing process, we are not focusing on the string of numbers selected; instead we are focusing on the number of PAT lines a coder creates -- that is, the number of violent interactions the coder perceives to exist in the program.

If all coders have the same number of PAT lines on their coding form for a show *and* if those PAT lines refer to the same acts, then there is perfect agreement. To reiterate, both conditions must be met for perfect agreement. If coders differ on the number of PAT lines, then there is not perfect agreement. If coders all have the same number of PAT lines, but if there is disagreement about what those PATs are, then there is not perfect agreement.

Table 5

Programs Randomly Selected for the Continuing Reliability Tests

Genre	Program Name
Children's Series	Ren & Stimpy
	Sailor Moon
	Ren & Stimpy
	Darkwing Duck
	Rocky & Bullwinkle
Drama Series	Homicide
	Heat of the Night
	Homicide
	All My Children
	The Commish
	Mike Hammer
Comedy Series	Married...with Children
	I Dream of Jeannie
	Married...with Children
Movie	Drop Dead Fred
	Fast Times at Ridgemont High
Music Video	Party Machine
	Big Eighties
Reality-Based	Geraldo Rivera
	Gordon Elliot

For each show coded, the determination of PAT level reliability began with the construction of a matrix. This matrix was composed of one column for every coder and one line for every PAT identified by those coders.

We report three descriptors: the Agreement Mode, the range of PATs, and a Close Interval around the Agreement Mode (CIAM). An example will illustrate what we mean by the "Agreement Mode." If we have ten coders and one reported 7 PAT lines, seven reported 8 PAT lines, one reported 9 PAT lines, and one reported 11 PAT lines, the mode would be 8 PAT lines because that is the number reported by the greatest number of coders. Thus 70% of the coders are at this mode. If all seven coders had the same 8 PAT lines, then the agreement mode is 8.

39

In many cases, not all coders were at the Agreement Mode, so we also report the range of PAT lines exhibited by the set of coders. The smaller the range, the tighter the pattern of agreement. But sometimes the range can be misleading as an indicator of how much variation there is in a distribution. For example, let's say that we have ten coders: three have 4 PAT lines, five have 5 PAT lines, one has 6 PAT lines, and one has 12 PAT lines. The range here is from 4 to 12 PAT lines, which appears to signal a wide range of disagreement. However, 90% of the coders are within one PAT line of the mode.

We also compute a Close Interval around the Agreement Mode (CIAM). We operationalized "close to the agreement mode" as those judgments that were within one PAT Line on either side of the agreement mode. For example, if the agreement mode were 4, we would include in the CIAM each of the following: (a) other coders who also saw 4 PATs but disagreed on one of the PATs, (b) other coders who saw only 3 PATs but each of those 3 match PATs in the set of the 4 PATs that determine the Agreement Mode, and (c) other coders who had 5 PATs where 4 of those 5 PATs were identical to the 4 that determine the Agreement Mode. When the Agreement Mode is greater than five, we establish the width of the CIAM as 20% on either side of the mode. For example, if the Agreement Mode is 10, we include coders who exhibit no more than two disagreements with the coders at the Agreement Mode.

The procedure explained above for determining the Agreement Mode and the CIAM for PAT lines is the same as that used to evaluate agreement for scenes. For each show coded, a scene level matrix was constructed, which included a column for each coder and a line for each scene identified. We then computed and report below an Agreement Mode, a range, and a CIAM for scenes for each program.

Selecting values on the coding variables. Finally, we turned our attention to the consistency among coders in choosing a value on each coding variable. Our coding scheme contains a total of 41 variables: 14 at the program level, 13 for each scene within each program, and 14 for each PAT within each scene.

The reliability for coding variables was assessed in the following manner. At the program level, the modal value was identified for each variable. The number of coders at the modal value was divided by the total number of coders, thus computing a percentage of agreement.

At the scene and PAT levels, each line of the matrix was examined for its modal value. All coders at the modal value were counted and this number was recorded in the margin. These margin numbers were summed down all the rows of a matrix. This sum was divided by all the decisions reflected in the matrix, and the resulting fraction was the percentage of agreement among coders on that variable.

The computation of the reliability coefficient for scene and PAT level is more complicated than the computation for the program level codes because of the unitizing issues described above. At the PAT level analysis, the first step starts with the PAT level matrix of coders. This becomes a template of cells. This template is used to build 14 PAT matrices, one for each variable coded at the PAT level. For each line in each matrix, the modal value is identified; thus the reliability testing is based on a norm determined by the coders, not a prescribed criterion value. The number of coders selecting the modal value is entered in the margin of the matrix. These margin numbers (one for each PAT line) are summed and then divided by the number of cells in the matrix. This proportion is the percentage of agreement. These percentages of agreement were then converted into reliability coefficients by using a PRE (proportional reduction of error) procedure.

The term "percentage of agreement" is used several times in the above section. This is simply the number of times coders actually agreed divided by the number of times they could have possibly agreed. The larger the number, the better the agreement.

Although percentage of agreement is often a useful indicator of consistency, it is an incomplete measure, particularly for complex judgments. With complex measures, some context is needed to better interpret the meaning of the statistic. We have two ways of providing this context: employing a proportional reduction of error technique and providing an inferential context for interpreting our reliability calculations.

In summary, three procedures were used for reliability testing. First, agreement on the unitizing for PATs was assessed for each show. Second, agreement on the unitizing for scenes was assessed for each show. And third, the selection of codes (at program, scene, and PAT levels) was assessed. We realize the importance of going beyond reporting simple percentages of agreement, because they can be misleading. In our procedures we do both of the following: (1) convert percentages of agreement into reliability coefficients by removing the error portion of the agreement, and (2) report the confidence level we have that each reliability coefficient could have occurred by chance alone.

Results of reliability testing. The results of the reliability testing indicate that coders were generally consistent in their decisions. Their consistency in unitizing was quite good given the complexity of the task and the number of coders involved (see Table 6). There was always a range in the number of scenes, but in over half of the tests, 75% of coders fell within the 20% interval around the mode. Likewise with PATs, there was always a range in the number of violent interactions, but coders usually clustered acceptably around the mode. Across all of the programs examined for reliability, most coders agreed on the number of PATs (68% median agreement) and scenes (78% median agreement) within the 20% interval around the mode.

As for the consistency of coding the variables within units, we first computed a level of confidence for each of our 738 reliability coefficients (41 variables on each of 18 programs in the reliability test). Out of those 738 coefficients, only 11 (approximately 1%) were too small to attain statistical significance ($p < .05$). This proportion is only one-fifth of what we should expect by chance alone.

The reliability on each of the 41 variables was quite high as indicated by the median level of agreement. With the exception of a few exceptionally low coefficients (e.g., .38) the median level of agreement generally ranged from a low of .60 to a high of 1.0 (see Tables 7-9). Half of these medians are above .90, which is very good for a task of this magnitude and with so many coders. More than three-fourths of the reliability coefficients are above .80.

Check for Fatigue in Coder Performance

Maintaining consistency over time in coding practices is also essential for establishing the reliability of the data. Therefore, as noted above, we conducted a continual check to spot instances of coder fatigue as soon as possible and to make any necessary corrections. Using the same reliability data as that reported in the preceding section, but analyzing it from a different perspective, we were able to assess the performance of individual coders relative to the performance of the overall group.

For each reliability test, three indexes of quality were constructed: one for program coding, one for scene coding, and one for PAT coding. Each time a coder was in the modal group on a coding decision, he/she earned a point. Thus, coders who amassed the greatest number of points on an index were ranked the highest on consistency and were regarded as the best coders. Each week during the reliability testing, the principal investigators and research associates met to examine the indexes of quality for the previous week's test. If all coders scored high on the indexes, then there was no need for concern for individual coders. But if some coders had low index scores, they were given additional training to improve their performance. If a coder was consistently scoring low on these diagnostic tests week after week, the coder was removed from the coding pool, and the tapes that he/she had coded up to that point were reassigned to other coders. During this third year of coding, only three coders of 56 had to be removed from the coding pool.

Summary of Reliability

The 20-week long reliability monitoring procedures resulted in evidence that our coders were consistently making decisions about identifying violence and assigning codes across the 41 contextual variables. The diagnostic procedures were able to identify coder fatigue and make immediate corrections. Thus we have a high level of confidence that all who were trained to apply our measures would have been able to generate the same data base.

Table 6

Reliability Coefficients for PAT and Scene Range and Mode

Title	PAT range	PAT mode/%	PAT mode +/- 20%	Scene range	Scene mode/%	Scene Mode +/- 20%
Ren & Stimpy (N=15)	2-7	5/27%	60%	2-5	4/33%	73%
Sailor Moon (N=14)	4-12	8/21%	43%	2-6	3/36 %	64%
Homicide (N=14)	2-6	5/50%	79%	2-5	5/43%	71%
Heat of the Night (N=14)	4-6	4/50%	93%	3-5	4/43%	100%
Married...with Children (N=15)	3-7	4/20%	67%	1-6	4/20%	80%
I Dream of Jeannie (N=11)	3-10	10/14%	29%	2-7	5/29%	57%
Drop Dead Fred (N=23)	6-19	15/-	31 %	5-13	5/15%	31%
Fast Times at Ridgemont High (N=14)	2-9	9/14%	64%	1-5	4/14%	86%
Party Machine (N=13)	1-4	1/31%	69%	1-4	1/31%	69%
Big Eighties (N=14)	1-2	2/57%	100%	1-2	2/57%	100%
Geraldo Rivera (N=13)	1-2	2/77%	100%	-	1/100%	100%
Gordon Elliot (N=10)	-	1/100%	100%	-	1/100%	100%
Ren & Stimpy (N=22)	2-10	8/9%	55%	2-7	6/27%	68%
Homicide (N=21)	4-9	6/10%	57%	3-7	4/24%	71%
Married...with Children (N=19)	2-7	6/16%	58%	2-5	5/47%	79%
All My Children (N=16)	1-3	2/19%	100%	1-3	2/19%	100%
Darkwing Duck (N=8)	6-11	18/13%	75%	15-24	8/25%	75%
The Commish (N=6)	7-8	8/33%	100%	3-4	3/67%	100%
Rocky & Bullwinkle (N=9)	5-13	11/11%	44%	4-10	8/22%	78%
Mike Hammer (N=7)	14-19	16/14%	86%	6-8	7/43%	100%
Overall Median			68%			78%

Table 7: Reliability Coefficients for PAT Context Variables

Title	Type of act	Means used	Extent of means used	Harm depicted	Harm likely	Pain	Visual depiction
Ren & Stimpy (N=15)	1.0	.83	.85	.72	.56	.63	.92
Sailor Moon (N=14)	1.0	.62	.74	.68	.62	.60	.98
Homicide (N=14)	.98	.92	.78	.88	.92	.75	.81
Heat of the Night (N=14)	1.0	.84	.92	.77	.78	.80	.89
Married...with Children (N=15)	1.0	.96	.90	.77	.67	.64	1.0
I Dream of Jeannie (N=14)	1.0	.81	.89	.92	.89	.95	.91
Drop Dead Fred (N=13)	.96	.96	.84	.75	.77	.72	.99
Fast Times at Ridgemont High (N=14)	1.0	.93	.98	.89	.89	.84	.98
Party Machine (N=13)	1.0	1.0	.93	.64	.61	.54	1.0
Big Eighties (N=14)	1.0	.95	.91	.55	.77	.59	1.0
Geraldo Rivera (N=13)	1.0	1.0	.63	.56	.56	*.38	.75
Gordon Elliot (N=10)	1.0	.80	.90	.70	.70	.60	*.60
Ren & Stimpy (N=22)	.99	.80	.85	.64	.78	.62	.90
Homicide (N=21)	.93	.88	.89	.93	.91	.81	.86
Married...with Children (N=19)	1.0	.95	.96	.80	.67	.64	1.0
All My Children (N=16)	1.0	.93	.89	.82	.71	.68	.71
Darkwing Duck (N=8)	1.0	.88	.82	.79	.70	.80	.97
The Commish (N=6)	1.0	.95	1.0	.95	.90	.87	1.0
Rocky & Bullwinkle (N=9)	1.0	.95	.91	.75	.81	.84	.99
Mike Hammer (N=7)	1.0	.96	.87	.75	.82	.78	.99
Overall Range	.93-1.0	.62-1.0	.63-1.0	.55-.95	.56-.91	.38-.95	.60-1.0
Overall Median	1.0	.93	.89	.76	.77	.70	.98

Title	Sexual assault	Justifi-cation	Perpetrator type	Perpetrator size	Perpetrator reason	Target type	Target size
Ren & Stimpy (N=15)	1.0	.93	.88	.96	.67	1.0	1.0
Sailor Moon (N=14)	1.0	.95	.97	.97	.81	.97	.97
Homicide (N=14)	1.0	.95	.95	.88	.83	.92	.95
Heat of the Night (N=14)	1.0	.89	.91	.66	.75	.94	.92
Married...with Children (N=15)	1.0	.92	1.0	1.0	.81	1.0	1.0
I Dream of Jeannie (N=14)	1.0	.98	.88	.86	.91	.97	.97
Drop Dead Fred (N=13)	1.0	.80	.98	.96	.74	.98	.99
Fast Times at Ridgemont High (N=14)	.99	.88	.95	.95	.98	.98	.97
Party Machine (N=13)	.96	.93	1.0	1.0	.57	.82	.86
Big Eighties (N=14)	1.0	.91	.68	.68	.82	1.0	1.0
Geraldo Rivera (N=13)	1.0	1.0	.63	.88	.75	.94	.94
Gordon Elliot (N=10)	.80	1.0	1.0	1.0	.80	1.0	1.0
Ren & Stimpy (N=22)	1.0	.81	.90	.98	.72	1.0	1.0
Homicide (N=21)	1.0	.87	.90	.85	.83	.95	.97
Married...with Children (N=19)	1.0	.83	1.0	1.0	.79	1.0	1.0
All My Children (N=16)	1.0	.89	.96	1.0	.79	1.0	1.0
Darkwing Duck (N=8)	1.0	.90	.85	.81	.75	.91	.81
The Commish (N=6)	1.0	.92	.97	.97	.97	.90	.92
Rocky & Bullwinkle (N=9)	1.0	*.68	.95	.89	.88	.79	.79
Mike Hammer (N=7)	.99	.95	.95	.98	.86	.95	.97
Overall Range	.80-1.0	.65-1.0	.63-1.0	.66-1.0	.57-.98	.79-1.0	.79-1.0
Overall Median	1.0	.91	.95	.96	.81	.97	.97

Key: * = p>.05   unstarred coefficients = p<.05

Table 8: Reliability Coefficients for Scene Character and Context Variables

Title	Character age	Rewards: self praise	Rewards: praise from other	Rewards: material praise	Punishments: self condemnation	Punishments: condemnation from other
Ren & Stimpy (N=15)	.80	.81	.98	.91	1.0	.98
Sailor Moon (N=14)	.75	.76	.84	1.0	.98	.78
Homicide (N=14)	.71	.96	.96	.91	1.0	.93
Heat of the Night (N=14)	.94	.93	.94	.91	1.0	.91
Married...with Children (N=15)	.85	.88	.98	.92	1.0	.95
I Dream of Jeannie (N=14)	.98	.83	.96	.96	.99	.81
Drop Dead Fred (N=13)	.89	.88	.94	1.0	.95	.76
Fast Times at Ridgemont High (N=14)	.97	.96	.98	.98	.96	.90
Party Machine (N=13)	.80	.75	1.0	1.0	1.0	1.0
Big Eighties (N=14)	1.0	.95	1.0	1.0	1.0	1.0
Geraldo Rivera (N=13)	1.0	1.0	1.0	1.0	1.0	.92
Gordon Elliot (N=10)	.80	1.0	1.0	1.0	1.0	.80
Ren & Stimpy (N=22)	.92	.90	.96	.91	1.0	1.0
Homicide (N=21)	.88	.97	.90	.93	1.0	.95
Married...with Children (N=19)	.85	.96	1.0	.89	1.0	.98
All My Children (N=16)	.88	1.0	1.0	1.0	1.0	.93
Darkwing Duck (N=8)	.77	.76	.99	.81	.97	.99
The Commish (N=6)	.91	1.0	.95	1.0	1.0	*.75
Rocky & Bullwinkle (N=9)	.84	.90	.97	1.0	1.0	.94
Mike Hammer (N=7)	.96	.90	1.0	.96	.98	.84
Overall Range	.71-1.0	.75-1.0	.84-1.0	.81-1.0	.95-1.0	.76-1.0
Overall Median	.88	.92	.98	.97	1.0	.93

Title	Punishments: nonviolent action	Punishments: violent action	Explicitness: violent action	Explicitness: focus on action	Graphicness	Humor
Ren & Stimpy (N=15)	1.0	.96	.91	.85	.98	.96
Sailor Moon (N=14)	.98	.90	.90	.96	1.0	.70
Homicide (N=14)	.94	1.0	.80	.83	.65	.80
Heat of the Night (N=14)	.89	.98	.85	.81	.81	.96
Married...with Children (N=15)	.97	1.0	.97	1.0	1.0	.95
I Dream of Jeannie (N=14)	.86	.94	.78	.78	.81	.90
Drop Dead Fred (N=13)	.89	.98	.93	.92	.99	.80
Fast Times at Ridgemont High (N=14)	.98	.94	.88	.84	.86	.70
Party Machine (N=13)	.96	1.0	.75	.82	1.0	.79
Big Eighties (N=14)	1.0	1.0	.91	.91	1.0	.86
Geraldo Rivera (N=13)	1.0	1.0	.69	.69	.92	1.0
Gordon Elliot (N=10)	1.0	1.0	.90	.80	.70	1.0
Ren & Stimpy (N=22)	1.0	.94	.88	.84	.89	.83
Homicide (N=21)	.96	.95	.80	.80	.51	.75
Married...with Children (N=19)	.93	.93	.96	.99	.99	.99
All My Children (N=16)	1.0	.89	1.0	1.0	.86	1.0
Darkwing Duck (N=8)	.99	.81	.82	.79	.85	.88
The Commish (N=6)	*.80	.85	.65	.65	.70	.90
Rocky & Bullwinkle (N=9)	1.0	.97	.84	.84	1.0	.94
Mike Hammer (N=7)	.96	.84	.94	.92	.92	.92
Overall Range	.80-1.0	.81-1.0	.65-1.0	.65-1.0	.51-1.0	.70-1.0
Overall Median	.98	.96	.88	.84	.91	.90

Key: * = p>.05   unstarred coefficients = p<.05

Table 9: Reliability Coefficients for Program Character and Context Variables

Title	Narrative Purpose	Realism	Harm/Pain	Style	Punish Pattern	Punish Bad	Punish Good
Ren & Stimpy (N=15)	1.0	.93	.73	1.0	.67	.53	.60
Sailor Moon (N=14)	1.0	.93	.93	1.0	.71	.86	.71
Homicide (N=14)	.79	.86	.79	1.0	.73	.86	.71
Heat of the Night (N=14)	.79	.86	.79	1.0	.70	.86	.71
Married...with Children (N=15)	1.0	1.0	.67	1.0	.72	.86	.71
I Dream of Jeannie (N=14)	1.0	.64	.57	1.0	.79	.93	.57
Drop Dead Fred (N=13)	1.0	.77	.77	.69	.69	.31	.54
Fast Times at Ridgemont High (N=14)	1.0	1.0	.93	1.0	.64	.50	.64
Party Machine (N=13)	1.0	.69	.54	1.0	.75	1.0	.46
Big Eighties (N=14)	1.0	1.0	.50	1.0	.86	.57	.93
Geraldo Rivera (N=13)	1.0	.92	.46	1.0	.63	.46	.92
Gordon Elliot (N=10)	*.70	.90	*.40	1.0	.85	.90	.90
Ren & Stimpy (N=22)	1.0	.95	.86	1.0	.85	.50	.55
Homicide (N=21)	.90	.95	.76	1.0	.88	.90	.86
Married...with Children (N=19)	1.0	.79	.68	1.0	.78	.58	.63
All My Children (N=16)	1.0	1.0	.69	1.0	.98	.81	.88
Darkwing Duck (N=8)	1.0	.88	1.0	1.0	.67	.75	.63
The Commish (N=6)	1.0	1.0	.66	1.0	.80	.50	.83
Rocky & Bullwinkle (N=9)	1.0	.89	.78	1.0	.78	*.33	*.44
Mike Hammer (N=7)	1.0	1.0	.83	1.0	.76	.50	*.33
Overall Range	.70-1.0	.64-1.0	.40-1.0	.69-1.0	.63-.98	.33-1.0	.33-.93
Overall Median	1.0	.93	.75	1.0	.76	.67	.68

Title	Punish Good/Bad	Primary Char.	Law Status	Char. type	Char. sex	Char. ethnicity	Char. good/bad	Char. hero status
Ren & Stimpy (N=15)	.73	.98	1.0	.78	.80	.70	.63	.97
Sailor Moon (N=14)	.86	.85	1.0	.51	.98	.92	.85	.91
Homicide (N=14)	.86	.78	.94	.96	.88	.82	.74	.85
Heat of the Night (N=14)	.86	.73	.94	.96	.88	.82	.74	.85
Married...with Children (N=15)	.53	.94	1.0	.93	1.0	1.0	.50	1.0
I Dream of Jeannie (N=14)	.93	.87	.97	.93	.89	.95	.90	.97
Drop Dead Fred (N=13)	.69	.84	.97	.95	.92	.91	.74	.93
Fast Times at Ridgemont High (N=14)	.50	.95	1.0	1.0	1.0	.94	.65	.98
Party Machine (N=13)	.69	.75	1.0	1.0	.95	.55	.65	.90
Big Eighties (N=14)	1.0	.71	1.0	1.0	.79	1.0	.50	1.0
Geraldo Rivera (N=13)	.54	1.0	1.0	1.0	1.0	.94	.69	1.0
Gordon Elliot (N=10)	1.0	.95	1.0	.85	.75	.75	.75	1.0
Ren & Stimpy (N=22)	.55	.90	.98	.83	.90	.68	.68	.97
Homicide (N=21)	.86	.84	.88	.96	.93	.82	.84	.94
Married...with Children (N=19)	.47	.78	.88	.96	.93	.82	.84	.94
All My Children (N=16)	.88	.67	.85	.94	.90	.94	.73	.90
Darkwing Duck (N=8)	.75	.96	.97	.82	.86	.82	.89	.85
The Commish (N=6)	.67	.77	.98	.93	.89	.86	.89	.80
Rocky & Bullwinkle (N=9)	.56	.90	.91	.94	.97	.79	*.63	1.0
Mike Hammer (N=7)	.67	.84	.99	1.0	.99	.94	.88	.93
Overall Range	.47-1.0	.67-1.0	.85-1.0	.51-1.0	.75-1.0	.55-1.0	.50-.90	.80-1.0
Overall Median	.71	.85	.98	.95	.91	.84	.74	.94

Key: * = p>.05   unstarred coefficients = p<.05

Three Year Assessment of the Methods

In this section we report on the sample and the measurement of coder reliability across the entire three years of the project. This multi-year assessment of the methods employed in this study is important because the results reported below will often include comparisons among our context variables across the full three year period. We have either reproduced exactly, or summarized information about the sample and coding reliability contained in the Year 1 and Year 2 reports and placed it alongside comparable Year 3 information.

The Sample

Sampling periods. Three sets of approximately 20 weeks each, beginning in October 1994 and ending in June 1997, were chosen as the sampling period. (See Table 10 for a list of the specific sample weeks).

Composite weeks of programming. The sampling procedure resulted in three seven-day composite weeks of programming for the 1994-95, 1995-96, and 1996-97 television seasons. Virtually all shows in the regular program schedule for each channel are represented in the final composite week for each year. Furthermore, program scheduling changes from year to year are now reflected in the composite weeks when we consider the sample of programs as a whole.

Total program count and error rate. The total taped sample includes 9,632 programs. A complete grid of all programs selected for inclusion in the sample appears in each of the yearly reports. Across the three year period a total of 342 programs (4%) were removed from the sample due to taping errors or other technical problems. Table 11 includes a breakdown of missing program blocks by individual channel.

Sample exclusions. As noted above, religious programs, game shows, "infomercials" or home shopping material, instructional programs, sports, and news were excluded from analysis in the study. In order to maintain the integrity of the sample design and its representativeness of the overall television environment, programs were included in the sample grid whenever they were selected by the random draw that created our composite week of programming. However, none of these program types were examined for violence. Of the total 9,632 programs selected across the three years, 1,432 (15%) fall into the excluded category and were not included in the coding analyses (see Table 12).

Table 10

Comparison of Sample Weeks Across Years

Week Number	Year 1 Dates	Year 2 Dates	Year 3 Dates
1	October 8-14, 1994	October 7-13, 1995	October 5-11, 1996
2	October 15-21	October 14-20	October 12-18
3	October 22-28	October 21-27	October 19-25
4	October 29-November 4	October 28-November 3	October 26-November 1
5	November 5-11	November 4-10	November 2-8
6	December 3-9	December 2-8	November 30-December 6
7	January 14-20, 1995	January 13-19, 1996	January 11-17, 1997
8	January 21-27	January 20-26	January 18-24
9	January 28-February 3	January 27-February 2	January 25-31
10	February 4-10	February 3-9	February 1-7
11	February 11-17	February 10-16	February 8-14
12	March 4-10	March 2-8	March 1-7
13	March 11-17	March 9-15	March 8-15
14	March 18-24	March 16-22	March 16-21
15	April 22-28	April 20-26	April 19-25
16	April 29-May 5	April 27-May 3	April 26-May 2
17	May 6-12	May 4-10	May 3-9
18	May 20-26	May 18-24	May 10-16
19	May 27-June 2	May 25-31	May 17-23
20	June 3-9	June 1-7	May 24-30
21			May 31-June 6

Table 11

Breakdown of Programs and Taping Errors in Sample Across Years

	Year One			Year Two			Year Three		
Channel	Number of Programs	Taping Errors	% Taping Errors	Number of Programs	Taping Errors	% Taping Errors	Number of Programs	Taping Errors	% Taping Errors
ABC	137	3	2%	137	4	3%	148	2	1%
CBS	143	6	4%	143	5	3%	138	7	4%
NBC	129	3	2%	132	1	1%	135	7	4%
FOX	163	14	9%	168	2	1%	189	6	3%
PBS	163	4	2%	169	3	2%	178	4	2%
KCAL	162	3	2%	150	2	1%	156	4	2%
KCOP	147	3	2%	135	2	1%	136	7	4%
KTLA	104	8	8%	152	0	0%	155	7	4%
A&E	95	3	3%	100	6	6%	107	2	2%
AMC	82	2	2%	80	9	11%	85	0	0%
BET	133	5	4%	124	2	2%	107	11	9%
CAR	171	9	5%	202	4	2%	211	9	4%
DIS	166	8	5%	172	0	0%	174	2	1%
FAM	174	5	3%	143	0	0%	124	5	3%
LIF	145	7	5%	139	1	1%	148	4	2%
MTV	153	4	3%	160	1	1%	156	8	5%
NIK	229	9	4%	224	3	1%	225	8	4%
TNT	94	7	7%	106	1	1%	100	2	2%
USA	143	3	2%	139	0	0%	147	13	7%
VH-1	181	11	6%	187	3	2%	138	37	26%
HBO	104	1	1%	94	1	1%	83	6	7%
MAX	81	3	4%	87	0	0%	82	6	7%
SHO	86	9	10%	92	3	3%	90	2	2%
TOTAL	3185	130	4%	3235	53	2%	3212	159	5%

49

Table 12

Breakdown of Programs and Exclusions in Sample Across Years

	Year One			Year Two			Year Three		
Channel	Number of Programs	Not Coded	% Not Coded	Number of Programs	Not Coded	% Not Coded	Number of Programs	Not Coded	% Not Coded
ABC	137	40	29%	137	56	41%	148	58	28%
CBS	143	54	38%	143	51	36%	138	42	23%
NBC	129	48	37%	132	44	33%	135	45	25%
FOX	163	26	16%	168	18	11%	189	29	13%
PBS	163	12	7%	169	22	13%	178	16	8%
KCAL	162	55	34%	150	49	32%	156	39	20%
KCOP	147	28	19%	135	20	15%	136	24	16%
KTLA	104	41	39%	152	20	13%	155	28	15%
A&E	95	0	0%	100	5	5%	107	4	4%
AMC	82	0	0%	80	0	0%	85	0	0%
BET	133	29	22%	124	23	19%	107	19	14%
CAR	171	0	0%	202	0	0%	211	0	0%
DIS	166	0	0%	172	0	0%	174	0	0%
FAM	174	58	33%	143	58	41%	124	41	25%
LIF	145	51	36%	139	53	38%	148	62	30%
MTV	153	13	8%	160	15	9%	156	14	8%
NIK	229	2	1%	224	4	2%	225	0	0%
TNT	94	2	2%	106	5	5%	100	2	2%
USA	143	33	23%	139	32	23%	147	35	17%
VH-1	181	0	0%	187	2	1%	138	4	3%
HBO	104	0	0%	94	0	0%	83	0	0%
MAX	81	0	0%	87	0	0%	82	0	0%
SHO	86	0	0%	92	1	1%	90	0	0%
TOTAL	3185	492	15%	3235	478	15%	3212	462	14%

Checking the Quality of Data

Procedure. Each year the coding process required roughly 20 weeks (excluding holidays and break periods) to complete. During each week when coding was conducted, roughly half of the active coders independently evaluated the same program. Their coding judgments were then compared for reliability assessment purposes. The programs selected for reliability assessments were randomly chosen within each genre. All genres were examined at least four times across the three year period. Several genres such as Drama Series and Children Series were examined up to 16 times because of the high level of violence within them. This large number of tests assures that estimates of reliability for these genres are extremely stable. Table 13 presents the list of randomly selected programs used for the reliability tests across the three years of the study.

Reliability

As we noted above, coders had to make decisions at two distinct levels. The first level focuses on unitizing, that is, coder identification of PATs and scenes. The second level is concerned with coders in choosing the same value for our context variables once the unitizing boundaries are established.

Unitizing. Unitizing refers to the process of identifying each PAT and each scene. If coders agree at the beginning and ending point of each PAT and each scene, then they are consistently identifying our units of analysis.

To measure the level of agreement among coders when unitizing we computed a Close Interval around the Agreement Mode (CIAM). We operationalized "close to the agreement mode" as those judgments that were within 20% on either side of the agreement mode. The procedure explained above for determining the Agreement Mode and the CIAM for PAT lines is the same as that used to evaluate agreement for scenes.

Selecting values on the coding variables. We also measured the consistency among coders in choosing a value on each coding variable. Our coding scheme contains a total of 41 variables: 14 at the program level, 13 for each scene within each program, and 14 for each PAT within each scene.

Results of reliability testing. The results of the reliability testing indicate that coders were remarkably consistent in their unitizing decisions. Table 14 displays the median level of unitizing agreement among coders for PATs and scenes across the three years of the study. The overall medians displayed in the table were computed by summing each of the individual medians from each of the reliability tests across the three years of the study and computing a "median of medians."

The median percentage of coders who fell within the 20% interval around the mode for scenes across the three years was 100%. There was a slightly wider range in the number of violent interactions or PATs identified, but overall, coders clustered

51

acceptably around the mode at a high level. Across all of the programs examined for reliability in the three year period, the median level of agreement on the number of PATs within the 20% interval around the mode was 76%.

As for the consistency of coding the variables within units, each year we computed a level of confidence for each of our reliability coefficients. A summary of these coefficients was also computed each year in the form of an overall median for each context variable. These summary coefficients for each year are displayed in the first three columns (Year One, Year Two, Year Three) of Table 15. An overall median that summarizes coder performance over the three-year period was also computed and is displayed in the fourth column of the table. As with the level of unitizing, the overall medians displayed in the table were computed by summing each of the medians from the three years of individual reliability tests of the variables coded and a median of medians was computed. For example, the overall median for the PAT level variable "Harm Depicted" was computed by summing all of the individual medians obtained for reliability tests of that variable over the three years of testing.

The reliability on each of the 41 variables, across the three years, was quite high as indicated by the median level of agreement. With the exception of one moderately low coefficient (.61), the median level of agreement for all of the context variables, across the three year period, ranged from a low of .71 to a high of 1.0. Over half of these medians are .90, or above and more than three-fourths of the median reliability coefficients are above .80. These reliabilities are very good for a task of this magnitude and with so many coders.

Summary of Methods

When we consider the results of our assessment of the methodology employed in this three-year study a remarkably solid research foundation was established for the evaluation of violence on television. The sampling procedure resulted in three, seven-day composite weeks of programming for the 1994-95, 1995-96 and 1996-97 television seasons. Nearly all shows in the regular program schedule for each channel are represented in the final composite week for each year. The total taped three-year sample includes over 9,600 programs. The results of the reliability testing indicate that coders were very consistent in their unitizing decisions in each year of the study. The reliability on each of the 41 variables, across the three years, was also quite high.

Table 13

Programs Randomly Selected for the Continuing Reliability Tests

Year One		Year Two		Year Three	
Genre	Program Name	Genre	Program Name	Genre	Program Name
Children's Series	Top Cat	Children's Series	Scooby Doo	Children's Series	Ren & Stimpy
	Captain Planet		Tazmania		Sailor Moon
			Jetsons		Ren & Stimpy
					Darkwing Duck
					Rocky & Bullwinkle
Drama Series	Rockford Files	Drama Series	Charlie's Angels	Drama Series	Homicide
	Lou Grant		Renegade		Heat of the Night
	Sherlock Holmes		MacGyver		Homicide
	Wild, Wild West		Star Trek: Deep Space 9		All My Children
	Days of Our Lives				The Commish
	Young and the Restless				Mike Hammer
Movie	God is my Co-Pilot	Movie	The Wild Life	Movie	Drop Dead Fred
	Coma		The Cowboy Way		Fast Times at Ridgemont High
			Colombo Movie		
			9 1/2 Weeks		
			Trapped in Paradise		
Comedy Series	Designing Women	Comedy Series	I Love Lucy	Comedy Series	Married...with Children
	Fresh Prince		Roseanne		I Dream of Jeannie
			Wayans Brothers		Married...with Children
Reality-Based	COPS			Reality-Based	Geraldo Rivera
	Highway Patrol				Gordon Elliot
Music Video	Yo MTV Raps	Music Video	MTV Videos	Music Video	Party Machine
	VH-1 Video		MTV's Most Wanted Jams		Big Eighties
			VH-1 Videos		

Table 14
Unitizing Across Years

	Year One	Year Two	Year Three	Overall Median
PAT mode +/- 20%	.80	.60	.68	.76
Scene mode +/- 20%	1.0	.97	.78	1.0

Table 15
Summary of Reliability Coefficients Across Years

		Year One	Year Two	Year Three	Overall Median
P A T	Type of Act	1.0	1.0	1.0	1.0
	Means Used	.90	.94	.93	.93
	Extent of Means Used	.88	.87	.89	.87
	Harm Depicted	.84	.83	.76	.81
	Harm Likely	.83	.77	.77	.78
	Pain	.81	.81	.70	.79
	Visual Depiction	.98	.99	.98	.98
	Sexual Assault	1.0	1.0	1.0	1.0
	Justification	*	.87	.91	.89
	Perpetrator type	.97	.96	.95	.96
	Perpetrator Size	.95	.94	.96	.95
	Perpetrator Reason	.75	.79	.81	.79
	Target Type	.98	.96	.97	.97
	Target Size	.93	.95	.97	.97
S C E N E	Character Age	.97	.96	.88	.95
	Self Praise	.93	.83	.92	.90
	Praise from Other	.95	.95	.98	.96
	Material Praise	.96	.94	.97	.97
	Self Condemnation	1.0	1.0	1.0	1.0
	Condemnation from Other	.92	.90	.93	.92
	Nonviolent Action	.86	.93	.98	.95
	Violent Action	.96	.95	.96	.95
	Explicitness-Violent Action	.89	.90	.88	.89
	Explicitness-Focus on Impact	.86	.89	.84	.86
	Graphicness	.88	.90	.91	.89
	Humor	.95	.83	.90	.91
P R O G R A M	Narrative Purpose	1.0	1.0	1.0	1.0
	Realism	.97	.96	.93	.95
	Harm/Pain	.70	.65	.75	.73
	Style	1.0	1.0	1.0	1.0
	Punish Bad	.64	.82	.67	.71
	Punish Good	.63	.56	.68	.61
	Punish Good/Bad	.81	.61	.71	.75
	Primary Character	*	.88	.85	.87
	Char. Type	1.0	.99	.95	1.0
	Char. Sex	.97	.97	.91	.96
	Char. Ethnicity	.96	.93	.84	.93
	Char. Good/Bad	.75	.79	.74	.75
	Char. Hero Status	.93	.96	.94	.96

* = variable was created in Year 2 of the project, therefore no data can be reported for Year 1

Chapter 3

RESULTS: YEAR THREE DATA

This chapter and the following two chapters present results. This chapter provides a comprehensive report of general descriptive patterns in the data from our third-year sample, based on programming that was presented in the 1996-97 television season. Chapter 4 compares this year's data patterns with those from last year (1995-96) as well as the year before (1994-95), highlighting changes and consistencies across the three year time-span. Finally, Chapter 5 presents a multivariate assessment that identifies violent portrayals that pose the highest risk for children's learning of aggressive attitudes and behaviors.

Before we present the year three findings, we remind the reader of four key methodological issues. First, not all programs that we sampled for our composite week of programming (encompassing 23 channels from 6:00 a.m. to 11:00 p.m.) are actually analyzed in the study. As mentioned previously in the Methods chapter, several types of programs were excluded from the analysis in our contract with the National Cable Television Association (e.g., news, sports, religious programming, instructional shows). These programs collectively represent 14% of all programs in the composite week sample. When these shows are subtracted from the total composite, the analysis sample this year involves 2,750 television programs.

Second, we want to underscore the importance of interpreting our findings accurately. **The results should always be framed in terms of the correct unit of analysis.** Some of the findings below pertain to *programs* as the unit of analysis, because a particular variable was coded at the program level. For example, style of presentation was coded at the program level so all results pertaining to this variable refer to the *percentage of programs* that feature animation or live action. In contrast, some of the findings pertain to *violent scenes* as the unit of analysis, because a particular variable was coded at the scene level. For example, graphicness was coded at the scene level so all results pertaining to this variable refer to *percentage of violent scenes* that feature graphic violence. Lastly, some of the findings pertain to *violent interactions* as the unit of analysis, because a particular variable was coded at the most micro level or unit of analysis in our study. For instance, the type of means employed in violence was coded at the interaction level, so all results pertaining to this variable refer to the *percentage of violent interactions* that involve a particular means like guns. We encourage the reader to consider carefully each finding in terms of its correct unit of analysis (i.e., program, scene, interaction).

Third, we have created two key "locator variables" that partition the total sample into meaningful subgroups. The locator variables allow us to determine where in the television landscape particular types of violence are most likely to occur. Our two locator variables are channel type and program genre. For channel type, the 23 channels in the sample were arranged into five primary groups as follows: (1) *broadcast network*, which includes ABC, CBS, Fox, and NBC; (2) *public broadcast*, which includes PBS; (3) *independent broadcast*, which includes the three VHF-licensed independents stations in Los Angeles, KTLA, KCOP, and KCAL; (4) *basic cable*, which includes Arts & Entertainment, American Movie Classics, Black Entertainment Television, Cartoon Network, The Family Channel, Lifetime, Music TV, Nickelodeon, Turner Network Television, USA Network, Video Hits-1, and The Disney Channel; and (5) *premium cable*, which includes Cinemax, Home Box Office, and Showtime. For the genre locator variable, we classified all programs in our sample into six groups: drama, comedy, movies, music videos, reality-based programs, and children's programs.

Fourth, in all analyses involving locator variables, we essentially are searching for differences between subgroups of programming. For example, does the prevalence of violence differ significantly across the five channel types or across the six program genres? To answer such questions, we considered two types of significance: statistical and practical. Statistical significance refers to how much confidence we have that the patterns we observe in the findings accurately reflect patterns in the entire population of television programming. To assess statistical significance, we computed a chi-square statistic for the pattern of data across each locator variable. Each chi-square has an accompanying probability value (p), which indicates the level of confidence we have that the pattern is not due to chance or error. For example, if the p-value is < .001, it means that there is less than one chance in 1,000 that this pattern is a result of error. Unless otherwise indicated, all reported differences involving locator variables included in this report are statistically significant at $p < .05$.

However, not all of the differences that are statistically significant are necessarily meaningful from a practical perspective. For instance, if our analysis reveals that a small but statistically significant difference exists on some comparison (for example, a table reveals that 55% of all programs contain violence whereas only 50% of comedy series contain violence), we would not assume that this finding has practical significance. We view 5% as being too small for us to regard as a substantive difference. To assess practical significance (our second type of significance), we examined the absolute magnitude of difference in percentages for our descriptive findings. Unless we observe a difference of at least 10% between the overall pattern across all programming (i.e., industry average) and the pattern found for a specific subgroup of programming, we are not prepared to assert that a difference of practical significance exists. Above that threshold, we differentiate two levels of meaning. Differences of 10% to 19% are regarded as *moderate* differences, whereas differences of 20% or more are regarded as *substantial*. Although these cut-points are somewhat arbitrary, we use them because they are a helpful tool in summarizing important differences that exist across our numerous analyses.

This chapter is organized to address two broad questions. First, how often does violence appear across the television landscape? Second, assessing program content at a more detailed level of analysis, what are the patterns in the context of the violence as it is presented on television?

57

The Presence of Violence: Prevalence, Saturation, and Rate

To what extent does violence appear in the television environment? There are three ways this question can be answered. One is to assess the distribution of violence *across* programs. This refers to the prevalence of violence on television. Another approach is to examine the concentration of violence *within* programs. This refers to the saturation of violence. A final way is to assess the amount of violence *per hour*. This refers to the hourly rate of violence on television.

Also important is the overall message about violence in television programming. Do violent programs feature aggression primarily for entertainment purposes or to emphasize the negative personal and social costs of violence? We answer this question by examining the frequency with which violent programs feature an "anti-violence theme" or not. All of these issues are addressed in this section, which then culminates in an assessment of adjusted prevalence.

Prevalence

The issue of prevalence raises the question: What percentage of the coded television programs contain violence? If a program contains one or more acts of violence, we regard it as violent for purposes of our prevalence analysis. By this criterion, 61% of all programs we coded contain some violence; the remaining 39% of programs contain no portrayals that qualified as violence given our definition.

Recall that our definition of violence has three main components: (1) behavioral acts, (2) credible threats, and (3) harmful consequences of unseen violence. A total of 17,638 interactions containing some type of violence were coded in our sample of programming.

What is the most prevalent form of violence in these interactions? Behavioral acts account for 67% of all violent interactions (see Figure 1). In other words, two thirds of all violent interactions involve a perpetrator committing an actual physical act of violence. Far fewer of the violent interactions involve credible threats (27%), where the perpetrator demonstrates a clear intent to harm the target physically and has the means ready to do so, but for some reason does not follow through immediately. Much more rare (3%) are interactions involving harmful consequences of unseen violence, or instances in which an injured victim is depicted but the violence itself is not shown on screen. Although most accidents were not coded because they lacked the most important element of our definition (intent to harm), accidental violence *was* included in situations where a character experienced unintentional harm as a result of ongoing violence. Such accidents are quite rare and account for only 3% of all violent interactions.

Prevalence by channel type. Does prevalence vary by channel type? The answer is yes. Programming on premium cable is *substantially* more likely to contain violence than the industry average of 61% (see Figure 2). In contrast, the percent of violent programs on public broadcast is *substantially* lower. Also, broadcast networks are *moderately* lower. All of the differences we highlight in the results section have met the statistical criterion of $p < .05$ according to a chi-square test of frequencies, as well as the more conservative criterion of practical significance indicated above. Recall that to be substantively significant, we stipulated that there must be a minimum of 10% difference between an observed percentage on a particular locator variable and the overall pattern or average across all programming.

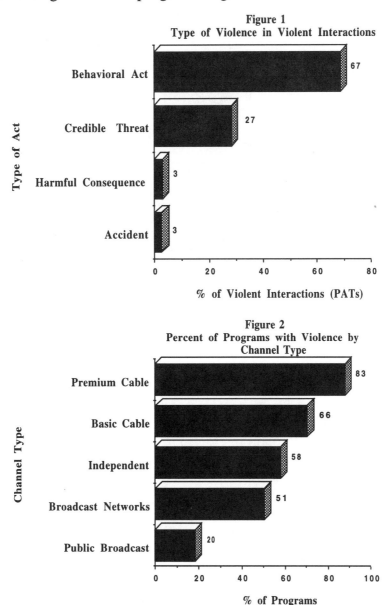

Figure 1
Type of Violence in Violent Interactions

Figure 2
Percent of Programs with Violence by Channel Type

<u>Prevalence by genre.</u> The prevalence findings also vary significantly by program genre. Movies feature *substantially* more programs with violence and dramas contain significantly more shows with violence than the industry average (61%). On the low end, comedy and reality-based shows each exhibit a *substantially* lower prevalence of violence (see Figure 3). It is not surprising that the movie genre would display the greatest prevalence given that premium cable, which is dominated by films, also has the highest prevalence among the channel types. Perhaps unexpectedly, reality-based programs are less likely to contain violence, although we must underscore that this genre not only includes programs like *Cops* and *American Justice*, but also talk shows and documentaries which often deal with topics other than violence.

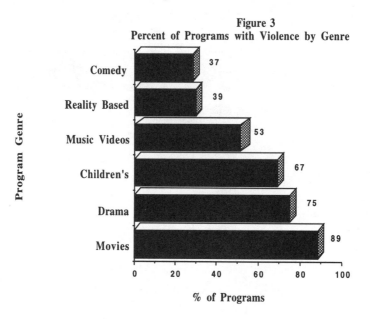

Figure 3
Percent of Programs with Violence by Genre

Saturation

The issue of saturation poses the question: Within each violent program, is there only one interaction of violence or are there many interactions? In the above analysis of prevalence, a program that contains only one violent interaction is treated the same as a program that contains 10 or 20 interactions. Clearly, violent programs can differ quite a bit in terms of the number of violent interactions, or perpetrator/target combinations, they contain. Our results show that many of the programs cluster at the lower end of the frequency distribution, with 18% of programs containing only one violent interaction, 15% containing two, and 9% containing three. Collectively, this means that 43% of all violent programs contain between one and three violent interactions. Another 26% contain between four and eight violent interactions. The remaining 32% fall into the category with the highest saturation of violence -- programs that feature nine or more different violent interactions or perpetrator/target combinations.

It is important to underscore that these data say nothing about the *extent* of individual violent behaviors within each of these incidents. A perpetrator could hit the same target once or 20 times in succession and it would still qualify as only one interaction. The findings on extensiveness or repetition of violent behaviors against the same target are reported in a subsequent section in this chapter.

Saturation by channel. Does saturation vary by channel type? Again, the answer is yes. Premium cable has the greatest saturation of violence with 60% of its violent programs displaying nine or more interactions (see Figure 4). Independent broadcast channels are also higher (43%) than the industry norm. Public broadcast is *substantially* below the industry average with only 11% of its violent programs containing nine or more violent interactions.

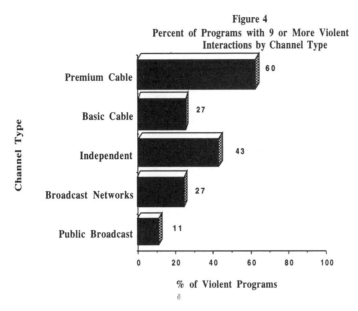

Figure 4
Percent of Programs with 9 or More Violent
Interactions by Channel Type

Saturation by genre. Movies have the highest saturation of violence with 59% of the violent films displaying nine or more interactions (see Figure 5). Reality-based programs are lower than the industry norm and comedy and music videos are *substantially* lower.

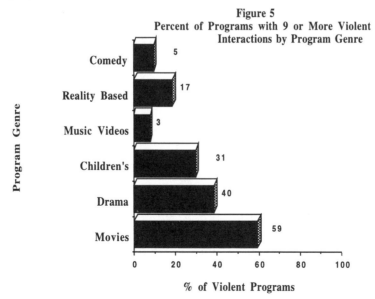

Figure 5
Percent of Programs with 9 or More Violent
Interactions by Program Genre

61

Rate

The issue of rate deals with the question: During an average hour of television programming, how many violent interactions are there? In the total sample of 2,586 hours of codeable programming, we found a total of 17,638 violent interactions (PATs). This computes to an average rate of 6.82 PATs per hour (total number of interactions/total number of hours). In other words, a viewer who sits down to watch television is likely to see at least six incidents of violence involving different perpetrator and target combinations per hour.

Rate by channel type. Premium cable channels have the highest rate of PATs per hour at 8.69. PBS has the lowest rate of violent interactions per hour (.76 PATs). In between these two extremes are the broadcast networks at 4.21 PATs per hour; basic cable channels at 7.07 PATs per hour; and independent channels at 8.09 PATs per hour.

Rate by genre. Children's programming has the highest rate of violence per hour at 13.37 PATs. The lowest rate can be found in reality shows with 1.69 PATs per hour. In between these extremes are comedy programs with 1.77 PATs per hour, music videos with 3.05 PATs per hour, drama series with 7.36 PATs per hour, and movies at 7.74 PATs per hour.

Prevalence of Programming with an Anti-Violence Theme

Even though a program contains violence, it could have an anti-violence theme. Programs were coded as having an anti-violence theme if the overall message emphasized that violence is destructive or wrong. This concept was operationalized using four different criteria. In order to be categorized as an anti-violence theme, at least one of the following patterns had to be a strong focus of the program's narrative: (1) alternatives to violence are emphasized; (2) the main characters show reluctance or remorse for committing violence; (3) pain and suffering are depicted throughout, and some attention is devoted to how the victims' family and/or the community is affected; or (4) on balance, there are many more punishments for violence throughout the program than there are rewards.

Of all programs containing violence, only 3% emphasize an anti-violence theme. This finding does not vary significantly across channel types or genre. Some examples of programs identified in the sample as reflecting an anti-violence theme are presented later in this chapter.

Adjusted Presence

In constructing a summary view for the presence of violence, we believe it is appropriate and informative to adjust our statistic regarding the overall prevalence of violence in a way that reflects the industry's use of responsible approaches to presenting violence on American television. Programs featuring an anti-violence theme should pose few if any concerns to viewers; the most probable viewing outcome would be to *reduce* the risk of a harmful effect such as learning of aggression. Thus, we believe it is proper in summarizing the prevalence of violence across the overall television landscape to *remove* this type of portrayal from consideration. To review, a total of 3% of programs (N = 62) containing violence in this year's sample feature an anti-violence theme.

Our initial finding on prevalence is that 61% of all programs analyzed contain some violent content. To compute adjusted presence, we simply subtracted all those programs that feature an anti-violence theme (N = 62) from the percentage of programs with violence. Our finding for adjusted prevalence of violence is that 59% of programs present violence primarily for entertainment purposes.

To summarize, we have devised a measure known as adjusted prevalence of violence that takes into account an important, indeed fundamental, program-level element associated with the context of certain violent portrayals. Our goal is to adjust our report of prevalence in a way that meaningfully reflects responsible efforts of the television industry to address the concern about violent depictions. The programs remaining after this screen has been applied reflect a percentage that we will call the "adjusted presence of violence." This is the statistic with which we should be most concerned from a frequency point of view. It should be noted that the adjusted prevalence figure does not change much even when those programs that use violence for prosocial purposes are eliminated.

Summary of Presence

The majority (61%) of programs in a composite week of television contain some violence. Furthermore, two thirds of the violent incidents on television involve behavioral acts of aggression rather than credible threats or implied violence. The highest percentages of violent programs are found on premium cable and within the genre of movies specifically; this is also where the highest frequencies of violent interactions are displayed. In contrast, broadcast networks are below the industry norm in terms of percentage of programs containing violence; public broadcast is substantially below the industry norm. Also, violence is less likely in reality-based programs and substantially less likely to be present in comedy.

Not all of the programs in the 61% displaying some violence are of equal concern. Some of these programs (3%) feature an anti-violence theme. When we remove these programs from consideration, an analysis we term Adjusted Presence of Violence, we find that 59% of the programs analyzed present violence primarily for entertainment purposes.

Context: The Meaning of the Violence

Even more important than the issue of prevalence of violence is the meaning of that violence for the audience. Meaning is derived from the context in which the violence is portrayed. Our contextual analysis is organized around the major variables introduced in Chapter 1, including the nature of the perpetrator of violence, the nature of the target, the reason for the violence, justification, means used (weapons), extent of violence, graphicness, realism, rewards/punishments, consequences, and humor. For each contextual variable, we present the overall pattern of findings across all programming, and then consider any important differences that emerge as a function of the locator variables.

When analyzing context, most programs were coded as a separate unit or narrative story. However, as we noted previously, some programs are segmented (i.e., *60 minutes*, *Looney Tunes*), meaning that they contain independent stories or narrative units within a larger framework. Because these segments each contain their own narrative purpose, different characters, and a different story line, they were treated as individual programs for purposes of applying the contextual variables. Thus, for all subsequent statistical analyses, the overall $\underline{N}$ (number of programs) is larger than the $\underline{N}$ in the preceding analyses, because segments are henceforth treated as independent programs.

Nature of the Perpetrator

Coders identified a perpetrator for each violent interaction in a program. Summing across all the violent interactions provides a profile of the characters that is weighted according to the number of interactions in which they are involved. For example, if a program features two characters, a male who is the aggressor in eight violent interactions and a female who is the aggressor in two violent incidents, we would report that 80% of the perpetrators are male and 20% are female. This weighting is appropriate, because our focus is a behavioral one. Thus, we are interested in describing the attributes (such as character demographics) associated with violent interactions, rather than focusing on characters independent of the extent of their behaviors.

Perpetrators could be classified as single individuals, groups of individuals, or implied (unidentified or unseen) individuals. Across the 17,638 violent interactions, 67% of the perpetrators are single individuals and therefore are relatively easy to code in terms of demographics and attributes. Most of the remaining perpetrators (28%) are groups of individuals. We represent each group as "one" perpetrator in our data because, by our definition, groups act collectively against a target. Like individuals, each group is assigned a value on the demographics and the character attribute variables. When individuals in a group are not homogenous on a particular characteristic (e.g., some men and some women), coders identified the perpetrator as "mixed" on that variable. As seen from the above breakdown, only 3% of the perpetrators of violence are implied or unknown. In subsequent analyses, percentages do not always add to 100, because implied as well as mixed perpetrators could not be assigned demographic and attribute characteristics. Also, some perpetrators were coded as "can't tell" when a trait or characteristic was impossible to ascertain (e.g., sex of an alien creature).

Type of character. Coders classified each perpetrator according to one of five character types: human, animal, anthropomorphized animal, supernatural creature, or anthropomorphized supernatural creature. As seen in Figure 6, 70% of perpetrators of violence are human characters. Two other categories account for nearly all the remaining perpetrators: anthropomorphized animals (11%) and anthropomorphized supernatural creatures (10%). Supernatural creatures (nonanthropomorphized) and animals are rarely involved as perpetrators of violence. In other words, most of the perpetrators of aggression on television are human or human-like characters, which presumably make them easier for viewers to identify with than non humans.

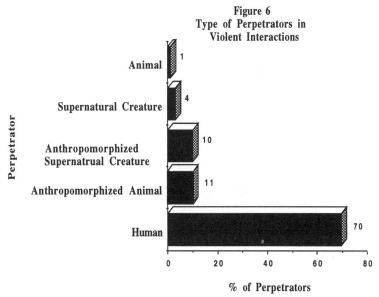

Figure 6
Type of Perpetrators in Violent Interactions

Type of perpetrator varies across channel type and genre. In terms of channel type, nearly all the perpetrators featured on premium cable are humans (see Figure 7). Public broadcast also displays a higher proportion of human perpetrators than the overall industry average. In comparison, independent broadcast is much less likely to feature human perpetrators and more likely to show anthropomorphized creatures as aggressors. Such a finding is indicative of a higher concentration of cartoons on this channel type.

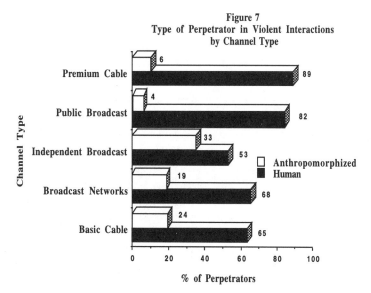

Figure 7
Type of Perpetrator in Violent Interactions by Channel Type

65

For every program genre except children's, nearly all perpetrators of violence are humans. In contrast, almost half (48%) of the perpetrators in children's programs are anthropomorphized and only 32% are humans (see Figure 8). This pattern is reflective of the high proportion of cartoons (89%) that constitute violent children's programming.

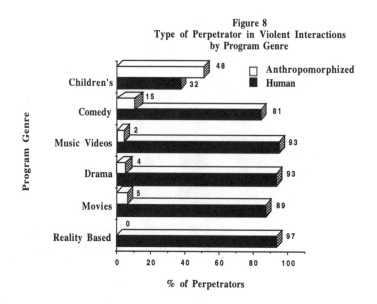

Figure 8
Type of Perpetrator in Violent Interactions
by Program Genre

Sex. A very high percentage (73%) of the perpetrators in violent interactions are male, whereas only 10% are female. In the remaining 17% of interactions, coders could not determine the sex of the perpetrator (e.g., character is not shown on screen) or the perpetrator was a group containing both sexes. Although this pattern does not differ by channel type, there is one difference as a function of genre: women are significantly more likely to be featured as perpetrators of violence in comedies (27%) than in all other genre types.

Age. Coders judged the approximate age of each perpetrator as one of the following: child (0-12 years), teen (13-20 years), adult (21-64 years), or elderly (65 years or older). As seen in Figure 9, 72% of the perpetrators in violent interactions are adults.

Although the vast majority of perpetrators are adults, premium cable features a higher proportion of perpetrators in this age group (83%) compared to the industry average. There are also important genre differences. When compared to the industry average (72%), drama programs contain a substantially higher proportion of adult perpetrators (92%) and music videos (82%) and reality-based programs (83%) feature a moderately higher proportion. In contrast, children's programming features a substantially lower proportion of adult perpetrators (50%). Nevertheless, the lower percentage of adults does *not* translate into more child or teen perpetrators in such programming, as might be expected. Instead, many of the perpetrators in children's series cannot be classified in terms of age, presumably because their supernatural or anthropomorphized qualities make chronological age impossible to ascertain.

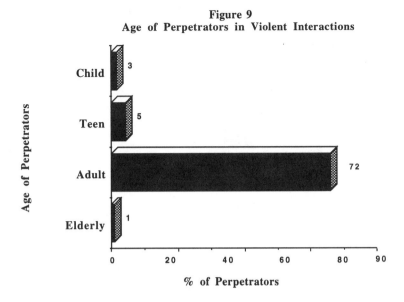

Figure 9
Age of Perpetrators in Violent Interactions

Apparent ethnicity. For human characters only, the perpetrator's apparent ethnicity was coded as: White, Hispanic, Black, Asian, Native American, or Middle Eastern. As seen in Figure 10, perpetrators of violence on television are predominantly White (71%).

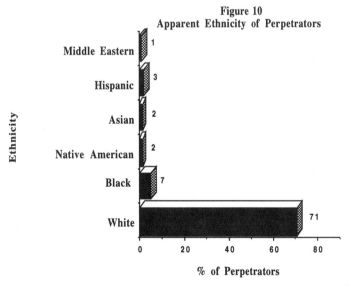

Figure 10
Apparent Ethnicity of Perpetrators

Character ethnicity does not vary much by channel type. Only one notable difference emerged, in this case for public broadcast. When compared to the industry average (71%), public broadcast presents a moderately lower proportion of perpetrators who are White (52%) and a moderately higher proportion of perpetrators whose ethnicity is not ascertainable (19%).

67

In terms of genre types, the vast majority of the perpetrators are White. However, Black perpetrators are substantially more likely to be featured in music videos and moderately more likely to be portrayed in comedy shows when compared to the overall industry average (see Figure 11).

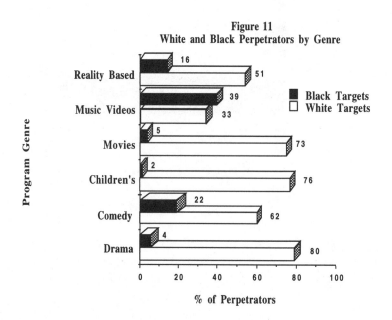

Figure 11
White and Black Perpetrators by Genre

Hero. Given our relatively stringent definition of the term, very few perpetrators qualify as heroes (10%), or primary characters who go above and beyond the call of duty to protect others from violence. No differences were detected in this pattern by channel type or genre.

Good/bad. Coders judged each perpetrator as good, bad, both good and bad (blended), or neutral (neither good nor bad). A bad character was defined as an animate being who is motivated primarily by self-interest, whereas a good character was defined as one who is motivated by a concern for others. Our findings reveal that nearly half of the perpetrators of violence on television are bad characters (43%). As seen in Figure 12, 28% of perpetrators are good characters. A much smaller proportion of perpetrators are both good and bad (10%). Taken together, then, approximately 40% of the perpetrators of violence have some good qualities with which a viewer might identify (percent for good plus percent for blended).

A few differences in this pattern occur as a function of channel type and genre. Public broadcast features moderately fewer perpetrators who are good (15%) compared to the industry average. In terms of program genre, music videos also feature a moderately lower proportion of perpetrators who have good qualities (17%). Furthermore, music videos (27%) and comedy series (29%) contain a lower proportion of perpetrators who are bad when compared to the industry average (43%).

68

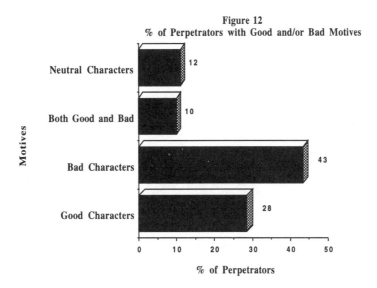

Figure 12
% of Perpetrators with Good and/or Bad Motives

Summary of Perpetrators

The typical perpetrator of violence on television is a human character who is adult, white, and male. Most often, the perpetrator is likely to be a "bad" rather than a "good" character. However, nearly 40% of all perpetrators have some good qualities that could make them attractive, and therefore potent role models for viewers.

Fewer differences are present for channel type. Premium cable and public broadcast are more likely than the norm to feature human perpetrators, whereas independent broadcast is less likely to show humans as perpetrators, primarily because of the number of cartoons on this channel type.

The profile of the typical perpetrator varies by genre. Children's programming is more likely to feature anthropomorphized or human-like perpetrators and less likely to feature actual humans as aggressors, compared to other genres. But this pattern is not surprising given the preponderance of cartoons within this genre. Music videos also show some differences in the nature of the perpetrator. In particular, they feature a higher proportion of Black perpetrators and a lower proportion of White perpetrators, compared to the overall pattern.

One final point should be emphasized regarding the findings. All of the percentages reported here refer *only* to perpetrators of violence and not to every character in a program. Because we coded only those characters involved in violence, we cannot use our data to describe the profile of all characters on television, nor can we directly compare our percentages to an overall base of all characters featured on television.

Nature of the Target

Coders identified a target for each violent interaction in a program. As was done with perpetrators, summing across all the violent interactions provides a profile of the characters that is weighted according to the number of interactions in which they are victims. For example, if a program features two characters, an adult who is the object of violence in nine interactions and a child who is the object in one violent interaction, we would report that 90% of the targets are adults and 10% are children.

Across the 17,638 violent interactions, 70% of targets are single individuals, and only 28% are groups. As with the perpetrator data, each group target is assessed as a single unit on the demographic and character attribute variables. If individuals in a group are not homogenous on a particular characteristic (e.g., ethnicity), then coders identified the target as "mixed" on that variable. The remaining 2% of the targets of violence are implied or unidentifiable. As a reminder, percentages reported below do not always add to 100 because of implied and "mixed" targets as well as those who were coded as "can't tell" for certain variables.

Type of character. As seen in Figure 13, the majority of targets in violent interactions are human characters (70%). Two other categories account for most of the other targets: anthropomorphized animals (12%) and anthropomorphized supernatural creatures (9%). Supernatural creatures and animals rarely are involved as targets of violence. It should be noted that this pattern is almost identical to that of the perpetrators. Overall then, most of the victims of aggression on television are humans or human-like characters who presumably are easier for viewers to identify with than non-humans.

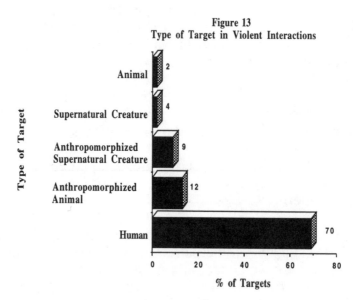

Figure 13
Type of Target in Violent Interactions

In terms of channel type, humans are even more likely to be targets on premium cable compared to the industry average of 70% (see Figure 14). In contrast, independent broadcast displays a smaller proportion of human targets, and a greater

70

proportion of anthropomorphized targets. Again, this pattern is indicative of more cartoons on this channel type.

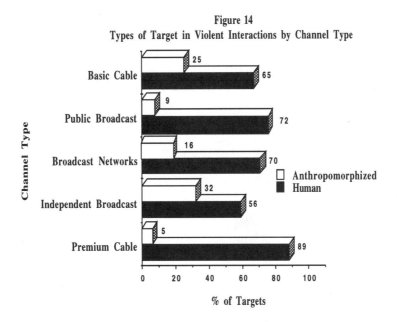

Figure 14
Types of Target in Violent Interactions by Channel Type

When examining genre, we see that humans are consistently the most frequent targets in drama, movies, comedy, reality-based programs, and music videos (see Figure 15). In contrast, children's programs feature a substantially lower proportion of human targets and a higher proportion of anthropomorphized characters as targets. Again, this difference is consistent with the fact that much of children's programming that is violent is comprised of cartoons.

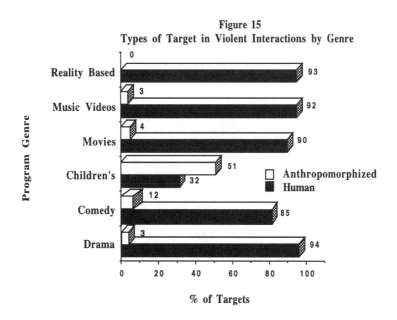

Figure 15
Types of Target in Violent Interactions by Genre

71

Sex. Just as with perpetrators, the vast majority of targets of violence are male (71%). Despite some public concern that women may be singled out as victims on television, only 10% of the targets in our sample are female. This pattern generally does not differ across channel type or genre.

Age. As with perpetrators, most of the targets of violence are adults (68%). The next most common victim is a teenager, but this age group makes up only 7% of all targets (see Figure 16). Very few of the victims of violence on television are children (4%) or elderly (1%).

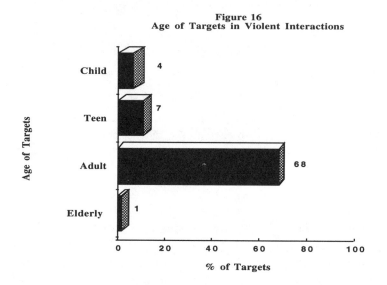

Figure 16
Age of Targets in Violent Interactions

The age of the target differs somewhat by both locator variables. In terms of channel type, targets are even more likely to be adults on premium cable (79%) when compared to the industry average (68%). In terms of genre, targets of violence are moderately more likely to be adults in music videos (81%) and movies (79%) and substantially more likely in dramatic series (90%). In children's programs, however, targets are much less likely (45%) to be adults and more likely to be coded as "can't tell."

Apparent ethnicity. As seen in Figure 17, a very high percentage (72%) of the targets of violence on television are White. Only 7% of the targets are Black and the remaining groups each account for 3% or less of the victims.

In spite of the overall predominance of White victims, ethnicity varies by channel type. On public broadcast, targets of violence are less likely to be White (59%) when compared to the industry average. Also, ethnicity varies by program genre. Music videos and reality-based programs are substantially less likely to feature White victims compared to the industry average (see Figure 18). Moreover, comedy is moderately more likely to portray Black victims of violence (25%) and music videos are substantially more likely (44%).

72

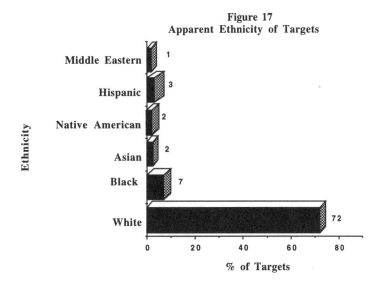

Figure 17
Apparent Ethnicity of Targets

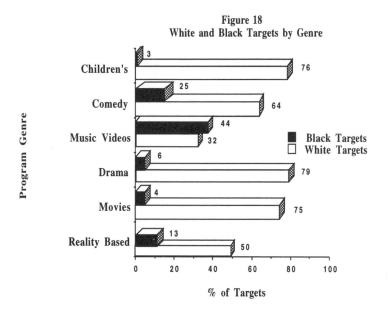

Figure 18
White and Black Targets by Genre

Hero. Targets of violence typically are *not* heroes. Only 11% of victims meet our strict definition of what constitutes this type of character (i.e., primary character who goes above and beyond the call of duty to protect others from violence in a program). This finding does not differ across genre or channel type.

Good/bad. Our findings suggest that over one third of targets (36%) can be described as good characters (see Figure 19). In contrast, 29% of targets are bad characters. Only 9% can be classified as both good and bad, and 19% are best described as neutral. Taken together, then, almost half of the victims of violence on television

73

(45%) possess some good or attractive qualities that might encourage a viewer to identify with them.

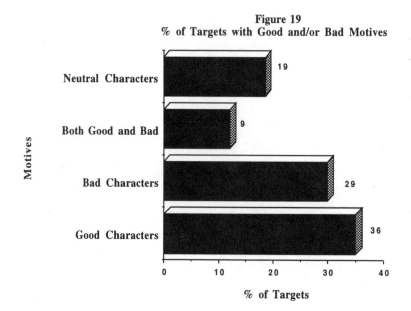

Figure 19
% of Targets with Good and/or Bad Motives

There are no differences on this variable as a function of channel type. In terms of genre, reality programs (16%) are moderately less likely to feature targets of violence who are good and music videos (15%) are substantially less likely compared to the industry norm. Also, targets of violence who are bad or motivated by self interest are less likely to appear on both comedy series (15%) and music videos (17%).

Summary of Targets

The profile of the typical target of television violence is nearly identical to that for the average perpetrator. Most targets are humans, or more specifically adult White males. Thus, the prototypical scenario for violence on television is an adult White male attacking another adult White male. Like perpetrators, very few targets are heroes. However, almost half of the targets of violence on television possess some good qualities that might encourage viewer identification. Indeed, targets are slightly more likely to be good characters than are perpetrators.

In terms of channel type, premium cable is more likely to feature human targets compared to the overall average, whereas independent broadcast is more likely to contain anthropomorphized victims. Again, these patterns are roughly parallel to the perpetrator findings.

The differences in the nature of the target across genre largely parallel the findings for perpetrators. Children's programs are more likely to feature anthropomorphized or human-like victims and less likely to feature actual humans as the target of violence compared to other genres. Even so, research reviewed above suggests that younger children are quite responsive to animated and unrealistic characters so we cannot conclude that such depictions are somehow less problematic in terms of viewer fear. Music videos and reality-based programs also show some differences in the nature of the target. Both genres feature a lower proportion of White victims, and music videos in particular display a higher proportion of Black victims compared to the overall pattern.

We must remind readers that the same caveat described in the perpetrator section holds for the target findings. All of the percentages here refer *solely* to targets of violence and not to every character in a program. Because we coded only those characters involved in violence, we cannot use our data to describe the profile of all characters on television.

Reasons for Violence

For every violent interaction, coders assessed the reason or motive for the perpetrator's aggression against a particular target. Reasons were coded into one of six categories: protection of life, anger, retaliation, personal gain, mental instability, or other. The "other" category was used whenever the perpetrator's motive did not fit into one of the five specific options, or whenever the program did not provide enough information to determine the perpetrator's reason (e.g., the perpetrator was not shown).

The findings reveal that violence on television is generally motivated by one of three reasons -- personal gain, anger, or protection of life (see Figure 20). Specifically, 28% of the violence is committed by perpetrators for personal gain, such as obtaining material goods (e.g., money), power, or affection. Another 28% of the violence is committed because the perpetrator feels anger over something the target did or said. And 24% of the violence is committed by a perpetrator in order to protect the self or another character.

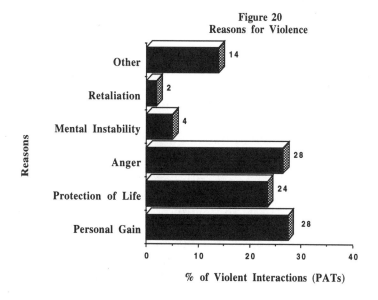

Figure 20
Reasons for Violence

Reasons for violence do not vary much across the types of channels, but there are some interesting differences across the program genres. Compared to the overall industry norm, violence in comedy programming is more likely to be committed because of anger (49%) and less likely to be committed to protect life (9%). In comparison, violence in music videos is less likely to be motivated by protection of life (13%), and more likely to occur for some "other" reason (36%). The fact that much of the violence in music videos was classified as "other" is not entirely surprising. Because of the brief nature and production format of most videos (e.g., quick cuts to numerous images), a perpetrator's reason for acting violently may be difficult to ascertain. And finally, anger is much less likely to be a motive for violence in reality programming (15%) and more likely to occur for some "other" reason (26%).

To summarize, over one fourth of the violence on television is committed for personal gain, and another one fourth is motivated by anger. In other words, perpetrators routinely use violence as a way to obtain resources or deal with their emotions. The only other reason that accounts for a substantial amount of violence (one fourth) is to protect life. This pattern is fairly consistent across different channels as well as different program genres.

Justification

For each violent interaction, the justification of aggression was assessed. By definition, justified violence is defined as those aggressive acts and or threats that are portrayed as "morally correct," "right," or "just" given the circumstances in the unfolding narrative. Each interaction was coded as justified, unjustified, or mixed.

Out of the 17,638 violent interactions coded, 28% portray violence as being justified, whereas 69% present aggression as unjustified. Justification was impossible to ascertain in only 2% of the interactions. This pattern is consistent across different channels. In terms of genre, however, an even lower proportion of violent interactions in comedy programs are portrayed as justified (18%) compared to the industry average (28%).

Means/Presence of Weapons

For each violent interaction, the means or method that a perpetrator used to engage in violence was coded. Means were classified into one of seven categories: natural means, unconventional weapon, handheld firearm, conventional handheld weapon other than a firearm, heavy weaponry, bombs, or means unknown. Coders recorded all the different means that a perpetrator used against the same target.

The most prevalent method that perpetrators use to enact violence is natural means (see Figure 21). Indeed, 39% of all violent interactions involve perpetrators using their own bodies to commit violence, such as hitting, punching, or kicking the target. When weapons are used, handheld firearms (i.e., guns) are the most common. In fact, guns are used in 26% of all violent interactions. The next most common form of weapon used is an unconventional object that is not traditionally associated with violence (e.g., rope, chair). Perpetrators use unconventional weapons in 19% of violent interactions. In contrast, bombs (2%), heavy weaponry like tanks and missiles (3%), and conventional handheld weapons other than guns (9%) are rarely used.

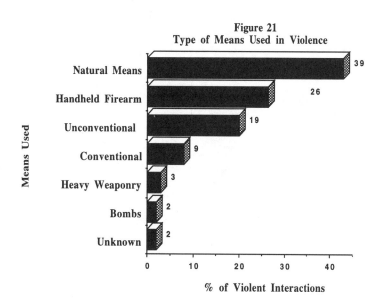

Figure 21
Type of Means Used in Violence

Because the two most prevalent means (natural means and guns) also are of interest theoretically, we will now focus on them more specifically. Violence by natural means warrants special attention because this form of violence is more imitatable by a viewer given that it does not require a special object or weapon. Guns have special significance because of the potential priming effect associated with such conventional weapons.

Do these two types of means differ across the locator variables? Our data indicate that there are no differences in the use of natural means or the use of guns across channel type, except for public broadcast which is less likely to portray the use of natural means than the industry average and more likely to employ conventional weapons. These data should be interpreted with caution though, because of the low number of violent interactions (n = 76) on this channel. There are, however, some significant differences in use of these two means across program genres. Compared to the overall average, natural means are used more often in comedy and music videos (see Figure 22). Guns, on the other hand, are used more often in drama as well as reality-based shows and *less* often in comedy and children's programs.

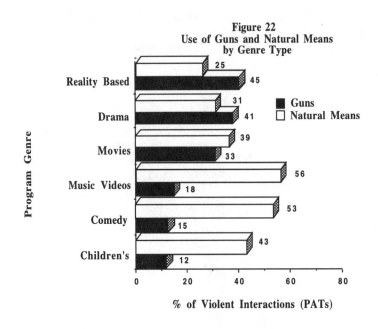

Figure 22
Use of Guns and Natural Means
by Genre Type

Program Genre

Reality Based	25 / 45
Drama	31 / 41
Movies	39 / 33
Music Videos	56 / 18
Comedy	53 / 15
Children's	43 / 12

■ Guns
□ Natural Means

% of Violent Interactions (PATs)

Extent of Violence

In this study, a violent interaction does not necessarily mean that a single act of violence occurs. Instead, it indicates that a particular perpetrator committed some amount of violence against a particular target. If, for example, a criminal fires a gun six times in rapid succession at a hero, coders recorded this as a single violent interaction rather than six independent acts of violence. The information about multiple gun shots is captured by a variable called "extent." Thus, when we report that one third of the programs feature nine or more violent interactions, we mean that these shows contain nine or more separate violent incidents involving different perpetrator and target combinations. This statistic tells us nothing about the number of individual behavioral acts *within* each incident, so it is not comparable to other studies that report on the rate of violent acts per hour or per program.

For each violent interaction in a program, the amount or extent of repeated violence was examined. This measure applies to behavioral acts only, and is not applicable to credible threats or harmful consequences. For extent, coders counted the number of times a behavioral act was repeated by a perpetrator against the same target within the same scene. The range was coded as follows: one, some (2 to 9 times), many (10 to 20 times), or extreme (21 or more times). For example, a perpetrator might punch a target 15 times and this would be coded as a single violent interaction involving "natural means" (punch with fist) with an extent of "many" (hitting 15 times). In cases where behavioral acts are interconnected and thus impossible to count individually, like a wrestling match or automatic gunfire, coders judged extent based on the amount of time the behavior lasted (i.e., seconds elapsed), using the same four categories (see Chapter 2).

Our data indicate that 39% of the violent interactions involve only one behavioral act of aggression (see Figure 23). Put another way, 61% of the violent interactions on television involve repeated or extended behavioral violence. In particular, 44% of the violent interactions feature "some" violence, 11% involve "many" acts of violence, and 6% involve "extreme" amounts of violence.

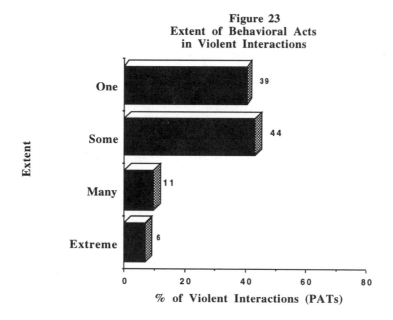

Figure 23
Extent of Behavioral Acts
in Violent Interactions

In terms of the locator variables, there are no differences in the extent or repetition of violence across the five channel types. In contrast, extent of violence differs as a function of program genre. In particular, reality-based programs are more likely to contain repeated violence than are the other genres whereas comedy programs are less likely to contain repeated acts of violence (see Figure 24).

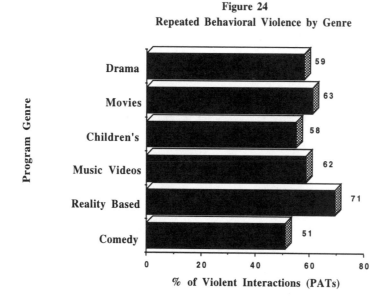

Figure 24
Repeated Behavioral Violence by Genre

79

Overall, a majority of violent interactions on television feature repeated or extensive aggression, though very few could be classified as extreme. Furthermore, reality-based programs are more likely than other genres to feature extended behavioral violence.

Graphicness of Violence

Graphicness of violence was subdivided into the concepts of (1) explicitness, and (2) blood and gore. Explicitness refers to the visual focus or concentration on the details of violence. Blood and gore refers to the amount of bloodshed and carnage shown. Both types of measures were assessed at the level of each violent scene. In other words, coders considered all violent interactions in a scene before judging overall explicitness and blood/gore.

Explicitness is applicable only to behavioral violence, and not to credible threats or harmful consequences of unseen violence, so the analyses in this section deal only with behavioral acts. Two types of explicitness were assessed: 1) explicitness of the violent behavioral act itself (i.e., the level of detailed focus on the perpetrator using the means or weapon), and 2) explicitness of means-to-target impact (i.e., the level of detailed, visual focus on the means or weapon impacting and damaging the target's body). Both types of explicitness were coded into one of three categories: close-up focus, long-shot focus, or not shown at all.

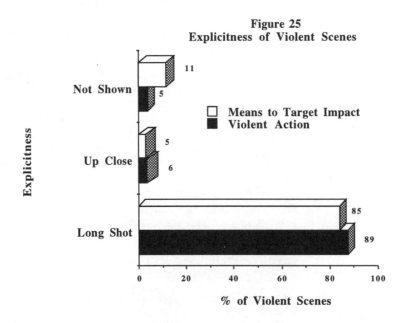

Figure 25
Explicitness of Violent Scenes

Our findings reveal that very little of the violence on television is explicit. In particular, only 6% of all violent scenes contain a close-up focus on behavioral acts of violence, and only 5% of violent scenes feature a close-up focus on the impact of violence on a target's body (see Figure 25). In other words, it is very rare to see a

80

close-up shot of a fist hitting a person or a bullet entering a body. The channel and genre locators revealed no differences in explicitness of the violent action. However, on the measure of explicitness of the means-to-target impact, there are some minor differences. Public broadcasting is substantially less likely when compared to the overall average to show a weapon impacting a target's body. We must interpret this finding with caution because there are so few violent scenes (n = 31) on this channel. Also, reality programming is substantially more likely to *not* show the means-to-target impact when compared to the industry norm.

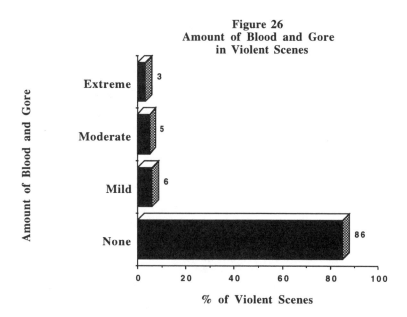

Figure 26
Amount of Blood and Gore
in Violent Scenes

Our second measure of graphicness deals with the amount of blood and gore shown. Amount of graphicness was classified into one of four categories: none, mild, moderate, or extreme. Our findings reveal that the vast majority of violent scenes on television depict no blood and gore (86%). As shown in Figure 26, few of the scenes contain a "mild" amount of blood and gore (6%), or a "moderate" amount (5%). And almost none of the scenes depict an "extreme" amount of blood and gore (3%).

Some variability exists, however, in where this bloodshed and carnage is found. For the analyses involving locator variables, the categories of "mild," "moderate," and "extreme" were combined because of their low frequencies. The analyses, then, look at the percent of scenes that contain *any* blood and gore versus *none*. Approximately 14% of all violent scenes contain some blood and gore. In terms of channel, viewers are more likely to encounter blood and gore in violent scenes featured on premium cable (see Figure 27). All other types of channels do not differ from the industry average on this measure.

As for genre, movies are more likely than the industry average to contain blood and gore within violent scenes. In contrast, bloodshed is virtually non-existent in comedy programs and children's programming (see Figure 28).

81

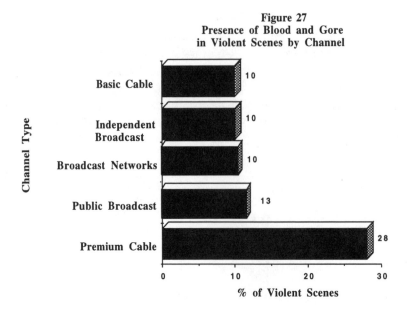

Figure 27
Presence of Blood and Gore
in Violent Scenes by Channel

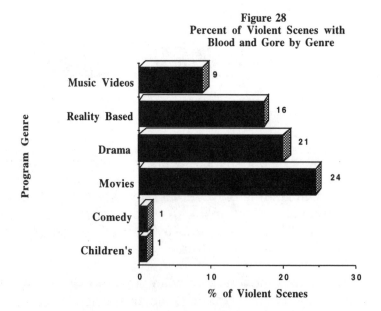

Figure 28
Percent of Violent Scenes with
Blood and Gore by Genre

To summarize, the most robust finding here is that only a small percentage of violent scenes on television can be described as graphic. There are very few close-ups of violent behaviors or of victims as they are injured. In addition, not much bloodshed and carnage is depicted. But this is not to say that all programming shares equally in this relatively positive pattern. When blood and gore is portrayed, it is most likely to be found on premium cable and in movies.

82

Realism

Research indicates that viewers who perceive television violence as realistic are more likely to be influenced by it. But what is real? Answering such a question requires that we consider several features of realism as well as the developmental level or age of the viewer. Consequently, we cannot simply label a particular portrayal as real or unreal, but we can array certain features of a program on a continuum where we can safely argue that some depictions reflect reality more than do others.

One feature of realism that we coded was the degree of authenticity of the characters and events on television. For each program, coders judged whether the characters and events represented actual reality, re-created reality, fiction, or fantasy. In the television world, some programs present actual events from real life (e.g., a documentary), and these portrayals usually are regarded as more realistic than re-enactments of real events (e.g., *Rescue 911*). Re-enactments typically are more realistic than fictional programs, which feature fabricated events. In turn, fictional programs are more realistic than fantasy shows, because the former portray events that are at least possible in real life.

Our findings reveal that nearly half (45%) of the violent programs in our sample can be classified as fantasy. As seen in Figure 29, most of the remaining programs fall into the fictional category (47%). Only 6% of violent programs involve actual reality and only 3% depict re-creations of reality.

For all subsequent analyses, we collapsed the later three categories into a "realistic" grouping which represents all programs based on events that could possibly occur in the real world (56% total).

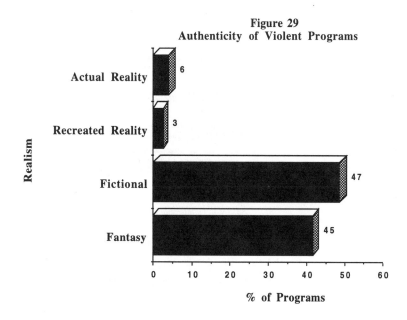

Figure 29
Authenticity of Violent Programs

When we analyze authenticity by channel type (Figure 30), we see that independent broadcast present significantly fewer programs involving realistic violence than the industry average. In contrast, broadcast networks and public broadcast are moderately more likely to feature violent programs in realistic settings, and premium cable is substantially more likely to feature violent programs in realistic settings than the industry average.

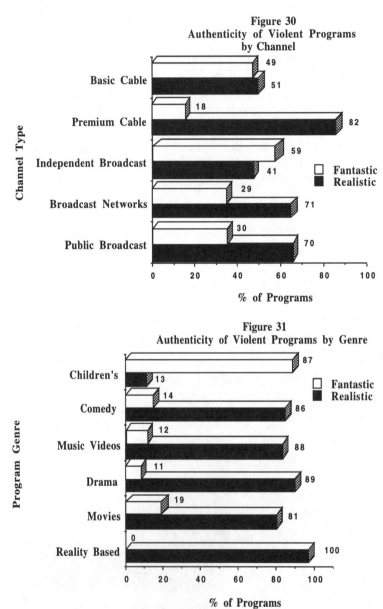

Figure 30
Authenticity of Violent Programs
by Channel

Figure 31
Authenticity of Violent Programs by Genre

The analysis by genre also reveals some differential patterns in terms of authenticity (see Figure 31). As might be expected, children's programs are substantially less likely to present violence in a realistic setting, whereas all other genres are substantially more likely. In other words, fantasy violence is almost exclusively found in programs targeted to young viewers.

Now we turn our attention to another feature of realism, the style of presentation. This variable refers to the production format that might influence how reality is assessed by viewers. Some producers use human actors in live-action scenes, whereas others use animated characters and settings. Still others use a combination of live action and animation. If characters and events are animated, it is more likely that mature viewers will regard them as being unrealistic. There are exceptions, however. Younger children respond to many animated characters as if they were real. Also, some animated characters like Bart Simpson may seem more realistic even to adult viewers compared to a non-animated character like the Terminator. Still, we contend that characters and events that are animated generally seem less real than human characters and live action. Coders rated the style of each violent program using three values: live action, animated action, or both live and animated action.

Violent programs are split primarily between live action (57%) and animated action (39%). Only 3% contain both live action and animation. This pattern differs a bit when we look at channel type (see Figure 32). Broadcast networks are moderately more likely to feature violence in live action and premium channels are substantially more likely when compared to industry average. Independent broadcast is significantly more likely to feature violence in animated action.

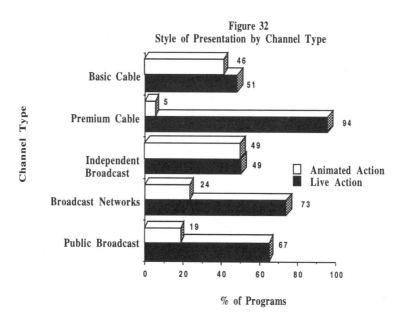

Figure 32
Style of Presentation by Channel Type

When we look at genre, nearly all the violence on children's programming is animated (see Figure 33). Furthermore, nearly all (89%) of the animated programs containing violence are in the single category of children's programs. The remaining

85

genres all are substantially more likely to feature live action violence compared to the industry average, which is lower simply because of children's programs.

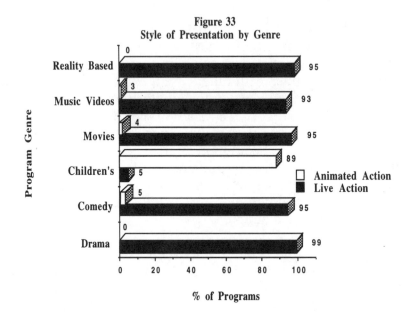

Figure 33
Style of Presentation by Genre

In summary, our two ways of assessing realism (degree of authenticity and style of presentation) result in very similar patterns. Overall, very few violent programs in our sample involve real or re-created events. Instead, most of the violent programs fall into one of two categories: fictional or fantasy. In terms of style of presentation, most violent programs are live action. However, the location of these depictions is very much tied to certain genres. Five of the six genres feature more realistic violence that is conveyed in live action. Alternatively, children's programs contain mostly fantasy violence shown in an animated style.

It may be tempting to conclude that children's programs are less problematic than other genres because their portrayals are so unrealistic (i.e., high degree of fantasy and animation). However, very young children have difficulty distinguishing fantasy from reality on television and often readily imitate animated characters who bear little resemblance to humans. Thus, we cannot exonerate this genre of programming when we consider the developmental capabilities of many of its viewers. It may also be tempting to conclude that much of the violence targeted to adult viewers poses little risk because it is not based on real-life events. Two caveats should be pointed out here. First, we did not assess any hard news programming so our findings surely under-represent the amount of real-life violence on television. Second, even fictional violence, which is the norm in adult programming, can seem realistic to a viewer because the events and characters are feasible in real life.

Rewards and Punishments

Rewards and punishments for violence were coded at the end of each violent scene as well as at the end of each program. The scene judgment allows us to examine reinforcements for violence that are delivered during or immediately after aggression occurs. The program judgment allows us to assess the pattern of reinforcements across the entire program.

In the majority of violent scenes (54%), aggression is neither rewarded nor punished when it occurs (see Figure 34). A much smaller proportion of scenes present violence as being explicitly punished (20%) or rewarded (17%), and even fewer depict violence as both rewarded and punished (9%). Violence that goes unpunished poses the greatest risk for viewers in terms of learning aggressive attitudes and behaviors. Taken together, our findings indicate that nearly three fourths of the violent scenes on television (71%) portray no punishments for violence within the immediate context of when it occurs. This robust pattern holds across all types of genres, including children's programs. The pattern also holds across the various types of channels.

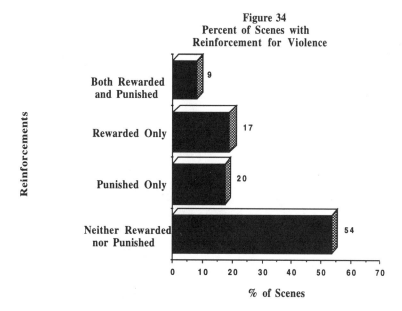

Figure 34
Percent of Scenes with
Reinforcement for Violence

What types of rewards and punishments typically are depicted? We classified rewards as involving self-praise that a perpetrator expresses after acting violently, praise from other characters, and material goods that are received as a consequence of violence (e.g., money, jewelry). A given violent scene could feature one or all of these types of rewards. Although rewards do not occur very often in the immediate context of violence, the most common forms involve self-praise and praise from others. In particular, the perpetrator expresses personal satisfaction for violence in 18% of all violent scenes, whereas other characters express approval in 11% of all scenes. Only 6% of all scenes depict material rewards for violence.

87

Punishments were classified as involving self-condemnation or remorse that a perpetrator expresses for acting violently, condemnation from others, nonviolent action to stop or penalize violence, and violent action by a third party to terminate further violence. A given scene could feature one or more of these types of punishments. Although punishments do not occur very often in the immediate context of violence, the most common forms involve condemnation expressed by characters other than the perpetrator (17% of all scenes) and violent action taken by a third party to stop violence (13% of all scenes). Only 9% of the violent scenes feature a nonviolent action to penalize violence, and virtually none of the scenes (4%) show a perpetrator feeling remorse over violence.

At the program level, reinforcements were examined as well. However, here we focused only on the presence or absence of punishment because of its importance for inhibiting viewers' learning of aggression. Coders assessed the overall pattern of punishments delivered to good perpetrators, to bad perpetrators, and to perpetrators who are both good and bad. It should be noted that reliabilities for these measures are somewhat lower than for other program-level variables so the data should be interpreted with some caution.

In a majority of programs (55%), bad characters are punished for violence sometime during the plot (see Figure 35). Another way of looking at this, however, is that a full 45% of programs contain bad characters who are never punished anywhere in the program.

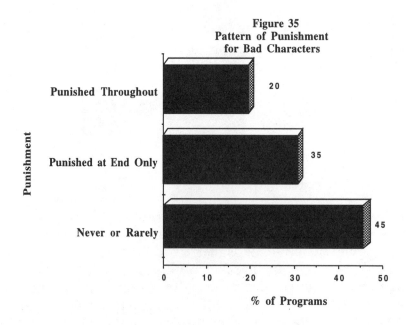

**Figure 35
Pattern of Punishment
for Bad Characters**

The pattern of punishments for bad characters generally holds across channel types. Several differences emerge when looking at the patterns of punishments by genre. Specifically, drama programs are more likely to show bad characters being punished whereas music videos are substantially less likely to depict bad characters as punished or disciplined in some way (see Figure 36).

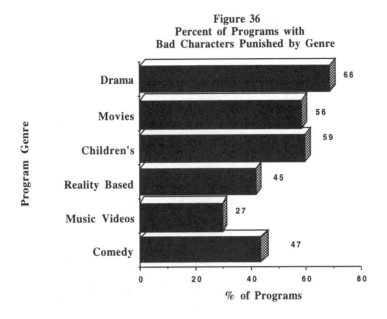

Figure 36
Percent of Programs with
Bad Characters Punished by Genre

The findings overall indicate that in well over half of the violent programs, bad characters are eventually punished. Yet the picture looks quite different for good characters. Good characters who engage in violence are punished in only 18% of all programs (see Figure 37). In other words, in the vast majority of programs good characters never feel remorse, nor are they reprimanded or hindered by others when they engage in violence. This robust pattern is stable across the five channel types and six genres of programming except for music videos (5%), which are even less likely than the industry average (18%) to portray good characters being punished.

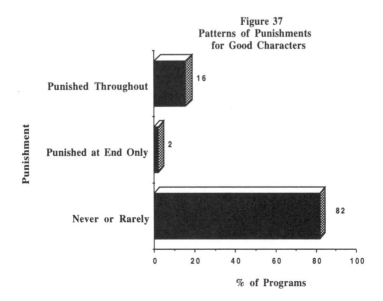

Figure 37
Patterns of Punishments
for Good Characters

89

Slightly fewer programs feature characters who are both good and bad. These blended characters (both good and bad) who engage in violence are punished in 31% of the programs (see Figure 38). There are no differences across channel type. As for genre, reality-based programs are less likely to show punishment of blended characters when compared to the industry average.

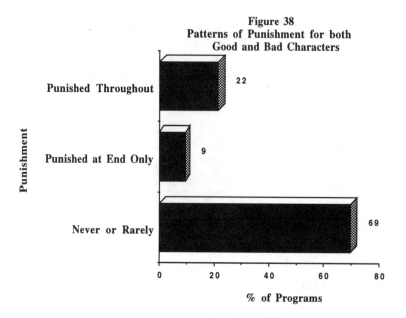

Figure 38
Patterns of Punishment for both Good and Bad Characters

In sum, the vast majority of violence on television is not punished at the time it occurs. Punishments more typically occur later in the program, particularly toward the end of the plot. But this pattern is true only for bad characters. Good characters who engage in violence are rarely punished at all on television, and characters who are both good and bad often are not punished either. Thus, the characters that children are most likely to identify with rarely show remorse for violence, and seldom are criticized or explicitly punished for acting aggressively. These patterns are fairly consistent across all locator variables, with a few exceptions pertaining to genre. Most importantly, drama programs are more likely to feature bad characters being punished for violence, whereas reality-based programs and music videos are less likely to portray bad characters as punished.

Consequences of Violence

Consequences refer to the harm and pain that result from violent actions. We measured the consequences of violence at both the interaction and the program level. Coding at the interaction level allows us to examine the immediate consequences of violence at the time that it occurs. Coding at the program level enables us to assess the aftermath of violence in terms of long-term pain and suffering.

For each violent interaction, we coded harm and pain separately. These two measures were applied to behavioral acts and harmful consequences only. By definition,

90

credible threats can not result in physical injury so pain and harm were not coded for any of these types of interactions. For harm, we assessed: (1) the amount of physical injury that is actually depicted on screen, and (2) the amount of likely injury that would have occurred if the violence had been enacted against a human in real life. Both of these measures of harm had four possible values: none, mild, moderate, or extreme. Coders also could choose a fifth option indicating that the target literally is not shown in the program, such that depicted harm could not be ascertained.

Our findings indicate that across all violent interactions, 33% depict no physical injury to the target. In an additional 10% of the violent interactions, the target is not even shown on screen (camera moves away or the scene changes abruptly). Thus, nearly half of violent incidents (43%) on television contain no observable indications of harm to the victim (see Figure 39). This finding is particularly important given that the research suggests that harm and pain cues inhibit viewers' learning of aggression.

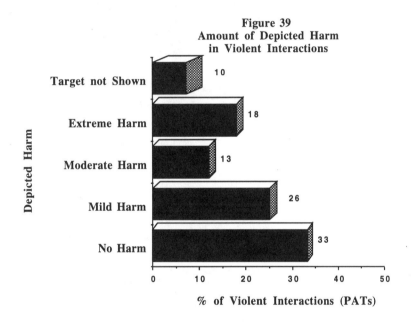

Figure 39
Amount of Depicted Harm
in Violent Interactions

Using this 43% figure as a basis of comparison, we found differences across channels and genres. In terms of channel type, public broadcast is less likely to show harm to the targets of violence (see Figure 40). Again, the findings on public broadcast should be considered cautiously, because the analysis included so few violent interactions. In terms of program genre, children's programs, comedy, and music videos are less likely to portray physical harm to victims of violence (see Figure 41).

In addition to depicted harm, we also measured likely harm or the amount of physical harm the violent interaction would have yielded in real life. Of greatest concern are those violent incidents that would result in serious physical harm were they to occur in real life. Overall, 54% of all PATs involve behavioral violence that would be "incapacitating" or "lethal" to a victim. This percentage of serious physical aggression is stable across channel types.

However, there are differences in seriousness of violence across program genres. Reality-based programs are more likely to feature incapacitating or lethal violence (64% of violent interactions) when compared to the industry average. In contrast, comedy is substantially less likely to involve physical aggression that would result in serious harm in real life (25% of violent interactions).

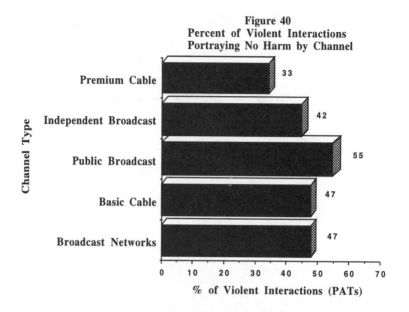

Figure 40
Percent of Violent Interactions
Portraying No Harm by Channel

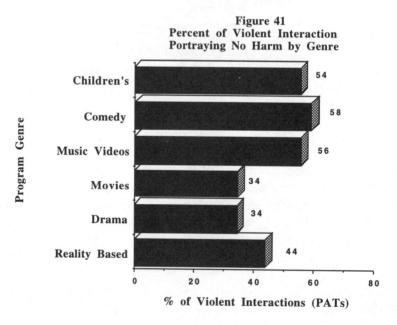

Figure 41
Percent of Violent Interaction
Portraying No Harm by Genre

We also computed a variable of realistic harm to assess if the portrayal of violence was depicted as resulting in an appropriate degree of harm to the target. Thus the variable of *unrealistic harm* was defined as any instance in which the degree of depicted harm (none, mild, moderate, extreme) is *less* than the degree of likely harm in real life (mild, moderate, extreme). An example would be a farcical depiction of a target who is hit over the head with a sledgehammer and walks away with only a small lump on the forehead. This type of injury would be coded as "mild" for depicted harm but "extreme" for likely harm in real life. Such a violent interaction would be characterized as showing an unrealistically low level of harm. This constructed variable allows us more accuracy in gauging the degree of authenticity of the harm depicted on television.

Overall, 34% of all violent interactions portray an unrealistically low amount of harm. To state this in a different way, 66% of the violent incidents feature a realistic portrayal of the degree of injury to the victim. The portrayal of unrealistic harm differs, however, across channel type. Compared to the overall pattern, premium cable is less likely to feature unrealistically low levels of harm (see Figure 42). The pattern for unrealistic harm also differs with respect to program genre. As seen in Figure 43, reality-based programs, movies, drama, and comedy are all less likely to feature unrealistic harm. In direct contrast, children's programs contain a substantially higher percentage of unrealistic depictions of harm. In fact, nearly 60% of the violent interactions in children's programming underestimate the amount of physical harm that would occur if the same violence happened in real life.

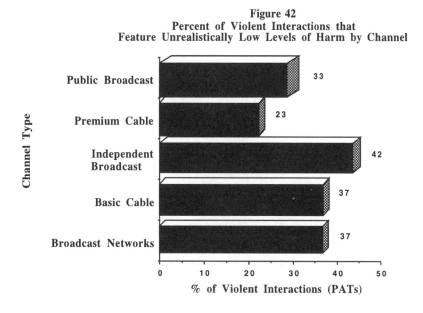

Figure 42
Percent of Violent Interactions that
Feature Unrealistically Low Levels of Harm by Channel

Like harm, depicted pain was coded at the level of each violent interaction. The amount of depicted pain ranged from none (no verbal or nonverbal expressions of pain, anguish, or suffering) to extreme (expression of intense, protracted pain and suffering). Our findings reveal that across all violent interactions, 41% depict the target experiencing no pain whatsoever. In an additional 10% of the interactions, the target is not even shown on screen so pain cues could not be assessed (i.e., camera moved away or the scene changed). Therefore, a total of 51% of all violent interactions show no observable pain to the victim (see Figure 44).

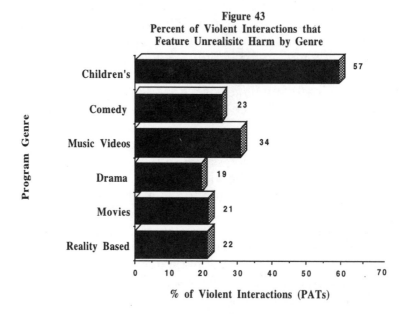

Figure 43
Percent of Violent Interactions that
Feature Unrealisitc Harm by Genre

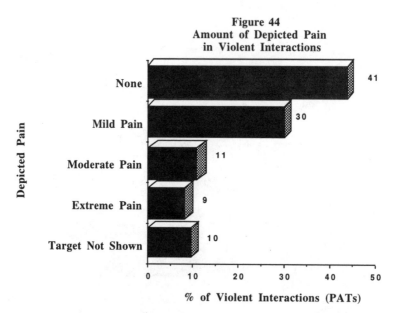

Figure 44
Amount of Depicted Pain
in Violent Interactions

There are no differences in pain across channel type. Some interesting differences emerge when we examine program genres, however (see Figure 45). Compared to the industry average, music videos and reality shows are even more likely to show no pain to the victims of violence.

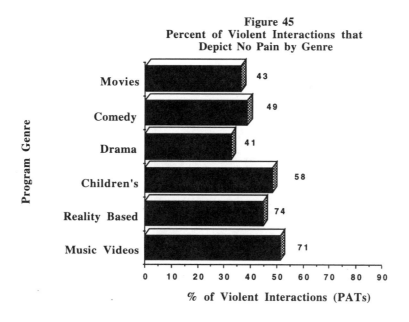

Figure 45
Percent of Violent Interactions that
Depict No Pain by Genre

Program Genre

Movies 43

Comedy 49

Drama 41

Children's 58

Reality Based 74

Music Videos 71

0 10 20 30 40 50 60 70 80 90

% of Violent Interactions (PATs)

In addition to coding harm and pain for each violent interaction, the consequences of violence were coded at the program level. This measure provided an overall judgment about harm and pain combined. It asked coders to consider not only the physical harm and pain experienced as a result of violence, but also the emotional, psychological, and financial costs to the participants, their families, and the community at large. Coders assessed the extent of harm and pain depicted across the entire program, indicating whether such consequences generally were: (1) not shown at all; (2) short-term or immediate in nature (limited to within the violent scene or immediately thereafter); or (3) long-term in nature (displayed throughout the program).

Our findings indicate that 29% of all programs can be characterized as showing no negative consequences of violence. As can be seen in Figure 46, over half of the programs depict short-term negative consequences of violence (55%), and only 16% depict more long-term pain and suffering associated with violence.

As for channel type, premium cable features substantially more programs that depict the long-term negative consequences of violence, and fewer programs that show no consequences at all compared to the industry average (see Figure 47). Public broadcast, compared to the industry average, is less likely to show the long-term consequences of violence. However, this finding is based on only 27 violent programs across the entire week on this channel so it should not be overinterpreted.

In terms of genre, music videos, reality shows, and comedy are more likely to show no negative outcomes of violence compared to the industry average. On the other hand, drama and movies are more likely to portray the long-term repercussions of violence than the industry norm (see Figure 48).

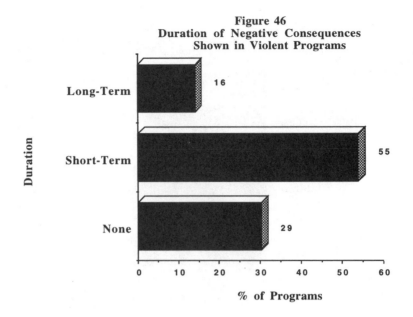

Figure 46
Duration of Negative Consequences
Shown in Violent Programs

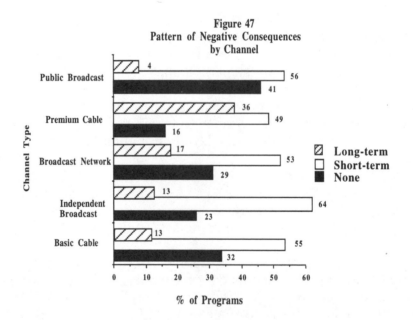

Figure 47
Pattern of Negative Consequences
by Channel

In summary, 43% of violent interactions on television contain no observable harm and 51% feature no pain cues to the victim. When we examine the depiction of harm on television in terms of its real-world accuracy, we see that children's programming is substantially more likely than any other genre to feature unrealistically low levels of physical injury to the victim. At the overall program level, almost one third of the programs do not portray any physical, emotional, psychological, or financial consequences of violence. When such consequences are shown, they are for the most part depicted as short-term in nature. Of all the channel types, premium cable is the most likely to portray the negative outcomes of violence. Of all genres, movies and drama are the most likely to feature the serious long-term repercussions of violence.

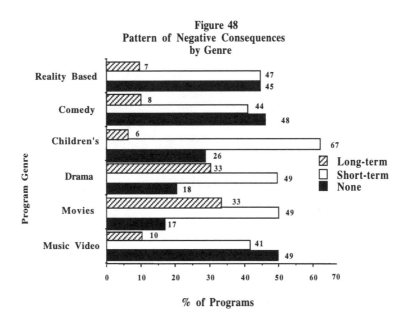

Figure 48
Pattern of Negative Consequences
by Genre

Humor

The presence or absence of humor was assessed within each violent scene. Our findings reveal that humor frequently accompanies violence on television. Indeed, humor is present in 42% of all violent scenes.   However, the presence of comedic violence varies across channel type. Only 22% of violent scenes are contextualized with humor on public broadcast and this is substantially below the industry norm. In contrast, independent broadcast contains more violent scenes presented with humor than the overall industry average (see Figure 49).

When we compare the use of humor across different genres, we also see some considerable differences (see Figure 50). As might be expected, humor accompanies violence substantially more often in children's programs and in comedy programs, and substantially less often in music videos, reality-based programs, and drama. Humor also is less likely to be present in violent scenes featured in movies, although this difference is not as great as for the other genres.

In sum, many of the violent scenes on television are portrayed in some form of comedic context which, according to research cited in Chapter 1, can serve to trivialize or undermine the seriousness of aggression. Humorous violence is especially concentrated in children's programming and in comedy.

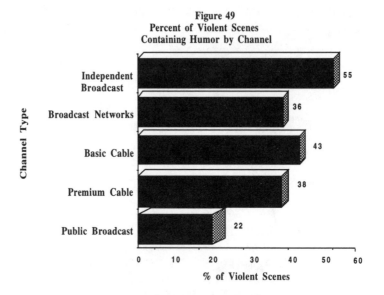

Figure 49
Percent of Violent Scenes
Containing Humor by Channel

Figure 50
Percent of Violent Scenes Containing
Humor by Genre

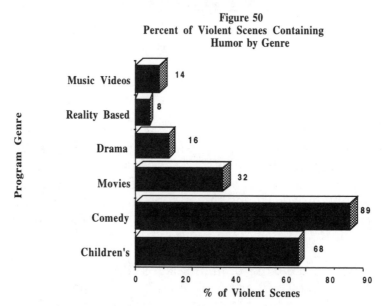

Sexual Violence

The probability of encountering a sexual assault within a violent incident is very low. On average, less than 1% of violent interactions in our sample involve a sexual assault. There are too few examples of these depictions to identify any variation by channel type or genre.

Programming with an Anti-Violence Theme

Programs were coded as having an anti-violence theme if the overall message was that violence is destructive or wrong. This concept was operationalized using four different criteria. In order to be categorized as an anti-violence theme, at least one of the following had to be a strong focus of the narrative: (1) alternatives to violence are presented, (2) the main characters show reluctance or remorse for committing acts of violence, (3) pain or suffering are depicted throughout, and attention is devoted to how the victims' family and/or the community is affected, or (4) on balance, there are many more punishments for violence throughout the program than there are rewards.

Of all programs containing some violence, only 3% emphasize an anti-violence theme. Table 16 contains examples of various types of programs that emerge from our sample as having an anti-violence theme.

Below we present a brief description of several of the programs in our sample that feature an anti-violence theme. We present these to illustrate how violence can be used in a responsible manner in entertainment programming. Such descriptions should be informative to parents and educators who want to distinguish violent programs that pose risks for children from those that are prosocial or educational. In addition, these descriptions should be informative for writers and producers who are seeking ways to portray conflict in a way that poses minimal risk to the viewer.

Drama Series

Touched by an Angel (CBS)   *Sunday 10/13/96*   *8:00-9:00 p.m.*

An ambitious female Secret Service agent is assigned to protect a U.S. Senator who is campaigning for the Presidency. An assassin who is stalking the politician pulls out a gun at a crowded campaign event and attempts to shoot the senator. The female agent reacts instantly, leaping to deflect the gunman's aim from the senator. She succeeds in subduing the suspect, but in the scuffle his gun discharges and seriously wounds a bystander in the crowd.

Amidst the pandemonium, the agent doesn't immediately learn that the wounded victim is a close friend of hers. The agent's responsibility is to get the senator to safety, which she does, heading immediately to Secret Service headquarters. There she learns that her heroic actions have convinced her superiors to promote her to the Presidential detail, the highest honor in the Secret Service.

In an ironic twist, however, the agent soon learns that her friend has been shot, and that he will require an immediate kidney transplant in order to survive. Because he has a rare blood type, there is little prospect of finding an acceptable donor in time to save the victim's life. Just hours after receiving news of her long-sought promotion, the agent discovers that she is a rare biological match as a possible kidney donor for her friend. But if she donates a kidney, she will be forced to resign from her career, because the Secret Service requires that all its agents have no physical impairments.

Table 16

Examples of Programs in Sample Containing an Anti-violence Theme by Genre

Genre	Title of Program	Channel
Children's Shows	Captain Planet	Cartoon Network
	Gummi Bears	Disney Channel
	Groundling Marsh	Disney Channel
	Johnny Quest	TNT
	Little Mermaid	Disney Channel
Comedy Shows	Family Matters	KTLA
	In the House	KCOP
	Steve Harvey Show	KTLA
Drama Series	Highway to Heaven	Family Channel
	Law & Order	A&E
	Quincy	A&E
	Touched by an Angel	CBS
Movies	A Family Divided	Cinemax
	Armed & Innocent	Lifetime
	Cooley High	Cinemax
	The Plainsmen	AMC
	When No One Would Listen	Lifetime
Reality-Based	Life & Times	PBS
	Rescue 911	Family Channel
	Top Cops	USA
	Unsolved Mysteries	Lifetime
Music Videos	"Freedom"	MTV
	"How Come, How Long"	VH-1
	"I Ain't Mad at Cha"	BET
	"Papparazi"	BET
	"We Didn't Start the Fire"	VH-1

The agent decides to donate the organ, sacrificing her career for her wounded friend. Throughout the program, emphasis is placed on the life-threatening nature of the shooting victim's plight. The story also depicts at length how the pain and suffering of victims of violence impacts their friends and family in tragic ways.

Comedy Series

In the House (UPN/KCOP)   *Monday 1/27/97*   *8:30-9:00 p.m.*

At about age 8, Austin is the youngest of several children in this family sit-com's household. Tyler, an older neighborhood child, steals away Austin's new remote-controlled electric car, threatening to beat him up if he tells anyone. Austin grapples with the issue of what to do, and the next day decides to go back and fight with Tyler. Using some newly learned karate skills, he wins the fight and succeeds in liberating the car.

There is no father figure in Austin's life, but the closest to that role is Marion, a young man in his twenties who rents a room from Austin's mother. Marion is an athlete, and obviously quite strong physically. When Austin returns home after his fight, he is followed shortly by Tyler's angry father. The father wants to pick a fight with someone, and he focuses his fury at Marion.

Marion's response is calm and cool, but Tyler's father keeps insisting on a physical confrontation, insulting Marion in order to provoke him. Even after being insulted, Marion refuses to resort to violence. To control his own rising anger, Marion pummels a nearby punching bag so hard that it shreds apart. Sensing the mismatch, Tyler's father backs off and finally both men agree it would be stupid to fight.

A poignant scene follows in which Marion gains the respect of others in the show for his non-violent approach, and Austin learns a valuable lesson about resolving conflict by talking rather than fighting. The show conveys the message that violence should be avoided and depicts a concrete example of a strong character who shows how to do it.

Reality Programming

Real World (MTV)   *Thursday 12/5/96*   *5:00-5:30 p.m.*

This cinema-verite style documentary series tells the story of how seven culturally diverse young adults (three women and four men) are brought together as strangers to live in one house. This episode begins with a practical joke that goes awry and leads to a major confrontation between two of the housemates. The situation culminates with one of the males, David, playfully barging into the room of one of the females, Tami, who shrieks and hides behind a bedsheet because she is undressed.

Tami screams loudly at David to leave her alone, but he continues to pull away her bedsheet, trying to expose her. Although David thinks they are just joking with one another, Tami is fiercely serious in her efforts to get him to stop. When David succeeds at pulling the sheet away, Tami flies into a rage. The situation has clearly escalated too far and, while screaming obscenities, Tami earnestly threatens David with physical harm, although no blows are struck as other housemates intercede to avoid the physical confrontation.

Following this opening scene, the entire remainder of the program is devoted to hearing all of the housemates reflect upon the conflict and seek ways to resolve the issues peacefully. Tami talks about how hard it was "for me not to kill him." The situation is complicated by the fact that David has previously fought with one of the other males in the house, and all the female residents now claim to feel unsafe with him. Tami felt as though David might have raped her if others had not been at home at the time of the incident.

The final scene shows all of the housemates except David meeting as a group and reaching a decision to ask David to move out. The ongoing nature of this serial program leaves the final resolution for a subsequent episode. Nonetheless, this episode placed significant emphasis on the importance of seeking alternatives to violence for conflict resolution. The final scene provides a calm, reasoned response to David's misbehavior that will obviously be stronger retribution than any physical assault.

Movies

A Family Divided (Cinemax)　　　　　*Friday 3/7/97*　　　　　*9:30-11:30 a.m.*

This film contains one act of violence, the rape of a 17-year-old girl by several members of a fraternity at a campus homecoming party. After the rape, the girl is left alone in a drunken state and dies from suffocation after vomiting.

The rape occurs in the first few minutes, with the rest of the film focusing on the remorse felt by two of the fraternity brothers, John and Chad. As a result of his growing guilt, John drops out of school. We learn near the end of the story that John has committed suicide. Chad initially suffers psychological pain as he fears getting punished by the police. He tells his father, a lawyer, what happened so that his father can help him and his friends avoid arrest. We see the father suffer the pain of trying to protect his son while hoping that he will do the right thing. We also see the father struggle with the issue of telling his wife about the incident. When he finally tells her, we see the mother's shock and grief. The film ends with Chad realizing that he cannot continue to hide from his responsibility to confess to police and be punished. Accompanied by his family, he finally turns himself in.

The movie has a clear theme that violence can have extreme consequences for perpetrators, and that this harm radiates to others close to those individuals. Nowhere in this film is violence ever glamorized; to the contrary, it is consistently characterized as painful and repugnant.

Children's Programming

The Little Mermaid (Disney Channel)   Tuesday 11/5/96   8:30-9:00 a.m.

Ariel, this program's star, is the daughter of the king of Atlantica, a land under the sea inhabited by many types of creatures. Denizens of Atlantica do not get along well with the creatures from a rival land, Olympia. The Olympians are brutal and war-like, whereas those who live in Atlantica are more kind and gentle. While Olympians are shown practicing how to attack, Atlanticans are shown taking art classes.

To gain peace between the two lands, Ariel's father suggests to the King of Olympia, who is the father of a young warrior prince, that their two offspring should marry. An agreement is reached and the prince is dispatched to visit Atlantica to meet his new fiancee. Ariel, a peace-loving mermaid, is aghast at the thought of marrying an aggressive fighter. When the prince arrives, he is the victim of many pranks and insults from Ariel's friends, who are trying to trick him into abandoning the plan.

The insults are too great, however, and lead the Prince of Olympia to declare war on Ariel's land of Atlantica. As the fighting begins, one of Ariel's friends is hurt and the prince sees Ariel cry intensely in response. Moved by her display of grief, the prince immediately halts the fighting. Recognizing that violence causes pain and harm, the prince announces that "war is a bad idea." All of the creatures from the two different lands agree not to fight, while Ariel and the prince exchange reasons to avoid violence in the world.

This program emphasizes an anti-violence theme by featuring a violent character who shows immediate remorse and eschews future aggression in response to a prominent display of pain and suffering.

Music Video

"I Ain't Mad at Cha," 2Pac   Monday 10/7/96   4:00-5:00 p.m.
  featuring Danny Boy (BET)

In this rap video, the singer Tupac Shakur is first shown "hanging out" with a friend when a loud gunshot rings out. No shooter is shown and no overt explanation for the attack is presented. Tupac is hit and the following scenes present the frenzied efforts of paramedics trying to save his life while riding in an ambulance with the siren screaming. Before arriving at the hospital, the singer dies in the ambulance, with a haunting voice intoning "patient is DOA."

The setting then shifts into visions of heaven, with Tupac arriving and meeting people who are already there. Meanwhile, his friend who was left behind on Earth is shown repeatedly grieving for Tupac. The tone is grim as both men reflect on their loss. The rap lyrics tell how the victim's death came from his ghetto life of crime and tragedy. The song bemoans gang violence, noting a common problem: "they forgot to see what's next -- in this world full of countless threats." The music video implores change from the gang life-style, and in the final scene the surviving character strips off his street attire and appears in a suit with a family, signifying abandonment of the gang. When you change for the better, Tupac raps, "nobody could be mad at you."

In this video, violence is shown only briefly and entirely off-screen. There is no glamorized perpetrator nor glorified action. After the shooting occurs at the outset, the entire remainder of the video presents metaphorically the sorrow and loss associated with the needless death of a young black man. This strong emphasis on the harmful consequences of violence reflects a clear anti-violence theme.

"Beat It," Michael Jackson (VH-1)   *Sunday 2/2/97*   *4:00-4:30 p.m.*

This music video shows Michael Jackson dancing in the streets while singing this song, interspersed with pictures of two separate groups of tough young men congregating in gangs and obviously beginning to look for trouble. The opposing gang members are shown preparing their weapons and staring down one another. Finally, violence breaks out when two individuals, one from each gang, engage in a knife fight that is presented as a choreographed dance, with the remaining members from each side performing like a dance troupe behind each combatant.

Michael Jackson appears and intercedes to end the knife fight. In time with the lyrics of the song, he separates the two gangs while singing "It doesn't matter who's wrong or right, just beat it..." This action breaks up the fight and triggers a metaphorical celebration of dancing involving members of both gangs dancing in unison for the remainder of the song. This video reflects an anti-violence theme because it features an influential character demonstrating alternatives to violence.

Analysis of Prime-time Programming

The audience for television generally builds throughout the day and reaches a peak in the prime-time hours, most widely defined as 8:00 to 11:00 p.m. (By television industry convention, prime-time hours in some portions of the country, largely the Midwest, is 7:00 to 10:00 p.m.) During this period, more than half of all households typically have their television sets turned on. Because of the size of the available audience, the economic stakes in the competition for prime-time viewers are great. The prime-time hours are unique not only because of their audience size, but also because they account for a large share of the overall production of new television content each year. Important shifts in program trends often emerge first in prime-time programming.

Given its prominence within the television landscape, we performed a separate analysis of the violent content presented during the prime-time hours. For our sample, which was gathered in the Pacific Time Zone, we included programs aired between 8:00 and 11:00 p.m. Monday through Saturday and 7:00 to 11:00 p.m. on Sunday. The focus of our analysis was to determine whether or not the amount of violence and/or the context in which violence is presented is different during the prime-time hours than at other times. We accomplished this by comparing the data for our sample of prime-time programs to the remaining data for all other programs.

Does the prevalence of violence or the context in which violence occurs change in prime time? From the perspective of practical significance, the answer is no, at least in terms of considering all television content collectively (see Table 17). The overall percentage of programs that contain violence is slightly higher in prime-time (67%) compared to non prime-time hours (60%), but this difference is not considered practically significant under our criteria for meaningful differences. At the level of individual channel types, however, the differences do become meaningful. The broadcast networks, independent broadcast, and premium cable all present a higher proportion of violent programming in prime time as compared to other hours of the day (due to a small sample size, data from public broadcasting are not included).

The pattern of context appears to raise fewer concerns during this high viewership time period. During prime time, there are more programs depicting the long-term negative consequences of violence, fewer violent interactions showing no pain to the victim, and a much lower incidence of unrealistic harm in violent interactions. In other words, the serious consequences of violence are more likely to be shown in prime time, and this pattern can inhibit the learning of aggression among viewers. In addition, prime time is much less likely to contain violent scenes in a humorous context, both in general and across all types of channels. This is a positive pattern because humor linked to violence has been found to increase the learning/imitation effect as well as the desensitization effect.

Balanced against these more positive indicators, however, are some findings that actually enhance the risk of negative effects. There is a higher proportion of programs with realistic settings (which contributes to learning and imitation) during prime time, as well as a greater percentage of scenes with blood and gore (which contributes to fear).

In summarizing the differences between violence in prime-time and non prime-time hours, we can conclude that when audiences are the largest, violence is less likely to be trivialized. That is, there is less of a humorous context and less of an under-statement of harm during prime time. Viewers are more likely to see victims suffer both in the short term and throughout the program. However, the violence is more likely to be in realistic settings and portrayed with blood and gore.

Table 17

Comparison of Prime-time and Non-Prime-time Hours Across Channel Types

		Broadcast Networks	Independent Broadcast	Basic Cable	Premium Cable	Overall Average
% Programs with Violence	Prime Time	67%	77%	64%	88%	67%
	Non Prime Time	47	56	66	82	60
% Programs w/ long term negative conseq	Prime Time	24	24	15	62	23
	Non Prime Time	15	11	13	29	14
% Programs w/realistic settings	Prime Time	93	71	58	81	68
	Non Prime Time	62	38	50	82	53
% Scenes w/un-punished violence	Prime Time	59	73	78	66	71
	Non Prime Time	72	73	71	68	71
% Scenes w/blood & gore	Prime Time	15	30	13	49	25
	Non Prime Time	7	7	9	21	11
% Scenes w/humor	Prime Time	22	34	35	20	29
	Non Prime Time	43	58	44	43	45
% Vio. PATs w/no pain	Prime Time	53	23	52	36	44
	Non Prime Time	51	48	57	43	52
% Vio. PATs w/unrealistic harm	Prime Time	19	18	29	20	24
	Non Prime Time	44	47	39	24	37

Summary of Results

This section provides an overview of the findings from our analysis focused solely on the third year sample (1996-97 programs) for this project. Two primary questions guided our study: 1) How much violence is on television and where is it located? and, 2) What is the nature or context of violence on television? In this summary section, we focus on the most robust findings across all the locator variables.

Presence of Violence

→ 61% of programs analyzed contain some violence

- Premium cable is substantially more likely to contain violence, whereas public broadcasting in particular as well as the broadcast networks are less likely to contain violence
- Movies are substantially more likely and drama programs are moderately more likely to contain violence than the industry average. Both comedy and reality-based programs are substantially less likely to contain violence

→ Two thirds of violent interactions on television portray actual behavioral acts of aggression against others

- About one fourth (27%) of the violent interactions involve credible threats alone, without any overt acts of aggression
- Very few violent interactions depict only harmful consequences of unseen acts

Saturation of Violence

→ About 32% of violent programs contain nine or more violent interactions

- The highest saturation of violent interactions are found:
  - on independent broadcast and especially on premium cable
  - in the genre of movies
- The lowest saturation of violent interactions are found
  - on public broadcast
  - in the reality-based, music video, and comedy genres

Rate of Violence

→ There is an average of 6.8 violent PATs per hour throughout the television landscape

- The highest rates are found:
  - on premium, independent, and basic cable channels.
  - in the genre of children's programming

- The lowest rates are found:
  - on public broadcasting
  - in the genres of reality and comedy programming

Protection from Violence

→ Only 3% of all programs with violence feature an anti-violence theme

→ When we adjust the overall presence of violence (61% of all programs) by removing those programs that feature an anti-violence theme, we are left with about 59% of all programs that present violence for primarily entertainment purposes

Context or Nature of Violent Portrayals

→ Perpetrators of violence are

  - overwhelmingly human, adult in age, white, and male
  - more often characterized as bad rather than good

→ Targets of violence are similar to perpetrators

→ Most violence is committed for one of three reasons

  - personal gain (28%)
  - anger (28%)
  - protection of life (24%)

→ Of all the violent interactions on television, 28% are portrayed as justified

→ Guns on television

  - are used in about one quarter (26%) of all violent interactions
  - are used most often in reality-based and dramatic programming

→ How extensive is violence?

  - The majority of violent interactions (61%) involve repeated behavioral acts of aggression
  - 17% of violent interactions include 10 or more acts of aggression against a victim

→ How graphic is violence?

- Very little violence is shown in close-up shots
- Blood and gore are rarely shown (14%) in scenes of violence
- When blood and gore do appear, such graphic portrayals are most often found on premium cable and in movies

→ How realistic is violence?

- Very little of TV violence is based on actual events in the real world, but most events seem fairly realistic in that they could happen in real life
- Fantasy violence is rare except in children's programs

→ Rewards and punishments

- In nearly three fourths of the violent scenes on television, there is no punishment (i.e., no remorse or condemnation) shown at the time that the violence occurs
- Good characters who engage in violence are rarely punished, meaning that they seldom show regret or are criticized
- The majority of bad characters are punished, but typically only at the end of the program

→ Consequences of violence

- Over 40% of the violent interactions on TV contain no observable harm or pain to the victim
- Children's programs are more likely than any other genre to feature unrealistically low levels of harm to the victim
- Very few programs depict the long-term negative repercussions of violence despite the fact that about half of all violent interactions featuring the actual use of physical force throughout the television landscape would likely result in incapacitating harm to the target if the violence occurred in real life.

→ Humor

- 42% of all violent scenes are presented in a humorous context
- Humor is more often linked to violence in children's and comedy programs

Chapter 4

ASSESSING CHANGE
IN TELEVISION VIOLENCE

In this chapter, we offer a comparison of Year 1 (1994-95), Year 2 (1995-96), and Year 3 (1996-97) results. Because the second year report focused on change from Year 1 to Year 2, this report will focus on trends across the entire three years of data collection. In most cases, these trends are analyzed by comparing the end-points of the study -- Year 1 and Year 3 -- with statistical tests. However, we also consider Year 2 results in order to confirm the consistency of any three year change trends identified.

We begin with a review of our approach from the Year 2 report for distinguishing a reliable or "true" change from any chance variation from year to year. Last year we developed a set of four criteria that must be met before we would conclude with confidence that violence on television has either increased or decreased in any meaningful way. We review these criteria below.

The philosophy that underlies the interpretation of the data reported in this chapter is to remain neutral on the question of whether television violence has changed over the three years of the study, until we are convinced otherwise by our data. We report only those changes that appear so substantial as to overcome this initial assumption of neutrality. We prefer caution in considering whether violence has either increased or decreased. It would be a serious error to report that violence had risen or fallen over the three years of this study when, in actuality, it had not. In order to avoid such an error we have set the hurdles for detecting change at rigorous, yet not unreasonable, levels.

After we define our criteria for accepting that a meaningful change has occurred, we report on three-year comparisons in several separate analysis sections. In the first section of this chapter, we compare the prevalence of violence from year to year. In the next section, we report the differences on character attributes for perpetrators and targets across all violent interactions. In the third section, we report overall differences from year to year on the major contextual variables that pose risk to viewers. In the remaining two sections, we examine the contextual differences in more detail, examining variation first by channel type and then by program genre. Finally, we report the results of an analysis of change during prime-time hours.

Thresholds for Detecting Change

To assist us in sorting through the year to year comparisons, we have developed a set of criteria or thresholds for detecting change. We pose four questions about the differences we observe.

1. Are they statistically significant?

2. Are they large enough to be of practical significance?

3. Where appropriate, do they form a consistent pattern?

4. Are we certain they are not a function of measurement error?

Only when the answer to all four of these questions is clearly "yes" for a given set of comparisons would we be comfortable in claiming that there has been "true" or meaningful change from Year 1 to Year 3. We elaborate on each of these criteria below.

Statistical Significance

Our first requirement is that any difference must be statistically significant. We use statistical tests to determine if differences between Year 1 and Year 3 are a function of reliable change or might be due to chance occurrence. The statistic we employ to test for significance is the binomial test. The binomial test is the most appropriate statistic for two reasons: 1) it is ideal for variables that have only two categories; and 2) it takes sample size into consideration.

In our summary of major findings presented in the NTVS first year report (see Wilson et al., 1997, p. 140), we reduced each variable to exactly two categories. For example, in Year 1, 25% of the violent interactions include use of a gun. Conversely, 75% of the interactions do not include use of a gun. The binomial test is well suited for comparisons of variables that are described in the form of proportions. The question we ask for each comparison across time is: Have the proportions found in 1994-95 changed significantly when compared to 1996-97? Applying the binomial test to the differences in proportions for these two end-point years allows us to answer this question.

There is another attractive element associated with the binomial test. This feature is best introduced by stating our general question about change in the following, slightly modified, form: Are the differences in proportions that we observe from year to year a function of *program sampling error* or a function of true change? Stated this way, our focus is on separating differences that may be the result of sampling error from reliable changes. Sampling error is an inverse function of sample size; as the sample size increases, the error decreases.

The mathematical formula for the standard error portion of the binomial test is as follows:

$$\sqrt{pq/n}$$

In the formula, p and q represent proportions and n represents the sample size. Because of the square root function in the formula, the error is reduced by half if the sample size is quadrupled. The larger the sample of units in a particular comparison the more confidence we may place in differences we observe.

The binomial test is very useful for screening out differences that may appear on their face to be substantial, but are actually unreliable because of the small sub-group of programs used in certain comparisons. This is a critical consideration for year to year contextual variable comparisons *within* channels.

For example, in this chapter, as in others, we consider public broadcasting as a separate channel type in our locator analyses. Because this is the only channel type that has just a single member in its "group," and because this channel has a relatively small number of programs that contain violence, the observations in this category have a greater risk of sampling error than do the observations for the other channel types. Year 1 to Year 3 comparisons on the violence contextual factors for this channel may show large differences (20-40%) from year to year. However, since sampling error is relatively high for this channel, even large fluctuations may not prove to be statistically significant. For other channels with larger numbers of cases (i.e., violent programs), sampling error will be lower and we may therefore place more confidence in the differences we observe.

In applying the binomial test to our data, we require that the conventional level of significance ($p < .05$) be reached before a difference may be considered as a meaningful change. Because we sampled by program, the sample size used for the computation of the binomial in all cases is the number of programs (as opposed to number of violent scenes or violent interactions) used in the comparison.

In summary, the binomial test allows us to evaluate differences that appear large in light of sampling error. If this error is too large, even formidable percentage differences from year to year would not be interpreted as true change.

Practical Differences

In a large and comprehensive sample of programming such as the one used in this study, there will be a number of small differences year to year that may, technically speaking, represent "statistically significant" change but are of little practical significance. To avoid being distracted by these small and inconsequential changes we have established a convention for detecting change at a 5% absolute difference level from Year 1 to Year 3. No difference below this minimum will be considered as indicative of a meaningful change over the three-year course of this study.

The Pattern of Differences

In addition to requiring an absolute difference of 5%, it is important to consider the overall pattern of Year 1/Year 3 differences within a given set of comparisons. We will be looking across 14 contextual variables in most of the analyses reported below. Making certain that we have a reliable pattern of differences year to year is particularly important when we consider the contextual variables as a group. Two factors are important for establishing that a reliable pattern is present: 1) the *number* of variables that demonstrate such differences; and 2) the *consistency* in the direction of these differences.

When we consider change over time on the contextual elements surrounding violent portrayals, we believe it is important to consider these attributes as a group rather than to microscopically examine each element in isolation. Given that our contextual analysis here considers 14 different variables, we have established the standard that roughly one third of the differences must exceed 5%. This translates into the following rule of thumb when we assess the contextual factors: At least four differences (among the 14 context variable comparisons) must emerge from the applicable comparisons (i.e., across the television environment as a whole, or within a particular channel group or genre) for us to be confident of identifying year to year change as meaningful.

Further, we require that these differences must all move in the same conceptual direction. For example, when examining differences within a particular channel or genre, we would be suspicious of a pattern of differences that included a decrease in the percentage of scenes with unpunished violence accompanied by an increase in the percent of violent interactions with use of a gun. Our suspicion would stem from two related concerns. First, differences that appear to "bounce around" in directionality are probably best explained as chance occurrences. Second, even if these differences were accurate, the social or practical significance of the change is diminished by the fact that they tend, in effect, to cancel each other out. In this instance, we could not reasonably speak of increases or decreases in television violence from year to year if it is being punished more on the one hand, but gun use is up on the other.

Measurement Error for the Contextual Variables

Another possible type of error we wish to guard against is concluding that there has been a true change on a contextual factor from year to year when the difference is actually a function of fluctuations in coder reliability. We should be more suspicious of any year to year differences for variables that have lower coder reliabilities than differences found for variables with higher reliabilities. If certain measures lack substantial coder agreement in any of the years, we may not be able to distinguish true changes from differences that stem from the lack of coder agreement.

A detailed description of Year 3 coder reliability is provided in Chapter 2 of this report. A comparable summary was provided in the first and second year reports. A summary comparison of coder reliability across all three years is also provided in Chapter 2. As we note in that chapter, the coding scheme developed in this project requires coders to make decisions at two distinct levels. The first level focuses on unitizing, that is, the identification of PATs and scenes. The second level is concerned with degree of consistency among coders in choosing the same value for our 41 context variables once the unitizing boundaries are established.

The median percentage of coders who fell within the 20% interval around the mode for PATs over the three year period was 76%. The median percentage of coders who fell within the 20% interval around the mode for scenes across the three years was 100%. A summary of the coefficients for each of the context variables within units was also computed. With the exception of one moderately low coefficient (.61; for a variable not reported), the median level of agreement for all of the context variables, across the three year period, ranged from a low of .71 to a high of 1.0. Over half of these medians are above .90 and more than three fourths of the median coefficients are above .80.

Coding reliability appears to be sufficiently high across all three years for the 14 variables we include in the change analyses. Consequently, we can be confident that differences we observe from year to year on the prevalence of violence as well as the contextual factors are not the result of coding errors.

In summary, only when the differences observed are statistically significant, of sufficient practical size, and the pattern of differences is clearly consistent will we conclude that meaningful change in the presentation of violence has occurred. All of the variables we will consider have been reliably coded so we can be confident that differences observed are not due to any inconsistency in coding procedures.

Prevalence Levels for Violent Programming

Overall Prevalence

In Year 1, violence was found on television for a majority, or more specifically, 58% of all programs analyzed. In Year 2, we found that the overall prevalence of violence remained virtually unchanged. Violence was found in 61% of programs. In Year 3 the prevalence of violence is once again 61%. **This is striking evidence that there is no increase or decrease in the overall prevalence of violence on television across the three-year course of this study.** It must be emphasized here that this analysis encompasses all channels and all day-parts included in the study. Later in this chapter, we offer a more detailed assessment of the change for certain channel types and in prime-time television programming, where change has arguably occurred.

In Year 1, slightly more than 18,000 violent interactions or PATs were observed across the content analyzed. In Year 2, more than 18,500 violent interactions were observed, although the Year 2 sample included 50 more shows than in Year 1 (3,235 vs. 3,185). This year more than 17,500 PATs were observed across 2,750 programs. Table 18 displays the range and breakdown of these violent interactions by type.

The definition of violence used in our study provides three primary components: credible threats, behavioral acts, and harmful consequences of unseen violence. As shown in the table, the largest share of violent interactions for all three years involved behavioral acts. Threats of violence represented most of the remaining interactions. Harmful consequences of unseen acts comprised a small percentage of violent interactions in both years. This pattern was relatively stable across the three years of the study.

In summary, the prevalence, range and type of violent interactions are remarkably similar from year to year. Although the number of violent interactions increased slightly in Year 2 and decreased slightly in Year 3, these numbers do not imply a meaningful change given the slightly larger number of shows in the Year 2 sample and the slightly smaller number in Year 3.

Table 18

Three-Year Comparisons:
Range and Type of Violent Interactions

	Year 1	Year 2	Year 3
Range of violent interactions	1-88	1-99	1-106
Type of violent interaction			
Behavioral acts	66%	69%	67%
Threats of violence	29%	24%	27%
Harmful consequences of unseen acts	3%	3%	3%

Prevalence by Channel and Genre

We also assessed prevalence by two locator variables: 1) the source of the violent content, represented by channel type; and, 2) the type of program, represented by commonly understood categories of television programs, or genres.

Figure 51 displays the three-year pattern of differences in the prevalence of violence by channel type. For the premium, independent, and public broadcast channel types, the level of violence has remained stable across the three years of this study. One shift in the percentage of programs containing violence meets our criterion for both our practical and statistical significance. The proportion of programs containing violence on basic cable increased from 60% in Year 1 to 64% in Year 2 and finally, to 66% this year. This represents an upward trend.

Last year we reported an increase of practical and statistical significance in the proportion of programs containing violence on the broadcast networks from 47% to 54%. In Year 3, the proportion of violent programs on broadcast television has dropped slightly (to 51%). This brings the Year 1 to Year 3 change to just 1% under the 5% practical significance level. In contrast, the basic cable findings place their increase at 1% over the 5% threshold.

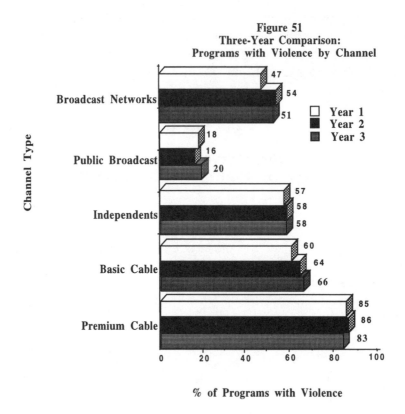

Figure 51
Three-Year Comparison:
Programs with Violence by Channel

% of Programs with Violence

Figure 52 displays the three-year differences in the prevalence of violence by program genres. We see from the figure that prevalence has remained relatively stable across the three years of the study for drama, children's programming, and movies.

Substantial differences are found in the music video, comedy, and reality-based genres. Last year, we detected a 22% increase in violence in music videos from Year 1 to Year 2. This increase was both practically and statistically significant. In Year 3 this increase has remained stable. (The reader should refer to the Year 2 report [p. 105] for an explanation of this dramatic increase.) Increases in violence that failed to attain practical significance for the comedy and reality-based genres in the Year 1 to Year 2 comparisons now appear to be practically and statistically significant trends toward more violence. In both cases, violence is now higher by approximately 10% from Year 1 to Year 3.

In summary, when we consider the trends across the years, there have been a few significant changes. The basic cable channels show a 6% increase in the prevalence of violent programs across their entire schedule. It also appears that the increase in the prevalence of violence in music videos we observed from Year 1 to Year 2 has remained stable. Examination of differences in prevalence by program genre shows two other consequential changes from Year 1 to Year 3: a 10% increase in the prevalence of violence in the comedy genre and a similarly sized increase for reality-based

116

programming[1]. Finally, despite no significant increases, the prevalence of violence in the drama, children's and movie genres, remains high and has changed little over the duration of the study. Violence is found widely across these genres and has remained stable across the three year period.

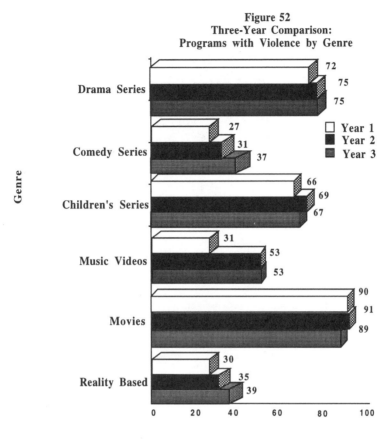

Figure 52
Three-Year Comparison:
Programs with Violence by Genre

% of Programs with Violence

Three-Year Comparison of Demographics and
Attributes of Perpetrators and Targets

The previous sections describe differences in the proportion of programs that contain violence. Such analyses, however, tell us nothing about changes in *how* that violence is portrayed from year to year. We now turn to analyses that provide us with that information. We deal first with the nature of the characters that were involved in violence.

---

[1] Our Year 1 percentage calculated for the prevalence of violence in reality programming differs from the percentage reported by the University of Texas study due to the inclusion of a slightly different number of reality-based programs in the two independent studies.

Table 19

Three Year Comparison:
Demographics and Attributes of Perpetrators and Targets
Across all Violent Interactions

	Nature of Perpetrators			Nature of Targets		
	Year 1	Year 2	Year 3	Year 1	Year 2	Year 3
Type of Character						
Human	71%	71%	70%	70%	70%	70%
Anthropomorphized Animal	12	14	11	14	15	12
Anthropomorphized Supernatural	10	7	10	9	7	9
Animal	1	1	1	2	2	2
Supernatural Creature	3	3	4	2	3	4
Sex						
Male	78%	77%	73%	75%	76%	71%
Female	9	10	10	9	10	10
Age						
Child	2%	4%	3%	3%	5%	4%
Teen	5	6	5	7	8	7
Adult	76	74	72	72	68	68
Elderly	1	1	1	1	1	1
Apparent Ethnicity						
White	76%	73%	71%	77%	75%	72%
Black	5	5	7	6	5	7
Asian	3	3	2	3	3	2
Hispanic	2	4	3	2	3	3
Native American	3	1	2	2	1	2
Middle Eastern	1	3	1	1	2	1
Hero						
No	93%	91%	86%	92%	91%	86%
Yes	6	8	10	6	8	11
Nature of Character						
Bad	45%	45%	43%	31%	32%	29%
Good	24	28	28	31	35	36
Blended (good & bad)	13	12	10	12	10	10
Neutral	14	10	12	21	17	19

Note. Demographic and attributive information was coded for each perpetrator and each target in every violent interaction. Variables do not always sum to 100% because some perpetrators/targets are implied or unidentified, and some cannot be classified according to a particular characteristic. Only those characters involved in violence were assessed in a program.

Demographic information was coded for each character involved as a perpetrator or target in each violent interaction. Summing across all of the violent interactions provides a profile of perpetrators and targets. Table 19 presents a comparison of Year 1, 2, and 3 on the demographics and related attributes of characters involved in violence.

The typical perpetrator and target of violence on television in Year 3 is overwhelmingly a human character whose apparent ethnicity is white, age is adult, and sex is male. However, there are several trends here that are both statistically and substantively significant. There is a 5% drop over the three years in the percentage of perpetrators and targets who are identified as male. Similarly the ethnicity of both perpetrators and targets involved in violent interactions appears to have changed from Year 1 to Year 3 with a 5% drop over the three years of the study in the percentage of whites who are portrayed in these roles. No other ethnicity appears to have gained disproportionately from this drop in the depiction of white males as perpetrators.

The percentage of perpetrators defined as "heros" has also changed from Year 1 to Year 3. A greater percentage of perpetrators and targets involved in violence are portrayed as heros in Year 3 compared to Year 1. On the other hand, the percentage of perpetrators characterized as "good," "bad" and "blended" generally remains the same from Year 1 to Year 3 with the exception of a 5% increase in the percentage of targets defined as "good."

By our criteria, then, there are several changes observed over the years for the demographic attributes of perpetrators and targets across all violent interactions. We have observed a 5% drop in the percentage of males and whites portrayed as both perpetrators and targets involved in violence and a similarly sized increase in the percentage of both targets and perpetrators defined as heros.

Assessing Change on the Major Contextual Variables in Television Programming Overall

In our first year report, we designed a summary framework for analyzing violent depictions that included operationalizing a set of key contextual factors that may either increase or decrease the risk of learning, desensitization, and fear. To review, these factors include: 1) the nature of the perpetrator; 2) the nature of the target; 3) the reason for the violence; 4) the presence of weapons; 5) the graphicness and extent of the violence; 6) the degree of realism of the violence; 7) whether the violence is rewarded or punished; 8) the consequences of the violence; and 9) whether humor is involved. In the previous chapter, we summarized our major findings for this year by these context or "risk" factors.

In this section, we now compare 14 different variables that operationalize these contextual factors across the three years of the study. First, we examine four program-level measures. Next, we assess three contextual variables measured at the scene level. Finally, we report on seven factors measured at the interaction (i.e., PAT) level.

119

Figure 53 displays the findings for 1994-95, 1995-96, and 1996-97 across the risk factors measured at the program level. There has been no improvement in the proportion of shows that feature an anti-violence theme by Year 3. This figure has remained stable at 3-4% of all violent programs. Likewise, there is no change in the portrayal of long-term negative consequences for violence over the three years and no change in the percentage of violent programs that present violence in realistic settings. However, there is an 8 percentage point increase in violent programs that feature "bad" characters who go unpunished for their aggressive actions from Year 1 to Year 3.

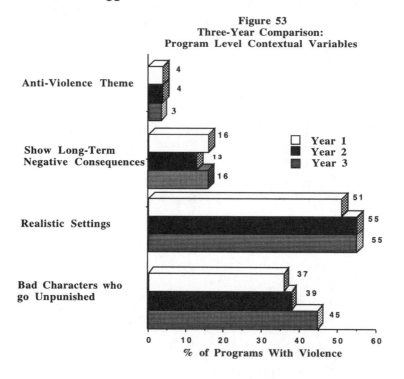

Figure 53
Three-Year Comparison:
Program Level Contextual Variables

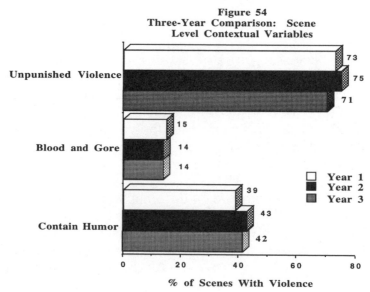

Figure 54
Three-Year Comparison: Scene
Level Contextual Variables

120

Figure 54 displays the three-year comparisons for three contextual variables measured at the scene level. Again, we find little change across the three years of data collection. The percentage of scenes where violence goes unpunished, that display blood and gore, and that include humor are unchanged from Year 1 to Year 3 by our 5% criterion.

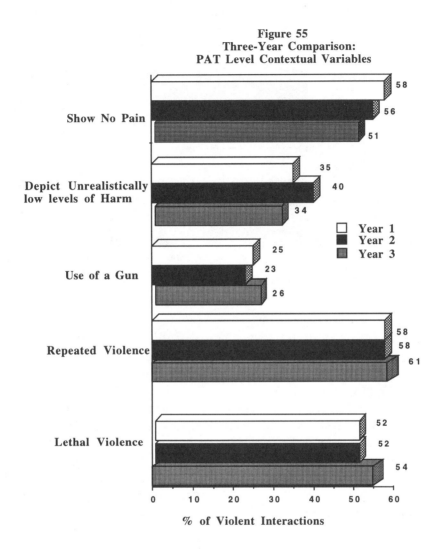

Figure 55
Three-Year Comparison:
PAT Level Contextual Variables

% of Violent Interactions

Figure 55 displays the three-year comparisons for five contextual factors measured at the violent interaction level. The percentage of interactions that portray the use of a gun, contain repeated behavioral violence, depict unrealistically low levels of harm, or portray lethal violence remain unchanged by our standards. The single meaningful difference we observe is a 7 percentage point decrease from Year 1 to Year 3 in violent interactions that show no pain.

121

Figure 56 displays the results of the three-year comparisons for characters involved in violence. No change, on a practical level, was observed from year to year in the percentage of attractive perpetrators or targets involved in violence.

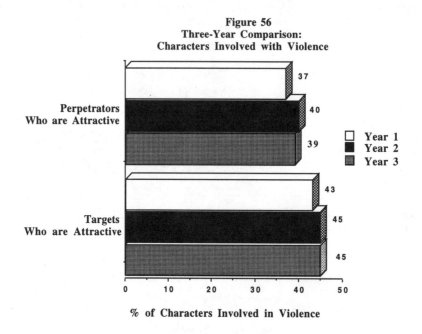

Figure 56
Three-Year Comparison:
Characters Involved with Violence

% of Characters Involved in Violence

In this section we examined a set of 14 variables that operationalized the key contextual features of violent programming: 1) the nature of the perpetrator; 2) the nature of the target; 3) the reason for the violence; 4) the presence of weapons; 5) the graphicness and extent of the violence; 6) the degree of realism of the violence; 7) whether the violence is rewarded or punished; 8) the consequences of the violence; and 9) whether humor is involved. In summary, the year to year comparisons on these variables generally fail to reach the 5% level of practical difference established for identifying meaningful change. With the exception of a 7 percentage point decrease in violent interactions that show no pain and a 8 percentage point increase in violent programs portraying bad characters who go unpunished for their aggressive actions, all other differences were in the range of 0 to 4%.

Thus, our final conclusion must be that there has been no consistent change for any of the major contextual variables from Year 1 to Year 3 for television programming overall. In every case across the three-year contextual comparisons, all of our concerns presented in Year 1 and Year 2 remain the same for Year 3.

Assessing Change on the Major Contextual Variables by Channel Type and Genre

The previous two sections addressed the issue of change at the level of the overall television environment. This section addresses year to year changes in the contextual factors by channel type and program genre.

Changes by Channel Type

Applying the criteria for identifying meaningful change, we find no reliable changes from Year 1 to Year 3 for any of the channel groups: broadcast networks, independent broadcast, public broadcast, basic cable, or premium cable.

Changes by Program Genre

Year 1 to Year 3 differences for the contextual factors broken down by program genre were also examined. Again, applying our criteria for change we find no consistent pattern in any of the genres that indicates a reliable change has occurred from Year 1 to Year 3.

Prime-time Analysis

A separate change analysis was undertaken for the prime-time period only. We defined the prime-time hours as 8:00 to 11:00 p.m. (P.S.T.) Monday thorough Saturday and 7:00 to 11:00 p.m. (P.S.T.) on Sunday, which is consistent with industry standards. There were several reasons for pursuing this analysis. First, this is the time when the largest number of viewers are in the audience. Second, prime time accounts for a significant share of all the new programming introduced on television, so any important shifts in program practices might be expected to emerge first during these hours. Finally, given that we have already identified a significant albeit modest increase in the overall prevalence of violence on broadcast network channels, it is important to examine what proportion of that shift, if any, is traceable to the prime-time schedule.

We applied the same criteria presented above for detecting change to these analyses. To review: Are the differences statistically significant, large enough to be of practical significance, and do they form a consistent pattern? With respect to the last criterion, consistency of pattern, we require that at least four context measures have shifted in similar conceptual directions among our list of key contextual variables.

In the two sub-sections that follow, we first report our findings for the prevalence of violence across programs, and then follow with our analyses of the major contextual variables.

Prevalence of Violence

When we consider the prime-time environment as a whole, encompassing all channels studied, we note an 8% increase in the amount of violence from 59% of all programs in Year 1 to 67% in Year 3.

The proportion of programs that contain violence in prime time has risen from Year 1 to Year 3 for two channel groupings that comprise the bulk of the channels in our sample. Examination of prevalence by channel type reveals an increase of 14% for the broadcast networks and 10% for the basic cable channels (see Table 20). There were no statistically significant changes for independent broadcast and premium channels.

Table 20

Three-Year Comparisons for Prime time:
Percent of Programs that Contain Violence by Channel Type

	Commercial Broadcast	Independent Broadcast	Basic Cable	Premium Cable	Overall
Year 1	53%	70%	54%	91%	59%
Year 2	63%	73%	63%	98%	66%
Year 3	67%	77%	64%	87%	67%

Note: We excluded public broadcasting from consideration because the number of programs containing violence in prime time was too low for any reliable statistical comparison to be made.

Major Contextual Variables

We found no consistent pattern of differences in prime time from Year 1 to Year 3 on any of the key variables that measure the context in which violence is presented. The implication here is that there were no industry-wide shifts in the primary ways in which violence is presented during prime-time hours.

We also examined the year to year changes in contextual variables within each of the individual channel groupings, to see if any differences would emerge from that perspective. We included four channel types in our analysis: broadcast networks, independent broadcast, basic cable, and premium channels. We excluded public broadcasting from consideration because the number of programs containing violence in prime time was too low for any reliable statistical comparison to be made.

Overall, these analyses produced no cluster of year to year differences within the channel types that can be reported with the high degree of confidence established by our change criteria: Are the differences statistically significant, large enough to be of practical significance, and do they form a consistent pattern?

Despite the lack of evidence for change, additional analyses were pursued to determine whether the relatively new programming appearing on the broadcast networks during prime time showed *any* tendency toward changes in the context within which violence is presented. It could be argued that if the context of violence is changing for the better that this improvement is most likely to be found in broadcast networks prime-time programming.

124

Table 21

Summary of Differences Across Three Years in Broadcast Networks Prime-Time Programming

	Yr 1	Yr 2	Yr 3	Significance Yr 1 to Yr 3
Of Programs that Contain Violence. . .				
% that show long-term negative consequences	35%	23%	24%	ns
Of Scenes that Contain Violence. . .				
% that show no regret, remorse, or sanctions	66%	64%	59%	ns
When a Violent Interaction Occurs. . .				
% that show no pain	67%	54%	53%	ns
% that use a gun	32%	44%	51%	*
% with repeated behavioral violence	32%	54%	62%	*

ns = the comparison from Yr 1 to Yr 3 is not statistically significant
* = the comparison from Yr 1 to Yr 3 is significant at $p < .05$.

Table 21 presents a summary of differences for the contextual variables across the three years of the study for broadcast prime-time programming. While there are only two differences between the percentages presented in the table that are statistically significant, examination of the trends among the contextual variables suggests that rather than improving, the changes in network broadcast prime-time programming are best described as "mixed." The percentage of programs that show long-term negative consequences for violence has declined from 35 to 24% from Year 1 to Year 3. Similarly, the percentage of violent interactions that show use of a gun has increased significantly from 32 to 51%. And, the percentage of violent interactions with repeated behavioral violence has increased significantly from 32 to 62% from Year 1 to Year 3. On the other hand, the percentage of violent scenes that show no regret, remorse, or negative sanctions has decreased by 7% and the percentage of violent interactions wherein the victim shows no pain has decreased from 67 to 53%. In summary, there is no evidence that the context in which violence is presented during prime time for broadcast programming has changed consistently over the three years of this study.

<u>Summary of Prime-time Analyses</u>

We detected an 8% increase in the overall amount of programs on television containing violence during this period. This increase is slightly larger on the broadcast networks and basic cable channel groups; smaller increases that were not of practical significance were found on the independent broadcast stations and on premium cable. We found no consistent pattern of differences in prime time from Year 1 to Year 3 on any of the key variables that measure the context in which violence is presented. Likewise, there is no evidence that the context in which violence is presented during prime time for broadcast programming has changed appreciably over the three years of this study.

Conclusions About Change in the Prevalence and Contextual Patterns of Violent Portrayals

Virtually all of our prevalence measures point to the conclusion that **violence across the television landscape has remained remarkably stable over the three-year period**. Our standard for detecting a true change from year to year consists of four criteria: 1) the difference in percentages on a variable from Year 1 to Year 2 must exceed 5% on an absolute scale; 2) the difference must be statistically significant; 3) the difference on one variable must join with others to show a consistent pattern, where appropriate; and 4) the variables involved must be free of measurement error. After applying this four-part test to all of our analyses, we can conclude with confidence that the overall prevalence of violence has remained constant over the three year period of the study. In Year 1, violence was found in 58% of all programs on television. In Year 2, we found that the overall prevalence of violence was 61% of programs. In Year 3, the prevalence of violence is once again 61%.

When we examine the prevalence of violence by channel type and genre, we find one notable source of increased violence. Compared to Year 1, we find that programs on the basic cable channels have increased by 6% overall in their likelihood of containing at least some violent material by Year 3.

Examination of differences in prevalence by genre locator variables shows three other consequential changes from Year 1 to Year 3. First, it appears that the increase in the prevalence of violence in music videos we observed from Year 1 to Year 2 has remained stable. Second, we detect a 10% increase in the prevalence of violence in the comedy genre and third, a similarly sized increase for reality-based programming. Despite no significant increases, the prevalence of violence in the drama, children's, and movie genres remains high and has changed little over the three years of the study.

We designed a summary framework for analyzing violent depictions that included the key contextual factors that may either increase or decrease the risk of learning, desensitization, and fear. These factors include: 1) the nature of the perpetrator; 2) the nature of the target; 3) the reason for the violence; 4) the presence of weapons; 5) the graphicness and extent of the violence; 6) the degree of realism of the violence; 7) whether the violence is rewarded or punished; 8) the consequences of the violence;

and 9) whether humor is involved. In the previous chapter, we summarized our major findings for this year by these context or "risk" factors.

When we consider the context in which violence is presented across the television environment overall, there has generally been no systematic change in the contextual factors with three exceptions -- none of which form a consistent pattern. We observed a 5% decrease in the number of violent interactions that feature males and whites as both perpetrators and targets and a 7% decrease in the amount of violent interactions that show no pain. Also, we found an 8% increase in the amount of violent programs that feature bad characters who are not punished for their violent actions.

Finally, when we assess the prime-time hours in particular, we find that the prevalence of programs containing violence is up somewhat (8%) overall. This shift is tied largely to increases in the prevalence of violence on the broadcast networks and basic cable channels. The context of violent portrayals on both the broadcast networks and basic cable channels during prime-time hours has remained stable over the three year period.

Chapter 5

HIGH-RISK PORTRAYALS THAT
ENCOURAGE LEARNING OF AGGRESSION

Throughout this report we have emphasized the importance of context, or the way in which violence is portrayed. Contextual factors such as the nature of the perpetrator and whether violence seems justified are crucial in determining how violence is likely to affect the audience. In Chapters 3 and 4, our analyses focused primarily on one contextual feature at a time. This univariate approach allows us to highlight the contribution of each context variable in its own right, and to point out that several features of violence must be considered independently in assessing whether a portrayal is problematic for the audience.

Nevertheless, a variable-by-variable approach does not tell the whole story. In actuality, portrayals of violence on television involve clusters of contextual features. Viewers have access to all the information in the cluster when constructing their meaning for observed violence. For example, a hero might be rewarded for engaging in violence that protects other characters. This type of theme or pattern involves three contextual variables: nature of the perpetrator, whether violence is justified, and whether it is rewarded or punished. Such a portrayal has a distinct meaning when compared to a depiction involving a good character who deeply regrets using physical force, even though lives are saved. Patterns such as these are the bases upon which plots are derived and represent how viewers interpret violent portrayals. To fully capture the meaning of violence on television, contextual variables need to be considered simultaneously.

The purpose of this chapter is to examine patterns of violence that emerge when contextual variables are appraised collectively. Consistent with our concern for harmful effects, we based the patterns on the idea of audience risk. In particular, our analysis focuses on those portrayals that include a combination of features that make them particularly risky or hazardous to the audience. In other words, we created *composites* of contextual features to reflect elevated risk. At this point, our high-risk assessment pertains only to the learning of aggressive attitudes and behaviors, and not to fear or desensitization. Of the three harmful effects of television violence, the learning of aggression continues to cause the greatest public policy concern (Murray, 1994; Reno, 1993; Windhausen, 1994). Additionally, there is more research on how the contextual factors affect learning than for how they affect fear or desensitization (see Wilson et al., 1997).

This chapter is divided into four sections. The first section outlines definitional issues for our risk composite involving the learning of aggressive attitudes and behaviors. The second section briefly overviews the units of analysis used in the construction of the composite. The third section provides a rationale for why we created two learning composites -- one for young children, and one for older children and adolescents. Finally, the fourth section presents the findings for the two risk composites. Overall patterns are discussed, and then each composite is further analyzed by genre, channel type, and daypart. Our goal is to describe where the highest risks are found in the television landscape, and to locate these risks in terms of certain types of programming, channels, and times of day. We also assess whether there have been any important changes in high-risk patterns since last year (1995-96 vs. 1996-97), and we conclude with some examples of what high-risk portrayals look like on television.

Two caveats are important before preceding. First, the contextual features have been tested primarily in isolation from one another in previous research, so we have little information on how they might interact or combine to produce an effect. Still, it is reasonable to assume that a portrayal containing several problematic contextual features poses more risk than a portrayal featuring only one. Consistent with this idea, we assume that combinations of contextual features reflect higher risk. Until further research is conducted, however, it is important to remember that our composites rest on a logical though untested assumption -- that combinations of contextual factors are more likely to encourage learning than any one factor alone.

Second, there are numerous ways to conceptualize risk as it relates to television violence. Our decision to focus on the learning of aggression as a harmful outcome is just one of many issues to consider. In our Year 2 Report (see Wilson et al., 1998), we explicated all the choices we made in creating our composites. But there are literally hundreds of alternative ways to assemble the contextual features. We constructed our composites in a conservative fashion, as will be explained below. We acknowledge that this approach is relatively new and certainly not the only way to think about risk. Our hope is that this type of analysis will encourage other media scholars to tackle the problem of assessing risk in the area of television violence.

Composite for Learning: Definitional Issues

As indicated in Chapter 1, there is a substantial body of evidence documenting that exposure to televised violence contributes to aggressive behavior (see Hearold, 1986; Paik & Comstock, 1994). Huesmann (1988) and other researchers (Berkowitz, 1984) explain this relationship in terms of a cumulative learning process. According to this view, children can learn aggressive scripts from watching violent models on television. These scripts or "programs for behavior" are stored in memory and become strengthened with repeated exposure to aggressive portrayals, especially those that normalize or condone violence.

Learning from televised violence can manifest itself in different ways. A young child may acquire a new script from a single violent portrayal, resulting in imitative or copycat behavior (Huesmann, 1988). In contrast, an older child who already possesses a repertoire of aggressive scripts in memory may be less likely to imitate, but instead may experience a triggering or reinforcement of previously learned tendencies from watching a violent depiction. Our use of the term learning should be thought of in this broad sense. It refers to all those processes involved in acquiring new aggressive attitudes and behaviors, reinforcing established aggressive tendencies, and generally reducing inhibitions against violence by making it seem normative.

The first step in constructing a risk composite for learning is to decide which variables to include. Table 1 on p. 13 of this report indicates that many of the contextual factors assessed in this project can impact aggressive attitudes and behaviors among viewers. We isolated those factors that have the strongest research support, particularly as documented in meta-analyses of multiple studies (for a review of this evidence, see Wilson et al., 1998). The five most influential features that increase the likelihood of learning aggression are: 1) an attractive perpetrator; 2) violence that is justified; 3) violence that is either explicitly rewarded or implicitly sanctioned (because it is not punished); 4) violence that shows no pain or harm; and 5) violence that seems realistic to the viewer.

Our approach is somewhat restrained because we focused only on those portrayals that contain all five of these risk features simultaneously. If any of the five characteristics is missing, a violent depiction did not qualify for our composites. In other words, depictions that have several but not all of the relevant risk factors would be screened out of the analysis. The composites, then, are a measure of *high risk* because they reflect a constellation of many problematic context features all present in a single portrayal.

Given our conservative screening rules, we end up identifying only a small percentage of violent portrayals as being of high risk. Yet this small percentage still translates into hundreds of extremely risky examples of violence appearing throughout the television landscape. For these portrayals, we can be confident that they raise serious concerns about negative effects on the audience. On the other hand, the many portrayals that do not meet our stringent criteria should not be considered as benign or risk free. Indeed, experimental evidence indicates that the presence of even one contextual feature can elevate the risk associated with a violent portrayal (see Wilson et al., 1997, for review). Thus, the findings reported in this chapter must be interpreted with caution; the data do not reflect all the portrayals that pose risk on television. Instead, the findings refer to the "worst offenders" on television -- those violent portrayals that contain a multitude of problematic features qualifying them as *high risk* for the audience.

Once the key variables are selected, the next step in building a composite is to determine how to combine the factors into an index. One option is to assign some numerical weight or score to each of the factors, and then to tabulate a total risk score for the violent portrayal. Such an approach is analogous to Gerbner's Violence Index, which is a summative score that reflects features of violence across all programming from year to year (see Gerbner & Gross, 1976).

The problem with this approach is twofold. The scores themselves are difficult to interpret and compare. In addition, the assignment of such values is somewhat arbitrary given that there is no solid empirical research on which to base such a scoring system (see Potter, 1997). Consequently, we turned to a more defensible method involving filters or thresholds. With a filter approach, a portrayal is deemed risky if it contains some predetermined level or amount of a contextual factor, but no attempt is made to quantify the factors. In other words, so long as the portrayal contains some facet of a contextual feature, then the threshold is achieved and the depiction meets that particular risk criterion. For example, if a perpetrator is coded as good *or* as both good and bad (blended), the threshold for attractiveness has been met because some aspect of that character presumably is appealing to the audience. However, no distinction or differential ranking is assigned to good versus blended perpetrators -- they both reach the threshold for attractiveness.

The particular thresholds that we established for each contextual factor are fully described in our Year 2 Report (Wilson et al., 1998).

Unit of Analysis: Violent Interactions Rather than Programs

Throughout this project we have stressed that the identification of specific programs as violent or as posing risk is not the focus of our research. Part of our reluctance is due to the fact that many of the newly scheduled series do not last very long because of low viewership ratings. If our project was to emphasize particular programs, many of the findings would be outdated from the moment they were released. Another reason we resist labeling programs is due to the nature of our sample. Our scientific sample is representative of a typical week of American television. Consequently, most of the regularly-scheduled prime-time programs are reflected by only a single episode in our sample. In other words, our sample is highly representative of a typical week of television, but not at all reflective of the scope and nature of a particular series across a year of programming. It would be scientifically inaccurate to make claims about an entire series based on only one episode.

For these reasons, our focus has been on the nature of violent *portrayals* on television rather than with specific episodes or titles. We have chosen to examine risk in a similar way. Our goal here is to assess where the high-risk portrayals are found in the weekly television landscape rather than to label particular episodes or programs as high risk. This type of information arguably is more beneficial to parents. Knowing that a particular formula, such as a hero engaging in justified violence, is problematic and most commonly found in certain genres or on certain channels is more useful in making future viewing decisions for children than having information about specific program titles that may or may not be continued the next season.

Consistent with this approach, the risk composites are based on profiling violent portrayals rather than violent program titles or series. The violent interaction represents the smallest unit or level of analysis in our study. It contains rich information about the types of characters involved, the nature of violence itself, and its consequences. Our goal is to identify all violent interactions across the television landscape that involve *an attractive perpetrator engaging in justified violence that*

131

does not get punished and that shows minimal consequences. The question to be addressed by our analyses in this chapter is where are these high-risk portrayals of violence located.

The Need for Two Composites: Developmental Considerations

In our high-risk analysis, we focus mostly on viewers under the age of 18. Although violent portrayals have been shown to facilitate aggression in adults (e.g., Berkowitz & Powers, 1979), the strongest effects of such content are found for younger age groups (Huesmann, 1988; Paik & Comstock, 1994). This pattern is consistent with the idea that young children are actively seeking new scripts for behavior and often do not appreciate the social norms against behaving aggressively. However, even older children and adolescents can be influenced by televised violence, indicating that such content can reinforce and disinhibit previously learned aggressive tendencies.

If teens as well as children can be affected, why create different composites for risk? A large body of research indicates that younger children attend to and interpret television content differently than do their older counterparts (Collins, 1983; Dorr, 1986). Several prominent perspectives on child development such as Piaget's (1952, 1960) theory of cognitive development and recent models of information processing (Flavell, 1985; Siegler, 1991) are consistent with this view. Given the natural variation in how and when children develop, it is difficult to specify precise ages associated with these changes. However, most research reveals marked differences between preschoolers and young elementary schoolers on the one hand and older elementary school children on the other in terms of the basic strategies that are used to make sense of the world (Siegler, 1991).

Given the importance of developmental level, we created two composites for risk: one that reflects risk for very young children, under the age of 7, and one that reflects risk for older children and adolescents. The two risk composites are based on differences in how these broad age groups will cognitively process and interpret television violence.

Two important changes in cognitive development are relevant to the risk composites. The first concerns perceptions of what is real on television. A growing body of research demonstrates that younger children tend to assume that anything that looks real on television is real (see Wilson et al., 1998 for review). Consequently, younger children are more susceptible to fantastic portrayals of violence and to animated depictions. As children mature, they increasingly judge television in terms of whether the depicted characters and events could possibly occur in real life. Thus, older children and adolescents are likely to discount portrayals that have no real-world corollaries.

The second cognitive change concerns the ability to integrate information and make sense of the unfolding storyline. Studies indicate that younger children are less

132

able than older children to link disjoint scenes together and infer connections among characters' motives, behaviors, and consequences of their actions (Collins, 1983). This developmental pattern has implications for the context factor dealing with rewards and punishments. Many programs feature perpetrators who engage in violence that is not immediately punished or discouraged. Although such behavior may be punished by the end of the program, younger viewers are likely to miss this connection. In other words, the timing of the punishment is a critical factor for younger children. In order to be an effective deterrent for a younger child, punishments must occur in close proximity to the violent action in a program (Collins, 1973).

In sum, although the reality of violence as well as the delivery of rewards and punishments impact all age groups, the way in which these two context features are interpreted differs for younger and older viewers. Children under the age of about 7 are likely to perceive fantasy depictions and animated violence as fairly realistic, and thus are more likely to learn from such portrayals than are older children and adolescents who will judge them as unreal. In addition, younger children will have difficulty taking punishments into account in a plot unless the penalty or remorse is shown at the same time as the violence.

We have incorporated these differences into the construction of our risk composites. Consistent with the research reviewed, there are two major differences between the risk composites for younger and older viewers: 1) the composite for young children includes fantastic or unrealistic portrayals of violence, whereas the composite for older children and teens does not; and 2) the composite for young children considers only those rewards and punishments that occur in close proximity to the violence, whereas the composite for older children and adolescents takes into account reinforcements throughout the program.

Filters for High Risk

Several stipulations were set forth in screening for high-risk portrayals for both age groups. First, we restricted all analyses to those portrayals involving *behavioral acts* of aggression rather than credible threats or harmful consequences of unseen violence. Behavioral acts are more problematic from a learning standpoint because the violence is actually carried out so it is presumably easier to model or imitate.

Second, we mandated that the portrayed violence has to be grave enough to result in *serious* physical harm if it were to occur in the real world. This stipulation screened out any aggressive behaviors that would ordinarily not cause harm in real life (e.g., pushing a character or stepping on someone's toe). The rule here is that the violence has to be grave enough that it would cause mild, moderate, or extreme harm if enacted in real life.

Finally, we eliminated from consideration all programs that prominently feature an anti-violence theme. Although they represent only a small fraction of our sample

(3% of all violent shows), such programs convey an overall message that violence is destructive and that alternatives to conflict should be explored. This message is brought about by emphasizing several broader contextual features that reduce the risk of learning aggression from a portrayal (e.g., punishments for violence, serious consequences of aggression).

To summarize, the initial stipulations for *both* risk composites are that:

- the violence must involve a behavioral act of aggression;
- the portrayed act must be capable of producing physical harm in real life; and
- the violence cannot be in a program that features an anti-violence theme.

Any violent interaction that did not meet these conditions was excluded from further consideration.

To identify high risk for younger children, the following filters were applied to violent interactions:

- *Perpetrator must be attractive*: the perpetrator is a primary character in the storyline, and is either good or blended (both good and bad). Strictly bad characters are excluded, as are any characters who are not primary in the plot.

- *Violence must be justified*: the violent behavior seems defensible or morally correct in the storyline. Any violence that seems unjustified is not included.

- *No immediate punishment for the violence*: there is no form of punishment (remorse, condemnation, or penalty) for the violent behavior either in the scene itself or immediately thereafter. If any form of immediate punishment does occur, the interaction is not included as part of high risk.

- *Violence results in minimal harm to the victim*: there is no harm or pain shown at all to the victims, or only short-term consequences are depicted in the program. Any portrayal that occurs in a program that features the long-term negative consequences to the victim is not included as part of high risk.

- *Violence seems realistic*: the portrayal of violence could be either fantasy-oriented or more realistic given younger children's difficulty in differentiating the two types of content.

In contrast, the risk composite for older children and adolescents was restricted to those portrayals that are more plausible or realistic in nature. Moreover, punishments throughout the program were taken into consideration rather than just those occurring in the immediate vicinity of the violence. To identify high risk for older children and adolescents, the following filters were applied to violent interactions:

• *Perpetrator must be attractive*: the perpetrator is a primary character in the storyline, and is either good or blended (both good and bad). Strictly bad characters are excluded, as are any characters who are not primary in the plot.

• *Violence must be justified*: the violent behavior seems defensible or morally correct in the storyline. Any violence that seems unjustified is not included.

• *No punishment throughout the program for violence*: attractive characters, who are the primary role models for viewers, are not punished (never show remorse, get condemned, or receive penalty) anywhere in the program for the violence they commit. If attractive characters do experience remorse or criticism anywhere in the program, the violent interaction is not included in high risk.

• *Violence results in minimal harm to the victim*: there is no harm or pain shown at all to the victims, or only short-term consequences are depicted in the program. Any portrayal that occurs in program that features the long-term negative consequences to the victim is not included as part of high risk.

• *Violence seems realistic*: the portrayal of violence involves characters and events that are at least possible in real life. Fantasy violence is not included.

For more details regarding how these thresholds for each age group were operation-alized, see the Year 2 Report (Wilson et al., 1998).

Results

This section of the chapter presents the findings from the two risk composites. For each age group, overall patterns of risk are described, and then risk is assessed in terms of different genres of programming and types of channels. Next, we examine whether there have been any notable changes in the patterns of high risk since last year's report (1995-96). The final part of this section provides descriptive examples of high-risk violent interactions identified in our sample.

High Risk for Young Children

The risk analysis for young children identified a total of 719 violent interactions that are highly likely to promote the learning of aggression. This figure represents 4% of the 17,638 violent interactions in our sample. At first glance, this percentage seems small and perhaps even inconsequential. However, the reader will recall that our composite is very conservative -- a violent interaction had to meet *all five* of the risk criteria outlined above to be included. Those interactions that met several but not all of these specifications did not qualify for the composite, even though they actually contain many facets of risk. In other words, **the interactions identified by our composite represent the most hazardous portrayals of violence on television for children under the age of 7.** In these depictions, attractive characters who are likely

135

to be role models for young children use violence in a morally defensible way to solve problems. The violence is not punished, regretted, or criticized, and it is sanitized in terms of consequences. The message in these interactions is that violence is a successful and an appropriate method for good people to solve problems, and that it rarely results in any serious harm to victims or their families.

Are these high-risk interactions all found in just a few programs? The answer to this question is no. The 719 interactions are distributed across 315 programs in our sample, which reflects 16% of the programs containing violence. In other words, one out of six programs with violence features dangerous portrayals that encourage the learning of aggression among young children.

As we indicated above, a listing of all 315 program titles is not appropriate given that the particular episodes we sampled are not necessarily representative of an entire series. Moreover, parents and educators arguably will be better equipped to predict the location of high risk on television from season to season if they understand broad programming patterns within specific types of channels and genres of programming rather than specific titles. Thus, we turn our attention now to where these high-risk portrayals are located in the television landscape, using our genre and channel type locator variables.

High risk for young children by genre. First, we can examine the 719 high-risk interactions in terms of our six types of programming: drama, comedy, children's, movies, reality-based, and music videos. As shown in Figure 57, fully half of these problematic portrayals (50%) are located in children's programs, and one third (33%) occur in movies. The remaining genres contain very few of these high-risk portrayals. In other words, most of the hazardous depictions of violence for young children are found in the very programs that are targeted to this age group.

One possible explanation for this high proportion in children's shows is that there simply may be more hours of children's programming in a week of television than there are other types of content. In order to control for this, we divided the number of high-risk interactions by the number of programming hours represented by each genre in our one-week sample. Figure 58 depicts these calibrations, which we will refer to as "risk ratios." Another way of understanding the risk ratio is to think of it as representing the number of high-risk interactions that occur per hour within a given genre. As Figure 58 demonstrates, despite this calibration, children's programming still contains the highest concentration of hazardous portrayals. In fact, the risk ratio for children's shows (.75) is roughly three times the size of those for drama programs (.25) and movies (.26), the next two highest ratios. In contrast, the risk ratios or probabilities of encountering such portrayals are quite low for comedy and reality-based programs, and comparatively small for music videos as well.

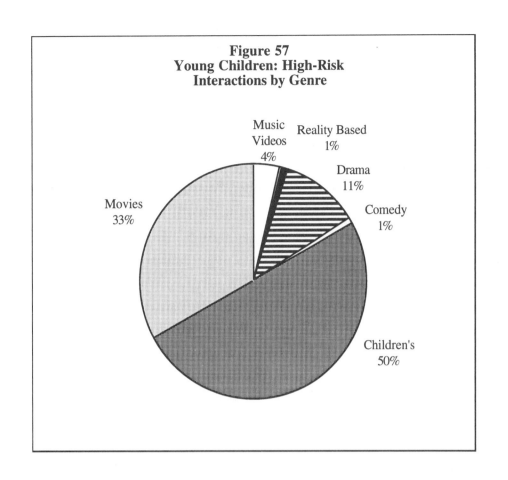

Figure 57
Young Children: High-Risk
Interactions by Genre

Music Videos 4%

Reality Based 1%

Drama 11%

Comedy 1%

Movies 33%

Children's 50%

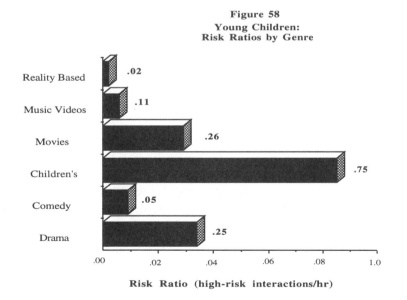

Figure 58
Young Children:
Risk Ratios by Genre

Reality Based .02

Music Videos .11

Movies .26

Children's .75

Comedy .05

Drama .25

Risk Ratio (high-risk interactions/hr)

137

We also can array the risk ratios by time of day to better pinpoint where a young child is most likely to encounter hazardous violence. Table 22 displays the risk ratios for each genre according to five time periods: before school (6:00 to 9:00 a.m.), during school (9:00 a.m. to 3:00 p.m.), after school (3:00 to 6:00 p.m.), early evening (6:00 to 8:00 p.m.), and prime time (8:00 to 11:00 p.m.). The single highest risk ratio (.81) in the table is for children's programs shown during early evening hours. However, risk in children's programming is not limited to this one time block. Relative to other genres and time blocks, children's shows during most periods of the day contain a high degree of hazardous interactions. This important finding is dramatically illustrated in Figure 59, which depicts the ratios in terms of degrees of shading (i.e., darker shades represent increasingly higher risk ratios). Children's shows are darkly shaded (i.e., feature the highest number of hazardous portrayals) during every time block except prime time. No other genre reaches this high level of risk throughout the day.

The only other area that stands out in the programming grid is for drama programs featured during the early evening. Here the risk ratio is .51, or almost twice the size of the ratios for drama during any other time period. This pattern suggests that parents should not limit their concerns solely to prime-time programming -- older dramatic series that are often sold in syndication and featured during early evening can pose risks for young viewers.

Several other findings are worth noting. First, the risk ratios for movies are fairly constant throughout the day, suggesting that high-risk portrayals for younger viewers can be found in the morning as well as the evening in this genre. Second, when broken down by time period, music videos contain very few high-risk portrayals until the prime-time period. Between 8:00 and 11:00 p.m., the ratio goes up to .22, indicating that the music content aired during late evening hours features more problematic violence for young children than do earlier time periods. Finally, looking at the far right column in the programming grid which reflects all genres combined (see Table 22), we can see that of all the time blocks, the before-school period (6:00 to 9:00 a.m.) contains the highest concentration of very risky portrayals for young children.

To summarize, most of the portrayals that pose high risk for young children are located in the very genre that attracts this age group: children's programming. In fact, children's shows during all times of the day and even during early evening contain a higher concentration of these problematic depictions than do any other genres or time periods. To explore this pattern further, we examined the high-risk interactions in children's shows and discovered that nearly all of them (92%) occur in animated programming. In other words, **cartoons are largely responsible for the concentration of problematic portrayals in children's programming.** These animated stories frequently feature the pattern of violence that is likely to encourage aggression in children under 7 years of age: an attractive perpetrator engaging in justified violence that is rarely punished and produces minimal consequences.

138

Table 22

High-Risk Findings by Genre and Time

TIME OF DAY	DRAMA	COMEDY	CHILDREN'S	MOVIES	MUSIC VIDEOS	REALITY-BASED	ACROSS GENRES
BEFORE SCHOOL (6 - 9 a.m.)							
# of high-risk interactions	5	0	109	33	5	2	154
# of programming hours	35	12.5	145.5	117.5	57.5	74	442
Risk ratio	.14	.00	.75	.28	.09	.03	.35
DURING SCHOOL (9 a.m. - 3 p.m.)							
# of high-risk interactions	40	2	139	82	11	0	274
# of programming hours	135	49.5	176	330.5	95	164.5	950.5
Risk ratio	.30	.04	.79	.25	.12	.00	.29
AFTER SCHOOL (3 - 6 p.m.)							
# of high-risk interactions	10	2	62	44	2	0	120
# of programming hours	43	26	88	177	42.5	85.5	462
Risk ratio	.23	.08	.70	.25	.05	.00	.26
EARLY EVENING (6 - 8 p.m.)							
# of high-risk interactions	14	0	33	19	2	6	74
# of programming hours	27.5	37	40.5	83.5	13	63.5	265
Risk ratio	.51	.00	.81	.23	.15	.09	.28
PRIME TIME (8 - 11 p.m.)							
# of high-risk interactions	8	4	16	61	7	1	97
# of programming hours	66	49.5	29.5	215.5	32	74	466.5
Risk ratio	.12	.08	.54	.28	.22	.01	.21
COLUMN TOTALS							
Total # of high-risk interactions	77	8	359	239	27	9	719
Total # of programming hours	306.5	174.5	479.5	924	240	461.5	2586
Overall Risk Ratio for Genre	.25	.05	.75	.26	.11	.02	.28

Figure 59

Young Children: High-Risk Patterns for Learning Aggression by Genre and Time

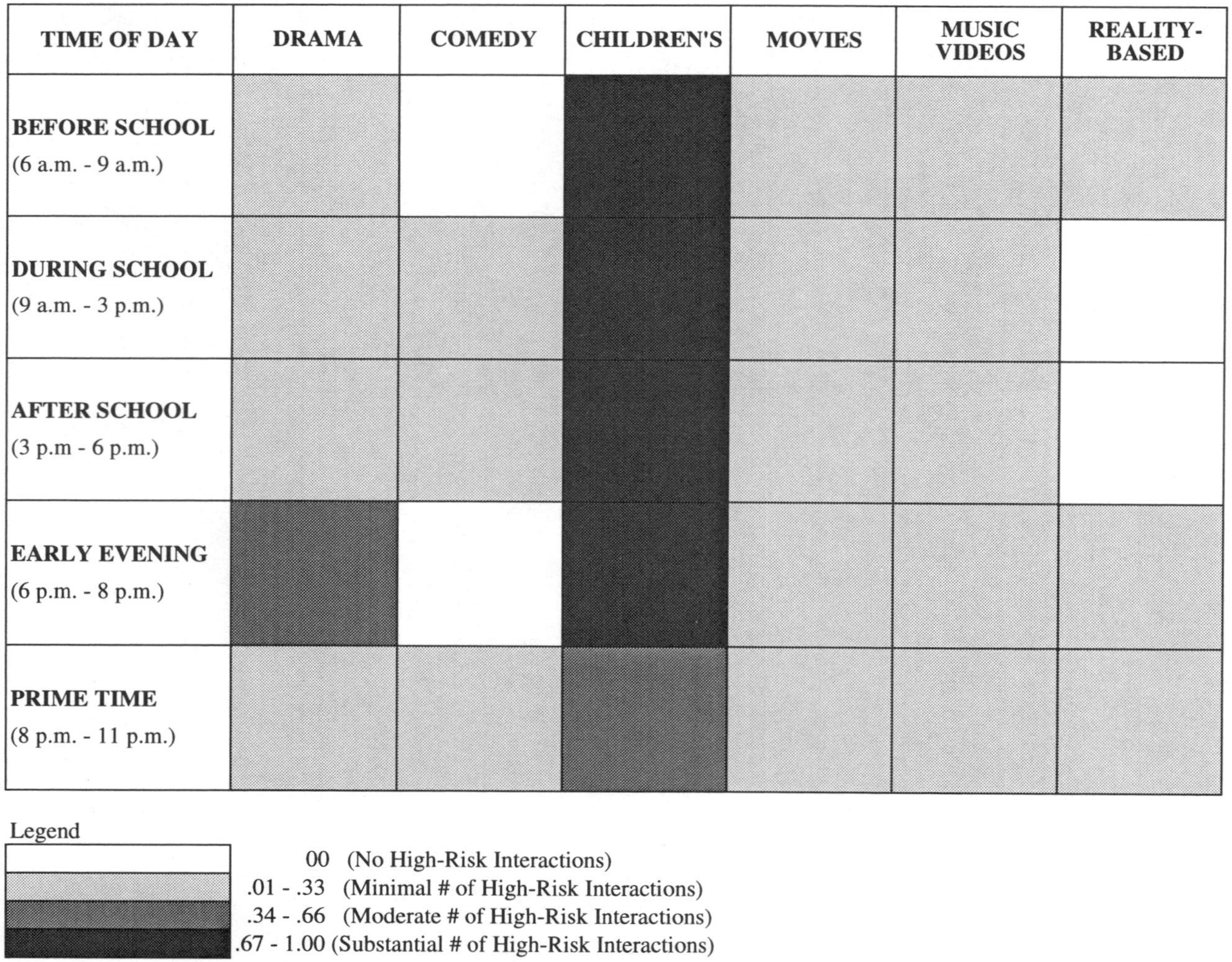

TIME OF DAY	DRAMA	COMEDY	CHILDREN'S	MOVIES	MUSIC VIDEOS	REALITY-BASED
BEFORE SCHOOL (6 a.m. - 9 a.m.)						
DURING SCHOOL (9 a.m. - 3 p.m.)						
AFTER SCHOOL (3 p.m - 6 p.m.)						
EARLY EVENING (6 p.m. - 8 p.m.)						
PRIME TIME (8 p.m. - 11 p.m.)						

Legend

00   (No High-Risk Interactions)

.01 - .33   (Minimal # of High-Risk Interactions)

.34 - .66   (Moderate # of High-Risk Interactions)

.67 - 1.00 (Substantial # of High-Risk Interactions)

High risk for young children by channel type. Next, we examined high risk for young children in terms of channels on television. In the previous chapters, we categorized channels into five types: broadcast networks, independent broadcast, public broadcast, basic cable, and premium cable. In this chapter, we subdivided basic cable because it consists of numerous channels (n=12) that may vary substantially in terms of risk. In particular, we grouped basic cable into three categories according to the predominant type of featured programming: general entertainment (A&E, AMC, Family Channel, Lifetime, TNT, USA), music-oriented (BET, MTV, VH-1), and child-oriented (Cartoon Network, Disney, Nickelodeon).

As seen in Figure 60, most of the high-risk interactions for young children can be found on child-oriented basic cable (27%), general-entertainment basic cable (24%), independent broadcast (19%), and premium cable (17%). However, when these interactions are normed by number of programming hours per channel type in the sample, the pattern changes substantially (see Figure 61). Two channel types stand out for high risk: child-oriented basic cable and independent broadcast. In fact, the risk ratios for these two channels (child-oriented basic cable, .54; independent broadcast, .50) are roughly twice the size of the next highest ratios, those for general-entertainment basic cable (.25) and premium cable (.26). In contrast, the risk ratio for the broadcast networks is quite low, and essentially zero or close to zero for public broadcast and music-oriented basic cable, meaning that these types of channels feature very little of the violence that poses high risk for young children.

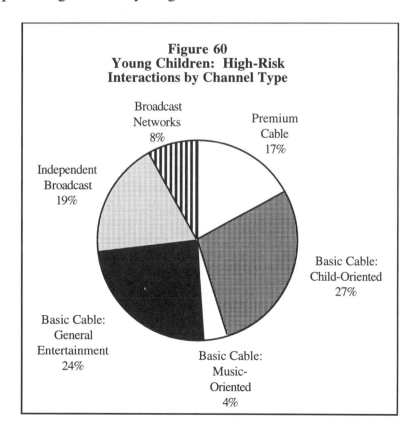

Figure 60
Young Children: High-Risk
Interactions by Channel Type

Broadcast Networks 8%

Premium Cable 17%

Independent Broadcast 19%

Basic Cable: Child-Oriented 27%

Basic Cable: General Entertainment 24%

Basic Cable: Music-Oriented 4%

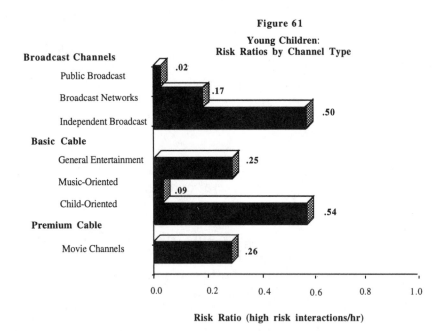

Figure 61

Young Children:
Risk Ratios by Channel Type

Broadcast Channels
Public Broadcast .02
Broadcast Networks .17
Independent Broadcast .50
Basic Cable
General Entertainment .25
Music-Oriented .09
Child-Oriented .54
Premium Cable
Movie Channels .26

Risk Ratio (high risk interactions/hr)

The findings for channel type are very consistent with those found for genre. That is, many of the most hazardous depictions of violence for children under 7 are found in the very places in the TV landscape that are likely to attract younger viewers: child-oriented basic cable. It should be noted, however, that child-oriented cable is comprised of three distinct channels (Cartoon Network, Disney, Nickelodeon) that vary somewhat in the types of children's shows that are scheduled. As indicated by the genre data, we would expect that risk is higher for those child-oriented channels that feature mostly cartoons.

For more information about risk, we can examine the channel types in terms of time of day. Table 23 contains the risk ratios for the seven channel types according to the time blocks identified above. As can be seen, the single highest risk ratio is for independent broadcast during the early morning hours (1.09). Such a pattern presumably reflects the high concentration of cartoons featured on such channels during the early morning period. The ratio of 1.09 tells us that a young viewer who watches programming aired on independent broadcast between 6:00 and 9:00 a.m. is likely to encounter one high-risk portrayal every hour. Put another way, an average American child who watches three hours of early morning television a day on such channels would be exposed to over 20 hazardous depictions a week, and over 1000 a year. These portrayals, again, contain a potent combination of contextual features that encourage the learning of aggressive attitudes and behaviors among young children.

Yet risk is not limited to this one area in the programming grid. As seen by the shadings in Figure 62, a substantial number of hazardous portrayals for young children also can be found on child-oriented basic cable during the hours of 9:00 a.m. to

142

Table 23

High-Risk Findings by Channel Type and Time

TIME OF DAY	BROADCAST CHANNELS			BASIC CABLE			PREMIUM CABLE	TOTAL
	Broadcast Networks	Public Broadcast	Independent Broadcast	General Entertainment	Music-Oriented	Child-Oriented	Movie Channels	
BEFORE SCHOOL (6 - 9 a.m.)								
# of high-risk interactions	4.00	2.00	44.00	35.00	5.00	34.00	30.00	154.00
# of programming hours	55.00	21.50	40.50	103.00	64.00	62.00	96.00	442.00
Risk ratio	.07	.09	1.09	.34	.08	.55	.31	0.35
DURING SCHOOL (9 a.m. - 3 p.m.)								
# of high-risk interactions	19.00	0.00	31.00	86.00	11.00	86.00	41.00	274.00
# of programming hours	124.50	40.00	109.00	259.00	119.50	127.50	171.00	950.50
Risk ratio	.15	.00	.28	.33	.09	.67	.24	0.29
AFTER SCHOOL (3 - 6 p.m.)								
# of high-risk interactions	15.00	0.00	41.00	20.00	2.00	23.00	19.00	120.00
# of programming hours	48.50	18.50	62.50	135.50	58.50	61.50	77.00	462.00
Risk ratio	.31	.00	.66	.15	.03	.37	.25	0.26
EARLY EVENING (6 - 8 p.m.)								
# of high-risk interactions	7.00	0.00	10.00	19.00	2.00	31.00	5.00	74.00
# of programming hours	31.00	12.00	35.00	80.50	28.50	46.00	32.00	265.00
Risk ratio	.23	.00	.29	.24	.07	.67	.16	0.28
PRIME TIME (8 - 11 p.m.)								
# of high-risk interactions	13.00	0.00	13.00	13.00	8.00	23.00	27.00	97.00
# of programming hours	84.00	19.50	28.50	124.50	53.50	66.00	90.50	466.50
Risk ratio	.15	.00	.46	.10	.15	.35	.30	0.21
COLUMN TOTALS								
Total # of high-risk interactions	58	2	139	173	28	197	122	719
Total # of programming hours	343	111.5	275.5	702.5	324	363	466.5	2586
Overall Risk Ratio for Genre	0.17	0.02	.50	.25	.09	.54	.26	.28

Figure 62

Young Children: High-Risk Patterns for Learning Aggression by Channel Type and Time

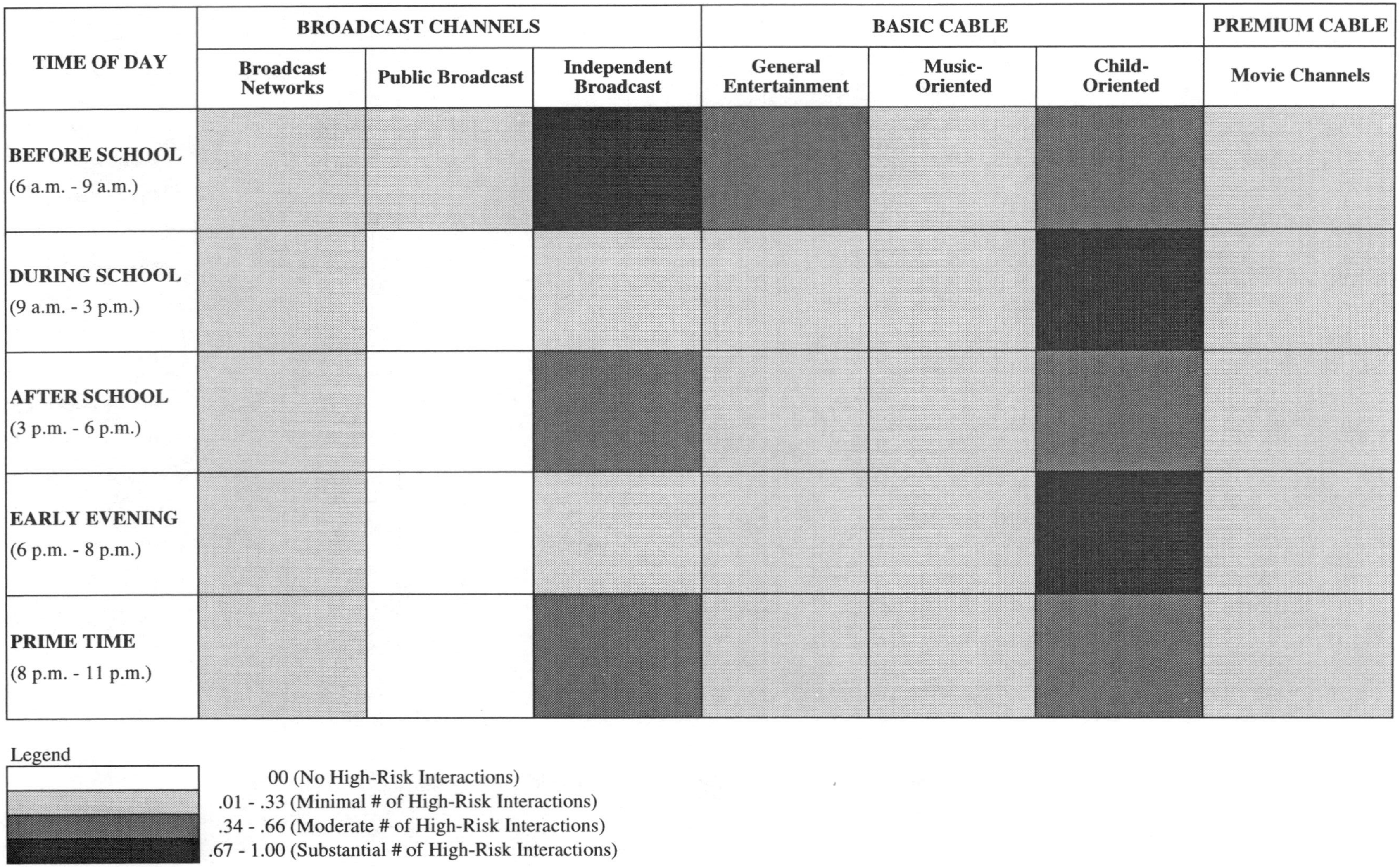

TIME OF DAY	BROADCAST CHANNELS				BASIC CABLE			PREMIUM CABLE
	Broadcast Networks	Public Broadcast	Independent Broadcast	General Entertainment	Music-Oriented	Child-Oriented		Movie Channels
BEFORE SCHOOL (6 a.m. - 9 a.m.)								
DURING SCHOOL (9 a.m. - 3 p.m.)								
AFTER SCHOOL (3 p.m. - 6 p.m.)								
EARLY EVENING (6 p.m. - 8 p.m.)								
PRIME TIME (8 p.m. - 11 p.m.)								

Legend

00 (No High-Risk Interactions)
.01 - .33 (Minimal # of High-Risk Interactions)
.34 - .66 (Moderate # of High-Risk Interactions)
.67 - 1.00 (Substantial # of High-Risk Interactions)

3:00 p.m, and during the early evening hours. Both of these time periods are accessible to children under 7, many of whom are not yet enrolled in school during the day and are still awake during the early evening. It should be noted that for children under 7, no other area in the programming grid can be characterized by a substantial amount of a high-risk interactions.

Figure 62 illustrates that other areas of high risk are scattered across the program grid. Not surprising, two remaining time blocks for child-oriented basic cable (before school and after school) contain moderate amounts of problematic portrayals. In addition, the after-school and prime-time periods on the independent broadcasters contain moderate amounts of high-risk interactions. The former pattern presumably is due to the cartoon programming that is regularly aired on these channels during the late afternoon. But the concentration of high-risk portrayals during prime time on independent broadcast cannot be accounted for by cartoons.

In contrast, the broadcast networks contain relatively few hazardous portrayals throughout the day. This is also true of music-oriented basic cable. Even more notable, public broadcast is literally free of high-risk portrayals during most times of the day.

Overall, then, our findings demonstrate that parents should be most concerned about young children watching child-oriented basic cable, especially between the hours of 9:00 a.m. and 3:00 p.m, and 6:00 and 8:00 p.m. Also, early-morning programming on independent broadcast contains a high number of dangerous portrayals for young children. Taking into account the genre findings, all of these patterns can be explained best in terms of cartoons. Those channels and times of day that feature animated children's programming pose the greatest risk of encouraging aggressive behavior for viewers under the age of 7. Though this type of unrealistic content would not be problematic for older viewers, young children are less able to distinguish reality from fantasy on television so they are more susceptible to violent cartoons.

High Risk for Older Children & Adolescents

The risk analysis for older children and adolescents identified a total of 383 violent interactions that are most likely to facilitate aggressive tendencies. This figure represents 2% of the 17,638 violent interactions in our sample. As a reminder, this percentage is relatively small because a violent interaction had to meet *all* of the criteria established in the risk composite for older viewers in order to be included here. Accordingly, 383 portrayals in our one-week sample can be described as realistic depictions of attractive perpetrators engaging in defensible violence that is not punished and results in no serious consequences.

We should note that the risk analysis for older viewers resulted in roughly half the violent interactions identified by the younger children's composite. This is consistent with the fact that the composite for older viewers is even more restrictive because it screens out unrealistic or fantasy portrayals of violence.

145

Are these 383 high-risk interactions concentrated in just a few programs?   The answer to this question is no; they are distributed across 141 programs in our sample, which reflects 7% of the programs containing violence. When compared with the data for young children, though, the probability of encountering a dangerous portrayal on television *is lower* for older viewers. There are fewer high-risk portrayals across the television landscape for older viewers (383 vs. 719), and these depictions are found in a relatively smaller proportion of violent programs (7% vs. 16%).

High risk for older children & adolescents by genre.   Next, we assessed these high-risk violent interactions in terms of our six program genres. As seen in Figure 63, more than two thirds of these dangerous portrayals (68%) are found in movies. The only other genre that features any sizeable number of high-risk interactions is drama (20%). However, when these interactions are normed by hours of programming in the sample, as seen in Figure 64, the risk ratios for movies (.28) and drama (.25) are nearly identical. Hence, movies and drama are the two genres most likely to contain high-risk portrayals that teach and reinforce aggression among older viewers. Again, we are referring here to realistic depictions of attractive perpetrators engaging in justified violence that is not punished and results in minimal consequences. The remaining genres have relatively low risk ratios. In fact, those for children's, reality-based, and comedy are zero or close to zero, meaning that they contain very few of these realistic, hazardous portrayals.

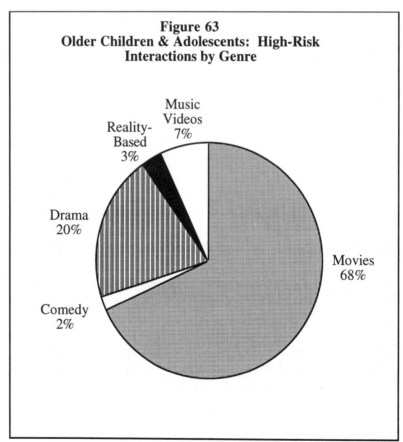

146

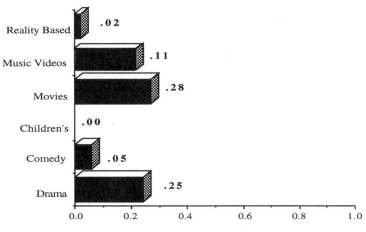

Figure 64
Older Children & Adolescents:
High-Risk Interactions by Genre

Risk Ratio (high-risk interactions/hr)

We also assessed the risk ratios for each genre in terms of time of day. As seen in Table 24, the ratios range in magnitude from 0 to .40. The two highest ratios are for drama programming featured during the early evening (6:00 - 8:00 p.m.) and for movies shown during the after-school period (3:00 - 6:00 p.m.). However, the shadings in Figure 65 demonstrate that the risk zones are distributed fairly evenly throughout the program grid, and none of the time blocks are marked by the sizable risk ratios found in the data for young children (see Figure 59 for comparison).

In general, then, movies and dramatic programming are the two genres most likely to contain high-risk portrayals for older viewers. In spite of this pattern, the risk zones generally are distributed more evenly across the programming grid for older viewers than was the case for younger viewers.

147

Table 24

High-Risk Findings by Genre and Time

TIME OF DAY	DRAMA	COMEDY	CHILDREN'S	MOVIES	MUSIC VIDEOS	REALITY-BASED	ACROSS GENRES
BEFORE SCHOOL (6 - 9 a.m.)							
# of high-risk interactions	6	0	0	21	3	2	32
# of programming hours	35	12.5	145.5	117.5	57.5	74	442
Risk ratio	.17	.00	.00	.18	.05	.03	.07
DURING SCHOOL (9 a.m. - 3 p.m.)							
# of high-risk interactions	37	2	0	108	16	1	164
# of programming hours	135	49.5	176	330.5	95	164.5	950.5
Risk ratio	.27	.04	.00	.33	.17	.00	.17
AFTER SCHOOL (3 - 6 p.m.)							
# of high-risk interactions	9	2	0	63	1	0	75
# of programming hours	43	26	88	177	42.5	85.5	462
Risk ratio	.21	.08	.00	.35	.02	.00	.16
EARLY EVENING (6 - 8 p.m.)							
# of high-risk interactions	11	0	2	11	2	6	32
# of programming hours	27.5	37	40.5	83.5	13	63.5	265
Risk ratio	.40	.00	.05	.13	.15	.09	.12
PRIME TIME (8 - 11 p.m.)							
# of high-risk interactions	13	4	0	57	5	1	80
# of programming hours	66	49.5	29.5	215.5	32	74	466.5
Risk ratio	.20	.08	.00	.26	.16	.01	.17
COLUMN TOTALS							
Total # of high-risk interactions	76	8	2	260	27	10	383
Total # of programming hours	306.5	174.5	479.5	924	240	461.5	2586
Overall Risk Ratio for Genre	.25	.05	.00	.28	.11	.02	.15

Figure 65

Older Children: High-Risk Patterns for Learning Aggression by Genre and Time

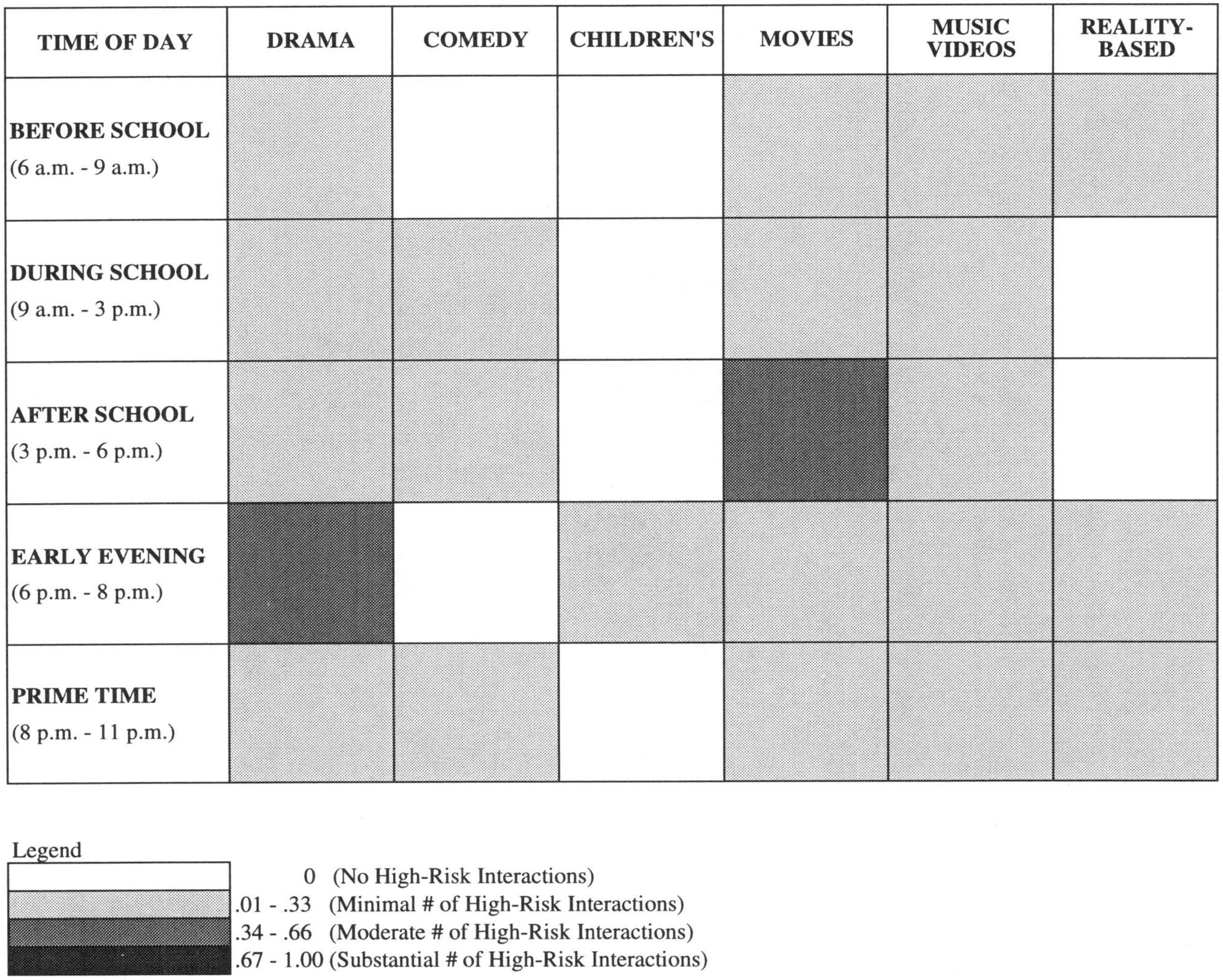

TIME OF DAY	DRAMA	COMEDY	CHILDREN'S	MOVIES	MUSIC VIDEOS	REALITY-BASED
BEFORE SCHOOL (6 a.m. - 9 a.m.)						
DURING SCHOOL (9 a.m. - 3 p.m.)						
AFTER SCHOOL (3 p.m. - 6 p.m.)						
EARLY EVENING (6 p.m. - 8 p.m.)						
PRIME TIME (8 p.m. - 11 p.m.)						

Legend

- 0 (No High-Risk Interactions)
- .01 - .33 (Minimal # of High-Risk Interactions)
- .34 - .66 (Moderate # of High-Risk Interactions)
- .67 - 1.00 (Substantial # of High-Risk Interactions)

High risk for older children & adolescents by channel type.   Risk also varies for older viewers in terms of channel type. As seen in Figure 66, most of the high-risk interactions for older children and teens can be found on general-entertainment basic cable (43%) and on premium cable (32%). This pattern persists even when the interactions are normed by number of programming hours in the sample (see Figure 67). Thus, premium cable and general-entertainment basic cable are responsible for most of the high-risk portrayals for older audiences. The only other channel type that has a risk ratio above .10 is independent broadcast (.15). Notably, public broadcast does not feature any high-risk portrayals that encourage aggression among older viewers. As readers will recall, this channel is almost void of dangerous portrayals for young children as well. Moreover, child-oriented cable channels have a low risk ratio because most of the violent portrayals on these channels are fantasy-oriented and thus would be discounted by more mature viewers.

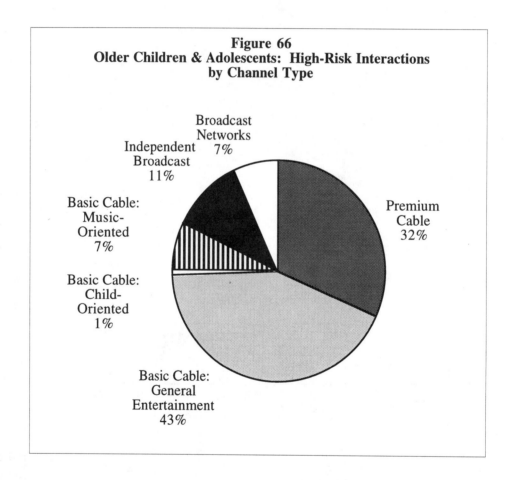

Figure 66
Older Children & Adolescents: High-Risk Interactions by Channel Type

Broadcast Networks 7%

Independent Broadcast 11%

Basic Cable: Music-Oriented 7%

Basic Cable: Child-Oriented 1%

Premium Cable 32%

Basic Cable: General Entertainment 43%

Finally, we can examine channel types in terms of time of day. Table 25 contains the risk ratios for the seven channel types according to time blocks. The highest risk ratios in the table are for independent broadcast during prime time (.46) and early evening (.34), for premium cable during after-school hours (.41), and for general-entertainment basic cable during school hours (.35). Other than these four slightly elevated zones, the shadings in Figure 68 demonstrate that the high-risk portrayals are distributed pretty evenly throughout the program grid.

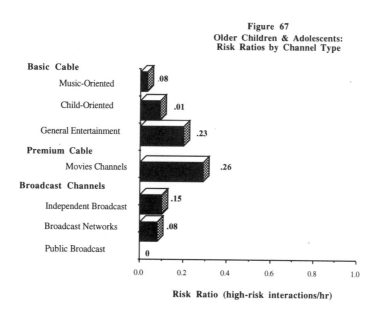

Figure 67
Older Children & Adolescents:
Risk Ratios by Channel Type

Risk Ratio (high-risk interactions/hr)

Two other patterns can be highlighted. The broadcast networks contain almost no high-risk portrayals throughout the day and into the early evening. Yet there is a notable increase in the number of these depictions during prime time (see Table 25 for risk ratios). Nevertheless, the ratio even here is relatively small (.25) compared to those cited above. Second, music-oriented basic cable contains relatively few high-risk portrayals that encourage aggression, and the risk ratios do not change much throughout the day.

In sum, then, premium cable and general-entertainment basic cable are the locations for most of the dangerous portrayals that promote aggressive tendencies among older children and teens. Consistent with the data for young children, public broadcast does not contain any of these high-risk depictions. Overall, however, the high-risk portrayals are distributed fairly evenly when considering channel type and time of day.

Table 25

High-Risk Findings by Channel Group and Time

TIME OF DAY	BROADCAST CHANNELS			BASIC CABLE			PREMIUM CABLE	TOTAL
	Broadcast Networks	Public Broadcast	Independent Broadcast	General Entertainment	Music-Oriented	Child-Oriented	Movie Channels	
BEFORE SCHOOL (6 - 9 a.m.)								
# of high-risk interactions	0	0	0	14.00	3.00	0	15.00	32
# of programming hours	55.00	21.50	40.50	103.00	64.00	62.00	96.00	442.00
Risk ratio	.00	.00	.00	.13	.05	.00	.16	0.07
DURING SCHOOL (9 a.m. - 3 p.m.)								
# of high-risk interactions	3.00	0	6.00	90.00	16.00	0	49.00	164
# of programming hours	124.50	40.00	109.00	259.00	119.50	127.50	171.00	950.50
Risk ratio	.02	.00	.05	.35	.13	.00	.29	0.17
AFTER SCHOOL (3 - 6 p.m.)								
# of high-risk interactions	1.00	0	10.00	31.00	1.00	0	32.00	75
# of programming hours	48.50	18.50	62.50	135.50	58.50	61.50	77.00	462.00
Risk ratio	.02	.00	.16	.23	.02	.00	.41	0.16
EARLY EVENING (6 - 8 p.m.)								
# of high-risk interactions	2.00	0	12.00	10.00	2.00	2.00	4.00	32
# of programming hours	31.00	12.00	35.00	80.50	28.50	46.00	32.00	265.00
Risk ratio	.06	.00	.34	.12	.07	.04	.13	0.12
PRIME TIME (8 - 11 p.m.)								
# of high-risk interactions	21.00	0	13.00	18.00	5.00	2.00	21.00	80
# of programming hours	84.00	19.50	28.50	124.50	53.50	66.00	90.50	466.50
Risk ratio	.25	.00	.46	.14	.09	.03	.23	0.17
COLUMN TOTALS								
Total # of high-risk interactions	27	0	41	163	27	4	121	383
Total # of programming hours	343	111.5	275.5	702.5	324	363	466.5	2586.00
Overall Risk Ratio for Genre	.08	.00	.15	.23	.08	.01	.26	.15

Figure 68

Older Children: High-Risk Patterns for Learning Aggression by Channel Type and Time

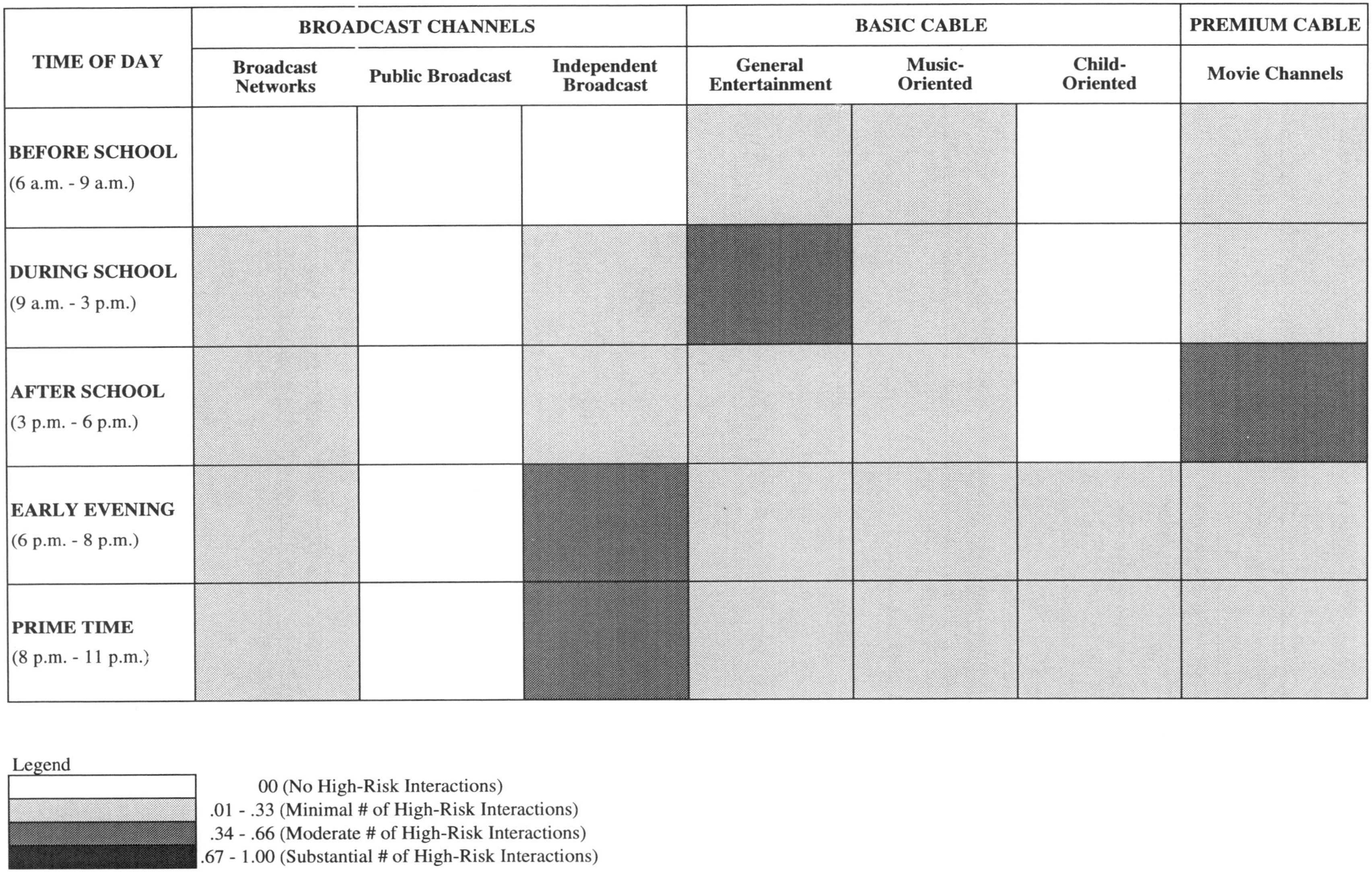

TIME OF DAY	BROADCAST CHANNELS			BASIC CABLE			PREMIUM CABLE
	Broadcast Networks	Public Broadcast	Independent Broadcast	General Entertainment	Music-Oriented	Child-Oriented	Movie Channels
BEFORE SCHOOL (6 a.m. - 9 a.m.)							
DURING SCHOOL (9 a.m. - 3 p.m.)							
AFTER SCHOOL (3 p.m. - 6 p.m.)							
EARLY EVENING (6 p.m. - 8 p.m.)							
PRIME TIME (8 p.m. - 11 p.m.)							

Legend

00 (No High-Risk Interactions)
.01 - .33 (Minimal # of High-Risk Interactions)
.34 - .66 (Moderate # of High-Risk Interactions)
.67 - 1.00 (Substantial # of High-Risk Interactions)

Change in High-Risk Patterns since 1995-96

Now that we have identified where the portrayals are in the television landscape that pose the highest risk of learning aggression, we can determine whether these patterns have changed over time. In this section, the results described above for 1996-97 will be compared to those we reported last year, representing 1995-96.[1] We will assess the degree of change in high risk as it related to both age groups.

Comparison over time in high risk for young children. Last year, we reported a total of 821 violent interactions that qualified as high risk for children under 7, and this year we found 719 interactions. As first glance, this looks like a drop in high-risk portrayals since 1995-96. However, when converted to a percentage of the total violent interactions each year, there is virtually no difference. In both 1995-96 and 1996-97, 4% of the violent interactions represent dangerous portrayals that encourage the learning of aggression in young children (see Table 26). Moreover, these high-risk portrayals are distributed across roughly the same percentage of violent programs each year (see Table 26).

Table 26

Amount of High Risk for Younger Children Over Two Years

	1995-96	1996-97
# of high-risk portrayals	821	719
# of total violent interactions	18,453	17,638
% of high-risk interactions	4%	4%
% of violent programs w/ high-risk interactions	19%	16%

We can also look at whether the location of these portrayals has changed over time. In terms of genre, children's programming by far contains the highest concentration of high-risk portrayals each year (see Table 27, risk ratios in bold). Moreover, the risk ratios for the six genres of programming are very similar across the two years. Overall, this represents a remarkable amount of stability over time, especially given the strict criteria for high-risk portrayals. Even one missing contextual feature means an interaction will not qualify as high risk. Yet two very different weeks of

---

[1]We did not look at high-risk portrayals in Year 1 of our study (1994-95) so change over time is assessed only in terms of Year 2 (1995-96) versus Year 3 (1996-97).

television, both representing random samples across two years, show the same patterns of high risk for type of programming.

Table 27

Genre Comparisons of High Risk for Younger Children Over Two Years

	1995-96	1996-97
Children's	**.85**	**.75**
Drama	.34	.25
Movies	.29	.26
Comedy	.09	.05
Music	.06	.11
Reality-Based	.02	.02

The same degree of consistency can be found in high risk for younger children as a function of channel type. For both years, child-oriented basic cable contains the highest concentration of dangerous portrayals (see Table 28). Again, the pattern of risk ratios is very similar across the two years.

Table 28

Channel Comparisons of High Risk for Younger Children Over Two Years

	1995-96	1996-97
Broadcast Channels		
Public Broadcast	.00	.02
Broadcast Networks	.19	.17
Independents	.39	.50
Basic Cable		
General Entertainment	.34	.25
Music Oriented	.04	.09
Child Oriented	**.64**	**.54**
Premium Cable		
Movie Channels	.33	.26

To summarize, the findings for high risk for younger children are very consistent over the last two years of this study. The overall amount of high risk is essentially identical and the location of most of these portrayals also has not changed: for genre, it is children's programming, and for channel type, it is child-oriented basic cable. Last year we concluded that vast majority of dangerous portrayals that encourage aggression in children under 7 are in the very places in the television landscape that target younger viewers. The same conclusion holds this year.

Comparison over time in high risk for older children and adolescents. In 1995-96, our data revealed a total of 378 violent interactions that qualified as high risk for older children and adolescents. This year we found 383 interactions. Obviously there has been no change in the amount of high-risk portrayals for older viewers, even when these figures are converted to percentages of all violent interactions (see Table 29). In addition, these high-risk portrayals are distributed across roughly the same percentage of violent programs each year (see Table 29).

Table 29

Amount of High Risk for Younger Children Over Two Years

	1995-96	1996-97
# of high-risk portrayals	378	383
# of total violent interactions	18,453	17,638
% of high-risk interactions	2%	2%
% of violent programs w/ high-risk interactions	7%	7%

Has there been any change in the location of these portrayals in terms of genre? The answer to this question is no. In both years, movies and drama contain the greatest concentration of high-risk depictions for older children and adolescents (see Table 30). As was the case for younger children, the risk ratios for the six genres of programming are very similar across the two years. Again, these findings reflect an extraordinary degree of stability over time.

The same degree of consistency characterizes the findings for channel type. For both years, premium cable and general-entertainment basic cable are responsible for most of the high-risk portrayals that encourage aggression in older viewers (see Table 31). Again, the pattern of risk ratios is very similar across the two years.

To summarize, the findings regarding high risk for older children and adolescents are extremely consistent over the last two years of our study. The overall amount of high risk is essentially identical and the location of most of these portrayals also has not changed: for genre, most portrayals of high risk are found in drama and movies; for channel type, most are on premium cable and general-entertainment cable.

Table 30

Genre Comparisons of High Risk for Older Children & Adolescents Over Two Years

	1995-96	1996-97
Children's	.06	.00
Drama	**.24**	**.25**
Movies	**.27**	**.28**
Comedy	.06	.05
Music	.03	.11
Reality-Based	.02	.02

Table 31

Channel Comparisons of High Risk for Older Children and Adolescents Over Two Years

	1995-96	1996-97
Broadcast Channels		
Public Broadcast	.00	.00
Broadcast Networks	.08	.08
Independents	.11	.15
Basic Cable		
General Entertainment	**.20**	**.23**
Music Oriented	.03	.08
Child Oriented	.09	.01
Premium Cable		
Movie Channels	**.29**	**.26**

Examples of High-Risk Violent Interactions

In this section we provide several examples of high-risk portrayals found in our sample that encourage the learning of aggression. These descriptions help to illustrate how the contextual factors can be combined in actual programming in ways that pose high risk to the viewer. The examples are not meant to be exhaustive or fully representative of the rich variety of plots and scenarios found in our high-risk data. Instead, the illustrations are offered as a way of providing parents with more concrete examples of the types of violent formulas to look for when identifying high-risk content for children. In addition, the descriptions may help writers and producers better appreciate which combination of plot features to avoid in violent programming if the goal is to minimize the risk of imitation and learning.

We provide four examples of high risk, described in generic terms (i.e., we do not identify program titles), two that pose risk for young children and two that pose risk for older children and adolescents. As readers will recall, the main differences between the two high-risk formulas or composites are that: 1) the composite for young children includes fantastic or unrealistic portrayals of violence, whereas the composite for older children and teens does not; and 2) the composite for young children considers only those rewards and punishments that occur in close proximity to the violence, whereas the composite for older children and adolescents takes into account these reinforcements throughout the program.

The two examples for younger children are both from animated children's series, which is consistent with our finding that more than 50% of high-risk portrayals for this age group are located in cartoons. The examples for older children and teens are from a movie and a dramatic program respectively, the two genres that contain most of the high-risk depictions for older viewers.

Example 1: younger children. One of the high-risk portrayals for younger children is from an animated children's series featuring three anthropomorphized cats who fight evil. In this particular episode, some bad guys, also anthropomorphized animals, are allegedly running a modeling school but in reality are scouting for young women to kidnap and train as soldiers. The high-risk portrayal features the hero cats using their ninja skills and sharp swords to battle the villains. After numerous sword slashes, several of the villains crumble to the ground but two of them escape from the scene.

This violent depiction has all the components that qualify it as high-risk for encouraging aggressive attitudes and behaviors in young viewers. The perpetrators are primary characters who are readily identifiable and attractive in nature. The violence seems justified because the heros have exposed the true purpose of the modeling school and are trying to save innocent young women from peril. Furthermore, there is no punishment or remorse for the violence. On the contrary, the heros are exalted in individual spotlights just prior to the battle scene, each being introduced by name. Finally, the repeated and potentially serious aggression against the bad characters does not produce any lasting harm. In fact, several of the bad characters appear later in the program, apparently unscathed by the sword attack. Though this portrayal involves anthropomorphized creatures in a cartoon setting, it still qualifies as high-risk for children under the age of 7 because such younger viewers have difficulty distinguishing fantasy from more realistic depictions.

Example 2: younger children. The second example is from an animated children's series as well, although this one features a squad of supernatural heros who look like humans rather than animals. The series is science fiction and involves female and male warriors who are "driven by purpose and bound by honor" in their struggle to protect earth. In this particular episode, enemy robots or "cybers" are invading the planet and threatening civilian life in nearby cities. The episode features several high-risk portrayals, two of which are in the early part of the 30-minute cartoon. In the first of these portrayals, a female warrior strikes back at a robot who has attacked her. Using a series of karate moves, she slams the enemy to the ground. As she stands over the robot, she says to it "You are nothing without soul and honor." Immediately thereafter, a new high-risk portrayal unfolds as the female is joined by a male comrade. In this interaction, the male warrior proceeds to battle two newly approaching robots. He, too, uses karate moves to knock down the robots. The scene ends as the female gazes longingly into the male hero's eyes and says with admiration, "Good form."

Both of these portrayals feature all the elements that are associated with increased risk of learning aggression. The two perpetrators are attractive heros with strong, muscular bodies who wear minimal clothing. They engage in repeated and lethal violence and yet the behaviors are portrayed as defensible. In fact, the group's code of honor seems to provide a formal justification for their aggression. The violence is not only *not* punished in the scene, but it is explicitly rewarded by group admiration and praise. The sexual overtones between the two warriors at the end of the scene reinforces this approval. And despite the seriousness of the physical violence, only minimal damage is depicted -- the robots fall to the ground, the camera moves away, and it is never clear whether the creatures are permanently damaged or are part of the forces who subsequently attack the warriors in later scenes (the robots all look identical). This portrayal is identified as posing high risk for children under 7 because it is animated and fantasy-oriented. However, the types of characters (i.e., human in appearance) and the events may be perceived as more plausible than those involved in the previous example. Because of this higher level of realism, such an animated depiction could reinforce aggression in slightly older children as well, though it probably poses little danger for teens.

Example 3: older children and adolescents. One example of a high-risk portrayal for older children and adolescents is from a movie about a young boy who moves to a new town shortly after his mother dies. The boy immediately feels alienated at his new school, particularly because he is belittled and teased by a group of bullies. In an early scene in the movie, the leader of the bullies torments the boy by stealing his kitten. After a bike chase, the boy catches up with the gang and demands his kitten back. The leader makes a wisecrack about the kitten being dead, just like the boy's mother. In the high-risk portrayal that follows, the boy glares in anger at the leader and then punches him in the nose. Though the punch hits him squarely in the face, the leader appears to be unscathed. He then retaliates by pummeling the boy in a fist fight. The boy loses the fight but in the end of the scene, one of the bullies hangs back and says with an admiring smile, "I've never seen anyone punch Clyde before."

This portrayal contains all the features that we have stipulated as part of the risk composite for older viewers. The perpetrator is a primary character who is young, good-looking, and portrayed in a sympathetic fashion. Any young viewer who has ever felt vulnerable or lonely presumably could identify with the character. In contrast, the bullies are crass and ugly. The leader has a strange hair cut and wears a long earring in one ear. The boy's attack on the leader seems justified in the context of this movie; the gang ruthlessly has taken the boy's kitten and made fun of the boy's dead mother. The boy feels no remorse for hitting the leader and he is never criticized for his violent response to the problem. In fact, he is praised by one of the bystanders in the gang, who later becomes the boy's best friend. So in a sense, the boy's physical aggression ends up winning him a friend. Lastly, the leader's face shows no blood or redness in spite of a direct blow to the nose, and the boy gets up and walks away painlessly after the pummeling. In other words, there are no serious consequences of this violence. It should be noted that compared to the two examples for younger children, this portrayal is presented in live action, involves human characters, and features events that could happen in real life (i.e., an authentic plot). In other words, this portrayal is more realistic in nature and thus would be more problematic than fantasy violence for older viewers.

Example 4: older children and adolescents. The next example of high risk for older viewers comes from a dramatic series rather than a movie. The program features a private investigator who often solves cases that have stymied the police. In this particular episode, a popular neighborhood candy store owner is killed by an unknown assailant. The investigator is called into the case by the store owner's daughter who fears that she too is in danger. In an early scene, the investigator goes to meet the daughter in a dark movie theater because she thinks she is being followed. Two suspicious-looking men enter the dark theater. The investigator boldly confronts the men and they jump him. In the high-risk portrayal, the investigator punches the men numerous times in the face and body, and in a dramatic move, knocks their heads together. The scene ends as the investigator throws one of the men through the movie screen. At that very moment, the film showing in the theater ends and the audience bursts into applause, seemingly clapping for the investigator.

This depiction qualifies as high risk for older viewers for several reasons. First, the violence is committed by the lead character of the series who is handsome and portrayed as very clever. In other words, he is an attractive perpetrator. Second, the investigator's physical aggression seems justifiable; he has just been attacked by the two men and he is also presumably trying to protect the woman. Third, the violence is not condemned or punished. On the contrary, the audience in the theater seems to be cheering as the body is thrown through the screen. Moreover, the investigator himself appears to be quite proud of his behavior, even taking a moment to bow slightly in the glare of light from the projection system. Thus, the violence results in both praise from bystanders as well as self-praise from the perpetrator. Fourth, the violence does not produce much in the way of serious consequences. The two bad guys who are hit repeatedly do not show any blood and do not seem to experience any pain. The camera pans away from the bodies immediately after they fall, avoiding any depiction of serious physical injury. In addition, the two men show up in a subsequent scene with no facial cuts or bodily harm, even though it is probably that same evening after the fight. Fifth, the characters and the events are fairly realistic, rendering the impact of such a portrayal more potent for older children and adolescents.

To summarize, all of the examples described here carry a particular theme that research demonstrates can encourage the learning of aggressive attitudes and behaviors in viewers. The message in these televised portrayals is that violence is a legitimate and successful method for benevolent individuals who are trying to combat evil, and that such action rarely produces any suffering or devastating consequences.

Summary

In previous chapters, we assessed the presence of important contextual factors that reflect the way in which violence is portrayed on television. Each of these elements can increase or decrease the risks associated with a violent portrayal. In this chapter, we take a different approach by appraising contextual features collectively. The goal of this chapter has been to identify patterns or formulas for televised violence that emerge when numerous contextual features all occur within the same portrayal. In particular, we identified risk composites, or combinations of contextual features, that increase the likelihood that a violent portrayal will teach and/or reinforce aggressive attitudes and behaviors in viewers.

It is important to recognize that our composites reflect only one of many possible ways to assess risk on television. Our approach focuses on the risk of children's learning of aggressive behavioral patterns, rather than two other harmful effects that could be analyzed in terms of risk: desensitization and fear. Moreover, our composites are based on the idea that contextual factors in combination pose a greater risk than any one factor alone, although this assumption has yet to be experimentally tested in social science research. Finally, our composites are conservatively defined because they encompass only those portrayals that contain five risk features simultaneously. Depictions that are missing any one of these problematic context factors are not tapped by our composites, even though such portrayals still pose some risk. The findings reflect only those portrayals that pose *high risk* to the audience because they involve a hybrid of plot features that encourage aggression.

In order to account for developmental differences in how television is interpreted, we created two composites -- one for young children under the age of 7, and one for older children and adolescents. Both composites were designed to identify those violent interactions that involve *an attractive perpetrator engaging in justified violence that does not get punished and that shows minimal consequences*. The major difference between the two composites is that risk for younger children includes fantasy portrayals, whereas risk for older viewers is confined to more realistic portrayals. This distinction reflects that fact that younger children have difficulty comprehending reality and fantasy on television, so they are more susceptible to unrealistic depictions.

The findings for young children (under age 7) indicate that:

- a week of television contains over 700 violent portrayals that qualify as *high risk* for children under 7, meaning that these depictions encourage the learning and imitation of aggression

- almost 20% of all programs with violence contain such portrayals

- most of these dangerous portrayals are located in the very genres and channels that are targeted to young children

    - of all genres, children's programming contains the most high-risk portrayals for young viewers
    - of all channel types, child-oriented basic cable (Cartoon Network, Disney, Nickelodeon) contains the most high-risk portrayals for young viewers

- the highest concentration of problematic portrayals for young children occurs during the early morning hours (6 - 9 a.m.) of television

- all these patterns can best be explained by the fact that nearly all of the high-risk portrayals (92%) for young children are found in cartoons

- none of the findings regarding high risk for younger children have changed over the last two years of this study

The findings for older children & adolescents indicate that:

- a week of television contains nearly 400 violent portrayals that qualify as *high risk* for older children and adolescents, meaning that these realistic depictions encourage and reinforce aggressive tendencies in such viewers

- about 7% of programs with violence contain such portrayals

- when compared with the findings for young children, the probability of encountering a high-risk portrayal on TV is lower for older viewers because only more realistic depictions are considered

- most of these realistic, high-risk portrayals are located in certain genres and channels

- of the genres, movies and dramatic programming contain the most high-risk portrayals for older viewers
- of the channel types, premium cable and general-entertainment basic cable contain the most high-risk portrayals

- none of the findings regarding high risk for older viewers have changed over the last two years of this study

In conclusion, our analysis suggests that television poses a great deal more risk for children under 7 than for older viewers. If a parent is concerned about a young child learning aggression from TV violence, the risk data suggest that cartoon programming should be avoided. Indeed, a preschooler who watches an average of 2 hours a day of such content will be exposed to at least 10 hazardous portrayals a week, and over 500 in a year. We invite readers to consider the following: even *one* televised depiction that encouraged a child to drink poison or play with fire undoubtedly would come under great public attack. We should be just as critical of recurrent portrayals of violence that encourage children to think of physical aggression as a legitimate and innocuous way to solve problems.

Chapter 6

DISCUSSION

We have conducted three primary types of analyses for our third year report on the overall state of violence on television. First, in Chapter 3, we analyzed the contextual factors associated with violent depictions solely as they were presented during the 1996-97 television season. Next, in Chapter 4, we compared the levels and types of violent portrayals found in Year 1 (1994-95) and Year 2 (1995-96) of the study to those we observed in Year 3 (1996-97). This aspect of the research sought to identify any meaningful changes in the presentation of violence that had occurred since the outset of the three-year study. Finally, in Chapter 5, we employed a means of identifying the violent portrayals that pose particularly high risk for influencing children's learning of aggressive behaviors.

In this chapter, which summarizes and interprets our major findings, we review our results across all three of these areas. First, we recap our evidence looking at the overall television landscape during the 1996-97 season. Next, we address the issue of change over time during the past three years in the presentation of violence on television. Then we compare the characteristics of violent portrayals presented on different types of channels and in different types of program genres. Finally, we examine the portrayals that are considered high risk for children's learning of aggression. After reviewing the full evidence and considering its implications, we offer recommendations to several important audiences: the television industry, public policy-makers, parents, and the academic community.

What Does Violence on Television Look Like?

Within the total sample of 2,750 programs coded in 1996-97, 61% contain at least some violent material. Of the shows portraying violence, most contain multiple violent interactions; over half of these programs (57%) contain four or more incidents and nearly a third (32%) contain nine or more. Of the approximately 17,600 violent interactions found in the composite week, most (67%) depict actual behavioral acts of aggression rather than credible threats (27%). Very few of the violent interactions involve harmful consequences of unseen violence or accidents that occur within an ongoing violent scenario. Overall, we can conclude that the majority of programs are violent, most shows with violence include multiple violent interactions, and most violent interactions involve overt behaviors in which one character attempts to harm another.

During the 1996-97 season, only 3% of the violent programs in our sample convey an overall anti-violence theme. A program is coded as containing such a theme when it emphasizes one of the following four elements: (1) alternatives to violent acts are presented and discussed; (2) the pain and suffering from violence go beyond the victim and perpetrator to have an impact upon their families, friends, and community; (3) main characters repeatedly discuss violence as having negative consequences;

164

and (4) on balance, there is a preponderance of punishment for violent actions when compared to rewards. If we subtract those programs featuring an anti-violence theme from the overall percentage of programs with violence, we still find that 59% of the programs contain violence that is shown without any pro-social purpose. In other words, the adjusted prevalence figure does not change much even when those programs that use violence for prosocial purposes are eliminated.

Our analysis of the context surrounding each violent portrayal reveals a number of important patterns of findings, as indicated below.

* Violence often goes without punishment.

Violence is seldom punished at the time that it occurs in a program. In fact, only 29% of violent scenes include clear punishment. Perpetrators rarely show remorse, and are seldom condemned by others or apprehended promptly. When looking across the entire program, nearly half (45%) of violent shows feature bad characters who are never or rarely punished anywhere in the plot; another 35% contain bad characters who are punished only at the end of the story. Good characters do not usually suffer any repercussions (i.e., remorse, criticism) for their violent actions, with 82% never or rarely punished for violence.

* Most violence is sanitized.

Violence is typically shown with little or no harm to the victim. In fact, more than half of the violent interactions depict no physical pain/injury to the victim. At the program level, only 16% of shows portray the long-term consequences of violence such as prolonged physical and psychological suffering.

* Most violent portrayals involve extended violent action.

Over half (61%) of all violent incidents on television feature repeated violent behaviors, and 17% show 10 or more different acts. In other words, it is rare to see a character fire a gun once or throw a single punch at a target. Instead, characters routinely use multiple acts of violence against their victims.

* It is extremely rare for a program to emphasize an anti-violence theme.

The study identified some noteworthy examples of programs that present strong anti-violence messages in all genres of programming. Yet this approach to the treatment of violence is rare, appearing in only 3% of all violent programs.

* Most violence is motivated by selfish reasons.

Selfish motives such as personal gain and anger account for more than half (56%) of the violence that is shown on television. Unselfish concerns such as the protection of life (24%) occur much less frequently.

165

* Guns are often used in violent interactions.

Roughly one out of four (26%) of all violent interactions involve a handgun. Guns are the most common type of weapon employed by violent perpetrators, other than using natural means, such as punching or kicking.

* Much violence is trivialized.

In 42% of all violent scenes, there is a humorous context. Humor tends to trivialize violence.

* Very little violence is explicit or graphic.

Only 5-6% of violent scenes include a close-up focus on the violent action or on the victims as they are attacked. In other words, it is unusual to see a close-up view of a gun firing or a bullet entering a victim's body. In addition, blood is not shown in most (86%) violent scenes and when it is, it is rarely (3%) in extreme amounts.

Viewed in light of the scientific research on effects, these findings imply a strong potential for learning of aggression, desensitization to violence, and fear among viewers who regularly see much of this violent content. In all but one of the points indicated above, the patterns we have identified reflect contextual features that raise rather than lower the risk of negative psychological effects. The sole exception to this trend is that violence is rarely presented graphically on television, and thus there is less risk of desensitization than would be the case if more explicit presentations were the norm. Yet for all other patterns, these contextual findings pose cause for concern.

Has Violence on Television Changed over the Past Three Years?

The most meaningful finding produced from the entire three-year study is the strong consistency identified in the patterns of violence presented on television since 1994. This stability encompasses nearly every measure we have employed to examine violent portrayals, from the overall frequency with which violence occurs to the more microscopic contextual features that surround each violent interaction and scene (see Figure 69). We first noted this trend in our Year 2 Report, yet find it more impressive now that these patterns have held so remarkably stable across an even more extended period of time. With only a few modest exceptions, the profile of violence on television we have observed in 1996-97 looks virtually identical to that seen two years earlier in 1994-95.

The evidence that establishes this pattern of stability begins with the data that indicate the overall prevalence of violence. Across a sample that averaged roughly 3,000 programs each year, the proportion of shows that contained violence varied year-to-year only 3%, from 58% to 61% of all programs sampled each year. The pattern for the types of violent acts portrayed was also highly consistent, with overtly depicted behaviors accounting for roughly two-thirds of all violent interactions (66-69%), and

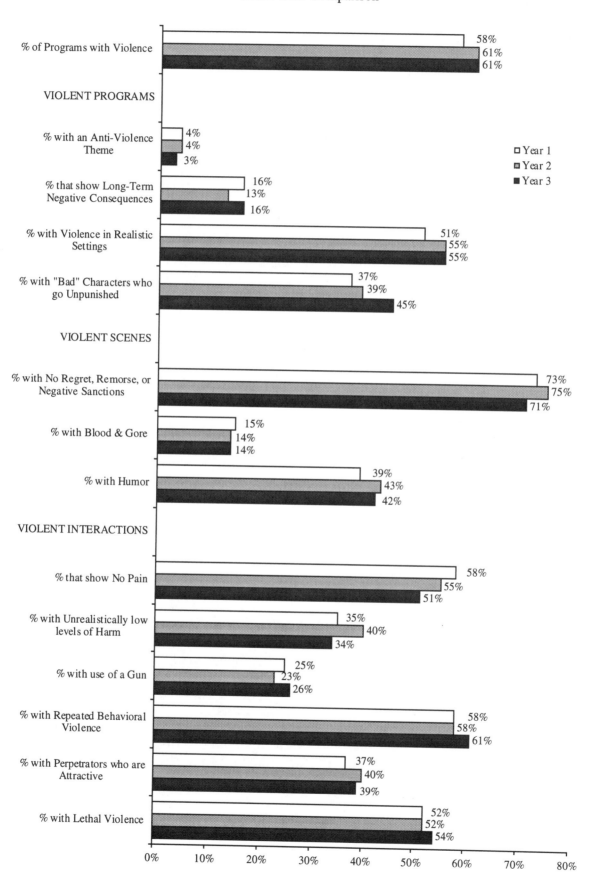

Figure 69
Overall Industry Average:
Three Year Comparison

the rest consisting primarily of credible threats of harm (24-29%). Violence that was implied but not shown to occur on-screen accounted for only 3% of all instances of violence in each of three years studied. These findings make clear that violence on television occurs with striking, indeed almost predictable, regularity in its frequency and basic form.

More important than the sheer frequency with which violence appears on television is the context in which it is presented. We have noted, for example, that positive effects on viewers are possible when violence is shown to have strong negative consequences or when alternatives to violence are emphasized within a program. Yet we find that the use of such anti-violent themes occurs only rarely. The proportion of programs with strong anti-violence story lines held at virtually the same level all three years of the study at 3-4% of all shows containing violence.

Across the entire range of important contextual features that are associated with violent depictions, we have identified only two changes in television programming overall across the past three years that appear to be meaningful. First, the patterns of punishment delivered to bad characters in violent programs show a significant change. In particular, the percentage of violent programs with bad characters who are never or rarely punished goes from 37% in 1994/95 to 39% in 1995/96, and now is at 45% in 1996/97. This change represents an increase in risk for the audience. Unpunished violence facilitates the learning of aggression in viewers. In this case, we see that fewer bad characters are being punished for violence in 1996/97 than in earlier years.

Second, the presence of violent interactions that show no pain declined for a second straight year, from 58% in 1994-95 to 55% in 1995-96 and now to 51% in 1996-97. Despite this change, the finding that a majority (51%) of all violent interactions still depict no pain for victims is a cause for concern. This approach to portraying violence enhances the risk of a harmful effect on viewers, and in particular children. When violence is presented without any pain cues from victims, viewers may begin to underestimate the harms of physical aggression, which can reduce inhibitions against violent behavior. In simple terms, violence seems easier to accept when it is sanitized in appearance, minimizing serious pain or harm.

With that said, our evidence across the last three years indicates that the industry is improving in this area by reducing the presence of violent depictions that lack any pain cues. Although the decline is relatively modest in size, it is statistically significant and meets the criteria established in Chapter 4 for being recognized as meaningful, so it is fair to view this as a positive development.

A related contextual feature involves depictions of harm that are unrealistically mild, such as a character being thrown out of a second-story window and walking away essentially unfazed. Our data show that this type of portrayal did *not* decline over the past three years in tandem with the reduction in portrayals of violence that show no pain. This finding may minimize the importance of the reduction in portrayals of violence that show no pain, as both of these factors are likely to shape the viewer's understanding of the negative consequences associated with violent behavior, and only one reflects a pattern of improvement.

Across all of the other contextual features reported in Figure 69, our results indicate a highly stable pattern of violent depictions over the past three years. Many of the individual measures were so consistent that the findings changed no more than a single percentage point from the beginning of the study in Fall 1994 until its conclusion in Spring 1997. That stability is remarkable given that it spans a total of more than 50,000 violent interactions identified during the three years of the study.

Our conclusion in assessing change over time in the presentation of violence across the television landscape as a whole is clear and firm: neither the frequency of violence nor the contextual elements that surround violent depictions have changed appreciably over the past three years. In terms of context, only two of the 14 major variables that we examined have shifted significantly across the three years. In one case, the pattern has gotten worse in terms of audience risk (i.e., less punishment of bad characters), and in the other case the pattern has gotten better (i.e., more depictions showing pain to victims). Thus, is impossible to argue that the industry has improved the depiction of violence given these contradictory patterns. Furthermore, these two isolated changes are undermined by the overall stability across the 12 remaining contextual variables. This impressive degree of consistency clearly suggests that the patterns the television medium employs in the presentation of violence are highly stable and formulaic. Most of these patterns contribute to the risk of harmful effects on the audience.

How is Violence Presented across Different Types of Channels?

The preceding section addresses the patterns of violent portrayals throughout the entire television world examined in this study. In this section, we review the key findings that emerge from our 1996-97 analysis when comparing each of the particular channel types included in the study to one another. Our sample encompasses most major sources of television content available to the American public: broadcast networks, independent broadcasting, public broadcasting, basic cable, and premium cable.

To facilitate comparisons across these five program sources, we will employ the same summary device that was presented in our previous annual reports. Table 32 presents a simplified picture of the important differences on the contextual variables across types of channels. The left-hand column of numbers reflects the overall industry-wide average for each variable listed. Deviations from these overall averages are indicated for each channel type by symbols that reflect any meaningful variation from the norm.

Moderate deviations (represented in the table by one circle) are defined as a difference of between 10-19 percentage points above or below the industry-wide average on any measure. Substantial deviations (represented in the table by two circles) require a difference of at least 20 percentage points from the average. We use symbols rather than numbers in order to make the patterns easier to discern. The darkened symbols represent deviations from the industry norms that hold adverse implications -- that is, they increase the risk of a harmful effect for viewers. The clear symbols represent deviations from industry norms in a positive, or socially desirable direction that minimize the risk of any possible negative effects.

In 1996-97, the *commercial broadcast networks* included violence in roughly half (51%) of their programs. While this finding indicates that violence is a common element in network programming, this level nonetheless falls 10% below the overall industry average, and thus we consider it a positive indicator, as shown in Table 32. With one exception (that being a moderately higher level of violence in realistic settings), however, the context in which violence is presented by the broadcast networks falls close to the norms across the television industry as a whole. We would conclude that the risk posed by viewing the violent depictions presented on network television is generally equivalent -- that is, no better or worse -- than that associated with violence on television programming overall.

Programs on *independent television channels* contain violence just about as often as the industry-wide average, and the context profile for their violent portrayals also looks very similar to the patterns established for programs overall. Independent channels are more likely to present programming with extensive violent depictions (i.e., nine or more violent interactions) and are substantially more likely to present aggressive incidents in humorous contexts. On the positive side, they are less likely to present violence in realistic settings.

Public broadcasting is noteworthy for producing one of the clearest and most beneficial findings in the entire study: its programs are far less likely to include violence than are the shows delivered by any other source. While more than half of the programs presented on all other channel types contain violence, public broadcasting includes violence in only 20% of its shows. In general, the contextual features associated with the relatively small number of violent portrayals on public television reflect positive indicators, as reported in Chapter 3. However, because the overall base of violent depictions on public broadcasting is so small, it is not informative to compare the contextual patterns as we have done with the other channels. Thus, we have omitted the contextual comparisons for public broadcasting in Table 32. Without qualification, the most important finding for this channel is the general avoidance of violence across its overall schedule of programs.

The cable industry was divided into two primary segments for analysis: basic and premium channels. Our findings indicate that the *basic cable* channels fell very close to the average for television programming overall on every single key measure during the past year, from the proportion of programs including violence to the complete range of contextual features for violent portrayals. In contrast, *premium cable* presents the highest proportion of programs with violence (83%), well above the industry average of 61% for all shows. Premium cable programs are substantially more likely to present violence in realistic settings, which facilitates aggressive reactions, and moderately more

Table 32

PROFILE OF VIOLENCE ACROSS CHANNEL TYPE

	Overall %	Broadcast Networks	Independent Broadcasts	Public Broadcast	Basic Cable	Premium Cable
Programs with Violence	61	○	⊙	○○	⊙	●●
Of Those Programs That Contain Violence...						
% with 9 or more violent interactions	32	⊙	●		⊙	●●
% with an Anti-Violence Theme	3	⊙	⊙		⊙	⊙
% that Show Long-Term Negative Consequences	16	⊙	⊙		⊙	○○
% with Violence in Realistic Settings	55	●	○		⊙	●●
% with "Bad" characters who go Unpunished	45	⊙	⊙		⊙	⊙
Of Those Scenes That Contain Violence...						
% with No Regret, Remorse, or Negative Sanctions	71	⊙	⊙		⊙	⊙
% with Blood & Gore	14	⊙	⊙		⊙	●
% with Humor	42	⊙	●●		⊙	⊙
When A Violent Interaction Occurs...						
% that Show No Pain	51	⊙	⊙		⊙	○
% with Unrealistically low levels of Harm	34	⊙	⊙		⊙	○
% with Use of a Gun	26	⊙	⊙		⊙	⊙
% with Repeated Behavioral Violence	61	⊙	⊙		⊙	⊙
% that Appear Justified	28	⊙	⊙		⊙	⊙
% with Perpetrators who are Attractive	39	⊙	⊙		⊙	⊙
% with Lethal Violence	54	⊙	⊙		⊙	⊙

○○ = Substantially Better than Industry Average
○ = Moderately Better than Industry Average
⊙ = Industry Average
● = Moderately Worse than Industry Average
●● = Substantially Worse than Industry Average

171

likely to display blood and gore, which contributes to viewer desensitization. On the positive side, programs featured on premium channels are substantially better than the industry average at showing the long-term consequences of violence, at avoiding violence that shows no pain to victims, and at avoiding the depiction of unrealistically mild harm from violent actions.

Despite the tremendous stability in both the frequency and contextual aspects of violence on television overall, it is conceivable that the consistency observed across all channels could mask important changes that have occurred within particular segments of the industry. Our data, however, make clear that this is not the case.

Using our criteria for identifying meaningful change, and analyzing the programming for each channel type independently, we find no indication of any shifts during the past three years in the frequency or context used for the presentation of violence.

How is Violence Presented across Different Types of Program Genres?

The sample of content examined in the study encompasses the complete diversity of television programming, with the exception of news, sports, and a handful of show types that seem unlikely to include any violence (e.g., game shows, religious shows, infomercials). We organized our sample of programs into six basic types or genres: drama, comedy, children's shows, movies, reality-based content, and music videos. It is not surprising that different genres exhibit different treatment of violence because they tend to employ different formulas in terms of plot and characterization. Like the preceding section on channel types, we have organized our discussion of these six genres by comparing each one's relationship to the industry-wide average on each applicable measure (see Table 33).

Drama programs are more likely to contain violence than the industry average. They also are more likely to depict the use of guns and substantially more likely to portray violence in realistic settings. On the positive side, they more frequently present the long-term consequences of violence, and avoid depicting unrealistically low levels of harm as well as violence without pain to victims.

Not surprisingly, *comedy* programs are much less likely to include violence and only rarely include it in extensive amounts. When violence is portrayed, its contextual features reflect many positive aspects that reduce the risk of harm to viewers. Comedy programs are less likely to feature guns or to show blood and gore than the industry average, and they also avoid violence that is justified or that results in unrealistically low levels of harm to victims. These shows are worse, however, in terms of presenting violence in a humorous context and depicting violence within realistic settings.

Children's programs do not differ substantially from the industry norm in the overall percentage of violent shows. They are substantially worse than average, however, in their use of humor with violence and in presenting unrealistically low levels of harm. Of all program genres, children's shows are the least likely to portray any long-term consequences of violence. The positive aspects are that blood and gore are below average, as is violence involving guns. The one substantially positive element is that most depictions of violence avoid realistic settings, although the importance of this factor is minimized by our knowledge that younger children have difficulty discriminating fantasy from reality in television programming. To them, all violence on television appears realistic and is understood as such, enhancing its risk for harmful effects.

Movies as a genre have the highest percentage of programs with violence (89%). Movies portray violence in realistic settings and include graphic blood and gore more often than the norm. Among the positive features of movies are that long-term consequences are portrayed substantially more often, and unrealistically low levels of harm less often than the industry average.

Reality-based programs include news magazines, documentaries, and talk shows as well as police-based reality programs. The diversity of the genre helps to explain why this category includes a substantially lower than average proportion of shows (39%) containing violence. However, the programs that do contain violence are of course substantially more likely to include realistic settings. They are also more likely than the industry norm to feature incidents involving the use of a gun and lacking any pain cues in victims. Furthermore, reality shows are more likely to feature bad characters who are never or rarely punished for their aggressive actions and behaviors when compared to the industry norm. The positive aspects are that these programs are below average in the use of humorous violence, depicting harm unrealistically low, and presenting attractive perpetrators.

Music videos are similar to the overall industry average with respect to their prevalence of violent material. Each music video can be considered a discrete narrative unit or segment, and most of these are relatively short in length. This helps account for the finding that this genre is substantially less likely to present numerous violent interactions within each segment. This genre, however, is substantially worse than average in terms of presenting violence in realistic settings, portraying bad characters that are never punished for their aggressive actions, as well as including depictions of violence that show no pain. The positive aspects are that the videos are low in violence with humor, and are less likely than the industry norm to depict attractive perpetrators of violence.

As was the case with our examination of channel type differences, our data indicate no meaningful shifts have occurred across the past three years in either the frequency or contextual aspects of violence within any of the basic program genres studied. This stability demonstrates the resiliency of violence as a staple in the diet of the complete range of television programming, albeit in slightly different dosages according to the program type involved.

Table 33

PROFILE OF VIOLENCE ACROSS GENRE

	Overall %	Drama Series	Comedy Series	Children's Series	Movies	Reality Based	Music Videos
Programs with Violence	61	●	OO	◉	●●	OO	◉
Of Those Programs That Contain Violence...							
% with 9 or more violent interactions	32	◉	OO	◉	●●	O	OO
% with an Anti-Violence Theme	3	◉	◉	◉	◉	◉	◉
% that Show Long-Term Negative Consequences	16	O	◉	●	O	◉	◉
% with Violence in Realistic Settings	55	●●	●●	OO	●●	●●	●●
% with "Bad" characters that go Unpunished	45	O	◉	◉	◉	●	●●
Of Those Scenes That Contain Violence...							
% with No Regret, Remorse, or Negative Sanctions	71	◉	◉	◉	◉	◉	◉
% with Blood & Gore	14	◉	O	O	●	◉	◉
% with Humor	42	OO	●●	●●	O	OO	OO
When A Violent Interaction Occurs...							
% that Show No Pain	51	O	◉	◉	◉	●●	●●
% with Unrealistically low levels of Harm	34	O	O	●●	O	O	◉
% with Use of a Gun	26	●	O	O	◉	●	◉
% with Repeated Behavioral Violence	61	◉	O	◉	◉	◉	●
% that Appear Justified	28	◉	O	◉	◉	◉	◉
% with Perpetrators who are Attractive	39	◉	◉	◉	◉	O	O
% with Lethal Violence	54	◉	OO	◉	◉	◉	●

OO = Substantially Better than Industry Average
O   = Moderately Better than Industry Average
◉   = Industry Average
●   = Moderately Worse than Industry Average
●● = Substantially Worse than Industry Average

What Portrayals Pose a High Risk for Children's Learning of Aggression?

Given the patterns observed on the contextual variables above, children and adults experience some risk of negative psychological effects when they view many if not most of the violent acts shown on television. Nonetheless, we have devised a multivariate analysis that we label a High-Risk Composite to identify the violent portrayals that place child-viewers at greatest risk of learning aggressive attitudes and behaviors. We have concentrated our attention on children because research suggests that younger age groups are more susceptible to the effects of televised violence. Assessing risk requires an understanding of how children of different ages interpret the meaning of sets of contextual variables.

Focusing specifically on the risk for learning aggressive behaviors, we identified five contextual features that are most salient for young children under age 7: (1) the perpetrator is attractive; (2) the violence seems justified; (3) the perpetrator is rarely or never punished for violent actions; (4) the victims are not shown as being harmed; and (5) the violence seems realistic to the child. When we focus on this most negative of contexts for young children, we find over 700 high-risk violent portrayals throughout our composite week of television.

A separate test was applied to identify high-risk portrayals for older children and adolescents. This audience can better recognize fantasy or fiction than their younger counterparts, and such understanding serves to reduce some of the risk from viewing violent depictions presented in unrealistic settings. Thus, we observed a smaller number of high-risk interactions for older children and adolescents, although we still found nearly 400 such cases in our composite week of television.

Most of our analyses categorize channels into five major groupings: broadcast networks, independent broadcast, public broadcast, basic cable, and premium cable. For the high-risk analyses, we further sub-divided basic cable because it consists of so many channels that could vary in terms of risk. In particular, we grouped basic cable into three classes of channels according to the predominant type of featured programming: general entertainment (A&E, AMC, Family Channel, Lifetime, TNT, USA), music-oriented (BET, MTV, VH-1), and child-oriented (Cartoon Network, Disney, Nickelodeon) programming.

The composite for younger children reveals that the majority of high-risk portrayals for this audience is found on two types of channels: child-oriented basic cable and independent broadcast stations. The composite for older children shows a different pattern in which general entertainment-oriented basic cable channels and premium cable account for the largest share of high-risk portrayals.

The findings regarding the high-risk composites are better understood as a function of program genre, as opposed to an analysis based strictly on channel type. For younger children, children's programs as a genre contain the greatest share (50%) of all high-risk violent interactions, as well as the highest ratio of interactions per hour (.75). In other words, most of the portrayals that pose particular concern for "teaching" aggressive attitudes and behaviors to young children are contained in the very programs

175

that are targeted to this age group. Furthermore, most of the children's programs that contain these portrayals are animated, or what people commonly label as cartoons.

These animated stories consistently emphasize the pattern of violence that is most likely to encourage aggression in young children: an attractive perpetrator engaging in justified violence that is rarely punished and produces minimal consequences. It is a sobering yet clear conclusion that the genre of children's programming contains many of the most problematic portrayals for young child viewers. To make sense of this, it is important to bear in mind that younger children lack the capability to distinguish fantasy from reality in television portrayals, and hence the impact of cartoon violence is not "discounted" in their minds as would be the case with older children or adult viewers.

The separate high-risk composite constructed for older children and adolescents yields a different pattern of concerns. For this age group, movies contain the largest proportion (68%) of high-risk violent interactions as well as the highest rate per hour (.28). Dramas also pose substantial cause for concern with a .25 rate per hour that is close to the level of high-risk portrayals found in movies. Most other genres present relatively few high-risk messages for this age group.

Recommendations

There are several distinct audiences for this report, including the television industry, public policy-makers, parents, and our colleagues in the academic research community. In this section, we turn to the task of considering the implications of our findings for each of these audiences, and offer recommendations that we believe are appropriate in light of the data produced by this study.

<u>For the Television Industry</u>

From the outset, one of the key functions of the NTVS project was to incorporate some degree of accountability for the television industry's performance in responding to public concern about television violence. Given the consistency of our findings about the risk of harm associated with the prevalent patterns of violent portrayals we observed in Year 1 (1994-95) and Year 2 (1995-96) of the study, we offered virtually identical recommendations in each of our first two annual reports. In this, our third and final report, our most significant finding is that the overall pattern for violence on television remains remarkably stable and virtually unchanged since 1994. That outcome means there is little new and meaningful evidence that would alter our previously stated recommendations to the industry for improving its use of violence on the screen.

Consequently, we reiterate what we believe are the most important suggestions for the industry to embrace to improve their social responsibility in this area. Each of the recommendations indicated below holds the potential to reduce substantially the risk of harm to America's youth that is posed by their cumulative exposure to thousands of violent acts across their formative years. Preceding each recommendation are the relevant findings from our three-year study that establish the need for the suggested actions on the industry's part.

Issue #1:   *Prevalence of Violence*

<u>Findings from the NTVS Study</u>:

There has been no reduction since 1994 in the percentage of programs that contain violence.

There has been no reduction since 1994 in the percentage of programs that contain nine or more violent interactions.

<u>Recommendation</u>

Produce more programs that avoid violence; if a program does contain violence, keep the number of violent incidents low.

The prevalence of violence on television has been high since its beginnings roughly 50 years ago. We do not advocate that all violence be eliminated from television, nor do we profess to know exactly how much is "too much." But we do know that the overall amount of violence on American television has not changed appreciably since this study began to measure it during the 1994-95 television season. It is still the case that more than half the programs in a composite week that consists of more than 2,500 hours of content contain some violence. Furthermore, most programs that contain violence feature numerous violent incidents rather than just an isolated act.

Our recommendation is to begin efforts to cut back. The need for a reduction is underscored by the fact that the average American child watches 2-3 hours of TV a day and thus is at risk for cumulative exposure to thousands of such portrayals over the course of her or his young life.

Issue #2:   *The Context of Violent Incidents*

<u>Findings from the NTVS Study</u>

There has been no increase since 1994 in the punishments shown for violent behavior.

There has been no increase since 1994 in portraying either the short-term or long-term negative consequences of violence.

There has been no decrease since 1994 in violence that is presented for justified reasons.

Recommendation

Program producers should make efforts to show:

- more frequent punishment associated with violent acts.

- more of the serious negative consequences of violence.

- less justification for violent actions.

These recommendations recognize that violence is not all the same; that some portrayals pose more risk to the audience than others. Conveying the message that violence gets punished, that it is not always justified, that there are alternatives to aggression, and that violence causes serious consequences (i.e., pain and suffering) for the victims are all ways to reduce the risk of a negative influence on viewers when violence is included in a story.

Unfortunately, our data indicate that most of the violence on television is formulaic, and the most common patterns include violence shown without punishment and without any emphasis on the suffering of victims. One of the chief explanations for violence shown without punishment is aggression that is practiced by "good guys" who are justified in bringing the "bad guys" to justice using violence. Should anyone in the industry misunderstand, let us be perfectly clear: this formula contributes to harmful psychological effects. Portrayals of glamorized heros who commit sanitized violence for justified reasons (i.e., catching "bad guys") contribute to the risk of viewers, especially children, learning aggressive attitudes and behaviors from television.

Issue #3: The Overall Message of Violent Programs

Findings From the NTVS Study

There has been no increase since 1994 in the percentage of violent programs that employ an anti-violence theme.

Recommendation

When violence is presented, consider greater emphasis on a strong anti-violence theme.

Since the outset of the NTVS project, we have encouraged the television industry to create more programs that: (1) present alternatives to violent actions throughout the program; (2) show main characters repeatedly discussing the negative consequences of violence; (3) emphasize the physical pain and emotional suffering that results from violence; and (4) show that punishments for violence clearly and consistently outweigh rewards. Whenever a program emphasizes one of these elements, we classify the show as containing an anti-violent theme.

Our data show that the use of an anti-violence theme on television continues to be rare. It has remained between 3-4% of all violent programs since 1994. This is one of the most disappointing findings of the study because this statistic is arguably the best indicator of a responsible, pro-social approach to depicting violence.

Some organized efforts to promote these approaches would seem to be required to accomplish any change. One way to stimulate such efforts might be an annual award for television given for the creative portrayal of an anti-violence theme. Workshops for writers and producers to sensitize them to these issues is another obvious possibility.

Issue #4: High-Risk Portrayals in Children's Programs

Findings from the NTVS Study

> **More portrayals that pose a high-risk for increasing young children's aggressiveness are found in children's programs than in any other type of TV content.**

> **There has been no change since 1995 in the patterns of high-risk portrayals found in children's programs.**

Recommendation

> **Reduce the number of high-risk portrayals of violence in children's cartoon programs.**

> **Ensure that any cartoons that present high-risk portrayals for young children are rated in a way that clearly warns parents.**

We have identified the kinds of portrayals that pose the greatest degree of risk for the learning of aggression among young viewers. Some might assume these would be the most explicit or graphic examples of violence on television, but that is not the case. Portrayals with the greatest risk of increasing young children's aggressive behavior are those that feature *an attractive perpetrator engaging in justified violence that goes unpunished and shows minimal consequences.* Our data indicate that a surprisingly large proportion of such portrayals are found in children's programming, particularly in certain types of cartoons. The frequent use of this formula in children's shows is a problem in and of itself, and one that the industry should address by actively avoiding such depictions.

In the meantime, with many children's shows on the air that include high-risk portrayals, it is important that parents are properly warned about the programs that contain material that is clearly problematic for younger children. Under the television industry's current V-chip rating system, children's shows can receive a designation of TV-Y7 (appropriate for all youth age 7 and above), as distinct from TV-Y (appropriate for all youth), as well as the content warning label "FV" for more intense fantasy violence. Thus, we would expect that programs which contain any high-risk portrayals would be

179

rated in the Y7 category with an FV label. Our data set this year, which was gathered prior to the full implementation of the current V-chip rating system, does not afford us the opportunity to examine this issue empirically.

The remaining sections of this chapter present recommendations for our three additional audiences: policy-makers, parents, and the academic community. Although we have previously provided recommendations to two of these groups (policy-makers and parents), our study is not designed to evaluate their performance as we do with the television industry, and thus we cannot offer any assessment of the response from these groups to our past recommendations. Instead, we simply present what we believe are the most important implications of our findings for each of the three audiences in turn below.

For Public Policy-makers

This study was stimulated in large part because of increasing policy concern about violence on television. Numerous regulatory alternatives have been proposed, and some action has been taken, such as the approval of legislation that led to the V-chip rating system. This study does not argue for or against any specific proposal to address the issue. Rather, it provides information to help policy-makers better understand the problems associated with violence on television. It also establishes a benchmark for comparisons over time in the levels of televised violence.

Because our data are oriented more to specifying the nature and extent of the problem of televised violence than to identifying the most appropriate solution, we cannot endorse any specific policy proposal. Our recommendations to policy-makers are therefore at a more fundamental level.

* Continue to monitor the nature and extent of violence on television.

Evidence of the harmful effects associated with televised violence was firmly established well before this study began. The unique contribution of the NTVS research is to apply that knowledge to track the presence of violence that poses a risk of harm. While some studies have focused on identifying the most violent program or the most violent network, we have consciously avoided that path. Our emphasis has been placed on tracking the presence of violence on television overall, encompassing all of the channels that people most frequently view. There is a compelling rationale for that strategy.

Programs come and go and, at least according to past research, random ebb and flow patterns occur across different television networks in their levels of violence. The stakes are high in terms of social implications in this realm not so much because of the effects of viewing any one violent program, but more from the fact that most everyone watches TV, most people watch a lot, and most of television contains violence. In other words, the effects are pervasive and cumulative. From a social policy perspective, the public is hardly well served when the overall pattern of violence on television remains the same, whether or not the levels are slightly up or down from one show to another or from one network compared to a competitor.

What should be of greatest interest to policy-makers is the pattern of violence presented across the television industry as a whole. Just as the concern about smoking and its risk of causing cancer would hardly be ameliorated by having one tobacco manufacturer significantly reduce the tar and nicotine in its cigarettes, improvements in reducing or more responsibly presenting televised violence cannot be judged effective if they involve only a limited number of channels or time slots, such as evening prime-time hours. People watch television at all times of day and increasingly view a wider and wider array of channels. Only when the overall profile of violence is reduced or improved across television programming as a whole will the concern about the issue diminish.

Therefore, we urge policy-makers not only to continue to monitor the nature and extent of violence on television, but in doing so to emphasize the overall patterns across the industry as a whole. The NTVS project has established an important benchmark for carefully calibrating the measurement of violence on television in a quantitative fashion that allows precise comparisons to be made over time. While our three-year project as initially sponsored by NCTA has now drawn to a close, we are optimistic that we will be able to pursue future efforts to apply our content measures to track television violence. And certainly there will be efforts from others to study this topic. The importance of the issue warrants continued attention to help sensitize the television industry as well as to help alert and inform the public.

* Recognize that context is an essential aspect of television violence.

Treating all acts of violence as if they are the same disregards a rich body of scientific knowledge about media effects. An appreciation of key contextual factors is crucial for understanding the impact of televised violence on the audience.

Consider the following example. Policy-makers, as well as television critics and others, often voice concern about "graphic" or "explicit" violence. Indeed, the new V-chip rating system reserves its most restrictive category (TV-MA) solely for graphic violence. At one level, this situation reflects a sensitivity to context; that is, it recognizes that graphic violence ought to be treated differently than other non-graphic portrayals. Yet because "graphic" or "explicit"violence is the *only* element that qualifies a portrayal for this most restrictive category, the special treatment accorded to graphic depictions may implicitly convey that other types of depictions are not as problematic for viewers. That is not necessarily true.

Our high-risk composite analysis demonstrates that portrayals that are not particularly explicit but that present violence as attractive, rewarding, and painless pose a significant threat of increasing children's aggressive behavior. From this perspective, such an array of context factors deserves to receive as much attention as that given to graphic portrayals. Unfortunately, this typically has not been the case. The lack of concern over such high-risk portrayals, we believe, results from inadequate attention to the scientific evidence regarding the influence of different context features associated with televised violence.

At the base of any policy initiative in this realm is the need to define violence and, assuming that not all violence is to be treated equally, to differentiate types of violent depictions that pose the greatest cause for concern. Accomplishing this task requires the careful consideration of the contextual elements we have identified in this study, as well as the elaborate base of empirical evidence that establishes their importance.

* Ensure that television program ratings accurately convey to parents the risks associated with different types of violent portrayals.

The contextual features identified in this study provide important information about the psychological risk for child viewers from any given portrayal of violence. It is important for parents to consider such factors in guiding viewing decisions for their children. Therefore, it is also important that a rating system designed to inform parents about violent material should be sensitive to the types of portrayals that pose the most significant risk of negatively affecting their children.

In assessing the efficacy of any ratings system, careful consideration should be given to whether or not the program labels or categories are consistent with the relevant scientific evidence about the effects of different types of violent portrayals on children. A rating system that ignores important risk factors associated with depictions of violence cannot adequately inform parents about the potential dangers of television content.

For Parents

Perhaps the most important consumers of this report are the nation's parents. It may take years to alter significantly the profile of violence on television. In contrast, parents can begin immediately to change the way they think about violence on television and the way they make decisions about their children's viewing. Last year we made three recommendations for parents that still hold.

* Be aware of the three risks associated with viewing television violence.

Evidence of the potential harmful effects associated with viewing violence on television is well established and fully documented in our Year 1 report. Perhaps the most troubling of these involves children's learning of aggressive attitudes and behaviors. Arguably more pervasive and often under-emphasized are the other two risks associated with television violence: fear and desensitization. An appreciation of these three effects will help parents recognize the role of television in children's socialization.

* Consider the context of violent depictions in making viewing decisions for children.

As demonstrated in both of our reports, not all violent portrayals are the same in terms of their impact on the audience. Some depictions pose greater risks for children than others, and some may even be prosocial. When considering a particular program, think about whether violence is rewarded, whether heroes or good characters engage in violence, whether violence appears to be morally sanctioned, whether the serious negative consequences of violence are avoided, and whether humor is used. These are the types of portrayals that are most harmful.

* Consider a child's developmental level when making viewing decisions.

Throughout this project, we underscore the importance of the child's developmental level or cognitive ability in making sense of television. Very young children are less able to distinguish fantasy from reality on television. Thus, for preschoolers and younger elementary schoolers, cartoon violence and fantasy violence cannot be dismissed or exonerated because it is unrealistic. Indeed, younger children identify strongly with superheroes and fantastic cartoon characters, and often learn from and imitate such portrayals. Furthermore, younger children have difficulty connecting non-adjacent scenes together and drawing causal inferences about the plot. Therefore, punishments, pain cues, or serious consequences of violence that are presented later in a plot, well after the violent act, may not be comprehended fully by a young child. For younger viewers, then, it is particularly important that contextual features like punishment and pain be shown within the violent scene, rather than solely at the end of the program.

To these recommendations, we add a fourth concerning high-risk portrayals.

* Recognize that certain types of violent cartoons pose particularly high risk for young children's learning of aggression.

Our findings suggest that certain animated programs can be particularly problematic for younger viewers. We have identified a type of portrayal that we label "high risk" because it contains an array of elements that encourage the learning of aggressive attitudes and behaviors. In particular, a high-risk portrayal for learning is one that features *an attractive character who engages in violence that is sanctioned and that does not result in any serious consequences to the victim.* Parents should closely monitor programming with an eye for this type of portrayal.

As it turns out, many of these high-risk depictions show up in cartoons. Adults often assume that violent cartoons are not a problem for children because the content is so unrealistic. However, this assumption is directly contradicted by research. Numerous studies show that animated programming such as *Batman* and *Superman* can increase aggressive behavior in young children (Ellis & Sekyra, 1972; Friedrich & Stein, 1973; Mussen & Rutherford, 1961; Steuer, Applefield, & Smith, 1971). Even more compelling, a recent meta-analysis of 217 experiments found that cartoons show the single largest effect for increasing aggression compared to six other types of television content (Paik & Comstock, 1994). Thus, animated programming cannot be dismissed as benign, particularly for children under 7 years of age who have difficulty distinguishing reality from fantasy.

Parents of older children and adolescents, on the other hand, should review movies and drama programs because these genres are most likely to contain realistic portrayals of the type defined above that pose high risk for more mature viewers. Such differences should be taken into account when monitoring children's viewing habits.

For the Academic Community

As scientists of all stripes well know, knowledge in any field tends to move forward in small, incremental steps. Thus, it is the hope of the authors of this study that our colleagues in the realm of communication and in other related disciplines will be able to build upon the foundation established by this research. Certainly, the ongoing social and policy concern with the issue of media violence insures that others will follow us in monitoring and analyzing the frequency and context of violent portrayals. As that work proceeds, we offer the following recommendations for other researchers to consider in shaping their own pursuit of the topic of television violence content and effects.

* There needs to be further research linking contextual features of violence to specific types of effects.

We already know that not all violence is the same in terms of its risk of harmful effects. While our understanding of how different contextual features contribute to the three primary types of harmful effects from viewing TV violence has developed to an intermediate state, there is still much more to be learned. Many of the studies that are relied upon in this realm are dated and would benefit from replication or confirmation. Some possible relationships seem to have escaped any investigation at all.

Table 1 on page 13 provides our assessment of the state of existing knowledge in the field in terms of linking particular contextual features to differing types of effects from exposure to violence. This table shows numerous empty cells, reflecting the fact that many of the possible relationships have not been adequately explored by research.

For example, some theorists have suggested that humor within a violent scene may decrease viewers' fear responses to aggressive portrayals, yet no research has systematically explored this issue. Another gap in knowledge involves the potential ameliorative influence of showing the harmful consequences of violence on viewer desensitization effects. It is possible that seeing a victim's physical injury and pain may short-circuit the desensitization process, though there is no empirical evidence on this important topic. Even beyond the empty cells in our summary table, there are certainly other contextual features that may be important but which have barely been explored by research, such as the use of music and the pacing of visual cuts.

Finally, it is important to bear in mind that the extent to which a context feature contributes to a particular type of effect might vary across different audiences. Children may interpret certain contextual features differently than adults, and thus the use of such elements could be more or less important depending upon the focus of a given study. In general, the field needs further investigation of the link between particular context features and the risk of harmful effects among important segments of the audience.

* There needs to be investigation of the relative strength of different contextual features in producing particular types of effects.

Most all of the research assessing the influence of a contextual feature on the audience has examined attributes individually. For example, we know that portraying violence without punishment heightens the risk for increasing viewers' aggressiveness. We also know that portraying violence as justified heightens the risk for the same type of effect. What we do not know is which of these two factors contributes more strongly to viewer aggression. In fact, we do not have much empirical evidence at all to help differentiate the relative strength of *any* one given contextual attribute as compared to another one in influencing viewer effects. Rather, researchers tend to have greater or lesser confidence in the importance of some attributes over others primarily as a function of a greater number of studies documenting the link between a particular context feature and a given effect, rather than any comparative assessment of the strength or power of that context feature as contrasted with the strength or power of other context features.

Simply put, researchers need to conduct studies that can help to isolate the independent and interactive contribution to the primary types of effects of each of the complete array of contextual features. This is potentially quite difficult because so many context features can be creatively intermingled in any given depiction of violence. But a careful researcher working systematically could manipulate one context factor at a time while holding the others constant in an experimental design that would yield highly valuable information. It is important to disentangle the most influential contextual features from those that seem to hold less significance for shaping viewer effects. With this type of information, scholars could more confidently develop scales of risk probabilities associated with exposure to different types of violent portrayals.

* There needs to be research on the content and effects of news programming that contains violence.

Roughly four years ago, then-Senator Paul Simon of Illinois argued that the television industry should take greater responsibility in limiting portrayals of violence that posed a risk of harm to children. His argument led the National Cable Television Association to commission this study, which represents an independent academic assessment of the overall industry's performance at presenting violence on television. In the funder's original Request for Proposals that solicited this study, it was stipulated that news would be excluded from examination. This exclusion mirrored political debate at the time in Congress, which was considering several pieces of legislation addressing TV violence, but which exempted this category from the proposed regulations' reach. Indeed, Senator Simon agreed publicly that it would be unwise to pursue any action, public or private, that might lead to any restraint on the free flow of information in the news reaching the American public.

Consequently, this study has not examined violence in nightly news programs that report "breaking news," although this exclusion was drawn as narrowly as possible. Other related types of public affairs programs and entertainment news shows were included in the analyses. Nonetheless, we believe that excluding the news in any form is an important omission. Although we do not support restrictions of any sort on news gathering or dissemination, we recognize the unavoidable fact that violence presented in television news certainly poses some risk of harmful effects on children. There is a growing body of research that documents this concern.

It is our view that research can and should be done examining violence in TV news, and that such evidence can have a positive impact on industry practices without threatening censorship. When any editor makes a judgment about what content to convey in a newscast, many factors are weighed. Certainly, one salient element here, albeit only one among many, is the potential impact of the content on children who may be watching.

Some have argued that television news has skewed its focus so heavily toward stories involving violence that the public's access to information actually suffers as a result, with more important but less attention-grabbing civic issues squeezed out of the news agenda. Thus, data that might identify such a trend could conceivably result in a more informed public, rather than any censorship efforts, depending upon the industry's response to such findings. Of course, such outcomes are unpredictable and a natural part of public debate and dialogue. We believe that the public is best served in this debate by bringing scientific information about the levels and types of violence presented in the news into public light. Those on all sides of the debate about how best to proceed can then argue from informed perspectives.

In conducting our three-year study, we sampled and taped all programs selected by the random draw, regardless of content. Thus, our archive is complete in containing a representative sample week that includes all aspects of television for each of the three years studied. In the future, that archive will be available to us as well as any qualified researcher who wishes to conduct studies in these areas that might complement the work presented in the NTVS reports. Arguably the most important complement to our findings reported across the past three years would be an examination of the violence contained in television news, and the risk it may pose to child viewers.

Final Thoughts

There have been few studies in the field of communication that parallel the rich investment of time and resources that have been devoted to this project. The UCSB research team involved five senior faculty who have devoted their primary efforts over three years to this work, along with the assistance of several graduate researchers and dozens of student assistants. This collective effort benefitted from the consultation and feedback provided by a national advisory board of diverse interested parties, many of whom are themselves accomplished experts in the area of media violence.

As a result, our research was able to incorporate a number of conceptual and methodological innovations. We examined the broad landscape of entertainment television, not just prime-time, and not only the broadcast networks. We sampled by individual programs, not intact days or weeks, so that each program had an equal chance of being selected. This increased independence for program selections meant that, more than in any previous study, the resulting sample represented a typical week of television content. Finally, we analyzed any violence within its context at multiple levels ranging from the individual violent interaction to the full program narrative so that various forms of its meaning could be assessed.

The merits and liabilities of our efforts will be judged over time by our peers as well as the other audiences addressed by our recommendations. It is our fervent hope that the evidence we have produced proves beneficial in some way to all who have important stakes in the issue of television violence.

REFERENCES

Atkin, C. (1983). Effects of realistic TV violence vs. fictional violence on aggression. Journalism Quarterly, 60, 615-621.

Bandura, A. (1965). Influence of models' reinforcement contingencies on the acquisition of imitative responses. Journal of Personality and Social Psychology, 1, 589-595.

Bandura, A. (1986). Social foundations of thought and action: A social cognitive theory. Englewood Cliffs, NJ: Prentice-Hall.

Bandura, A. (1994). Social cognitive theory of mass communication. In J. Bryant & D. Zillmann (Eds.), Media effects (pp. 61-90). Hillsdale, NJ: Erlbaum.

Bandura, A., Ross, D., & Ross, S. A. (1961). Transmission of aggression through imitation of aggressive models. Journal of Abnormal and Social Psychology, 63, 575-582.

Bandura, A., Ross, D., & Ross, S. A. (1963). Vicarious reinforcement and imitative learning. Journal of Abnormal and Social Psychology, 67, 601-607.

Baron, R. A. (1971a). Aggression as a function of magnitude of victim's pain cues, level of prior anger arousal, and aggressor-victim similarity. Journal of Personality and Social Psychology, 18, 48-54.

Baron, R. A. (1971b). Magnitude of victim's pain cues and level of prior anger arousal as determinants of adult aggressive behavior. Journal of Personality and Social Psychology, 17, 236-243.

Baron, R. A. (1978). The influence of hostile and nonhostile humor upon physical aggression. Personality and Social Psychology Bulletin, 4, 77-80.

Berger, A. A. (1988). Humor and behavior: Therapeutic aspects of comedic techniques and other considerations. In B. D. Ruben (Ed.), Information and Behavior (Vol. 2, pp. 226-247). New Brunswick, NJ: Transaction Books.

Berkowitz, L. (1970). Aggressive humor as a stimulus to aggressive responses. Journal of Personality and Social Psychology, 16, 710-717.

Berkowitz, L. (1984). Some effects of thoughts on anti- and prosocial influences of media events: A cognitive-neoassociation analysis. Psychological Bulletin, 95, 410-427.

Berkowitz, L. (1990). On the formation and regulation of anger and aggression: A cognitive-neoassociationistic analysis. American Psychologist, 45(4), 494-503.

Berkowitz, L., & Alioto, J. T. (1973). The meaning of an observed event as a determinant of its aggressive consequences. Journal of Personality and Social Psychology, 28, 206-217.

Berkowitz, L., & Geen, R. G. (1967). Stimulus qualities of the target of aggression: A further study. Journal of Personality and Social Psychology, 5, 364-368.

Berkowitz, L., & Powers, P. C. (1979). Effects of timing and justification of witnessed aggression on the observers' punitiveness. Journal of Research In Personality, 13, 71-80.

Berkowitz, L., & Rawlings, E. (1963). Effects of film violence on inhibitions against subsequent aggression. Journal of Abnormal and Social Psychology, 66, 405-412.

Berndt, T. J., & Berndt, E. G. (1975). Children's use of motives and intentionality in person perception and moral judgment. Child Development, 46, 904-920.

Bryant, J., Carveth, R. A., & Brown D. (1981). Television viewing and anxiety: An experimental examination. Journal of Communication, 31 (1), 106-119.

Carlson, M., Marcus-Newhall, A., & Miller, N. (1990). Effects of situational aggression cues: A quantitative review. Journal of Personality and Social Psychology, 58, 622-633.

Cline, V. B., Croft, R. G., & Courrier, S. (1973). Desensitization of children to television violence. Journal of Personality and Social Psychology, 27, 360-365.

Collins, W. A. (1973). Effect of temporal separation between motivation, aggression, and consequences. Developmental Psychology, 8, 215-221.

Collins, W. A. (1983). Interpretation and inference in children's television viewing. In J. Bryant & D. R. Anderson (Eds.), Children's understanding of television (pp. 125-150). New York: Academic Press.

Comisky, P., & Bryant, J. (1982). Factors involved in generating suspense. Human Communication Research, 9, 49-58.

Comstock, G., & Paik, H. (1991). Television and the American child. New York: Academic Press.

Dorr, A. (1986). Television and children: A special medium for a special audience. Beverly Hills, CA: Sage.

Ellis, G. T. & Sekyra, F. (1972) The effects of cartoons on the behavior of first grade children. Journal of Psychology, 81, 37-43.

Feshbach, S. (1972). Reality and fantasy in filmed violence. In J. P. Murray, E. A. Rubinstein, & G. Comstock (Eds.), Television and social behavior: Vol. 2. Television and social learning (pp. 318-345). Washington, DC: U.S. Government Publication Office.

Feshbach, N. D., & Roe, K. (1968). Empathy in six- and seven-year-olds. Child Development, 39, 133-145.

Flavell, J. H. (1985). Cognitive development (2nd ed.). Englewood Cliffs, NJ: Prentice-Hall.

Friedrich, L. K. & Stein, A. H. (1973). Aggressive and prosocial television programs and the natural behavior of preschool children. Monographs of the Society for Research in Child Development, 38 (4), Serial No. 151.

Geen, R. G. (1975). The meaning of observed violence: Real vs. fictional violence and consequent effects on aggression and emotional arousal. Journal of Research in Personality, 9, 270-281.

Geen, R. G., & Rakosky, J. J. (1973). Interpretations of observed aggression and their effects on GSR. Journal of Experimental Research in Personality, 6, 289-292.

Geen, R. G., & Stonner, D. (1973). Context effects in observed violence. Journal of Personality and Social Psychology, 25, 145-150.

Geen, R. G., & Stonner, D. (1974). The meaning of observed violence: Effects on arousal and aggressive behavior. Journal of Research In Personality, 8, 55-63.

Gerbner, G., & Gross, L. (1976). Living with television: The violence profile. Journal of Communication, 26 (2), 172-199.

Goransen, R. E. (1969). Observed violence and aggressive behavior: The effects of negative outcomes to observed violence. Dissertation Abstracts International, 31 (01), DAI-B. (University Microfilms No. AAC77 08286).

Gunter, B. (1983). Do aggressive people prefer violent television? Bulletin of the British Psychological Society, 36, 166-168.

Gunter, B. (1985). Dimensions of television violence. Aldershots, England: Gower.

Gunter, B. (1994). The question of media violence. In J. Bryant & D. Zillmann (Eds.), Media effects (pp. 163-211). Hillsdale, NJ: Lawrence Erlbaum Associates.

Hearold, S. (1986). A synthesis of 1043 effects of television on social behavior. In G. Comstock (Ed.), Public Communication and Behavior, Vol. 1. (pp. 65-133). New York: Academic Press.

190

Hoffner, C., & Cantor, J. (1985). Developmental differences in responses to a television character's appearance and behavior. Developmental Psychology, 21, 1065-1074.

Hoffner, C., & Cantor, J. (1991). Perceiving and responding to mass media characters. In J. Bryant & D. Zillmann (Eds.), Responding to the screen (pp. 63-101). Hillsdale, NJ: Lawrence Erlbaum Associates.

Hoyt, J. L. (1970). Effect of media violence "justification" on aggression. Journal of Broadcasting, 14, 455-464.

Huesmann, L. R. (1986). Psychological processes promoting the relation between exposure to media violence and aggressive behavior by the viewer. Journal of Social Issues, 42 (3), 125-140.

Huesmann, L. R. (1988). An information processing model for the development of aggression. Aggressive Behavior, 14, 13-24.

Huesmann, L. R., Eron, L. D., Lefkowitz, M. M., & Walder, L. O. (1984). The stability of aggression over time and generations. Developmental Psychology, 20, 1120-1134.

Jo, E., & Berkowitz, L. (1994). A priming effect analysis of media influences: An update. In J. Bryant & D. Zillmann (Eds.), Media effects (pp. 43-60). Hillsdale, NJ: Lawrence Erlbaum Associates.

Lazarus, R. S., & Alfert, E. (1964). Short-circuiting of threat by experimentally altering cognitive appraisal. Journal of Abnormal and Social Psychology, 69, 195-205.

Lazarus, R. S., Opton, E. M., Jr., Nomikos, M. S., & Rankin, N. O. (1965). The principal of short-circuiting of threat: Further evidence. Journal of Personality, 33, 622-635.

Lazarus, R. S., Speisman, M., Mordkoff, A. M., & Davidson, L. A. (1962). A laboratory study of psychological stress produced by a motion picture film. Psychological Monographs: General and Applied, 76, (34) Whole No. 553.

Leyens, J. P., & Parke, (1974). Aggressive slides can induce a weapons effect. European Journal of Social Psychology, 5 (2), 229-236.

Linz, D. G., Donnerstein, E., & Penrod, S. (1988). Effects of long-term exposure to violent and sexually degrading depictions of women. Journal of Personality and Social Psychology, 55, 758-768.

Liss, M. B., Reinhardt, L. C., & Fredriksen, S. (1983). TV heroes: The impact of rhetoric and deeds. Journal of Applied Developmental Psychology, 4, 175-187.

Mueller, C., & Donnerstein, E. (1977). The effects of humor-induced arousal upon aggressive behavior. Journal of Research In Personality, 11, 73-82.

Mueller, C. W., & Donnerstein, E. (1983). Film-induced arousal and aggressive behavior. The Journal of Social Psychology, 119, 61-67.

Mullin, C. R., & Linz, D. (1995). Desensitization and resensitization to violence against women: Effects of exposure to sexually violent films on judgments of domestic violence victims. Journal of Personality and Social Psychology, 69, 449-459.

Murray, J.P. (1994). The impact of televised violence. Hofstra Law Review, 22, 809-825.

Mussen, P. & Rutherford, E. (1961). Effects of aggressive cartoons on children's aggressive play. Journal of Abnormal and Social Psychology, 62, 461-464.

Network Television Association (December, 1992). Standards for Depiction of Violence in Television Programs.

Ogles, R. M., & Hoffner, C. (1987). Film violence and perceptions of crime: The cultivation effect. In M. L. McLaughlin (Ed.), Communication yearbook (Vol. 10, pp. 384-394). Newbury Park, CA: Sage.

Paik, H., & Comstock, G. (1994). The effects of television violence on antisocial behavior: A meta-analysis. Communication Research, 21, 516-546.

Piaget, J. (1952). The origins of intelligence in children. New York, NY: International Universities Press.

Piaget, J. (1960). The child's conception of the world. London, England: Routledge.

Potter, W. J. (1997). The problem of indexing risk of viewing television aggression. Critical Studies in Mass Communication, 14, 228-248.

Reno, J. (1993, October 20). Statement concerning violent television programming. Hearings before the U.S. Senate, Committee on Commerce, Science, & Transportation.

Sander, I. (1995). How violent is TV violence? An empirical investigation of factors influencing viewers' perceptions of TV violence. Paper presented at the International Communication Association conference, Albuquerque, NM.

Sanders, G. S., & Baron, R. S. (1975). Pain cues and uncertainty as determinants of aggression in a situation involving repeated instigation. Journal of Personality and Social Psychology, 32, 495-502.

Schmutte, G. T., & Taylor, S. P. (1980). Physical aggression as a function of alcohol and pain feedback. Journal of Social Psychology, 110, 235-244.

Siegler, R. S. (1991). Children's thinking (2nd ed.). Englewood Cliffs, NJ: Prentice-Hall.

Speisman, J. C., Lazarus, R. S., Mordkoff, A., & Davison, L. (1964). Experimental reduction of stress based on ego-defense theory. Journal of Abnormal and Social Psychology, 68, 367-380.

Steuer, F. B., Applefield, J. M., & Smith R. (1971). Televised aggression and the interpersonal aggression of preschool children. Journal of Experimental Child Psychology, 11, 442-447.

Tannenbaum, P. H., & Gaer, E. P. (1965). Mood change as a function of stress of protagonist and degree of identification in a film-viewing situation. Journal of Personality and Social Psychology, 2, 612-616.

Thomas, M. H., & Tell, P. M. (1974). Effects of viewing real versus fantasy violence upon interpersonal aggression. Journal of Research In Personality, 8, 153-160.

Whitney, C., Wartella, E., LaSorsa, D., Danielson, W., Olivarez, A., Lopez, R., & Klijn, M. (1997). Television violence in "reality" programming: University of Texas, Austin Study. National Television Violence Study Volume 1 (pp. 269-359). Thousand Oaks, CA: Sage.

Wilson, B. J., Linz D., & Randall, B. (1990). Applying social science research to film ratings: A shift from offensiveness to harmful effects. Journal of Broadcasting & Electronic Media, 34 (4), 443-468.

Wilson, B., Kunkel, D., Linz, D., Potter, J., Donnerstein, E., Smith, S., Blumenthal, E., & Gray, T. (1997). Television violence and its context: University of California, Santa Barbara study. National Television Violence Study Volume 1 (pp. 5-268). Thousand Oaks, CA: Sage.

Wilson, B., Kunkel, D., Linz, D., Potter, J., Donnerstein, E., Smith, S., Blumenthal, E., & Berry, M. (1998). Television violence and its context: University of California, Santa Barbara study. National Television Violence Study Volume 2 (pp. 5-208). Thousand Oaks, CA: Sage.

Windhausen, J. (1994). Congressional interest in the problem of television and violence. Hofstra Law Review, 22, 783-791.

Wotring, C. E., & Greenberg, B. S. (1973). Experiments in televised violence and verbal aggression: Two exploratory studies. Journal of Communication, 23, 446-460.

Zillmann, D. (1980). Television viewing and arousal. In D. Pearl, L. Bouthilet, & J. Lazar (Eds.), <u>Television & behavior: Ten years of scientific progress and implications for the eighties: Vol 2</u> (pp. 53-67). U.S. Public Health Service Publication No. ADM 82 1196. Washington, DC: U.S. Government Printing Office.

Zillmann, D. (1991). Empathy: Affect from bearing witness to the emotions of others. In J. Bryant & D. Zillmann (Eds.), <u>Responding to the screen</u> (pp. 135-167). Hillsdale, NJ: Lawrence Erlbaum.

Zillmann, D., & Bryant, J. (1991). Responding to comedy: The sense and nonsense in humor. In J. Bryant & D. Zillmann (Eds.), <u>Responding to the screen</u> (pp. 261-279). Hillsdale, NJ: Lawrence Erlbaum.

Zillmann, D., & Cantor, J. R. (1977). Affective responses to the emotions of a protagonist. <u>Journal of Experimental Social Psychology, 13,</u> 155-165.

Appendix 1

National Television Violence Study

Sample of Programs for Content Analysis

1996 - 1997

NATIONAL TELEVISION VIOLENCE STUDY

SAMPLE OF PROGRAMS FOR CONTENT ANALYSIS

The following scheduling grid displays the 3,212 programs that were randomly sampled across 23 channels from the time period of October 1996 to June 1997. Of the total 3,212 programs, 14% (N = 462) were classified as religious programs, game shows, infomercials, instructional shows, or breaking news. As specified by contract with the National Cable Television Association, these five program types were not coded, but were included in the sample so that a representative week of television programming could be compiled. A total of 159 programs (5%) were removed from the sample due to taping errors or other technical problems. The time slots they occupy on the grid are left blank. The total number of programs coded for violence is 2,750.

Overlap among programs within time slots occurs in the composite week due to the sampling procedure employed. Approximately 15% of programs in the sample overlap with other programs. Overlapping programs contain their start and end times on the grid. All statistical comparisons are based on proportions, therefore the effects of program overlap are controlled for in the study's analyses. For further explication of the sampling procedures see the Methods section of the UCSB report.

Legend for Scheduling Grid

= PARENTAL GUIDELINE

The TV Parental Guidelines include the following ratings: TVY, All Children; TVY7, Directed to Older Children; TVG, General Audience; TVPG, Parental Guidance Suggested; TV14, Parents Strongly Cautioned; and TVMA, Mature Audiences Only. Each rating is indicated by a precise numerical value (TVY = 1, TVY7 = 2; TVG = 3; TVPG = 4, TV14 = 5, and TVMA = 6) on the grid.

¥ = MOTION PICTURE ASSOCIATION OF AMERICA (MPAA) RATING

MPAA Ratings refer to those ratings given to movies by the Motion Picture Association of America. The only MPAA ratings that were observed in this sample were "G: General audiences," "PG: Parental discretion advised," "PG-13: Parents strongly cautioned," and "R: Restricted."

«» = VIOLENCE CODE

Violence codes refer to those specific content codes developed to indicate the nature of the content to appear in the program. Although the codes used in the sample apply to language, adult content, nudity, and rape, as well as violence, only the violence codes are displayed on the grid. They are "MV: Mild violence," "V: Violence," and "GV: Graphic violence."

Δ = ADVISORY

Advisories refer to those short messages that precede programs. Advisories can take a variety of forms, but typically involve advocating caution or discretion regarding the upcoming program (e.g., "viewer discretion advised").

ABC

	SATURDAY	SUNDAY	MONDAY	TUESDAY	WEDNESDAY	THURSDAY	FRIDAY
6:00 am	Nick News 10/26	3 This Old House 2/2	News 12/2	News 4/29	News 3/12	News 5/8	News 5/2
6:30 am	New Doug 11/30	3 This Old House 3/2	News 5/19	News 3/4	News 3/12	News 5/22	News 1/31
7:00 am		News 1/12	Good Morning America 2/10	Good Morning America 10/8	Good Morning America 12/4	Good Morning America 10/17	Good Morning America 11/1
7:30 am	Healthy Kids 3/8						
8:00 am	Mighty Ducks 10/26	Good Morning America 1/26					
8:30 am	2 Mighty Ducks 3/15						
9:00 am	Bugs Bunny 10/19	News 11/3	3 Regis & Kathie Lee 2/3	Regis & Kathie Lee 10/15		3 Regis & Kathie Lee 1/23	Regis & Kathie Lee 2/14
9:30 am	1 Bugs Bunny 9-10am 5/31						
10:00 am	Bone Chillers 11/2	This Week 10/27	4 Caryl & Marilyn 3/10	3 Caryl & Marilyn 1/28	4 Caryl & Marilyn 1/15	3 Caryl & Marilyn 2/13	3 Caryl & Marilyn 5/16
10:30 am	2 Gargoyles 2/1						
11:00 am	1 Winnie the Pooh 4/19	Wall Street Journal Report 11/3	The City 11/4	4 A Day Time 4/22	5 The City 3/5	4 The City 1/16	4 The City 3/21
11:30 am	1 Weekend Special 4/26	3 Vista L.A. 2/2	News 3/17	News 12/3	News 3/19	News 3/20	News 1/24
12:00 pm	4 Extremists 10/19	3 Main Floor 4/20	4 All My Children 1/13	All My Children 10/22	All My Children 11/6	4 All My Children 1/30	All My Children 12/6
12:30 pm	1 Educating Mom 3/15	Extremists 4/27					
1:00 pm		American Sportswomen 10/6	One Life to Live 12/2	One Life to Live 11/5	One Life to Live 10/16	One Life to Live 10/31	One Life to Live 10/11
1:30 pm							
2:00 pm	College Basketball 1-3pm 1/11	Soccer 1:30-4pm 3/16	5 General Hospital 3/3	4 General Hospital 2/4	General Hospital 10/30	5 General Hospital 3/6	General Hospital 11/8
2:30 pm							
3:00 pm	Bowling 4/19	Hispanic Heritage Awards 10/13	Oprah 10/7	5 Oprah 2/11	Oprah 10/23	Oprah 11/7	4 Oprah 2/7
3:30 pm							
4:00 pm		Disney's Halloween 3:30-5pm 10/20	News 4-5pm 5/12	News 3/11	News 2/12	News 3/13	News 1/31
4:30 pm			ABC News 11/4				
5:00 pm	Wide World of Sports 1/18	3 TV.Com 5/11	News 4/21	News 10/29	News 10/9	News 12/5	News 3/7
5:30 pm		ABC News 3/2					
6:00 pm	News 2/8	News 5/4	News 5/19	News 10/22	News 3/19	News 5/8	News 5/2
6:30 pm	ABC News 2/1	Siskel & Ebert 12/1	ABC News 4/28	ABC News 4/29	ABC News 4/23	ABC News 4/24	ABC News 3/21
7:00 pm	Jeopardy! 11/2	3 Funniest Home Videos 4/20	Jeopardy! 5/5	3 Jeopardy! 5/20	3 Jeopardy! 1/22	3 Jeopardy! 3/20	Jeopardy! 10/25
7:30 pm	3 Wheel of Fortune 2/8	Funniest Home Videos 5/4	3 Wheel of Fortune 5/26	Wheel of Fortune 12/3	3 Wheel of Fortune 5/14	3 Wheel of Fortune 4/24	3 Wheel of Fortune 1/24
8:00 pm	Second Noah 10/12	Vanessa Williams 12/1	3 Spy Game 3/17	4 Home Improvement 5/6	3 Grace Under Fire 4/23	4 High Incident 5/1	Δ Family Matters 10/25
8:30 pm				4 Life's Work 5/27	4 Coach 1/29		3 Boy Meets World 5/23
9:00 pm	4 Δ Boomerang 9-11pm 3/1	4 Seduction in a Small Town 2/9	4 Tell Me No Secrets 1/20	3 Home Improvement 3/4	4 Drew Carry 3/5	Murder One 10/24	Sabrina 10/18
9:30 pm				4 Drew Carey 5/20	5 Ellen 5/7		Clueless 10/18
10:00 pm	Behind Closed Doors 1/25			5 Δ NYPD Blue 1/21	Primetime Live 2/5	4 Murder One 9-11pm 5/29	20/20 5/23
10:30 pm							

Key: # Parental Guideline (1 = TVY, 2 = TVY7, 3 = TVG, 4 = TVPG, 5 = TV14, 6 = TVMA) ¥ MPAA Rating «» Violence Code Δ Advisory

CBS

	SATURDAY	SUNDAY	MONDAY	TUESDAY	WEDNESDAY	THURSDAY	FRIDAY
6:00 am	Field Trip 1/25	Singsation 4/27	News 3/10	News 11/5	News 4/23	News 5/1	News 5/9
6:30 am	Δ PE TV 4/19	From the Heart Ministries 4/20					
7:00 am	2 The Mask 2/8	Key of David 10/27	This Morning 6/2	This Morning 3/11	This Morning 10/9	This Morning 4/24	This Morning 2/14
7:30 am							
8:00 am	The Mask 11/30	CBS Sunday Morning 5/11	This Morning 5/12	This Morning 6/3	This Morning 6/4	This Morning 5/29	This Morning 5/16
8:30 am	Project Geeker 10/26						
9:00 am	College Basketball 9-11am 2/8	Face the Nation 10/27	Guiding Light 10/14	5 Guiding Light 4/22	Guiding Light 11/6	5 Guiding Light 5/8	5 Guiding Light 5/16
9:30 am		Bob Navarro's Journal 4/20					
10:00 am	Skiing 1/11	Basketball Championships 10am-12pm 3/9	3 Price is Right 1/20	3 Price is Right 2/11	3 Price is Right 3/12	3 Price is Right 3/6	Price is Right 11/8
10:30 am							
11:00 am	NCAA Basketball 11am-1pm 3/15		5 Young & the Restless 4/21	5 Young & the Restless 1/21	5 Young & the Restless 3/19	5 Young & the Restless 2/6	5 Young & the Restless 5/2
11:30 am							
12:00 pm		College Basketball 11am-1:30pm 1/26	News 5/5	News 3/18	News 1/22	News 5/22	News 5/23
12:30 pm	College Basketball 1/18		5 Bold & the Beautiful 5/5	5 Bold & the Beautiful 5/20	5 Bold & the Beautiful 5/7	Bold & the Beautiful 10/31	5 Bold & the Beautiful 5/23
1:00 pm			5 As the World Turns 4/21	5 As the World Turns 5/13	As the World Turns 12/4	As the World Turns 11/7	5 As the World Turns 3/21
1:30 pm							
2:00 pm	Golf 1-3pm 4/26	Olympic Winterfest 1/19	5 Gordon Elliot 4/28	Gordon Elliot 1/14	4 Gordon Elliot 4/30	Gordon Elliot 1/16	Gordon Elliot 10/11
2:30 pm							
3:00 pm	Infomercials 3/1	4 Entertainment Tonight 6/1	4 Hard Copy 5/5		4 Hard Copy 1/22	4 Hard Copy 5/8	4 Hard Copy 4/25
3:30 pm		Martha Stewart Living 11/3		Highway Patrol 5/20	Highway Patrol 5/7	Highway Patrol 5/22	Highway Patrol 5/23
4:00 pm	Beakman's World 1/25	4 Psi Factor 4-5pm 5/4	Day & Date 12/2	3 Geraldo 3/4	4 Geraldo 1/15	Day & Date 10/10	3 Geraldo 6/6
4:30 pm	1 Δ Storybreak 4/19	Face the Nation 3/2					
5:00 pm	Coastguard 11/2	4 Fire Rescue 3/9	News 3/3	News 10/15	News 3/5	News 5/1	News 4/25
5:30 pm	CBS News 10/12	CBS News 3/2					
6:00 pm	News 3/8	News 11/3	News 11/4	News 4/22	News 5/21	News 10/31	News 5/2
6:30 pm							
7:00 pm	Entertainment Tonight 10/19	60 Minutes 10/20	Hard Copy 4/28	Hard Copy 5/6	Hard Copy 12/4	4 Hard Copy 5/8	4 Hard Copy 5/16
7:30 pm			Entertainment Tonight 10/28	4 Entertainment Tonight 5/6	4 Entertainment Tonight 5/21	Entertainment Tonight 1/30	4 Entertainment Tonight 5/23
8:00 pm	Dr. Quinn, Medicine Woman 10/26	Touched by an Angel 10/13	3 Cosby 5/12	Promised Land 10/8	4 The Nanny 5/7	Diagnosis Murder 10/17	4 Jag 5/23
8:30 pm			Ink 10/28		4 Dave's World 5/7		
9:00 pm	Early Edition 10/5		4 Cybil 4/28			Moloney 12/5	Disney's Beauty & the Beast 12/6
9:30 pm			4 Ink 5/19	3 Too Close to Home 4/29	5 Δ The Last Don 5/14		
10:00 pm	5 Walker, Texas Ranger 4/19		Chicago Hope 10/7			48 Hours 5/29	5 Nash Bridges 1/17
10:30 pm							

Key: # Parental Guideline (1 = TVY, 2 = TVY7, 3 = TVG, 4 = TVPG, 5 = TV14, 6 = TVMA) ¥ MPAA Rating «» Violence Code Δ Advisory

199

FOX	SATURDAY	SUNDAY	MONDAY	TUESDAY	WEDNESDAY	THURSDAY	FRIDAY
6:00 am	3 Flintstones 1/18	3 Infomercial 1/26	News 10/21	News 10/8	News 10/16	News 12/5	News 3/7
6:30 am	1 Sky Dancer 2/1	3 In Touch 1/12					
7:00 am	C-Bear & Jamal 10/19		Good Day L.A. 4/21	Good Day L.A. 11/5	Good Day L.A. 10/9	Good Day L.A. 2/6	Good Day L.A. 10/18
7:30 am	Fox Kids Monsterama 10/26	3 In Touch 7-8am 6/1					
8:00 am	2 △ Power Rangers 4/19	Fox News Sunday 10/13					
8:30 am	Spider-Man 11/30						
9:00 am	△ Goosebumps 11/2	Midday Sunday 4/27	3 After Breakfast 3/17	3 After Breakfast 5/6	3 After Breakfast 3/19	3 After Breakfast 3/6	3 After Breakfast 3/14
9:30 am	1 △ Eerie, Indiana 3/8	3 Infomercials 9:30-11am 5/4					
10:00 am	1 △ Life with Louie 4/19		4 Dating Game 4/28	Infomercial 1/21	Dating Game 5/7	Dating Game 1/16	Dating Game 1/24
10:30 am	2 X-Men 1/11	Infomercial 1/19	Newlywed Game 10/28	Newlywed Game 10/15	Newlywed Game 2/12	Newlywed Game 10/17	Newlywed Game 2/7
11:00 am	1 C-Bear & Jamal 1/25	Midday Sunday 2/9	I Love Lucy 10/7	3 I Love Lucy 1/14		I Love Lucy 11/7	3 I Love Lucy 5/16
11:30 am	3 WMAC Masters 2/8	Andy Griffith 2/2	3 I Love Lucy 2/3	I Love Lucy 2/11	I Love Lucy 4/30	I Love Lucy 3/13	3 I Love Lucy 3/21
12:00 pm	WCW Wrestling 10/12	3 Andy Griffith 6/1	3 Andy Griffith 4/28	Andy Griffith 10/29	3 Andy Griffith 5/7	3 Andy Griffith 2/13	3 Andy Griffith 1/17
12:30 pm		3 Andy Griffith 6/1	Andy Griffith 12/2	3 Andy Griffith 3/18	Andy Griffith 10/30	Andy Griffith 10/24	3 Andy Griffith 5/16
1:00 pm	3 Gilligan's Island 3/15	3 Gilligan's Island 6/1	Beverly Hillbillies 10/28	3 Beverly Hillbillies 2/4	3 Beverly Hillbillies 4/23	3 Beverly Hillbillies 1/23	Beverly Hillbillies 10/11
1:30 pm	Gilligan's Island 10/19	3 Gilligan's Island 6/1	3 Beverly Hillbillies 5/5	3 Beverly Hillbillies 1/14	3 Beverly Hillbillies 5/14	3 Beverly Hillbillies 3/20	3 Beverly Hillbillies 5/23
2:00 pm	3 Wonder Years 5/10	3 Wonder Years 3/16	1 △ Spider-Man 5/19	Brady Bunch 4/29	Brady Bunch 4/30	Bobby's World 10/24	1 Spider-Man 5/16
2:30 pm	Wonder Years 11/30	3 Wonder Years 5/25	Peter Pan & the Pirates 11/4	1 Peter Pan & the Pirates 2/11	Brady Bunch 1/22	2 △ Batman & Robin 4/24	
3:00 pm	3 Happy Days 1/11	3 Happy Days 1/19		1 △ Bobby's World 5/20	2 Batman & Robin 2/5	2 △ Batman & Robin 3/13	2 Batman & Robin 1/24
3:30 pm	3 Happy Days 4/26	Happy Days 12/1	1 △ Life with Louie 5/12	Spider-Man 12/3	1 △ Spider-Man 4/23	1 Spider-Man 1/30	1 △ Casper 5/23
4:00 pm	I Love Lucy 10/26	I Love Lucy 11/3	Big Bad Beetleborgs 11/4	1 △ Big Bad Beetleborgs 5/13	Big Bad Beetleborgs 11/6	1 △ Big Bad Beetleborgs 5/1	Big Bad Beetleborgs 12/6
4:30 pm	3 Mr. Belvedere 5/10	3 I Love Lucy 4/20	Power Rangers 12/2	2 △ Power Rangers 4/29	2 △ Power Rangers 3/19	Power Rangers 12/5	2 △ Power Rangers 5/23
5:00 pm		I Love Lucy 5/11	3 Hangin' with Mr. Cooper 5/19	Hangin' with Mr. Cooper 10/29	3 Hangin' with Mr. Cooper 6/4	Hangin' with Mr. Cooper 1/23	Hangin' with Mr. Cooper 10/11
5:30 pm	I Love Lucy 10/5	I Love Lucy 11/3	Happy Days 1/20	4 Married with Children 5/20	4 Married with Children 5/21	Married with Children 2/13	4 Married with Children 5/16
6:00 pm	I Love Lucy 5/3	4 Outer Limits 4/20	3 Home Improvement 5/19	Home Improvement 12/3	Home Improvement 12/4	3 Home Improvement 1/16	3 Home Improvement 5/2
6:30 pm	3 I Love Lucy 5/3		4 Simpsons 1/13	4 Simpsons 5/20	Simpsons 12/4	Simpsons 11/7	4 Simpsons 4/25
7:00 pm	3 Home Improvement 3/15	5 △ X-Files 7-8pm 1/26	3 Home Improvement 5/19	Simpsons 1/21	3 Home Improvement 2/12	3 Home Improvement 5/1	Home Improvement 12/6
7:30 pm	Married with Children 10/5	Married with Children 12/1	Simpsons 10/7	4 Simpsons 5/20	4 Simpsons 1/15	4 Simpsons 4/24	4 Simpsons 1/31
8:00 pm	4 △ Cops 5/17	4 Simpsons 5/11	4 Melrose Place 1/27	Coneheads 10/15	4 Beverly Hills, 90210 1/22	5 △ World's Scariest 8-9pm 5/15	Sliders 11/8
8:30 pm	4 △ Cops 1/25	4 King of the Hill 2/2				Hangin' with Mr. Cooper 10/10	
9:00 pm	Cops 11/2	5 X-Files 9-10pm 3/16	4 Ned & Stacey 1/20		4 Party of Five 9-10pm 2/5	Simpsons 10/10	
9:30 pm	4 Most Wanted 9-10pm 5/10	Worlds Funniest Outakes 10/6	5 Married with Children 1/13		Home Improvement 10/9	5 N. Y. Undercover 9-10pm 6/5	
10:00 pm	News 1/18	News 10/20	News 10/14	News 10/22	News 10/30	News 10/31	News 11/1
10:30 pm							

Key: # Parental Guideline (1 = TVY, 2 = TVY7, 3 = TVG, 4 = TVPG, 5 = TV14, 6 = TVMA) ¥ MPAA Rating «» Violence Code △ Advisory

NBC

	SATURDAY	SUNDAY	MONDAY	TUESDAY	WEDNESDAY	THURSDAY	FRIDAY
6:00 am / 6:30 am	Today 5-7am 10/26	Today 1/19	News 10/28	News 12/3	News 10/9	News 5/15	News 10/11
7:00 am / 7:30 am	News 10/5	Meet the Press 2/2	Today 12/2	Today 2/4	Today 10/30		Today 2/7
8:00 am / 8:30 am	News 2/8	News 11/3					
9:00 am / 9:30 am	Saved by the Bell 10/12 — Hang Time 10/19		4 Leeza 3/3	4 Leeza 4/22	5 Leeza 2/12	4 Leeza 3/13	Real Life 11/8
10:00 am / 10:30 am	Saved by the Bell 10/12 — 2 California Dreams 3/1	Making Love Work 10/27	4 Maureen O'Boyle 2/3	Leeza 10/8	Leeza 12/4	4 Maureen O'Boyle 5/8	4 Maureen O'Boyle 3/21
11:00 am	2 NBA Inside Stuff 2/1	Basketball 11am-12pm 5/25	News 5/5	News 5/6	News 4/23	News 5/22	News 1/31
11:30 am	1 News for Kids 5/17	NBA Showtime 3/9	4 Extra! 4/28	4 Extra! 5/13	Court TV 1/29	4 Extra! 5/22	4 Extra! 5/16
12:00 pm / 12:30 pm	NBA Showtime 5/3 — 2 NFL Youth Special 1/25	NBA Playoff 12-2:30pm 5/4	5 Another World 3/17	Days of Our Lives 11/5	5 Another World 3/5	5 Another World 2/6	5 Another World 5/9
1:00 pm / 1:30 pm		NBA Basketball 12:30-3pm 3/2	Another World 10/7	5 Days of Our Lives 3/4	Another World 11/6	5 Days of Our Lives 3/20	5 Days of Our Lives 1/17
2:00 pm / 2:30 pm	Gymnastics 1-3pm 4/19	NFL Playoff 1-4pm 1/12	5 Sunset Beach 1/13	5 Sunset Beach 4/29	Maureen O'Boyle 10/16	5 Sunset Beach 1/30	Maureen O'Boyle 10/18
3:00 pm / 3:30 pm	2 △ News for Kids 3/15 — NBC News 10/5		3 Rosie O'Donnell 1/20	Rosie O'Donnell 10/15	Rosie O'Donnell 10/23	Rosie O'Donnell 10/24	Rosie O'Donnell 11/1
4:00 pm / 4:30 pm	3 Travels with Chuck Henry 1/11 — 3 Big Spin 3/1	News 4/20	News 10/21	News 1/21	News 2/5	News 3/6	News 4-5pm 5/23 — NBC News 10/11
5:00 pm / 5:30 pm	News 3/8	NBC News 3/16	News 1/27	News 3/11	News 1/15	News 5/15	News 5/2
6:00 pm / 6:30 pm	NBC News 2/1 — McLaughlin Group 4/26	News 2/9	News 11/4	News 2/11	News 1/22	News 6/5 — NBC News 1/23	News 1/24
7:00 pm / 7:30 pm	Extra! 11/2	Dateline NBC 10/20	4 Extra! 4/21 — 4 Access Hollywood 3/10	4 Extra! 1/14 — Access Hollywood 10/22	4 Extra! 3/12 — 4 Access Hollywood 4/23	4 Extra! 1/16 — 4 Access Hollywood 3/13	4 Extra! 5/23 — 4 Access Hollywood 5/23
8:00 pm / 8:30 pm	Dark Skies 10/19	3rd Rock from the Sun 10/20 — 4 Boston Common 3/9	4 3rd Rock from the Sun 2/10	4 Mad About You 5/6 — 4 Caroline in the City 5/13	4 △ Ace Ventura 8-10pm 4/30 — John Larroquette 10/9	4 Friends 5/22 — 4 3rd Rock from the Sun 5/22	Unsolved Mysteries 12/6
9:00 pm / 9:30 pm	4 Pretender 1/11	Night Visitors 10/13	A Kiss so Deadly 10/14	4 Frasier 1/14 — 4 Access Hollywood 5/27	4 Wings 3/12 — 4 Men Behaving Badly 1/29	Seinfeld 10/17 — 4 Naked Truth 1/23	Dateline NBC 3/14
10:00 pm / 10:30 pm	TV Censored Bloopers 11/30			Dateline NBC 10/29	4 Pretender 3/19	ER 10/17	Homicide 10/25

Key: # Parental Guideline (1 = TVY, 2 = TVY7, 3 = TVG, 4 = TVPG, 5 = TV14, 6 = TVMA) ¥ MPAA Rating «» Violence Code △ Advisory

KCET	SATURDAY	SUNDAY	MONDAY	TUESDAY	WEDNESDAY	THURSDAY	FRIDAY
6:00 am / 6:30 am	Sesame Street 3/1	Sesame Street 10/13	Sesame Street 11/4	Sesame Street 1/21	Sesame Street 11/6	Sesame Street 1/30	Sesame Street 1/17
7:00 am	Reading Rainbow 11/30	Kidsongs 11/3	Barney & Friends 4/21	Mister Rogers 12/3	Barney & Friends 2/5	Mister Rogers 1/16	Barney & Friends 2/14
7:30 am	Big Comfy Couch 3/8	Magic School Bus 2/9	Storytime 2/10	Storytime 4/22	Storytime 10/30		Storytime 11/1
8:00 am	Barney & Friends 11/30	Magic School Bus 11/3	Lamb Chop's Play Along! 4/28	Puzzle Place 2/4	Lamb Chop's Play Along! 5/21	Lamb Chop's Play Along! 2/6	Lamb Chop's Play Along! 5/2
8:30 am	Big Comfy Couch 2/1	Puzzle Place 3/16	Arthur 1/13	Arthur 10/29	Arthur 10/9	Arthur 1/23	Arthur 4/25
9:00 am	Storytime 1/18	Storytime 2/2	Barney & Friends 4/28	Barney & Friends 11/5	Barney & Friends 4/30	Barney & Friends 1/16	Barney & Friends 1/31
9:30 am	Crossroads Cafe 4/26	Donna's Day 2/9	Puzzle Place 10/28	Puzzle Place 2/11	Puzzle Place 1/22	Puzzle Place 10/10	Puzzle Place 3/21
10:00 am	Victory Garden 1/25	Life & Times 10/27	Sesame Street 12/2	Sesame Street 10/15	Sesame Street 2/12	Sesame Street 12/5	Sesame Street 10/11
10:30 am	Victory Garden 4/26	Life & Times 3/16					
11:00 am	Jacques Pepin's Kitchen 3/8	Mystery! 10/20	Storytime 5/12	Storytime 4/22	Storytime 10/16	Storytime 5/1	Storytime 2/14
11:30 am	Taste of Africa 4/19		Shining Time Station 5/26	Shining Time Station 1/28	Shining Time Station 4/30	Shining Time Station 3/6	Shining Time Station 5/2
12:00 pm	Baking with Julia 1/11	M. Theatre 1/19	Puzzle Place 1/27	Puzzle Place 5/13	Puzzle Place 2/5	Puzzle Place 3/20	Puzzle Place 11/1
12:30 pm	Frugal Gourmet 10/26		Mister Rogers 5/26	Mister Rogers 3/4	Crossroads Cafe 10/30	Mister Rogers 5/29	Mister Rogers 5/9
1:00 pm	To the Contrary 10/5	Alchemy in Light 3/2	Reading Rainbow 3/3	Reading Rainbow 12/3	Magic School Bus 1/29	Reading Rainbow 3/13	Reading Rainbow 5/9
1:30 pm	Rights & Wrongs 10/19	American Experience 1:30-3:30pm 1/26	Magic School Bus 4/21	Arthur 1/28	Magic School Bus 12/4	Magic School Bus 5/1	Arthur 1/24
2:00 pm	Firing Line 10/26		Spilled Milk 1/20	Arthur 10/8	Faces of Culture 3/12	Arthur 10/31	Crossroads Cafe 2/7
2:30 pm	John McLaughlin's One on One 11/2			Parent Puzzle 5/20	America in Perspective 4/23	Time to Grow 4/24	
3:00 pm	Life & Times 10/19	M. Theatre 2-4pm 1/12	Newshour with Jim Lehrer 10/14	Newshour with Jim Lehrer 10/22	Newshour with Jim Lehrer 12/4	Newshour with Jim Lehrer 2/13	Newshour with Jim Lehrer 3/7
3:30 pm	Tony Brown's Journal 2/8						
4:00 pm	Think Tank 2/1	Chicano! 4-5pm 4/27	Wishbone 2/10	Wishbone 4/29	Wishbone 1/29	Wishbone 10/10	Wishbone 3/21
4:30 pm	Voices in Harmony 4:30-6pm 3/15	National Geographic 12/1	Carmen San Diego 5/12	Carmen San Diego 11/5	Carmen San Diego 10/23	Carmen San Diego 10/17	Carmen San Diego 12/6
5:00 pm			Bill Nye 1/13	Bill Nye 2/4	Bill Nye 10/9	Kratt's Creatures 2/6	Kratt's Creatures 10/18
5:30 pm	New Yankee Workshop 1/25		America's Family Kitchen 1/27	Modern Thai Cuisine 5/13	Cooking with Caprial 10/16	Cooking at the Academy 3/6	Frugal Gourmet 10/25
6:00 pm	California's Gold 1/18		Nightly Business Report 3/17	Nightly Business Report 3/4	Nightly Business Report 3/5	Nightly Business Report 4/24	Nightly Business Report 1/24
6:30 pm	Visiting with Huell Howser 1/11	Ancestors 1/12	Newshour with Jim Lehrer 2/3	Newshour with Jim Lehrer 10/8	Newshour with Jim Lehrer 5/7	Newshour with Jim Lehrer 10/17	Newshour with Jim Lehrer 3/14
7:00 pm	Nova 10/12						
7:30 pm		California's Gold 10/27	Life & Times 3/3	Life & Times 5/20	Life & Times 1/22	Life & Times 10/31	Life & Times 10/25
8:00 pm	Keeping Up Appearances 2/8	American Experience 10/6	John Tesh Concert 8-10pm 3/10	A Laugh, A Tear, A Mitzvah 3/11	Δ More Straight Talk on Menopause 3/19	Great Railway Journeys 11/7	Washington Week 1/17
8:30 pm	As Times Go By 4/19						Wall Street Week 4/25
9:00 pm / 9:30 pm	Δ Network 10/5		Great Performances 10/21	Frontline 9-10pm 1/14	Great Performances 5/14	Mystery! 10/24	David Frost 1/31
10:00 pm							
10:30 pm				Entrepreneurial Revolution 5/6	Bill T. Jones 1/15	Δ P.O.V. 5/8	

Key: # Parental Guideline (1 = TVY, 2 = TVY7, 3 = TVG, 4 = TVPG, 5 = TV14, 6 = TVMA) ¥ MPAA Rating «» Violence Code Δ Advisory

202

KTLA

	SATURDAY	SUNDAY	MONDAY	TUESDAY	WEDNESDAY	THURSDAY	FRIDAY
6:00 am	Infomercial 2/1	Pacesetters 1/19	News 2/10	News 1/28	News 12/4	News 2/6	News 11/8
6:30 am	2 PC4U 4/19	Making It 2/2					
7:00 am	All Dogs Go to Heaven 1/18	Creflo A. Dollar 10/27	Morning News 1/13	Morning News 10/29	Morning News 3/5	Morning News 10/17	Morning News 12/6
7:30 am	1 Richie Rich 4/26	Kenneth Copeland 2/9					
8:00 am	Infomercial 3/8						
8:30 am	1 Animaniacs 1/25	Oscar's Orchestra 12/1					
9:00 am	2 Superman 3/1	3 Gladiators 2000 1/12	4 Sally Jesse 3/17	Sally Jesse 10/22	4 Sally Jesse 1/22	Sally Jesse 12/5	Sally Jesse 10/18
9:30 am	1 Road Rovers 4/19	Dodgers Pregame 3/16					
10:00 am	1 Waynehead 4/26	Saved by the Bell 12/1		Scoop 1/14	Scoop 11/6	Scoop 10/24	Scoop 10/11
10:30 am	Pinky & the Brain 11/30	Saved by the Bell 10/27					
11:00 am	Animaniacs 11/30		News 4/21	News 2/4	News 4/30	News 10/31	News 11/1
11:30 am	Earthworm Jim 10/12		Charles in Charge 6/2	Sally Jesse 12/3	Charles in Charge 4/30	Infomercial 3/13	Honeymooners 2/7
12:00 pm	Saved by the Bell 1/25	Alice in Wonderland 11/3	Hunter 12-1pm 2/3		Brady Bunch 5/21	Hunter 3/6	Sally Jesse 11:30-12:30pm 10/25
12:30 pm	Saved by the Bell 3/1		Pat Bullard 10/14	Brady Bunch 12-1pm 4/22	Brady Bunch 5/21		Brady Bunch 5/30
1:00 pm	California Dreams 3/8			Sally Jesse 1-2pm 2/11	Sally Jesse 2/5	4 Sally Jesse 1-2pm 4/24	5 Sally Jesse 3/14
1:30 pm	Charles in Charge 10/26		4 Sally Jesse 1-2pm 5/12	Blossom 11/5		Blossom 10/10	
2:00 pm	Soul Train 1/18	Adventures of Sinbad 10/13	Blossom 4/28	Blossom 3/18	Dinosaurs 12/4	Blossom 2/13	
2:30 pm			Dinosaurs 3/3	Dinosaurs 3/4	Dinosaurs 4/23	Dinosaurs 3/20	Dinosaurs 2/14
3:00 pm	4 Adventures of Sinbad 3/15	Superman III 10/6	1 Bugs 'n' Daffy 3/10	Bugs 'n' Daffy 10/22	Bugs 'n' Daffy 10/16	Bugs 'n' Daffy 10/31	1 Bugs 'n' Daffy 4/25
3:30 pm			1 Animaniacs 4/28	1 Animaniacs 1/21	1 Animaniacs 5/7	Animaniacs 10/24	1 Animaniacs 5/23
4:00 pm	Hercules 10/5		Beverly Hills, 90210 12/2	Beverly Hills, 90210 10/8		Beverly Hills, 90210 1/23	Beverly Hills, 90210 1/31
4:30 pm							
5:00 pm	Xena 10/19	Alice in Wonderland 10/20	Saved by the Bell 2/3	Saved by the Bell 12/3	Saved by the Bell 10/9	Saved by the Bell 10/10	Saved by the Bell 11/1
5:30 pm			Family Matters 3/17	Family Matters 11/5	Family Matters 2/5	Family Matters 3/13	Family Matters 4/25
6:00 pm	She's in the Army Now 10/26		Fresh Prince 5/5	Fresh Prince 3/4	Fresh Prince 5/21	Fresh Prince 12/5	Fresh Prince 6/6
6:30 pm			Fresh Prince 5/5	Fresh Prince 2/11	Fresh Prince 10/30	Fresh Prince 1/30	Fresh Prince 5/23
7:00 pm		3 Brotherly Love 3/2	Bzzz 11/4	4 Bzzz 3/11	4 Bzzz 5/21	Bzzz 3/20	3 Bzzz 2/7
7:30 pm		3 Nick Freno 3/9	4 Seinfeld 3/10	Seinfeld 1/21	4 Seinfeld 5/7	Seinfeld 1/23	4 Seinfeld 6/6
8:00 pm	4 Hercules 5/3	3 Sister, Sister 1/26	7th Heaven 10/21	Medicine Man 10/15	3 Sister, Sister 1/22	¥ △ FX 2 1/16	¥ «» Delta Force II 1/24
8:30 pm		3 Steve Harvey 2/2			3 Steve Harvey 5/28		
9:00 pm	Xena 1/11	4 Unhappily Ever After 2/9	△ Savannah 10/7		△ Wayans Bros. 10/30		
9:30 pm		4 Life with Roger 3/2			Jamie Foxx 10/9		
10:00 pm	News 2/8	News 1/12	News 1/27	News 10/15	News 10/16	News 11/7	News 1/17
10:30 pm							

Key: # Parental Guideline (1 = TVY, 2 = TVY7, 3 = TVG, 4 = TVPG, 5 = TV14, 6 = TVMA) ¥ MPAA Rating «» Violence Code △ Advisory

203

KCOP	SATURDAY	SUNDAY	MONDAY	TUESDAY	WEDNESDAY	THURSDAY	FRIDAY
6:00 am	Infomercials 10/26	2 Jumanji 3/2	700 Club 12/2	700 Club 5/6	700 Club 1/22	700 Club 2/13	700 Club 1/24
6:30 am		Real Life...Religion that Works 3/9					
7:00 am		Why Why Family 12/1	2 Mega Man 2/3	2 Mega Man 3/11	2 Mega Man 4/30	2 Mega Man 1/23	
7:30 am		Δ L.A. Kids 4/27	Samurai Pizza Cats 4/21	Samurai Pizza Cats 10/29	Samurai Pizza Cats 10/9	Samurai Pizza Cats 5/29	Samurai Pizza Cats 5/9
8:00 am	Infomercials 8-10am 1/25	Adventures of Oliver Twist 10/20	3 In the House 4/28	Pink Panther 3/18	Pink Panther 3/19	Pink Panther 1/16	Dinobabies 1/17
8:30 am		Dragon Flyz 10/6	Step by Step 10/7	Step by Step 5/27	Step by Step 4/30	Step by Step 12/5	Step by Step 5/30
9:00 am	Infomercial 10/26	2 Jumanji 4/27	Jenny Jones 11/4		Jenny Jones 10/9	Jenny Jones 10/17	Dr. Quinn 5/30
9:30 am	Infomercials (con't) 1/25	Mouse & the Monster 10/20					
10:00 am	Infomercials 1/11	2 Incredible Hulk 3/16	Dr. Quinn 10/14	Everyday Living 1/21	Everyday Living 3/12	Everyday Living 3/20	Dr. Quinn 11/8
10:30 am		2 B.A.D. 3/9					
11:00 am		Dream Big 11/3	News Scope 10/7	News Scope 11/5	3 Jenny Jones 4/23	News Scope 10/24	4 Jenny Jones 3/21
11:30 am		Ghostwriter 12/1					
12:00 pm	Across the Tracks 10/5	4 Baywatch 1/26	Baywatch 10/21	Ricki Lake 1/28	Baywatch 12/4	Baywatch 11/7	4 Montel Williams 3/14
12:30 pm							
1:00 pm		Blazing Saddles 10/13	Ricki Lake 1/27	Ricki Lake 2/4	Richard Bey 10/16	Ricki Lake 3/6	Richard Bey 10/18
1:30 pm							
2:00 pm	Honeysuckle Rose 11/30		5 Jenny Jones 2/10	Jenny Jones 10/22	3 Jenny Jones 3/5	Jenny Jones 12/5	4 Jenny Jones 1/31
2:30 pm							
3:00 pm		The Man in the Iron Mask 10/27	Judge Judy 10/28	Judge Judy 3/11	Judge Judy 2/12	Judge Judy 3/13	3 Judge Judy 5/30
3:30 pm			News 3/10	News 3/18	News 1/29	News 5/8	News 5/23
4:00 pm	Tootsie 10/19		4 Montel Williams 2/3	4 Montel Williams 2/11	Montel Williams 10/30	Montel Williams 10/31	4 Montel Williams 3/7
4:30 pm							
5:00 pm		4 Crocodile Dundee 2/2	Ricki Lake 3/3	Ricki Lake 10/29	Ricki Lake 11/6	Ricki Lake 1/30	Ricki Lake 10/11
5:30 pm							
6:00 pm	Δ Lethal Weapon 11/2		Mad About You 1/13	Martin 4/22	Martin 5/7	Martin 10/10	Martin 5/30
6:30 pm			Roseanne 3/17	Martin 4/22	Roseanne 2/12	Martin 5/8	Martin 5/30
7:00 pm			Martin 1/20	Deep Space Nine 10/15	Martin 3/19	Martin 1/16	Deep Space Nine 11/1
7:30 pm			Roseanne 5/5		Martin 1/29	Roseanne 5/1	
8:00 pm	Δ Extreme Prejudice 10/12	4 Star Trek: Voyager 4/20	In the House 1/13	Them 10/8	4 The Sentinel 2/5	4 Deep Space Nine 4/24	
8:30 pm			3 In the House 1/27				
9:00 pm		News 1/26	3 Moesha 3/10		4 Star Trek: Voyager 1/15	Babylon 5 10/10	FX: The Series 10/25
9:30 pm		Talking About Sports 3/16	3 Moesha 3/17				
10:00 pm	News 1/18	News 11/3	News 10/28	News 12/3	News 10/23	News 2/6	News 4/25
10:30 pm							

Key: # Parental Guideline (1 = TVY, 2 = TVY7, 3 = TVG, 4 = TVPG, 5 = TV14, 6 = TVMA) ¥ MPAA Rating «» Violence Code Δ Advisory

KCAL	SATURDAY	SUNDAY	MONDAY	TUESDAY	WEDNESDAY	THURSDAY	FRIDAY
6:00 am	Infomercial 2/8	Harvest Fire 3/9	Dennis the Menace 12/2	Dennis the Menace 5/6	Dennis the Menace 2/5	Yogi & Friends 3/13	Dennis the Menace 5/30
6:30 am	Eagle Riders 11/2	Rod Parsley 4/20	1 Bananas in Pajamas 4/28	Bananas in Pajamas 11/5	1 Bananas in Pajamas 4/23	1 Bananas in Pajamas 3/6	1 Bananas in Pajamas 5/30
7:00 am	Dragon Ball Z 1/25	Coral Ridge 10/13		The Mask 1/28	The Mask 3/5	The Mask 11/7	The Mask 10/25
7:30 am	Sing Me a Story 4/19		Masked Rider 4/28	Masked Rider 11/5	Masked Rider 10/23	Masked Rider 10/10	Masked Rider 12/6
8:00 am	Infomercial 2/8		2 Beast Wars 3/3	Beast Wars 10/8	Vor-Tech 12/4	1 Reboot 4/24	Beast Wars 12/6
8:30 am	Feed the Children 5/31	Ever Increasing Faith 10/6	B.R.U.N.O. the Kid 1/27	B.R.U.N.O. the Kid 4/22		B.R.U.N.O. the Kid 2/6	B.R.U.N.O. the Kid 3/21
9:00 am	Infomercials 11/30	It is Written 4/27	Are You Lonesome 9-11am 6/2	Toon Town Kids 10/8	3 Crook & Chase 2/12	Crook & Chase 1/23	Toon Town Kids 10/11
9:30 am							
10:00 am		3 Hour of Power 1/26	△ Love Kills 1/13	High Risk 2/11	Grand Theft Auto 1/22	Beauty & Denise 10/31	Dark Night of the Scarecrow 11/8
10:30 am							
11:00 am	Infomercials 1/11	CMN Championships 6/1					
11:30 am							
12:00 pm	△ Bounty Hunters 10/26	Bill Nye 10/20	News 4/21	4 News 1/14	News 1/29	News 12/5	News 2/7
12:30 pm		Flash Gorden 10/20					
1:00 pm	Eye of the Storm 10/12	Skysurfer Strike Force 2/2	Maury Povich 10/28	4 Maury Povich 3/11	Maury Povich 10/30	4 Maury Povich 1/16	3 Maury Povich 1/31
1:30 pm		Street Sharks 3/9					
2:00 pm		Bill Nye 1/19	News 3/17	News 10/15	News 10/9	News 2/13	News 1/17
2:30 pm		Street Sharks 3/2					
3:00 pm	△ Bejewelled 2-4pm 3/15	Night Angel 11/3	Dennis the Menace 10/7	Bewitched 5/13	Dennis the Menace 3/12	Bewitched 12/5	Bewitched 1/24
3:30 pm			Darkwing Duck 11/4	Darkwing Duck 2/4	Darkwing Duck 12/4	Darkwing Duck 10/10	Darkwing Duck 3/21
4:00 pm	Baywatch Nights 1/18		Gargoyles 1/20	Gargoyles 10/15	Gargoyles 3/5	Gargoyles 10/17	Gargoyles 5/2
4:30 pm			Aladdin 3/10	Aladdin 3/18	Aladdin 1/15	Aladdin 3/13	Aladdin 5/30
5:00 pm	Never Cry Wolf 4-6pm 5/31	Young Frankenstein 12/1	Timon & Pumba 5/19	Quack Pack 1/28	Quack Pack 4/23	Quack Pack 3/6	Mighty Ducks 6/6
5:30 pm			Funniest Home Videos 3/3	Funniest Home Videos 4/29	Funniest Home Videos 3/19	Funniest Home Videos 4/24	Funniest Home Videos 10/25
6:00 pm	Tarzan 11/2		Funniest Home Videos 1/27	Funniest Home Videos 5/6	Funniest Home Videos 4/30	Funniest Home Videos 11/7	Funniest Home Videos 5/9
6:30 pm			4 Real TV 5/19	Real TV 10/22	Real TV 5/7	4 Real TV 5/1	4 Real TV 1/24
7:00 pm	Funniest Home Videos 3/1	Flipper 10/27	Inside Edition 12/2	Inside Edition 4/29	Inside Edition 2/5		Inside Edition 5/16
7:30 pm	Funniest Home Videos 3/8		American Journal 1/20	American Journal 5/13	American Journal 5/7	American Journal 10/17	American Journal 5/30
8:00 pm	News 2/1	News 1/12	News 10/14	News 5/27	News 5/28	News 1/30	News 4/25
8:30 pm							
9:00 pm	4 Real TV 3/1	National Geographic 2/2	News 2/3	News 12/3	News 11/6	News 3/20	News 2/14
9:30 pm	Inside Edition Weekend 4/19						
10:00 pm	News 10/19	Tarzan 2/9	News 11/4	News 10/22	News 10/16	News 10/24	News 10/18
10:30 pm							

Key: # Parental Guideline (1 = TVY, 2 = TVY7, 3 = TVG, 4 = TVPG, 5 = TV14, 6 = TVMA) ¥ MPAA Rating «» Violence Code △ Advisory

A&E	SATURDAY	SUNDAY	MONDAY	TUESDAY	WEDNESDAY	THURSDAY	FRIDAY
6:00 am	3 Wildlife Mysteries 1/18	3 Breakfast with the Arts 6/1	3 Columbo 5-6:30am 4/28	3 McMillan & Wife 5-6:30am 4/29	3 McCloud 5-7am 5/7	3 Columbo 5-7am 2/6	3 McMillan & Wife 5-7am 5/9
6:30 am							
7:00 am	2 Biography For Kids 2/1		Columbo 10/7	3 Banacek 3/11	3 Lovejoy 1/29	Lovejoy 10/24	Lovejoy 12/6
7:30 am							
8:00 am	3 Voyages 3/1	Dr. Jekyll & Mr. Hyde 10/27	Mike Hammer 10/28	4 Mike Hammer 1/14	Mike Hammer 2/12	4 Mike Hammer 5/8	4 Mike Hammer 3/14
8:30 am							
9:00 am	Ancient Mysteries 11/30		Quincy 3/3	Quincy 12/3	Quincy 10/9	Quincy 12/5	Quincy 11/1
9:30 am							
10:00 am		Too Good to Be True 10/13	4 Equalizer 1/20	4 Equalizer 1/28	4 Equalizer 3/5	4 Law & Order 5/1	Equalizer 10/25
10:30 am							
11:00 am	20th Century 1/11		3 Columbo 3/10	McMillan & Wife 10/22	3 McCloud 2/5	Columbo 10/10	3 McMillan & Wife 1/17
11:30 am							
12:00 pm	Investigative Reports 10/19	Biography 12/1					
12:30 pm							
1:00 pm	American Justice 11/2	American Justice 10/20	3 Columbo 2/3	3 Banacek 4/22	Lovejoy 12/4	Lovejoy 11/7	3 Lovejoy 3/7
1:30 pm		4 American Justice 2/9					
2:00 pm	3 America's Castles 1/25	3 Unexplained 1/12	Mike Hammer 10/21	Mike Hammer 10/29	Mike Hammer 10/16	4 Mike Hammer 1/30	4 Mike Hammer 1/24
2:30 pm							
3:00 pm	3 Bob Vila's Home Again 3/8	3 Bob Vila's Home Again 3/2	3 Quincy 1/13	3 Quincy 1/21	Quincy 10/30	3 Quincy 3/20	3 Quincy 2/14
3:30 pm	3 Bob Vila's Home Again 3/15	Bob Vila's Home Again 10/6					
4:00 pm	3 Mysteries of the Bible 3/15	3 Ancient Mysteries 1/19	4 Equalizer 3/17	4 Equalizer 2/4	Equalizer 10/23	4 Equalizer 1/16	4 Equalizer 3/21
4:30 pm							
5:00 pm	Biography 10/5	3 Great Escapes of WWII 2/2	Biography 11/4	Biography 5-7pm 11/5	3 Biography 3/19	3 Biography 3/13	3 Biography 1/31
5:30 pm							
6:00 pm	Investigative Reports 3/8				American Justice 1/22	3 Ancient Mysteries 5/15	Murphy's Romance 10/11
6:30 pm				3 Columbo 5/6			
7:00 pm	John Denver 10/12	America's Castles 11/3	3 Miss Marple 2/10		20th Century 3/12	4 Unexplained 1/23	
7:30 pm							
8:00 pm		Straight Dope 10/20	4 Law & Order 4/21	Law & Order 10/15	Law & Order 11/6	Law & Order 10/17	4 Law & Order 2/7
8:30 pm		3 Mysteries of the Bible 8-9pm 4/20					
9:00 pm	Biography 5/31	3 Irish In America 3/16	3 Biography 5/5	3 Biography 2/11		3 Biography 2/13	3 Biography 4/25
9:30 pm							
10:00 pm	3 Pride & Prejudice 10pm-1am 2/8		Δ House of Cards 10pm-12am 12/2	Scales of Justice 10pm-12am 10/8	4 American Justice 4/23	Nightmare 10/31	The Shadow Riders 10pm-12am 11/8
10:30 pm							

Key: # Parental Guideline (1 = TVY, 2 = TVY7, 3 = TVG, 4 = TVPG, 5 = TV14, 6 = TVMA) ¥ MPAA Rating «» Violence Code Δ Advisory

AMC

	SATURDAY	SUNDAY	MONDAY	TUESDAY	WEDNESDAY	THURSDAY	FRIDAY
6:00 am	The Night Riders 5:30-7am 3/8	The Gang's All Here 4:30-6:30am 2/9	Since You Went 4:30-7:30am 3/3	Beau James 5:30-7:30am 10/15	The Egg & I 5:30-7:30am 1/29	Carousel 6-8:30am 1/23	Welcome Stranger 6-8am 12/6
6:30 am					Stormy Weather 1/22		
7:00 am		Blondie in the Dough 1/19	Jim Thorpe 1/27				Susannah of the Mountains 3/7
7:30 am				Cobra Woman 2/11			
8:00 am	Betty Boop 10/5				Flesh & Fury 7:30-9am 10/9	Big Jim McLain 2/13	
8:30 am	Laurel & Hardy 5/31	The Little Princess 11/3					Singapore 8:30-10am 10/18
9:00 am	Unusual Occupations 4/19		Stranger in my Arms 9-11am 11/4	Oklahoma! 8:30-11am 11/5			
9:30 am	Flash Gorden 11/30				House on Haunted Hill 2/12	Stormy Weather 9-10:30am 2/6	3 Runaround 9-11am 5/30
10:00 am	Apache Drums 11/2	Prince of Foxes 10/13		The Brave One 10am-12pm 4/29			
10:30 am			All About Eve 10/21				
11:00 am					Golden Earrings 10am-12pm 12/4	The Seventh Victim 10am-12pm 10/31	Joe Butterfly 10:30-12:30pm 11/8
11:30 am	Chief Crazy Horse 1/18	The Farmer's Daughter 12:30-2:30pm 3/2		A Street Car Named Desire 11:30am-2pm 10/29	Rodgers & Hammerstein 11:30-1:30pm 11/6	4 You Gotta Stay Happy 12-2pm 1/16	
12:00 pm							
12:30 pm			Maid of Salem 12/2				The Best of Everything 12:30-3pm 1/17
1:00 pm		The Prince & The Showgirl 1-3:30pm 1/12		A Guide for the Married Man 1:30-3:30pm 3/4			
1:30 pm	Long, Long Ago 1-2:30pm 3/15				Slightly Scarlet 1:30-3:30pm 2/5	My Gal Sal 10/17	
2:00 pm							Kitty 11/1
2:30 pm	Friendly Persuasion 2/1	Northwest Mounted Police 10/27	No Time for Sergeants 3/10	The Incredible Shrinking Man 4/22	South Pacific 2-5pm 10/30		
3:00 pm							
3:30 pm			Curly Top 2:30-4pm 1/20			My Gal Sal 12/5	
4:00 pm			Blue Steel 1/13	Beau Geste 3-5pm 1/28	April Love 3-5pm 10/23		A Christmas Carol 3:30-5:30pm 2/7
4:30 pm				East of Sumatra 3:30-5:30pm 10/8			
5:00 pm	Titanic 4-6pm 10/26	Man Without a Star 5-7pm 3/9	Pandora & the Flying Dutchman 10/14		Remember Wenn 3/19	No Time For Sergeants 5-7:30pm 10/10	A Streetcar Named Desire 10/25
5:30 pm				Jane Eyre 5-7pm 10/22	Gentleman's Agreement 5:30-8pm 10/16		
6:00 pm	Remember Wenn 11/30	Foxfire 10/6					
6:30 pm							
7:00 pm	My Darling Clementine 10/19			Unconquered 6/3		Captain Horacio Hornblower 7-9:30pm 3/6	The Glenn Miller Story 7-9pm 1/31
7:30 pm					The Glenn Miller Story 7:30-9:30pm 3/12		
8:00 pm		The Thornbirds 7-10pm 1/26					
8:30 pm	Invasion 8:30-10pm 2/8		Flash Gorden 7-11:30pm 10/28			The Perfect Furlough 8:30-10:30pm 1/30	The Agony & the Ecstasy 1/24
9:00 pm					Remember Wenn 10/16		
9:30 pm	Riders of Destiny 9-10pm 1/25	O'Henry's Full House 9-11:30pm 10/20		Reap the Wild Wind 1/14	How Green Was My Valley? 9:30pm-12am 3/5		
10:00 pm	Remember Wenn 4/19					The Plainsman 9-11pm 11/7	
10:30 pm	Zorba the Greek 10:30pm-1am 10/12						

Key: # Parental Guideline (1 = TVY, 2 = TVY7, 3 = TVG, 4 = TVPG, 5 = TV14, 6 = TVMA) ¥ MPAA Rating «» Violence Code △ Advisory

BET

Time	SATURDAY	SUNDAY	MONDAY	TUESDAY	WEDNESDAY	THURSDAY	FRIDAY
6:00 am	Hit List 10/26	Bobby Jones Gospel 1/12	Screen Scene 3/10	Origins of the Ghost 1/21	Screen Scene 2/5	Screen Scene 2/13	Real Business 5/30
6:30 am	Hit List 10/26	Bobby Jones Gospel 1/12	Sanford 2/10	Benson 2/11	Sanford 1/29	Sanford 5/22	Sanford 3/21
7:00 am	Hit List 10/26	Video Gospel 11/3	Hit List 3/3	Hit List 2/4	Hit List 11/6	Hit List 10/31	
7:30 am	Hit List 10/26	Lead Story 2/2	Hit List 3/3	Hit List 2/4	Hit List 11/6	Hit List 10/31	
8:00 am	Rap City Top 10 1/18	Our Voices 10/27	Video Vibrations 1/13	Video Vibrations 10/22	Video Vibrations 2/12	Video Vibrations 1/16	Video Vibrations 10/11
8:30 am	Rap City Top 10 1/18	Our Voices 10/27	Video Vibrations 1/13	Video Vibrations 10/22	Video Vibrations 3/5	Video Vibrations 1/16	Video Vibrations 10/11
9:00 am	Teen Summit 3/1	Real Business 5/25	Video Vibrations 1/13	Video Vibrations 10/22	Video Vibrations 2/12	Video Vibrations 1/16	Video Vibrations 10/11
9:30 am	Teen Summit 3/1	Infomercial 1/19	Video Vibrations 1/13	Video Vibrations 10/22	Videos 10/16	Video Vibrations 1/16	Video Vibrations 10/11
10:00 am	Teen Summit 3/1	Infomercial 4/27	Unreal 10/21	Video Vibrations 3/18	Unreal 10/23	Video Vibrations 1/30	Unreal 10/18
10:30 am	Benson 1/11	Infomercial 5/4	Unreal 10/21	Video Vibrations 11am-1pm 3/4	Unreal 10/23	Video Vibrations 1/30	Unreal 10/18
11:00 am	Caribbean Rhythms 2/8	Infomercials 12/1	Unreal 10/21	Video Vibrations 11am-1pm 3/4	Unreal 10/23	Video Vibrations 1/30	Unreal 10/18
11:30 am	Caribbean Rhythms 2/8	Infomercials 12/1	Unreal 10/21	Video Vibrations 11am-1pm 3/4	Unreal 10/23	Video Vibrations 1/30	Unreal 10/18
12:00 pm	Infomercials 10/12	Infomercials 12/1	Δ Rap City 11/4	Δ Rap City 10/29	Rap City 12/4	Rap City 11/7	Planet Groove 11am-1pm 5/2
12:30 pm	Infomercials 10/12	Infomercial 2/2	Δ Rap City 11/4	Δ Rap City 10/29	Rap City 12/4	Rap City 11/7	Planet Groove 11am-1pm 5/2
1:00 pm	Infomercials 10/12	Infomercial 5/4	Δ Rap City 11/4	Δ Rap City 10/29	Rap City 12/4	Rap City 11/7	Δ Rap City 1-3pm 3/7
1:30 pm	Infomercials 10/12	Infomercial 5/4	Δ Rap City 11/4	Δ Rap City 10/29	Rap City 12/4	Rap City 11/7	Δ Rap City 1-3pm 3/7
2:00 pm	Rap City Top 10 2-3pm 3/15	Infomercials 1:30-3:30pm 10/20	Videos 2/3	Teen Summit 10/8	Teen Summit 10/30	Videos 3/13	Teen Summit 12/6
2:30 pm	BET Shop 11/30	Infomercials 1:30-3:30pm 10/20	Videos 2/3	Teen Summit 10/8	Teen Summit 10/30	Videos 3/13	Teen Summit 12/6
3:00 pm	Teen Summit 3-4:30pm 5/3	Infomercials 2-5pm 6/1	Videos 2/3	Teen Summit 10/8	Teen Summit 10/30	Sanford 2/13	Teen Summit 12/6
3:30 pm	Teen Summit 3-4:30pm 5/3	Infomercials 3/9	Screen Scene 12/2	Screen Scene 1/14		Screen Scene 3/6	BET News 5/16
4:00 pm	BET Shop 10/19	Infomercials 3/9	Hit List 10/7	Hit List 12/3	Hit List 10/9	Hit List 10/10	Hit List 3/14
4:30 pm	BET Shop 10/19	Infomercials 3/9	Hit List 10/7	Hit List 12/3	Hit List 10/9	Hit List 10/10	Hit List 3/14
5:00 pm	Hit Videos 3/8	Infomercial 3/2	Unreal 10/28	Unreal 10/15	Unreal 1/15	Planet Groove 1/23	Planet Groove 1/31
5:30 pm	Hit Videos 3/8	Infomercial 2/9	Unreal 10/28	Unreal 10/15	Unreal 1/15	Planet Groove 1/23	Planet Groove 1/31
6:00 pm	Hit Videos 3/8	Lead Story 4/27	Unreal 10/28	Unreal 10/15	Unreal 1/15	Planet Groove 1/23	
6:30 pm	Hit Videos 3/8	Bobby Jones Gospel 11/3	Unreal 10/28	Unreal 10/15	Unreal 1/15	Planet Groove 1/23	
7:00 pm	Comic View 11/2	Bobby Jones Gospel 11/3	Comic View 1/20	Comic View 11/5		Comic View 10/17	Comic View 1/17
7:30 pm	Comic View 11/2	Dance Mix USA 4/20	Comic View 1/20	Comic View 11/5		Comic View 10/17	Comic View 1/17
8:00 pm		Infomercials 10/6	Talk 12/2	Talk 2/11	Talk 6/4	Talk 5/29	BET News 4/25
8:30 pm		Infomercials 10/6	Benson 2/10	Sanford 4/22	Benson 1/29	Thea 5/15	Benson 5/9
9:00 pm	Caribbean Rhythms 11/30	Infomercials 10/6	Δ Rap City 10/14	Δ Rap City 1/28	Rap City 1/22	Rap City 12/5	Rap City 11/8
9:30 pm	Caribbean Rhythms 11/30	Infomercials 10/6	Δ Rap City 10/14	Δ Rap City 1/28	Rap City 1/22	Rap City 12/5	Rap City 11/8
10:00 pm	Midnight Love 5/31		Δ Rap City 10/14	Δ Rap City 1/28	Rap City 1/22	Rap City 12/5	Rap City 11/8
10:30 pm	Midnight Love 5/31		Δ Rap City 10/14	Δ Rap City 1/28	Rap City 1/22	Rap City 12/5	Rap City 11/8

Key: # Parental Guideline (1 = TVY, 2 = TVY7, 3 = TVG, 4 = TVPG, 5 = TV14, 6 = TVMA) ¥ MPAA Rating «» Violence Code Δ Advisory

FAM

	SATURDAY	SUNDAY	MONDAY	TUESDAY	WEDNESDAY	THURSDAY	FRIDAY
6:00 am	Infomercials 5-7am 3/15	This Is Your Day 1/19	3 Fit TV 3/10	Fit TV 12/3	Fit TV 11/6	Fit TV 12/5	Fit TV 4/25
6:30 am		Zola Levitt 2/9					
7:00 am	American Baby 10/26	Changed Lives 1/19					
7:30 am	Healthy Kids 5/3	Coral Ridge 3/2					
8:00 am	2 The Bugaloo's 3/1	In Touch 12/1	Highway to Heaven 10/28	3 Highway to Heaven 3/4	3 Highway to Heaven 1/22	Highway to Heaven 10/24	Highway to Heaven 2/14
8:30 am							
9:00 am	Sigmund & the Sea Monsters 10/19	World of Sid & Mary Krofft 10/27	3 Waltons 2/3	3 Waltons 1/14	Waltons 1/29	3 Waltons 2/6	Waltons 1/17
9:30 am	2 H.R. Pufnstuf 3/1						
10:00 am	Family Challenge 1/11	Sparkling Cyanide 10am-12pm 1/12	700 Club 2/10	700 Club 10-11:30am 4/22	700 Club 2/5	700 Club 11/7	700 Club 11/1
10:30 am				700 Club 10/8		700 Club 10-11:30am 6/5	
11:00 am	Young Riders 1/25	Snowy River 10/20					
11:30 am			Fit TV 4/21	Fit TV 6/3	Fit TV 2/12	Fit TV 1/23	Fit TV 11/8
12:00 pm	4 King Rat 11am-1pm 5/31	4 Having Babies 11am-1pm 5/4	Rescue 911 1/27	Rescue 911 10/29	Rescue 911 10/9	4 Rescue 911 2/13	Rescue 911 10/11
12:30 pm							
1:00 pm	Paradise 10/26	Hart to Hart 10/27	3 Home & Family 6/2	3 Home & Family 1/28	Home & Family 10/23	Home & Family 10/17	3 Home & Family 3/21
1:30 pm							
2:00 pm	Big Valley 2/1						
2:30 pm							
3:00 pm	Rifleman 10/12	4 Carson's Comedy Classics 1/26	3 Shop 'til You Drop 3/3		3 Shop 'til You Drop 3/19	Shop 'til You Drop 10/31	Shop 'til You Drop 5/9
3:30 pm	Rifleman 11/30	3 How I Spent My Summer Vacation 2:30pm-4:30pm 6/1	3 Shopping Spree 3/17	Shopping Spree 12/3	3 Shopping Spree 3/5	3 Shopping Spree 3/6	3 Shopping Spree 5/16
4:00 pm	3 High Chapparal 2/8		3 It Takes Two 3/10	3 It Takes Two 4/29	3 Wait till You Have Kids 1/22	Small Talk 10/31	
4:30 pm		3 Carol Burnett & Friends 1/26	3 TV's Bloopers 4/21		3 TV's Bloopers 4/23	3 TV's Bloopers 4/24	Wait till You Have Kids 11/1
5:00 pm	Bonanza 11/2	The Night of the Twisters 10/13	Family Challenge 10/21	3 Before They Were Stars 3/11	Santa Claus is Coming 12/4	4 Carson's Comedy Classics 3/20	3 TV's Bloopers 1/31
5:30 pm						4 Carson's Comedy Classics 4/24	
6:00 pm	The Big Red One 11/30		3 Carol Burnett & Friends 3/17	3 Carol Burnett & Friends 5/6	Carol Burnett & Friends 10/30	3 Carol Burnett & Friends 1/23	3 Carol Burnett & Friends 5/9
6:30 pm			Carol Burnett & Friends 10/21	3 Carol Burnett & Friends 5/20	Carol Burnett & Friends 3/5	3 Carol Burnett & Friends 3/6	3 Carol Burnett & Friends 5/16
7:00 pm		Tonight Show's 19th Anniversary 11/3	3 Waltons 1/13	3 Waltons 1/21	3 Waltons 3/12	Waltons 10/10	3 Waltons 2/7
7:30 pm							
8:00 pm	Panic in the Skies 10/19		Highway to Heaven 11/4	Highway to Heaven 10/15	Highway to Heaven 10/16	Highway to Heaven 1/16	Highway to Heaven 12/6
8:30 pm							
9:00 pm		4 Columbo 2/2	Δ Rescue 911 10/7	Rescue 911 3/18	4 Rescue 911 3/19	4 Rescue 911 1/30	4 Rescue 911 3/7
9:30 pm							
10:00 pm	4 Who is Killing? 10pm-12:30am 1/18		3 700 Club 1/20	3 700 Club 5/13	700 Club 10/30	3 700 Club 5/1	3 700 Club 5/2
10:30 pm							

Key: # Parental Guideline (1 = TVY, 2 = TVY7, 3 = TVG, 4 = TVPG, 5 = TV14, 6 = TVMA) ¥ MPAA Rating «» Violence Code Δ Advisory

CAR	SATURDAY	SUNDAY	MONDAY	TUESDAY	WEDNESDAY	THURSDAY	FRIDAY
6:00 am	3 Addams Family 3/15	1 Big Bag 1/19	3 Fantastic Max 4/21	3 Fantastic Max 2/4	Fantastic Max 4/30	3 Fantastic Max 1/30	3 Fantastic Max 2/7
6:30 am	Dexter's Lab 1/18		Bear Brunch 10/7	3 Snorks 1/28	Snorks 3/5	Snorks 11/7	Snorks 12/6
7:00 am	3 Flintstones 5/10	3 Tom & Jerry 1/26	3 Paw Paws 4/28	3 Paw Paws 1/21	3 Paw Paws 4/23	3 Paw Paws 2/13	Paw Paws 12/6
7:30 am	Scooby Doo 11/2	3 Tex Avery 4/27	3 Pound Puppies 2/10	3 Pound Puppies 3/11	Small World 10/16	3 Pound Puppies 1/23	3 Pound Puppies 3/7
8:00 am	3 Scooby Doo 4/26	3 Rocky & Bullwinkle 2/9	3 New Scooby Doo Movies 2/3	New Scooby Doo Movies 10/8	3 New Scooby Doo Movies 3/12	New Scooby Doo Movies 10/10	New Scooby Doo Movies 1/31
8:30 am	3 Jetsons 4/19	Underdog 10/13					
9:00 am	Taz-Mania 11/30	New Scooby Doo Movies 1/12	3 Smurfs 4/28	2 Captain Planet 4/22	3 Smurfs 4/30	3 Smurfs 3/6	Smurfs 1/24
9:30 am			Tom & Jerry 12/2	Tom & Jerry 12/3	Tom & Jerry 10/9	Tom & Jerry 10/17	Tom & Jerry 10/25
10:00 am	2 Super Adventures 10-11am 5/3	3 Don Coyote 2/9	3 Flintstone Kids 3/10	3 Flintstones 4/29	3 New Scooby Doo Movies 5/21	Flintstones 12/5	Flintstones 10/18
10:30 am	Space Ghost 1/11	3 Young Robin Hood 4/27		3 Flintstone Kids 1/21		3 Flinstone Kids 5/1	Flintstones 1/17
11:00 am	2 Swat Kats 3/8	Pirates 10/13	3 New Scooby Doo Movies 1/13	Tom & Jerry 5/6	A Pup Named Scooby Doo 10/16	A Pup Named Scooby Doo 10/24	3 Yogi Bear 5/23
11:30 am	2 Centurions 4/26	3 George of the Jungle 4/20	3 Bugs & Daffy 5/5	3 Bugs & Daffy 2/11	3 Bugs & Daffy 1/29	3 Bugs & Daffy 5/29	3 Bugs & Daffy 3/21
12:00 pm	G-Force 10/19	2 What a Cartoon Show 1/26	2 Godzilla 1/20	3 Tom & Jerry 5/20	2 Speed Racer 3/19	2 Godzilla 1/30	2 Godzilla 2/14
12:30 pm	2 Thundarr the Barbarian 3/8	3 Dexter's Lab 4/20	2 Godzilla 5/19	Captain Planet 11/5	2 Godzilla 5/7	Captain Planet 10/10	2 Godzilla 5/23
1:00 pm	2 Super Friends 3/15	The Phantom Tollbooth 10/6	2 Centurions 3/3	2 Centurions 3/11	Centurions 12/4		Centurions 10/11
1:30 pm	Centurions 11/2		2 Super Adventures 1/27	2 Captain Planet 4/22	2 Voltron 6/4	2 Super Adventures 1/23	2 Voltron 5/30
2:00 pm	3 Misadventures of Ed Grimley 5/10		Birdman 3/17	Speed Racer 1/14	2 Speed Racer 2/5	2 Speed Racer 3/6	Space Ghost 5/16
2:30 pm	The Hillbilly Bears 1/25		2 Jonny Quest 5/12	2 Super Adventures 2/4	2 Jonny Quest 5/14	Super Adventures 11/7	Super Friends 11/8
3:00 pm		3 Phooey 2/2	Garfield & Friends 10/21	Garfield & Friends 10/29	3 Garfield & Friends 2/12	3 Garfield & Friends 2/6	Super Friends 6/6
3:30 pm	Bugs & Daffy 11/30	Clue Club 11/3	3 Taz-Mania 3/10	3 Taz-Mania 5/6	3 Taz-Mania 3/5	Taz-Mania 10/17	Taz-Mania 11/8
4:00 pm	Addams' Family 10/12	Inch High Private Eye 12/1		Jetsons 10/22	Jetsons 10/23	Halloween is Grinch Night 10/31	Jetsons 10/25
4:30 pm	Scooby Doo 10/19	Chan Clan 10/20		A Pup Named Scooby Doo 10/22		2 Jonny Quest 2/13	Scooby Doo 10/11
5:00 pm	3 Taz-Mania 1/18	3 Scooby Doo & Jaberjaw 5-6pm 3/9	3 Scooby Doo 5/19	3 Scooby Doo 1/14	3 Scooby Doo 1/29	3 Scooby Doo 5/15	3 Scooby Doo 1/17
5:30 pm	3 Dexter's Lab 3/1	Jabberjaw 10/27	Flintstones 10/21	3 Bugs & Daffy 5/13	3 Dexter's Lab 5/14	3 Flintstones 1/16	3 Bugs & Daffy 5/9
6:00 pm	2 Jonny Quest 2/8	3 Flintstones 3/2	3 Flintstones 5/26	Bugs & Daffy 12/3	2 What a Cartoon Show 5/14		3 Bugs & Daffy 3/7
6:30 pm	What a Cartoon Show 10/12	3 Tom & Jerry 3/9	3 Tom & Jerry 3/3	Tom & Jerry 10/29	Space Ghost 11/6	Tom & Jerry 12/5	3 Jetsons 5/2
7:00 pm	Bugs & Daffy 10/26	Flintstones 10/27	Speed Racer 10/28	3 Tom & Jerry 3/18	3 Looney Toons 2/12	2 Speed Racer 3/13	3 Tom & Jerry 5/9
7:30 pm		Jetsons 11/3	2 Speed Racer 5/12	2 Speed Racer 5/13	Scooby Doo 10/9	2 Speed Racer 5/8	2 Super Friends 1/24
8:00 pm			Rocky & Bullwinkle 10/7	2 Jonny Quest 3/4	2 Jonny Quest 5/21	Rocky & Bullwinkle 10/24	2 Space Ghost 5/23
8:30 pm		3 Roger Ramjet 2/2	3 Rocky & Bullwinkle 4/21	3 Rocky & Bullwinkle 1/28	Cartoon Planet 12/4	3 Rocky & Bullwinkle 3/13	Cartoon Planet 10/18
9:00 pm	2 Space Ghost 1/11	Tom & Jerry 12/1	2 Wait till Your Father Gets Home 5/19	3 Snorks 2/11	3 Snorks 2/5	Jonny Quest 10/31	2 Jonny Quest 5/2
9:30 pm	2 Speed Racer 1/25		Jetsons 10/14	Jetsons 10/15	Jetsons 10/23	3 Jetsons 1/16	2 Jonny Quest 2/14
10:00 pm	2 Super Friends 5/31	3 Popeye 3/16	3 Scooby Doo 2/10	Scooby Doo 11/5	3 Scooby Doo 5/21	3 Scooby Doo 3/20	3 Scooby Doo 3/14
10:30 pm			2 Stupid Dogs 10/28	2 2 Stupid Dogs 5/20	2 2 Stupid Dogs 1/15	2 2 Stupid Dogs 2/6	

Key: # Parental Guideline (1 = TVY, 2 = TVY7, 3 = TVG, 4 = TVPG, 5 = TV14, 6 = TVMA) ¥ MPAA Rating «» Violence Code Δ Advisory

LIF	SATURDAY	SUNDAY	MONDAY	TUESDAY	WEDNESDAY	THURSDAY	FRIDAY
6:00 am	Infomercials 4:30-6:30am 3/15	Infomercials 5-7am 3/16	Infomercials 5-7am 10/28	Infomercials 4:30-6:30am 4/29	Infomercials 5-7am 6/4	Infomercials 4:30-6:30am 3/20	Infomercials 4:30-6:30am 5/2
6:30 am	Infomercials 10/19			Infomercial 3/11	Infomercials 10/23	Infomercials 1/23	Infomercial 5/16
7:00 am		Ever Increasing Faith 1/26	Infomercial 12/2	4 Everyday Workout 2/11			3 Everyday Workout 5/30
7:30 am			3 Denise Austin's Workout 4/21	3 Denise Austin's Workout 1/21	Everyday Workout 10/16	3 Denise Austin's Workout 1/30	3 Denise Austin's Workout 5/23
8:00 am		Infomercials 10/20	3 What Every Baby Knows 1/13		What Every Baby Knows 5/21	3 What Every Baby Knows 4/24	3 What Every Baby Knows 1/17
8:30 am	Infomercial 11/30		3 Kids These Days 3/3	3 Kids These Days 1/28	3 Kids These Days 2/12	3 Kids These Days 3/6	3 Kids These Days 2/7
9:00 am	Infomercial 2/1		4 Sisters 3/10	Sisters 12/3	4 Sisters 1/22	4 Sisters 1/16	4 Sisters 1/31
9:30 am	Infomercial 1/25						
10:00 am	Infomercial 3/1	What Every Baby Knows 12/1	Designing Women 10/7	3 Debt 3/4	3 Debt 3/12	Designing Women 10/24	Debt 2/14
10:30 am	Infomercial 1/25	Kids These Days 12/1	Our Home 11/4	3 Our Home 1/21	3 Our Home 3/5	Our Home 11/7	Our Home 12/6
11:00 am	3 Frugal Gourmet 2/8		3 Main Ingredient 3/17	3 Main Ingredient 1/14	Main Ingredient 10/23	3 Main Ingredient 1/30	3 Main Ingredient 1/24
11:30 am	3 Handmade by Design 3/1	Mommy 10/27	Handmade by Design 10/14	3 Handmade by Design 1/28	3 Our Home 4/23	Handmade by Design 12/5	Handmade by Design 11/8
12:00 pm	Martha Stewart Living 10/12		3 Martha Stewart Living 3/3	Martha Stewart Living 10/22	3 Martha Stewart Living 1/29	3 Martha Stewart Living 3/13	3 Martha Stewart Living 3/7
12:30 pm	3 Our Home 1/18		Main Ingredient 4/21	Our Home 12/3	Our Home 10/16	3 Main Ingredient 5/22	3 Our Home 2/7
1:00 pm	3 Supermarket Sweep 2/1	5 The Mean Season 12-2pm 1/12	Class of '96 10/14	Designing Women 10/8	4 Designing Women 2/12	Designing Women 10/24	4 Designing Women 3/14
1:30 pm	3 Debt 5/31			4 Nurses 2/11	4 Nurses 2/5	3 Debt 4/24	Nurses 12/6
2:00 pm	4 Designing Women 1/18	4 One West Waikiki 1/19	Between Two Women 10/7	Mommy 10/29	Men Don't Tell 10/9	Haunted Honeymoon 10/31	Prince of Bel Air 10/11
2:30 pm	Jewels' (Part 1) 2:30-5pm 11/2						
3:00 pm	Unsolved Mysteries 10/12	Δ Dances with Wolves 3-7pm 10/13					
3:30 pm							
4:00 pm	Manhunt: Search for the Night Stalker 10/26		4 L.A. Law 2/3		L.A. Law 11/6	L.A. Law 10/17	L.A. Law 10/25
4:30 pm							
5:00 pm		Aftermath 5-7pm 10/6	4 Commish 2/10	4 Commish 1/14	Commish 12/4	4 Commish 2/6	Commish 11/1
5:30 pm							
6:00 pm	Jewels' (Part 2) 5-7:30pm 11/2	Δ When No One Would Listen 3/2	Supermarket Sweep 12/2	Supermarket Sweep 10/8	3 Supermarket Sweep 3/12	Supermarket Sweep 12/5	3 Supermarket Sweep 3/7
6:30 pm			3 Debt 1/13	3 Debt 3/18	3 Debt 1/29	Debt 10/17	3 Debt 3/14
7:00 pm	4 Nightmare in Daylight 6-8pm 4/19		Hope & Gloria 10/28	4 Designing Women 3/4	3 Intimate Portrait 7-8pm 5/21	4 Designing Women 3/6	The Dish 3/21
7:30 pm			Designing Women 11/4	4 Designing Women 2/4	Designing Women 3/5	3 Intimate Portrait 7-8pm 6/5	
8:00 pm	Δ Indictment: The McMartin Trial 11/30	Δ Fire! Trapped on the 37th Floor 11/3	Unsolved Mysteries 10/21	Δ Unsolved Mysteries 10/22	4 Unsolved Mysteries 1/15	Unsolved Mysteries 10/10	Intimate Portrait 10/18
8:30 pm							
9:00 pm			5 When No One Would Listen 1/27	5 When No One Would Listen 9-11pm 3/11	Jekyll & Hyde 10/30	4 Making Mr. Right 2/13	5 Δ Armed & Innocent 1/17
9:30 pm							
10:00 pm	4 Sisters 1/11	3 Intimate Portrait 2/9		Color Me Perfect 10pm-12am 11/5			
10:30 pm							

Key: # Parental Guideline (1 = TVY, 2 = TVY7, 3 = TVG, 4 = TVPG, 5 = TV14, 6 = TVMA) ¥ MPAA Rating «» Violence Code Δ Advisory

MTV	SATURDAY	SUNDAY	MONDAY	TUESDAY	WEDNESDAY	THURSDAY	FRIDAY
6:00 am	Video Countdown 1/11	Videos 1/26	Rude Awakening 11/4	Rude Awakening 1/28	Rude Awakening 12/4	Rude Awakening 2/6	Rude Awakening 2/14
6:30 am							
7:00 am		4 Video Countdown 2/9	4 The Grind 3/10	4 The Grind 4/29	The Grind 1/15	4 The Grind 4/24	4 The Grind 4/25
7:30 am			4 Videos 4/21	Jams 2/4	4 Jams 3/12	Jams 1/23	Jams 3/21
8:00 am	4 Videos 4/26		Rude Awakening 12/2	Rude Awakening 11/5	Rude Awakening 11/6	Rude Awakening 10/17	Rude Awakening 1/31
8:30 am	2 Ren & Stimpy 3/15	MTV Sports 11/3					
9:00 am	3 MTV Sports 5/3	Gameworks Premiere Party 3/16					
9:30 am	Singled Out 11/2						
10:00 am		MTV Jams 9:30-10:30am 10/13	4 Videos 4/28	MTV Jams 12/3	MTV Jams 10/9	MTV Jams 10/24	MTV Jams 1/24
10:30 am	Singled Out 1/18	Singled Out 11/3	Videos 5/12				
11:00 am	3 MTV Sports 3/8		4 Jams 3/17				
11:30 am	4 Daria 5/10	△ Buzz Kill 10/20					
12:00 pm	Real World 2/1	4 Real World 5/18	Videos 10/7	Videos 2/11	Videos 3/5	Videos 1/16	Video Countdown 12-2pm 11/1
12:30 pm	5 △ Beavis & Butt-Head 4/26	Week In Rock 12/1	Videos 5/5	Videos 10/15	Videos 1/22	Videos 3/20	
1:00 pm	Fashionably Loud II 2/8	1997 Preview Saturday 1/19	Indie Outing 4/21	Videos 10/22	Videos 1/29	4 Videos 3/6	Videos 10/18
1:30 pm			Videos 2/10	Videos 1/14	Videos 4/23	Michael Jackson Concert 2/13	Videos 1/17
2:00 pm	Road Rules 10/19	5 △ Beavis & Butt-Head 4/27	4 Videos 4/28	Videos 2/4	Videos 11/6		Videos 2/7
2:30 pm	4 Break Down 5/17	1997 Preview Saturday (con't)	Videos 3/3	Videos 4/22	Videos 4/30	Videos 1/23	Videos 4/25
3:00 pm	4 Making of Private Parts 3/1	4 Videos 3-4:30pm 5/11		4 △ Videos 5/6	4 Videos 3/12	Videos 5/15	4 Videos 5/2
3:30 pm		Beavis & Butt-Head 4/27	Videos 2/3	Videos 3/4	Videos 10/23	Videos 1/16	Singled Out 3/21
4:00 pm	4 Real World Reunion 3/15	Video Music Awards 10/6	Most Wanted Jams 1/13	Most Wanted Jams 3/11	MTV Jams 10/30	Most Wanted Jams 10/10	Weekend Warm-up 11/8
4:30 pm				Top 500 Videos 5/20			
5:00 pm	MTV Movie Awards 4-6pm 10/5		One on One 10/28	Real World 1/21	MTV News 2/12	Real World 12/5	MTV Jams 10/25
5:30 pm				4 Videos 5:30-6:30pm 5/13	MTV News: Unfiltered 3/19	MTV News: Unfiltered 3/6	
6:00 pm	MTV Movie Special 3/8		Ren & Stimpy 1/20	2 Ren & Stimpy 2/11	Top 500 Videos 5/21	4 Top 500 Videos 5/22	4 Summer Movie Showcase 5/23
6:30 pm	△ Week In Rock 4/19	Week In Rock 6/1	Top 500 Videos 5/19	4 Road Rules 3/4	Superock 10/16		
7:00 pm	Road Rules 2/1	Road Rules 10/20	4 Singled Out 2/10	My So Called Life 7-8pm 6/3	4 Singled Out 3/19	4 Singled Out 3/13	Singled Out 10/11
7:30 pm		Singled Out 10/27	4 Singled Out 5/5	Top 500 Videos 5/20	Idiot Savants 1/29	4 Idiot Savants 4/24	4 House of Style 5/23
8:00 pm	Rock N' Jock B-Ball Jam 8-9:30pm 10/26	Videos 3/9	Prime Time 10/21	Straight Dope 10/8	Videos 4/23	My So Called Life 10/31	U2: Tickets First 3/7
8:30 pm							
9:00 pm	4 Videos 5/17	Videos 1/12		Unplugged 1/21		Yo! 9-11pm 1/30	
9:30 pm	3 Slam-N-Jam Wrap Up 9-10pm 5/31						Ren & Stimpy 10/18
10:00 pm	4 Singled Out 3/1		Dreamtime 2/3	4 Buzz Kill 3/11	Real World 10/23	Yo! 11/7	5 △ Beavis & Butt-Head 2/7
10:30 pm	Real World 11/2	MTV Sports 12/1		5 Rodman World Tour 3/18	Real World 1/22		3 MTV Sports 3/14

Key: # Parental Guideline (1 = TVY, 2 = TVY7, 3 = TVG, 4 = TVPG, 5 = TV14, 6 = TVMA) ¥ MPAA Rating «» Violence Code △ Advisory

NIK

	SATURDAY	SUNDAY	MONDAY	TUESDAY	WEDNESDAY	THURSDAY	FRIDAY
6:00 am	Mr. Wizard's World 2/8	1 Mr. Wizard's World 6/1		1 Blue's Clues 2/11	Blue's Clues 1/15	2 Adventures of Tintin 3/20	
6:30 am	Alvin & the Chipmunks 10/5	1 Alvin & the Chipmunks 3/2	1 Beetlejuice 3/17	1 Beetlejuice 3/11	1 Beetlejuice 4/23	Alvin & the Chipmunks 10/17	1 Gullah Gullah Island 2/7
7:00 am	1 Arcade 4/26	1 Arcade 4/20	Weinerville 12/2	1 Inspector Gadget 4/22	Weinerville 10/9	Weinerville 1/16	1 Inspector Gadget 5/9
7:30 am	1 Rocko's Modern Life 5/10	Family Double Dare 1/19	Beetlejuice 10/7	Beetlejuice 10/29	1 Alvin & the Chipmunks 6/4	1 Alvin & the Chipmunks 3/6	Alvin & the Chipmunks 1/17
8:00 am	1 Doug 3/15	1 Muppet Babies 5/11	1 Looney Tunes 8-9am 4/21	Looney Tunes 12/3	Looney Tunes 11/6	Looney Tunes 12/5	
8:30 am	1 Rugrats 5/10	1 Tiny Toon Adventures 5/11	Looney Tunes 8:30-9:30am 2/3				
9:00 am	Tiny Toon Adventures 10/19	Looney Tunes 1/26	Rugrats 1/20	1 Little Bear 5/6	1 Little Bear 5/14	1 Rugrats 2/13	Rugrats 1/17
9:30 am	1 Tiny Toon Adventures 5/17		Richard Scarry 11/4	Richard Scarry 10/22	Richard Scarry 10/30	Richard Scarry 11/7	1 Richard Scarry 3/14
10:00 am	1 Muppet Babies 4/26	1 Rugrats 3/9	1 Rupert 1/27	1 Rupert 5/6	Rupert 10/16	1 Rupert 4/24	1 Rupert 5/16
10:30 am	Muppet Babies 1/25	AAAHH!!! Real Monsters 10/27		Muppet Babies 11/5	1 Muppet Babies 1/29		Muppet Babies 10/11
11:00 am		Ren & Stimpy 10/20	Allegra's Window 1/13	Allegra's Window 10/8	1 Allegra's Window 4/23	1 Allegra's Window 5/15	1 Allegra's Window 3/7
11:30 am	2 Ren & Stimpy 2/1	1 AAAHH!!! Real Monsters 5/4	Gullah Gullah Island 10/28	Gullah Gullah Island 3/4	Gullah Gullah Island 10/30	1 Gullah Gullah Island 4/24	Gullah Gullah Island 10/25
12:00 pm	1 Salute Your Shorts 3/1	Adventures of Pete & Pete 10/20	2 Little Bear 2/10	Little Bear 1/14	1 Little Bear 2/12	Little Bear 10/31	Little Bear 12/6
12:30 pm	Hey Dude 1/11	All That 1/19	1 Blue's Clues 4/28	Blue's Clues 10/8	Blue's Clues 12/4	Blue's Clues 11/7	Blue's Clues 10/25
1:00 pm	Looney Tunes 10/12	My Brother & Me 11/3	Richard Scarry 1/20	1 Richard Scarry 5/13	1 Flintstones 2/5	Richard Scarry 10/10	Richard Scarry 11/8
1:30 pm		My Brother & Me 10/13	1 Papa Beaver Stories 3/3	Papa Beaver Stories 1/21	1 Papa Beaver Stories 5/7	Papa Beaver Stories 10/17	Papa Beaver Stories 10/18
2:00 pm	Doug 11/30	2 What Would You Do? 2/9	1 Looney Tunes 4/28	Tiny Toon Adventures 10/22	Looney Tunes 3/5	Tiny Toon Adventures 10/31	Tiny Toon Adventures 11/8
2:30 pm	1 Wild & Crazy Kids 5/3	Rugrats 12/1	1 Beetlejuice 5/5	Alvin & the Chipmunks 11/5	Muppet Babies 1/15	1 Beetlejuice 5/1	Alvin & the Chipmunks 10/11
3:00 pm	1 Ship to Shore 3/15	1 Inspector Gadget 5/4	AAAHH!!! Real Monsters 10/14	1 Tiny Toon Adventures 2/4	1 Tiny Toon Adventures 4/30	AAAHH!!! Real Monsters 10/24	Tiny Toon Adventures 1/24
3:30 pm	Weinerville 1/11	Welcome Freshmen 10/6	1 Muppet Babies 3/17	1 Muppet Babies 3/18	Rugrats 10/16	1 Muppet Babies 1/30	1 Muppet Babies 2/7
4:00 pm	1 Hidden Temple 3/8	1 Hidden Temple 4/20	1 Alvin & the Chipmunks 5/12	Alvin & the Chipmunks 1/14	1 Alvin & the Chipmunks 2/12	Alvin & the Chipmunks 1/23	1 Alvin & the Chipmunks 1/31
4:30 pm	Ship to Shore 11/2	Global Guts 10/27	1 Inspector Gadget 2/10	Mystery Files of Shelby Woo 10/15	Inspector Gadget 1/22	1 Inspector Gadget 5/8	1 Inspector Gadget 5/16
5:00 pm	Beetlejuice 10/26	Land of the Lost 10/13	2 Are you Afraid of the Dark? 2/3	Are you Afraid of the Dark? 10/15	Are you Afraid of the Dark? 10/9	2 △ Are you Afraid of the Dark? 2/6	Are you Afraid of the Dark? 11/1
5:30 pm	2 Ren & Stimpy 2/8	1 Space Cases 3/9	1 Rocko's Modern Life 1/27	2 Rocko's Modern Life 3/4	1 Rocko's Modern Life 2/5	Rocko's Modern Life 10/10	1 Adventures of Pete & Pete 2/14
6:00 pm	Rocko's Modern Life 11/2	2 Are you Afraid of the Dark? 2/2	Clarissa Explains it All 10/14	1 Clarissa Explains it All 3/11	1 Clarissa Explains it All 3/12	1 Clarissa Explains it All 2/13	1 Clarissa Explains it All 4/25
6:30 pm	Kablam! 11/30	1 Secret World of Alex Mack 4/27	Tiny Toon Adventures 11/4	1 Tiny Toon Adventures 4/29	Tiny Toon Adventures 11/6	1 Tiny Toon Adventures 3/6	1 Tiny Toon Adventures 5/23
7:00 pm	1 Doug 3/1	1 My Brother & Me 2/9	1 Doug 3/10	Doug 12/3	1 Doug 3/19	1 Doug 5/1	1 Doug 5/2
7:30 pm	Adventures of Pete & Pete 10/26	AAAHH!!! Real Monsters 1/12	1 Rugrats 5/5		Rugrats 10/23	Rugrats 10/24	1 Rugrats 5/23
8:00 pm	Kenan & Kel 10/19	1 Dr. Seuss 5/18	Hey Arnold! 10/7	Secret World of Alex Mack 1/21	1 Hey Arnold! 4/30	Secret World of Alex Mack 1/16	1 Kablam! 5/2
8:30 pm	1 All That 5/31	1 Nick News 5/18	3 Happy Days 5/12	3 Happy Days 1/28	3 Happy Days 3/12	3 Happy Days 5/8	Happy Days 12/6
9:00 pm	Mystery Files of Shelby Woo 1/25	Happy Days 12/1	I Love Lucy 10/21	3 I Love Lucy 2/4	I Love Lucy 1/22	3 I Love Lucy 5/15	3 I Love Lucy 1/31
9:30 pm	1 Kablam! 3/8	Munsters 11/3	Addams Family 10/28	3 Flip Wilson 4/29	3 Munsters 3/5	3 Munsters 2/6	Munsters 10/18
10:00 pm	I Love Lucy 1/18	3 Odd Couple 3/16	3 Mary Tyler Moore Show 3/10	Mary Tyler Moore 1/28	3 Mary Tyler Moore 1/29	3 Odd Couple 6/5	Munsters 11/1
10:30 pm	3 Lucy-Desi 10:30-11:30pm 2/1	Taxi 2/2	Rhoda 1/13	3 Rhoda 2/11	Rhoda 10/23	Rhoda 12/5	3 Odd Couple 5/30

Key: # Parental Guideline (1 = TVY, 2 = TVY7, 3 = TVG, 4 = TVPG, 5 = TV14, 6 = TVMA) ¥ MPAA Rating «» Violence Code △ Advisory

213

TNT

Time	SATURDAY	SUNDAY	MONDAY	TUESDAY	WEDNESDAY	THURSDAY	FRIDAY
6:00 am	How the West Was Won 10/26	1 Scooby Doo 5:30-6:30am 1/19	1 Flintstones 1/13	1 Flintstones 2/4	Flintstones 12/4	1 Flintstones 1/23	1 Flintstones 4/25
6:30 am		3 Gilligan's Island 2/9					
7:00 am	Wild Wild West 10/19	4 In the Heat of the Night 1/26	3 Gilligan's Island 3/17	3 Gilligan's Island 3/11	3 Gilligan's Island 3/12	3 Gilligan's Island 2/6	3 Gilligan's Island 5/2
7:30 am			3 Gilligan's Island 4/21	Gilligan's Island 1/21	3 Gilligan's Island 3/12	3 Gilligan's Island 3/13	3 Gilligan's Island 5/2
8:00 am	Brisco County Jr. 11/2	In the Heat of the Night 10/13	4 Spencer: For Hire 8-10am 3/10	Knots Landing 10/15		4 Knots Landing 1/30	Knots Landing 10/18
8:30 am							
9:00 am	4 Brisco County Jr. 3/8	All Dogs Go to Heaven 9-11am 12/1	3 Chips 1/27	3 Chips 1/21	3 Chips 2/12	3 Chips 3/6	3 Chips 5/9
9:30 am							
10:00 am	Δ Weird Science 11/30	Δ The Great Outdoors 10/6	Thunder in Paradise 10/7	4 Thunder in Paradise 2/11	Thunder in Paradise 10/23	Thunder in Paradise 10/17	Thunder in Paradise 10/11
10:30 am							
11:00 am			How the West Was Won 11/4	The Gunfighter 10/22	3 How the West Was Won 2/5	3 How the West Was Won 2/13	3 How the West Was Won 6/6
11:30 am							
12:00 pm	3 The Naked Jungle 1/11	3 The Comancheros 12-2:30pm 3/2	Wild Wild West 10/14	3 Wild Wild West 1/14	3 Wild Wild West 3/5	Wild Wild West 10/24	Wild Wild West 11/8
12:30 pm							
1:00 pm		Poltergeist III 12:30-2:30pm 10/27	The Indian Fighter 2/10	4 Hangman's Knot 1/28	Many Rivers to Cross 11/6	4 Δ Red Sun 1/16	3 Pony Express 1-3pm 3/21
1:30 pm							
2:00 pm	2 Jonny Quest 1/25	4 Last Stand 1:00-3:00pm 2/2					4 In the Heat of the Night 1/17
2:30 pm	1 Bugs Bunny 2/1						
3:00 pm	1 Flintstones 2/1	4 Δ Summer School 1/12	In the Heat of the Night 12/2	In the Heat of the Night 11/5	In the Heat of the Night 10/16	4 In the Heat of the Night 2/6	4 In the Heat of the Night 2/14
3:30 pm	1 Bugs Bunny 1/18						
4:00 pm	4 In the Heat of the Night 1/25		4 In the Heat of the Night 3/17	In the Heat of the Night 12/3	In the Heat of the Night 10/30	In the Heat of the Night 11/7	NBA Tipoff 11/1
4:30 pm							
5:00 pm	In the Heat of the Night 10/5	Δ The Exorcist 11/3	WCW Wrestling 10/21	Invasion of the Body Snatchers 10/29	Salem's Lot 10/9	Δ The Outlaw Josey Wales 5-8pm 12/5	4 Δ National Lampoon's Vacation 2/7
5:30 pm							
6:00 pm	Police Academy III 10/12						
6:30 pm							
7:00 pm		Δ The River 10/20	3 New Adventures of Robin Hood 3/3				Δ Football America 10/25
7:30 pm				Inside the NBA 3/11		5 Δ Bright Lights, Big City 7-9:30pm 5/29	
8:00 pm	5 Δ For a Few Dollars More 1/18		Inside the NBA 5/19	4 Airplane! 8-10pm 3/4			
8:30 pm							
9:00 pm			WCW Wrestling 2/3	The Outsiders 10/8	4 The Sacketts 9pm-1am 1/29	4 The Birds 9pm-12:30am 6/5	5 Δ Motel Hell 8:30-11pm 5/23
9:30 pm							
10:00 pm			4 Hollywood Nights 10pm-12am 4/21				4 Δ Back to the Future 9:30pm-12:30am 3/7
10:30 pm		5 Δ Alien 9:30pm-12:30am 6/1					

Key: # Parental Guideline (1 = TVY, 2 = TVY7, 3 = TVG, 4 = TVPG, 5 = TV14, 6 = TVMA) ¥ MPAA Rating «» Violence Code Δ Advisory

214

USA

	SATURDAY	SUNDAY	MONDAY	TUESDAY	WEDNESDAY	THURSDAY	FRIDAY
6:00 am	Bloomberg Information TV 5:30-7am 2/8	3 C/Net 3/2	Bloomberg Information TV 5-7am 10/7	Bloomberg Information TV 5-7am 12/3	Bloomberg Information TV 5-7am 2/12	Bloomberg Information TV 5-7am 3/20	Bloomberg Information TV 5-7am 3/7
6:30 am		1 Dennis the Menace 2/2					
7:00 am	Infomercial 11/30	1 Mighty Max 4/27	1 Super Mario Bros. 4/21	1 Super Mario Bros. 3/18	Sonic the Hedgehog 10/23	1 Super Mario Bros. 1/30	Sonic the Hedgehog 11/1
7:30 am	Infomercial 2/1	Double Dragon 12/1	1 Street Sharks 4/21	Street Sharks 10/15	1 Street Sharks 1/29	1 Street Sharks 2/13	2 Wing Commander Academy 6/6
8:00 am	Infomercial 4/19	2 Action Man 5/11	1 Mighty Max 4/28	1 Mighty Max 4/22	1 Mighty Max 3/19	1 Mighty Max 1/23	1 Mortal Kombat 5/9
8:30 am	Infomercial 3/1	2 Ultra Force 4/20	1 Sonic the Hedgehog 2/10	1 Sonic the Hedgehog 3/4	1 Sonic the Hedgehog 2/5	Sonic the Hedgehog 10/10	1 Sonic the Hedgehog 3/21
9:00 am	Infomercial 4/19	Street Fighter 10/13	MacGyver 10/21	Murder, She Wrote 10/29	MacGyver 10/9	3 Murder, She Wrote 3/13	Murder, She Wrote 1/24
9:30 am	Infomercial 5/24	2 Savage Dragon 3/9					
10:00 am	4 △ WWF Livewire 1/18	2 Savage Dragon 5/4			△ Survive the Night 12/4	4 Wings 4/24	4 Almost an Angel 10am-12pm 1/31
10:30 am		Wing Commander Academy 10/13		Last Resort 1/14		French Open 9am-12pm 6/5	
11:00 am	2 Street Fighter 3/1	4 △ WWF Wrestling 1/12				Magnum P.I. 10/24	4 National Lampoon's Vacation 6/6
11:30 am	2 Wing Commander Academy 3/8						
12:00 pm	2 Mortal Kombat 1/25	4 Wings 1/19	3 Major Dad 1/13	Major Dad 10/8	Major Dad 11/6	4 Wings 6/5	Major Dad 10/18
12:30 pm	2 Savage Dragon 3/8	4 Leap of Faith 12:30-2:30pm 2/2	3 Major Dad 3/17	French Open 10am-1pm 5/27	3 Major Dad 1/22	Major Dad 12/5	National Lampoon's Vacation (con't)
1:00 pm	△ The Substitute 1/11	Pacific Blue 10/27	People's Court 3/10	People's Court 10/15	4 People's Court 3/12		People's Court 2/14
1:30 pm			4 People's Court 1-2pm 5/5	4 Love Connection 1:30-2:30pm 6/3	Love Connection 1:30-2:30pm 4/23	People's Court 10/17	People's Court 10/11
2:00 pm		Best Little Whorehouse in Texas 1-3:30pm 12/1	Love Connection 10/21	4 Love Connection 5/20	4 Big Date 4/30		
2:30 pm						4 Big Date 2/6	4 Big Date 3/14
3:00 pm	Reasons of the Heart 10/12		4 Uncle Buck 3-5pm 5/26	Big Date 4/29	Big Date 10/30	Big Date 10/24	4 Big Date 3/21
3:30 pm		4 Working Girl 3-5:30pm 4/27		Big Date 4/29	4 Big Date 1/29	4 Big Date 5/29	4 Big Date 5/2
4:00 pm			4 America's Most Wanted 1/20	4 America's Most Wanted 1/21	4 America's Most Wanted 3/12	4 Macgyver 4-5pm 5/29	Golf 4-6pm 4/25
4:30 pm		Amazing Stories: The Movie V 4-6pm 10/6	7 Top Cops 3/10	4 Macgyver 4-5pm 6/3	Top Cops 10/23	4 Top Cops 2/13	4 △ Top Cops 2/7
5:00 pm	△ Halloween 10/26		Wings 1/13	Wings 10/29	4 Wings 1/22		4 Wings 2/14
5:30 pm			4 Wings 2/10	4 Wings 4/22	4 Wings 5/7	4 Wings 1/23	Wings 12/6
6:00 pm		△ Trilogy of Terror II 11/3	4 Renegade 1/27	4 Renegade 2/4	Renegade 11/6	Renegade 10/31	Renegade 10/25
6:30 pm							
7:00 pm			Highlander 12/2	4 Highlander 2/11		4 Highlander 3/6	4 Highlander 2/7
7:30 pm					Chipmunk Halloween 10/30		
8:00 pm		4 Pacific Blue 1/26	4 WWF Wrestling 8-10pm 3/3	3 Murder, She Wrote 3/11	3 Murder, She Wrote 3/5	Murder, She Wrote 11/7	5 △ Pet Semetary Two 8-10pm 1/17
8:30 pm							
9:00 pm	Pacific Blue 10/19	5 Silk Stalkings 2/9	△ WWF Wrestling 10/14	The Crying Child 10/22	4 Dying to Remember 1/15	5 △ Pet Semetary 1/16	Switching Channels 11/8
9:30 pm							
10:00 pm	Weird Science 10/5	The Big Easy 10/20					
10:30 pm	Duckman 11/30						

Key: # Parental Guideline (1 = TVY, 2 = TVY7, 3 = TVG, 4 = TVPG, 5 = TV14, 6 = TVMA) ¥ MPAA Rating «» Violence Code △ Advisory

VH1	SATURDAY	SUNDAY	MONDAY	TUESDAY	WEDNESDAY	THURSDAY	FRIDAY
6:00 am	Infomercial 2/8	Infomericals 12/1		Videos 10/8	House Blend 10/16		Infomercial 4/25
6:30 am	Infomercial 11/30						
7:00 am	Big 80's 10/26		4 Videos 4/28	Videos 5/6	Cross Roads 11/6	House Blend 10/24	Videos 5/9
7:30 am	Videos 1/25						
8:00 am	Videos 5/31						
8:30 am	Videos 4/26						
9:00 am	Top 10 Video Countdown 10/19	4 Groovin with the Tube 3/16	Soul of VH-1 1/20	Music Matinee 11/5	Music Matinee 10/30	Flix Flash 1/16	VH-1 to One 1/17
9:30 am	Pop-Up Videos 5/17	Videos 1/26		Video Break 9-10am 3/18			Greatest Hits 6/6
10:00 am	4 Videos 3/15	Sunday Brunch 10am-12pm 4/20	3 Monkees Marathon 4/21		Videos 10-11am 5/7	Sex Appeal 1/30	Videos 5/30
10:30 am				4 Videos 5/27	Music Matinee 10/9		Greatest Hits (con't)
11:00 am	Fashion TV 3/8		Music Matinee 10:30am-1pm 1/27		Music Matinee 10/9	House Blend 10/31	Music Matinee 10/18
11:30 am	3 Best of American Bandstand 5/24	Jackson 5 Cartoon 1/12		3 Videos 4/29	Videos 6/4	Music Matinee 10/10	
12:00 pm	4 Top Ten Countdown 5/24		Music Matinee 10/7		4 Soul of VH-1 3/19	4 Best of Midnight Special 5/22	Soul of VH-1 12/6
12:30 pm		4 Best of American Bandstand 3/9	Big 80's 10/7				
1:00 pm		John Lennon Live in NY 10/13	4 Videos 5/5	Videos 12/3	Videos 3/5	4 Sex Appeal 2/6	Videos 5/30
1:30 pm				8 Track Flashback 10/8	Videos 4/30	Videos 10/31	
2:00 pm	4 Paul McCartney 2-3pm 5/17	Baywatch Countdown 1/26	Fashion TV 10/21	Videos 1/14	Video Break 2/5	Music Matinee 11/7	Fashion TV 10/18
2:30 pm	Sex Appeal 3/1		Video Break 10/14				Video Break 2-3pm 1/24
3:00 pm	4 Number Ones 5/17		Fashion TV (con't)	Video Break 2-4pm 1/28			Videos 1/31
3:30 pm	Archives 10/5	Videos 6/1			4 Here's Donny 3/12		
4:00 pm		Mega #1 Week 2/2	American Bandstand 2/3	American Bandstand 2/4	American Bandstand 1/22	Marcia, Marcia, Marcia 10/17	3 American Bandstand 3/7
4:30 pm		4 Storytellers 4-5pm 6/1	4 Big 80's 5/5	8 Track Flashback 1/21			8 Track Flashback 11/1
5:00 pm			Videos 2/10	4 Attack of the Bradys 3/11	Videos 5-6pm 3/5	4 A Very Jefferson Reunion 3/13	Top Ten Countdown 2/14
5:30 pm					Videos 12/4		
6:00 pm	4 Videos 6-7pm 5/17	4 Pop-Up Videos 4/27	Videos 3/3	Videos 10/29		4 Interview with Mathew Perry 2/13	4 Dance Machine 5/23
6:30 pm	4 Pop-Up Videos 3/8	Archives 10/20			Videos 5/21		
7:00 pm		4 Pop-Up Videos 3/9	1996 Lifebeat Concert 11/4	4 Videos 4/22	4 Videos 5/28	4 Sex Appeal 7-8pm 4/24	Sex Appeal 1/24
7:30 pm		Whitney Houston 1/12			4 8 Track Flashback 2/12	Best of American Bandstand 10/10	Taking Care of Business 3/14
8:00 pm		4 Hard Rock Live 4/27		4 Top Ten Countdown 2/11	Big 80's 1/22		4 Top Ten Countdown 5/2
8:30 pm	Party Machine 10/19				4 Big 80's 8-9pm 2/12	Videos 5/15	Beatles Today 12/6
9:00 pm	Flix Flash 1/11	8 Track Flashback 11/3	3 Selena 3/17	3 The Beatles Collection 5/13	Archives 1/29	Week with Elvis 2/6	
9:30 pm		Rupaul Show 12/1	Rupaul Show 10/28	4 8 Track Flashback 5/20	8 Track Flashback 11/6	4 8 Track Flashback 5/1	
10:00 pm	3 Barry Manilow 5/31	4 Storytellers 6/1		4 INXS Rocks the Rockies 3/4	3 The Monkees 5/21	VH-1 to One 1/23	
10:30 pm			3 Archives 5/12		4 Archives 5/21	4 Archives 5/29	

Key: # Parental Guideline (1 = TVY, 2 = TVY7, 3 = TVG, 4 = TVPG, 5 = TV14, 6 = TVMA) ¥ MPAA Rating «» Violence Code Δ Advisory

MAX

Time	SATURDAY	SUNDAY	MONDAY	TUESDAY	WEDNESDAY	THURSDAY	FRIDAY
6:00 am	¥ «» Crosscut 5:30-7:30am 2/1	¥ «» Cooley High 11/3	5 Love at First Sight 3/3	3 Molly & Me 3/4	¥ «» Improper Conduct 5-6:30am 11/6	¥ Drive In 10/10	Playmates 6-7:30am 2/14
6:30 am							
7:00 am	The Vengeance of Fu Manchu 7-9am 10/5		«» I Mitici 6:30-8:30am 10/14	¥ «» Dracula A.D. 1972 6:30-8:30am 11/5	Artists & Models 6-8am 1/22		¥ The Nutcracker Prince 1/17
7:30 am							
8:00 am		¥ It Takes Two 8-10am 3/16			¥ Days of Thunder 8-10am 3/5	¥ Valley of the Dolls 8-10am 2/6	
8:30 am	¥ Δ Miracle on 34th Street 8-10am 3/8		¥ «» Nine Months 8:30-10:30am 3/17	Young Mr. Lincoln 1/28			¥ High Spirits 8-10am 3/14
9:00 am		¥ Leonard Part 6 8:30-10am 10/27			A Night to Remember 10/16	¥ Silent Movie 1/23	
9:30 am			¥ «» The Carpetbaggers 9-11:30am 1/27				4 «» A Family Divided 9:30-11:30am 3/7
10:00 am	The True Story of Jesse James 10/26	¥ Necessary Roughness 10/20					
10:30 am			¥ «» The Wolves 10-11:30am 10/28	¥ Stuart Saves His Family 10:30am-12:30pm 1/21			¥ «» Born to Be Wild 10am-12pm 11/1
11:00 am					Murderers' Row 11am-1:30pm 1/29	¥ «» Congo 10am-12pm 10/24	
11:30 am			¥ «» The Last Dragon 11am-1pm 10/7				
12:00 pm	¥ Driving Miss Daisy 1/11	So Big 12-2pm 1/26		¥ «» Explorers 11am-1pm 12/3	Call Me Mister 10/23	«» Oblivion 10/31	
12:30 pm							
1:00 pm		Tremors 2 1:30-3:30pm 5/4	¥ «» Brainstorm 12:30-2:30pm 2/10	¥ Forever Young 11:30-2pm 10/15			
1:30 pm	¥ «» Far From Home 1/25					¥ Nothing In Common 1-3pm 1/16	
2:00 pm		¥ «» Lady in White 2:30-4:30pm 1/19	¥ «» It's Alive 1:30-3pm 12/2	¥ «» Shadow of the Wolf 2-4pm 3/11	¥ «» Crime Wave 1:30-3pm 3/12		¥ Miracle on 34th Street 2-4pm 12/6
2:30 pm							
3:00 pm			Δ Grace Kelly 3-5pm 1/20		¥ «» Sidekicks 3-5pm 1/15		¥ There Goes the Neighborhood 10/18
3:30 pm	«» Δ Deliver Them From Evil 11/2	¥ «» Night of the Comet 3-5pm 12/1		¥ «» Free Willy 2 2:30-4:30pm 1/14		¥ The Thing Called Love 11/7	
4:00 pm							
4:30 pm			¥ La Bamba 10/21	¥ «» Brainstorm 4:30-6:30pm 2/4	¥ «» American Shaolin 4:30-6:30pm 12/4		
5:00 pm	¥ Man Trouble 4:30-7pm 10/12						¥ The Big Picture 1/24
5:30 pm		¥ «» Armed & Dangerous 3/2				¥ A Fine Mess 2/13	
6:00 pm							
6:30 pm	¥ A River Runs Through It 5:30-8pm 3/1	¥ Modern Problems 1/12	¥ Meatballs Part 2 11/4	Don't Tell Mom The Babysitter's Dead 10/22	Forever Young 10/9	¥ Trapped In Paradise 6-8pm 1/30	¥ «» Bushwhacked 2/7
7:00 pm							
7:30 pm							
8:00 pm							
8:30 pm	¥ «» Timecop 1/18	¥ St. Elmo's Fire 10/6	¥ Tommy Boy 1/13	¥ «» Hear No Evil 8-10pm 10/29	¥ «» The Lost Boys 2/12	¥ «» Mirage 10/17	
9:00 pm							
9:30 pm				¥ «» Wes Craven Presents Mind Ripper 9:30-11:30pm 2/11		¥ «» Goodfellas 9:30-12am 3/6	¥ «» Fair Game 10-12am 1/31
10:00 pm	¥ «» Rage 10-12am 11/30	¥ «» Rambo: First Blood Part II 9:30-11:30pm 10/13	¥ «» Pure Danger 10-12am 3/10		¥ «» Brainscan 9:30-11:30pm 10/30	¥ «» The Net 10-12am 12/5	
10:30 pm							

Key: # Parental Guideline (1 = TVY, 2 = TVY7, 3 = TVG, 4 = TVPG, 5 = TV14, 6 = TVMA) ¥ MPAA Rating «» Violence Code Δ Advisory

	SATURDAY	SUNDAY	MONDAY	TUESDAY	WEDNESDAY	THURSDAY	FRIDAY
6:00 am		1 Mouse Tracks 1/12	Mouse Tracks 12/2	1 Mouse Tracks 3/11	1 Mouse Tracks 2/12	1 Mouse Tracks 1/16	1 Mouse Tracks 1/24
6:30 am	Dumbo's Circus 10/26	Wuzzles 12/1	1Tale Spin 3/17	1 Tale Spin 2/4	1 Tale Spin 1/15	Tale Spin 1/30	1 Tale Spin 3/21
7:00 am	1 Pooh Corner 2/1	1 Ducktales 1/19	1 Quack Attack 3/3	1 Goof Troop 1/21	1 Quack Attack 3/19	1 Goof Troop 1/23	Goof Troop 10/11
7:30 am	1 Grounding Marsh 1/11	Charlie Brown & Snoopy 10/13	Chip 'n Dale 12/2	Chip 'n Dale 10/8	1 Chip 'n Dale 1/29	1 Chip 'n Dale 2/6	1 Goof Troop 3/7
8:00 am	Secret Life of Toys 11/30	1 Goof Troop 1/12	1 Chip 'n Dale 3/10	Winnie the Pooh 10/15	1 Chip 'n Dale 4/23	1 Winnie the Pooh 2/13	Winnie the Pooh 12/6
8:30 am	1 Amazing Animals 1/11	1 Amazing Animals 2/9	1 Little Mermaid 1/20	Little Mermaid 11/5	Little Mermaid 12/4	Little Mermaid 10/10	Little Mermaid 10/25
9:00 am	1 Real Wild Animals 3/15	Chip 'n Dale 10/13	1 Adventures in Wonderland 2/10	1 Adventures in Wonderland 1/14	1 Winnie the Pooh 3/5	1 Winnie the Pooh 4/24	1 △ Adventures in Wonderland 2/7
9:30 am	1 Animal Adventures 3/15	1 Animal Adventures 3/16	Under the Umbrella Tree 10/7	Under the Umbrella Tree 10/15	1 Under the Umbrella Tree 2/12	Under the Umbrella Tree 12/5	1 Mouse Tracks 3/14
10:00 am	Rainbow Brite & The Star Stealer	Scooby Doo Meets the Boo Brothers 10/27	1 Groundling Marsh 1/27	1 △ Adventures in Wonderland 3/11	1 Groundling Marsh 2/5	1 Groundling Marsh 2/13	1 △ Adventures in Wonderland 3/21
10:30 am	Under the Umbrella Tree 10/26		Pooh Corner 11/4	Pooh Corner 12/3	Pooh Corner 10/23	Pooh Corner 10/17	Pooh Corner 10/25
11:00 am	Rainbow Brite (con't) 11/2		1 Gummi Bears 4/21	1 Ducktales 2/11	Ducktales 10/9	Ducktales 10/10	1 Ducktales 1/17
11:30 am			Dumbo's Circus 10/21	Care Bears 10/8	1 Care Bears 4/30	Care Bears 10/31	1 Care Bears 3/14
12:00 pm	The Neverending Story II 10/19	3 The Santa Claus 11am-2pm 4/27	1 Dumbo's Circus 2/10	1 Dumbo's Circus 1/14	1 My Little Pony Tales 3/12	1 Dumbo's Circus 2/6	1 Dumbo's Circus 1/31
12:30 pm			Adventures in Wonderland 10/21	1 Little Mermaid 4/22	1 Little Mermaid 3/5		1 Adventures in Wonderland 1/31
1:00 pm	1 Baby-Sitters Club 3/1	1 Baby-Sitter's Club 2/2	Gummi Bears 10/14	1 Gummi Bears 2/4	1 Gummi Bears 1/29	Gummi Bears 10/17	Gummi Bears 11/1
1:30 pm	2 Flash Forward 1/18	2 Flash Forward 1/26	1 Charlie Brown & Snoopy 1/20	Charlie Brown & Snoopy 10/22	Charlie Brown & Snoopy 12/4	Charlie Brown & Snoopy 11/7	Charlie Brown & Snoopy 11/1
2:00 pm	2 Torkelsons 2/8	2 Torkelsons 3/2	1 Quack Attack 1/27	1 Winnie the Pooh 3/18	1 Winnie the Pooh 4/23	1 Quack Attack 1/23	1 Quack Attack 1/24
2:30 pm	2 Ready or Not 1/25	2 Ready or Not 3/9	1 Quack Attack 3/17	1 Winnie the Pooh 1/21	Winnie the Pooh 10/16	1 Winnie the Pooh 1/30	1 Quack Attack 3/7
3:00 pm	2 Ocean Girl 2/1	2 Ocean Girl 1/26					
3:30 pm	2 Spellbinder 2/8		Old Yeller 11/4	3 Cinderella 1/28	3 Brave Little Toaster 1/22	Suzie Q 10/24	Stanley's Dragon 10/11
4:00 pm		Mary Poppins 10/20					
4:30 pm	The Ugly Dachshund 10/5		1 Charlie Brown & Snoopy 2/3	1 Charlie Brown & Snoopy 2/11	Charlie Brown & Snoopy 10/16		
5:00 pm			1 Tale Spin 3/10	Tale Spin 11/5	1 Tale Spin 5/21	2 Tale Spin 3/20	Tale Spin 11/8
5:30 pm			1 Ducktales 3/3	1 Ducktales 3/18	Ducktales 10/9	Ducktales 12/5	Ducktales 11/8
6:00 pm	Avonlea 10/12	1 Amazing Animals 2/9	Chip 'n Dale 10/7	Chip 'n Dale 10/29	1 Chip 'n Dale 3/19	Chip 'n Dale 10/31	Chip 'n Dale 12/6
6:30 pm		1 Animal Adventures 2/2	Goof Troop 10/14	Goof Troop 10/29	1 Goof Troop 2/5	1 Goof Troop 3/13	1 Goof Troop 1/17
7:00 pm							
7:30 pm	3 A Kid in King Arthur's Court 1/25	A Mom for Christmas 12/1	The Dark Crystal 7-9pm 10/28	The Misadventures of Merlin Jones 10/22	Susie Q 10/30	3 The Parent Trap 7-9:30pm 1/16	3 Cinderella 2/14
8:00 pm							
8:30 pm				The Making of 101 Dalmations 12/3	3 Summertime 8:30-10pm 6/4	3 Jetsons Meet the Flintstones 8:30-10:30pm 5/8	Step Monster 8:30-10pm 10/18
9:00 pm	3 Peter Pan 1/18	Avonlea 10/6			△ Waging Peace 11/6		
9:30 pm			3 Young Again 5/12	3 The Wiz 9-11:30pm 3/4			
10:00 pm							
10:30 pm	3 Love Bug 10-12am 5/17	Road to Utopia 10-11:30pm 11/3			4 Dark Crystal 10-12am 5/21	3 Ugly Dacshund 10:30-12:30 am 6/5	3 Gus 10:30-12:30am 2/7

Key: # Parental Guideline (1 = TVY, 2 = TVY7, 3 = TVG, 4 = TVPG, 5 = TV14, 6 = TVMA) ¥ MPAA Rating «» Violence Code △ Advisory

HBO	SATURDAY	SUNDAY	MONDAY	TUESDAY	WEDNESDAY	THURSDAY	FRIDAY
6:00 am			¥ Naked In New York 5-7am 2/3		Damon Wayans 5-6:30am 2/12		
6:30 am	¥«» D.A.R.Y.L. 11/2	¥ Short Circuit 2 3/2		¥«» Hiding Out 10/29	¥ «» Andre 6:30-8:30am 10/23	¥«» Clash of the Titans 6:30-8:30am 1/30	¥«» Absence of Malice 11/8
7:00 am			¥«» Blankman 10/28				
7:30 am						¥ Bebe's Kids 7:30-9am 10/31	
8:00 am	Neverending Story 10/26	Neverending Story 1/26		«» Making of Drop Zone 10/29			¥«» Fast Getaway II 8:30-10am 2/7
8:30 am	Wizard of Oz 10/26	2 Animated Hero Classics 3/16					
9:00 am	¥ «» Wild Thing 9-10:30am 10/12	¥«» Ghost 9-11:30am 4/27	¥ A Walk In The Clouds 8:30-10:30am 12/2		¥«» Forrest Gump 10/30	¥«» The Adventures of Yellow Dog 8:30-10am 3/20	¥«» 1492: Conquest of Paradise 11/1
9:30 am				¥ A Million to Juan 1/14			
10:00 am	The Making of Richie Rich 10:30-11:30am 2/8	¥ «» Iron Eagle II 9:30-11:30am 10/27				¥ Necessary Roughness 9:30-11:30am 12/5	
10:30 am			¥ «» Iron Eagle II 10/21				
11:00 am	Inside the NFL 1/18	4 In the Gloaming 11:30am-1:30pm 5/11					
11:30 am				¥ Sense & Sensibility 11:30am-2pm 1/21	¥ Made In America 11am-1pm 10/16	¥«» Last of the Dogmen 11:30am-1:30pm 2/6	America Undercover 3/7
12:00 pm	¥«» Folks 11:30-1:30pm 3/15	¥ The Bridges of Madison County 12:30-3pm 10/13					
12:30 pm							
1:00 pm			¥ A Chorus Line 12-2pm 11/4	¥«» Last of the Dogmen 12:30-2:30pm 2/11	¥ Nell 3/5	¥«» Fast Forward 12:30-2:30pm 10/10	¥«» Sweet Dreams 10/11
1:30 pm	¥ Little Women 12:30-2:30pm 2/1	¥«» Legend of Billie Jean 1-3pm 10/6					
2:00 pm			America Undercover 1/13				
2:30 pm				¥ A Little Princess 2:30-4:30pm 2/4	¥ Sense & Sensibility 1:30-4pm 1/29	¥«» Merlin 11/7	¥«» Warrior Spirit 3/14
3:00 pm	¥ Made in America 10/19	¥ Peggy Sue Got Married 3-5pm 2/9	¥«» A Time of Destiny 2:30-4:30pm 3/10				
3:30 pm							
4:00 pm		¥ Made in America 3:30-5:30pm 1/19		¥«» Pontiac Moon 1/28	Δ Heartsounds 4-6:30pm 12/4		Lifestories 3:30-4:30pm 1/31
4:30 pm							Warrior Spirit (con't)
5:00 pm	¥ Man Trouble 1/11	¥ It Takes Two 4-6pm 1/12				¥«» Nine Months 1/23	
5:30 pm				¥«» Airheads 5-6:30pm 10/22			¥ French Kiss 10/18
6:00 pm			¥ Bye, Bye Love 1/20				
6:30 pm					¥ Peggy Sue Got Married 2/5	¥«» Odd Jobs 5:30-7:30pm 10/24	
7:00 pm	¥«» Richie Rich 6-8pm 10/5	¥ Steel Magnolias 10/21		¥«» Dr. Jekyll & Ms. Hyde 10/15			Inside the NFL 10/25
7:30 pm			Testament 2/3				
8:00 pm	¥«» Eye For An Eye 1/25	¥«» 48 Hours 12/1	¥«» Above Suspicion 10/14	¥«» To Die For 8-10pm 12/3	¥«» Jade 11/6	¥ Lady Bugs 8-9:30pm 2/13	¥«» The Professional 2/14
8:30 pm							
9:00 pm				6 George Carlin 9:30-10:30pm 3/4			
9:30 pm						Past Perfect 10/17	
10:00 pm	Comic Relief's 10th Anniversary 10-11pm 11/30	¥«» Δ Head Above Water 10-12am 4/20	Tracey Takes On 1/27	¥«» Tremors 2 10:30-12:30am 11/5	Larry Sanders 2/5		¥«» The Getaway 9-11pm 12/6
10:30 pm					Undercover 10:30-11:30pm 1/15		

Key: # Parental Guideline (1 = TVY, 2 = TVY7, 3 = TVG, 4 = TVPG, 5 = TV14, 6 = TVMA)   ¥ MPAA Rating   «» Violence Code   Δ Advisory

SHO

	SATURDAY	SUNDAY	MONDAY	TUESDAY	WEDNESDAY	THURSDAY	FRIDAY
6:00 am	¥Δ Powder 5-7am 1/11	Mima 5:30-7am 12/1	¥«»Δ Terminal Velocity 5-7am 1/27	¥Δ Hackers 5-7am 1/28	The Song Spinner 5:30-7:30am 12/4	¥«»Δ The House on Carroll Street 5-7am 10/31	
6:30 am							
7:00 am	1 Richard Scarry 3/8	Mrs. Piggle Wiggle 1/26	Richard Scarry 3/3	1 American Heroes & Legends 2/11		Treasure Island 1/16	Ship to Shore 11/8
7:30 am		Treasure Island 1/19		1 American Heroes & Legends 2/4	Paddington's Birthday 10/16		2 Degrassi Junior High 2/7
8:00 am	¥«»Δ Far & Away 1/25	Treasure Island 1/26	The Angry Red Planet 11/4	¥ Speed Zone 8-10am 3/18	¥Δ Princess Caraboo 11/6	Daisies in December 1/16	3 The Two Little Bears 2/7
8:30 am							
9:00 am		¥Δ What About Bob? 10/6	¥Δ The Owl & the Pussycat 8:30-10:30am 2/10	Twelve Hours to Kill 9-11am 10/8			
9:30 am							
10:00 am	¥«»Δ The Adventures of Baron Munchausen 10/19				¥Δ The American President 1/22	¥Δ Chaplin 9am-12pm 10/10	¥ Breaking Away 8:30-10:30 am 10/11
10:30 am		¥«»Δ Golden Eye 10am-12:30pm 4/27	Bugs Bunny/Road Runner Movie 9:30-11:30am 10/21	Fate is the Hunter 10:30am-12:30pm 10/15			
11:00 am						The Lady from Shanghai 11/7	Whiskers 10am-12pm 1/31
11:30 am		¥«»Δ Mommie Dearest 12-2:30pm 1/12	¥Δ Bagdad Cafe 3/3				
12:00 pm				¥«»Δ Tough Enough 12-2pm 10/29	¥Δ Tough Enough 11am-1pm 10/9		¥«»Δ Jumanji 11am-1pm 2/14
12:30 pm	¥Δ High Spirits 12:30-2:30pm 2/8						
1:00 pm		¥«»Δ Super Mario Bros. 2/2				¥Δ A River Runs Through It 12:30-3pm 3/20	¥«»Δ The Last American Hero 1-3pm 1/17
1:30 pm			¥«»Δ Tap 10/7	Muscle Beach Party 10/22	¥Δ End of the Line 10/16		
2:00 pm	¥Δ Drop Dead Fred 1-3pm 10/5						¥ Annie O 1:30-3:30pm 11/1
2:30 pm		Δ Making of Donnie Brasco 3/9				¥Δ Mother, Jugs & Speed 1:30-3:30pm 10/24	
3:00 pm	¥Δ Camp Nowhere 11/2	¥Δ Only You 2-4pm 3/16	¥«»Δ Harmony Cats 2:30-4:30pm 10/28	3 Bye Bye Birdie 2:30-4:30pm 3/4			¥«»Δ 100 Rifles 2-4pm 3/21
3:30 pm						¥Δ Chu Chu & The Philly Flash 3:30-5:30pm 2/13	
4:00 pm		¥Δ Princess Caraboo 3:30-5:30pm 2/9			¥«»Δ Urban Cowboy 2/5		
4:30 pm				¥ Captain Nuke & The Bomber Boys 1/21			¥«»Δ Obsessed 10/18
5:00 pm	¥Δ Things Change 4:30-6pm 3/15	¥Δ Canadian Bacon 4:30-6:30pm 10/13	¥Δ A Month In the Country 1/20			¥«»Δ A World Apart 4:30-6:30pm 2/6	
5:30 pm							
6:00 pm	¥«»Δ Hook 5:30-8pm 3/1						¥«»Δ King Kong Lives 11/8
6:30 pm		Prisoner of Zenda, Inc. 10/27	¥«»Δ Far & Away 5:30-8pm 1/13	¥Δ A Pyromaniac's Love Story 2/4	¥Δ What About Bob? 10/23	Prisoner of Zenda, Inc. 10/17	
7:00 pm	¥Δ La Bamba 6-8pm 1/18						
7:30 pm							
8:00 pm	¥«»Δ Get Shorty 8-10pm 11/30		¥«»Δ Never Talk to Strangers 10/14	¥«»Δ Dolores Claiborne 8-10:30pm 1/14	¥«»Δ Silence of the Lambs 8-10pm 10/30	«»Δ Silver Strand 8-10pm 12/5	¥Δ Roommates 10/25
8:30 pm		¥Δ Full Body Massage 11/3					
9:00 pm	¥«»Δ Skyscraper 10-12am 2/1				¥«»Δ Funny Bones 9:30-11:30pm 2/12	¥«»Δ Men of War 10-12am 3/13	
9:30 pm			¥Δ The Baby-Sitters Club 9:30-11:30pm 2/3				
10:00 pm	«»Δ Black Scorpion II 10:30-12am 10/26	¥«»Δ Judge Dredd 9:30-11:30pm 5/4		«» Alien Avengers 12/3	¥Δ Powder 10:30-12:30am 1/29	¥Δ Man of the House 10:30-12:30am 3/6	«»Δ Outer Limits 1/24
10:30 pm							

Key: # Parental Guideline (1 = TVY, 2 = TVY7, 3 = TVG, 4 = TVPG, 5 = TV14, 6 = TVMA) ¥ MPAA Rating «» Violence Code Δ Advisory

PART II

TELEVISION VIOLENCE IN "REALITY" (NON-FICTIONAL) PROGRAMMING: UNIVERSITY OF TEXAS AT AUSTIN STUDY

Dr. Charles Whitney
Dr. Ellen Wartella
Dr. Dominic Lasorsa
Dr. Wayne Danielson
Adriana Olivarez
Nancy Jennings
Rafael Lopez

SUMMARY

Some 526 non-fictional reality programs from a constructed 1996-1997 sample week on 23 television and cable channels were analyzed for the nature and context of their violent portrayals. The results were compared with similar analyses of 1995-1996 and 1994-1995 programs.

As a genre of television programming, reality shows are substantially less violent than television programming overall. As we show in this report, and as is true of television programming overall, there is great stability in our findings across the three-year study period. However, both in considering reality programming, and most especially in examining violence in reality programming, a number of contextual considerations must be addressed. Among them are where these programs appear in the broadcast universe, when they appear, and some special considerations that the reality genre demands attention to.

** *Where:* In sheer prevalence, reality programs tend to be concentrated on network stations and, to an increasing extent across the study period, on basic cable; public television programs proportionately more reality fare but in most television markets constitutes but a single channel. Premium cable focuses almost exclusively on entertainment, not reality, programming. Consistently for three years, we have found that public television reality programs contain the least violence and network-affiliated stations the most.

** *When:* Reality shows are more a daytime than a nighttime phenomenon. We have consistently found over three years, however, that prime-time reality programs are more violent than daytime shows, and, in fact, in Years 2 and 3, early prime-time programs appear slightly more violent than 8-11 p.m. reality shows. Of concern in Year 3 is a significant increase in levels of visual violence in the late afternoon (3-6 p.m.), a time when children and adolescents are an important segment of the audience.

** *Violence in Reality Genres:* Overall, 61 percent of 1996-1997 reality programs contained no visual violence. We have argued, and now have three years of data to support the notion, that "reality programs" as a genre merit special consideration for both formal and discursive reasons. We now have compelling evidence to support our notion that examining not just visual depictions of violence but also the nature and structure of *Talk About Violence* provides richer context in understanding violence in reality programs. Some 10 percent of Year 3 reality programs contained Talk About Violence without visual depictions. Moreover, we have consistent evidence that "reality" as a genre itself is too broad. Police Shows are clearly the most violent reality programs, and Talk Shows the least violent. Tabloid news programs are more likely to feature violence than other News and Public Affairs programs, and "entertainment-reality" genres represent something of a hybrid between the entertainment television analyzed by our Santa Barbara colleagues and "real reality" programs.

TELEVISION VIOLENCE IN 'REALITY' (NON-FICTIONAL) PROGRAMMING:

UNIVERSITY OF TEXAS AT AUSTIN STUDY

"Reality" programming constitutes a significant--and growing--portion of the television landscape, and while much of the criticism of television violence has concerned fictional programming, shows depicting the "real world" raise concerns of their own.

We have noted in the past two years (NTVS, 1997, Part II, NTVS, 1998, Part II), "reality" programming manifests some distinct differences from other forms of programming that require distinct forms of analysis, and our goal here is to explain, and provide that analysis for the 1996-1997 television season, making comparisons with the two prior years where such comparisons are informative.

Moreover, our data indicate that reality programming may indeed be an area of increasing interest, for it represents an increasing portion of the content of television: the 526 reality programs in the 1996-1997 sample represent a six percent increase from the 1995-1996 (n=494), and a 34 percent increase from the first year (n=393 in 1994-1995).

Our report is divided as follows: we first define "reality" programming and explain and provide a rationale for its analysis; we then describe our methods (see NTVS, 1997, for a more complete account), including the assessment of the reliability of our coding; data from the 1996-1997 season (Year 3) are presented and compared with the previous years, with special attention to the various genres of reality programming; and we conclude with recommendations for the industry, policymakers, and the public.

Our overall finding for the current year is that reality programming in 1996-1997 is on most particulars very similar to what we have found in the two prior seasons. This gives us some comfort, for it suggests that the methods we have been using to describe reality television and its violent aspects yield reliable results.

Reality Programming Defined

Reality programs on television are defined as nonfictional programming in which the portrayal is presumed to present current or historical events or circumstances. The production presents itself as being a realistic account.

Included are news and public affairs programming[1], interview and talk shows, entertainment news-and-review programs, documentaries, and other programs presenting themselves as recreations of "real-world" events, such as those depicting

---

[1] Regularly scheduled news programs (e.g., *ABC World News Tonight*), national and local news "drop-ins" on morning news programs, and news preemptions of regularly scheduled programming are not coded, a proviso included as part of the original contract between NCTA and the researchers. Other exclusions (e.g., game shows) are noted in the Santa Barbara report.

scenes of police or emergency workers, or humorous events or circumstances. Programs may be either actual or recreated depictions of events or circumstances, but in the case of the latter, the context must make it clear that efforts have been made to recapture a past event as it happened. Although not coded for this project, sporting events and roundups, instructional programs, and quiz and game shows also are considered reality programs.

Excluded are "docu-dramas" featuring invented or composite characters or dialogue which it can be reasonably inferred did not occur, and other programming in which the dramatic or humorous intent of the program outweighs intent to re-present actual events or circumstances; docu-dramas were coded as dramatic or movie programming by the Santa Barbara team.

The boundaries between reality and unreality are not always clear, and television producers may even exploit this lack of clarity. Programs dealing with paranormal and extraterrestrial phenomena, for example, may take pains to present as plausible "events" which are extremely unlikely ever to have occurred. As we have previously noted, *all* mediated versions of reality, both on television and in other media, are re-presentations, and a rich critical and cultural literature explores the degree to which media representations "in fact" recapture reality. Most writers would agree, however, that "reality" as a concept is one of great importance, for the interpretive frames that audience members, particularly those past early childhood, bring to such content may vary significantly from those they bring to programming recognized as fictional. Indeed, the research literature suggests that realism as a contextual feature of television programs *heightens* involvement, arousal and aggression, may sharpen viewer perceptions of the real world, leading viewers to perceive the real world as violent. At least one study, moreover, found both short-term (immediate post-test) and longer term (three days later) increases in both personal judgments of crime victimization and in societal-level risk for a televised crime documentary, while two different fictionalized dramas showed no enduring impact. For more complete discussions of research on the effects of televised messages on viewers, particularly those involving reality viewing, see NTVS, 1997 and 1998.

Reality *programming,* moreover, is different from other programming in key respects. First, relatively little reality programming is directed at young children.[2] However, while most reality shows are not *intended* for children, they are widely available when children may be in the audience--during the day for preschool children, in the afternoon for all children, in early prime time, and on weekends.

Many reality programs vary *in form* from other television programs, and in ways that affect how those programs must be assessed. First, we again note that to a far greater extent than is true of fictional programming, reality shows are *segmented*, meaning that one program may include several "mini-programs" on differing topics, as do magazine-style news shows such as *20-20* and police and emergency shows such as *Rescue 911.* Moreover, narratively, reality shows are far more likely than their fictional

---

[2] Indeed, one subgenre, news and public affairs, skews older than any other category of television programming, and, as we note below, child- and family-oriented cable channels present almost no reality programming.

counterparts to recreate events by *describing* them orally rather than by depicting them visually. In part, this stems from unavailability of "real" images, in news and public affairs programs and in talk shows alike, because visual images of scenes were not captured as they occurred, and they may only be retold. In news and public affairs programs in particular, too, there is a journalistic proscription against the recreation of "real events," and from producers' points of view, part of the appeal of reality programming in general is its relatively low cost: talk is cheap; visuals are not.

For a variety of reasons, then, there are several arguments for detailed study of televised reality programs, most especially aspects of those programs related to their violent content.

In principle, there is every reason to expect reality-based television to have the same cognitive, affective and behavioral impacts on audiences as fictional television. Indeed, one recent analysis (Oliver & Armstrong, 1995) found that punitive attitudes about crime, higher levels of racial prejudice and higher levels of authoritarianism were associated with more frequent viewing of, and enjoyment of reality-based police programs but not with enjoyment of fictional crime programming. Further, a recent study of agenda-setting on crime in the state of Texas, has found that newspaper and television news coverage of crime is a far stronger predictor of public *salience*, or judgment of civic importance, of crime as an issue, than is actual incidence of crime (Ghanem & Evatt, 1995), evidence that the medium's depictions may have attitudinal effects on matters related to the issues here.

MEASURING VIOLENCE IN REALITY PROGRAMS

Violence Defined

The definition of televised violence for reality programs is the same as it is for entertainment programs: *Evidence of a credible threat of physical force or the actual use of such force intended to physically harm or intimidate an animate being or group of beings. Violence also includes certain depictions of physically harmful consequences against an animate being that occur as a result of violent means.*

There is one exception. In reality programming, *Talk About Violence* is also coded. *Talk About Violence* is defined as *the verbal recounting of threats, acts and/or harmful consequences by a person or person-like character appearing on screen or heard from off screen. Verbal abuse* per se *is not coded as Talk About Violence.*

We would note in passing that in reality programming (as in all other programming), accidental or unintentional physical harm is not considered violence. Hence in a reality program such as *America's Funniest Home Videos,* unintentional harm is not considered a violent act or consequence, unless accidental harm occurs in an otherwise violent sequence. Moreover, our intention, as in prior years, is to analyze the presentation of violence in reality programs in the *context* in which it occurs.

Levels of Analysis

Reality-based programs are analyzed at three levels--the *program*, the *segment* and the *violent sequence*. Unlike the Santa Barbara coders, we do not code at the

Perpetrator-Action-Target level, but many of the context variables coded at the PAT level in their analysis were coded at the sequence level in the Texas study.[3]

Program: At the program level of analysis, coding is virtually identical with that described in the Santa Barbara report: Genre, Network, Time of Broadcast, Program Name, Day and Date, Program Length, and Presence of Ratings and Advisories. One variable, identifying whether programs were programs were originally produced for the channel or network on which the appeared or not (e.g., syndicated programs) was added for the second year.

Segment: As noted above, reality programming is frequently segmented. A segment is defined as "a coherent part of a broadcast, a partitioned narrative within a program that exhibits unity within itself and separation, by topic and/or central focal character, from other segments within a program." For instance, separate "stories" within a news magazine program or police-reality show are coded as separate segments.

We were interested in describing the nature of the topics discussed in these segments. For example, we coded the main theme, subject or issue under discussion in each segment, as well as secondary themes that might be present.[4] Secondly, segments were coded for the *locale* of the main topic--where the action described occurred--within or outside the United States, or both--and for *social setting*--whether the segment took place outside the United States, in a U.S. city, suburb, small town or rural area. The locale and social setting were coded as context variables, in that they may influence viewer *identification* with the violence described; presumably violence in a circumstance with which a viewer might identify would be more pertinent than that which occurs at a great remove (cf. M. Tulloch & J. Tulloch, 1992).

All segments, whether they contain violence or not, are coded for topic, locale and social setting, in order to give us a basis of comparison for describing violent and nonviolent reality segments. Coders then identify segments as containing visual violence sequences and/or talk-about violence sequences, both, or neither.

Several contextual variables are coded at the *segment* level: the presence of reenactments; rewards and punishments; program realism; pain cues; and overall harm and pain.

When Talk About Violence or Visual Violence is present in a segment or program, that violence is further described by sequence coding.

The Violent Sequence: The first determination made at the sequence level is whether that sequence is to be coded as a Talk About Violence or a Visual Violence sequence. In a Year 2 coding change from the first year, we also added a third possibility--that a sequence could contain both Visual and Talk About Violence.

---

[3] See the Codebook for further details on coding of the variables; changes in the codebook are noted in the text.

[4] See NTVS, 1996, Ch. 2, for further details.

We decided that in addition to determining talk about violence and visual depictions of violence it was important to identify when we had a sequence that had both talk about violence and visual violence. For purposes of this report, the sequences that were identified as having both will *only* be analyzed as sequences with visual depictions of violence because we decided, from the beginning, that visual violence took precedence over talk about violence. Definitions for each type of sequence are as follows:

A visual violence sequence is a related sequence of violent behaviors, actions, or depictions that occur without a significant break in the flow of actual or imminent violence. A related sequence means that one behavior, action or depiction complements another, or is a direct response to another. The important aspect about a violence sequence is that it represents a narrative flow of events or depictions that are connected to one another. Because of this relational aspect, violent sequences typically occur in the same general setting among the same characters or types of characters. A violence sequence begins with an initial depiction of violence such as 1) a credible threat that occurs, 2) a violent behavior that occurs, or 3) physically harmful consequences. A violent sequence ends when a significant break in the flow of action occurs. A break is considered significant when either 1) the threat of violence, the actual violent behavior and/or the harmful consequences of violence stop or cease within a scene or 2) the primary setting shifts in time or place in a way that extensively interrupts the flow of related action in the sequence.

A talk about violence sequence is a conversation related to violence, as elsewhere defined. A sequence begins with an initial utterance concerning a violent credible threat, behavior, or physically harmful consequence and continues so long as the discussion or conversation is centered on that act or closely related acts. The introduction of a new character or speaker may or may not signal the end of a sequence; it signals the end of a sequence if the new character changes the direction of the discussion, either by introducing a new topic or by changing the focus of the discussion.

A visual and talk about violence sequence begins with an initial visual depiction of violence as defined under visual violence sequence and turns into a talk about violence sequence as defined under talk about violence sequence at some point, either simultaneously with the visual depiction or right after it. In a talk show for example, a sequence might start with a short visual depiction of a violent act and then continue as a discussion related to the visual. A Visual And Talk About Violence sequence begins as defined under a visual violence sequence and ends when the discussion related to the visual (talk about violence) and the visual depiction are over and there is a shift to a non-violent or unrelated topic. The important aspect about a visual and talk about violence sequence is that it represents a narrative flow of events or depictions that are connected to one another. However, any discussion related to the visual before it is shown is coded as a separate talk about violence sequence. Thus, a Visual and Talk About Violence sequence never begins with talk about violence.

Violent talk is coded for the *graphicness of the discussion of violence,* as being either concrete and physical in detail or as being general and vague and for the *level of testimony*--whether the account involves *first person* description, of a violent act that involved the speaker as perpetrator or victim, an eyewitness or *second-person* account of the observation of violence or its aftermath, or a *third-person* account of violence which occurred elsewhere. As with our segment-level coding of locale and setting, we suggest that first- and second-person reports are more involving than third-person ones (cf. Davison, 1983).

Several other sequence variables were added to the codebook for the second year: 1) A summary measure of the predominant form of violence in a sequence in which multiple forms of violence were present; 2) a measure of the predominant or most salient weapon in a violent sequence, where multiple violent means were present; and 3) for Talk About Violence sequences, an indicator of whether the sequence was followed by a related Visual And Talk About Violence sequence.

Finally, *characters involved in violence* are coded at the sequence level, by gender, age, race, citizenship or national origin, and their authority or official status (e.g., whether they are a program's narrator or host, another journalist, an expert or professional, a police or law enforcement official, military personnel, other government authority, or have no official status). In the first year, these data were coded at the segment level (though not analyzed by segment in our report); these codes were brought to the sequence level to increase coder reliability. Also at the sequence level, characters are coded for their relationship to violent acts--whether they are victims, relatives of or spokespersons for victims, perpetrators[5] of violence, relatives of or spokespersons for perpetrators, or witnesses of violent acts. These are "dummy codes," meaning that someone who was, in a sequence, both a perpetrator and a victim or target of violence, would be coded as both. Finally, in addition, perpetrators of violence are coded for sixteen reasons or motivations for violent activity.

SAMPLING

The sampling procedure is described in detail in the Santa Barbara report. Once programs were sampled and taped, a determination was made as to whether a program was to be considered an entertainment program or a reality program. In cases where there was a question or disagreement as to whether programs were entertainment or reality, or whether a sample program was to be coded at all, a resolution was reached by conferral between the two sites.

As elsewhere noted, not all sampled reality programs were coded. Excluded were regularly scheduled news programs such as the *CBS Evening News,* instructional programs, religious programs, or quiz shows. In addition, commercials in all programming, and news "drop-ins" in reality programming were excluded. When breaking news preempted sampled programs, the programs, but not the news preemptions, were coded if the interruption was 10 minutes or less. When preemptions were longer, the program slot was returned to the sample pool and the program was not coded.

The total number of reality programs sampled across the 1996-97 season on 23 network, independent, basic cable and premium cable channels was 1,052 (1995-96 = 908; 1994-1995 = 620). Exactly 50 percent of sampled reality shows were not coded because the programs fell into uncoded categories, compared with 47 percent in Year 2 and 36 percent in Year 1. Our 1995-1996 sample thus comprises 526 coded programs.

---

5 In all cases, characters were coded as perpetrators if they were *actual or alleged* perpetrators of violence; thus a defendant in a case of violent crime would be considered a perpetrator.

METHODS[6]

The University of Texas at Austin research team consisted of four professors who began working on the project from the onset. Some 20 University of Texas undergraduate and graduate students served as coders on the project, supervised by three graduate research assistants and one undergraduate student coding supervisor, and an additional four students worked only on data entry. Coders were paid at an hourly rate and were expected to work on coding for a minimum of 10 hours per week and a maximum of 19 hours per week. The research assistants trained the coders and supervised coding sessions. The bulk of the coding was done in the spring of 1997.

Typical coding sessions lasted from about one hour to four hours. During a coding session, the coder would be assigned certain programs, segments or sequences to watch and to code. Coding was done in three "passes" through a program: a) In the first pass, a graduate research assistant coded all program-level codes and identified the beginning and ending times of each segment. b) In the second pass, a senior, experienced, coder coded the segment-level variables and identified sequences containing Visual and Talk-About violence. c) In the third pass, a coder coded violent sequences and characters. All coding was done in the project office on the University of Texas campus.

Coders received a copy of the reality program codebook, a 32-page document covering all coding procedures.

RELIABILITY

The reliability of the coding process was calculated by examining the agreements and disagreements among the coders in the various decisions they made in coding a subsample of reality television programming used in this project. Reliability was tested at all four levels of analysis.

For program and segment reliability testing, the 18 coders working at the time of the tests identified the beginning and end times of programs and segments and coded these same three programs for the program coding test. Moreover, all coders were tested on the same previously identified segments for the segment test. The three programs for the program test represented two genres of reality programming in the sample: Entertainment News and Review shows and Documentaries. During the segment testing, one Entertainment Non-News show and one Police show were selected to expand the genre selection from the program testing. An attempt was made during the segment testing to select segments with different levels and kinds of violent programming. Of the ten segments tested in two programs, four segments contained only talk about violence, two segments contained only visual violence, two segments contained both talk about and visual violence, and two segments contained neither talk about nor visual violence.

For sequence and character at sequence reliability testing, 14 coders were involved. The reduction of coders resulted from attrition. The three programs for the sequence and

---

6 Coding methods parallel those in the first two years of the study; see NTVS, 1998, Part II, and 1997, Part II.

character at sequence test represented three genres of reality programming in the sample: Entertainment News and Review shows, Documentaries, and Talk Shows. An attempt was made during both tests to select segments with different levels and kinds of violent programming. Of the seven sequences selected for the testing, three sequences contained only visual violence, three sequences contained only talk about violence and one sequence contained both talk about and visual violence.

The percentage of intercoder agreement was computed by adding the number of times each pair of coders agreed in their coding, divided by the total number of variables codes. When one coder did not code a particular variable, the corresponding data were considered as missing and, therefore, were not included in the total percentages. For example, if Coder A did but Coder B did not identify a perpetrator in a violent sequence, the two were considered to have disagreed on the presence of a perpetrator. However, if Coder A left the variable for presence of perpetrator blank, then this would be considered missing, not a disagreement between Coder A and Coder B.

During the reliability assessment, we discovered that coders were doing better than last year identifying the beginning and ending times of sequences. The solution to last year's problem seemed to be limiting the number of coders who identified sequences to only those who had been with the project an extended time and who had been trained together as a group. Similarly with last year's testing, we did discover that coders were looking at the same section of the segment, whether they identified one or more sequences. For example, Coder A may identify only one sequence and Coder B may identify 2 sequences. However, both coders are looking at the same space of time, Coder B identifying two sequences in the same time frame of Coder A's one sequence.

The following table shows the improvement. As can be seen, coders had a stronger agreement on the number of sequences in each program. The only exception would be with Program B, Coder B. This coder was unable to complete coding the program due to logistical problem with the tape. However, Coder B does show similar identification of sequences with other coders in the other two programs.

Coder	Program A	Program B	Program C	Total
Coder A	12	8	3	23
Coder B	9	3	3	15
Coder C	10	9	3	22
Coder D	10	10	4	24
Coder E	9	10	5	24

Moreover, as can be seen in the following table, coders who had located similar time frames had similar total amounts of time for each grand sequence, whether they identified one or more sequences for Program A.

In addition, we discovered that coders were also having a difficult time identifying characters. Coders generally identified the same main characters of the sequence, including the perpetrator and victim, but had difficulty discriminating minor characters. Again, the problem seemed to be not with the code itself but with the training the coders had received to help them locate minor characters. However, of the characters that the coders identified, strong agreement (80-100%) prevailed among the perpetrators and victims.

	Coder A	Coder B	Coder C	Coder D	Coder E	Mean	Median	Standard Dev.
Sequence A	0.05	0.15		0.23	0.03	0.12	0.10	0.09
Sequence B	0.08	0.05	0.18	0.33	0.33	0.19	0.18	0.13
Sequence C	0.03	0.02	0.02	0.38	0.08	0.11	0.03	0.16
Sequence D	0.08	0.10	0.10			0.09	0.10	0.01
Sequence E	0.32		0.38	0.40	0.40	0.38	0.39	0.04
Sequence F	0.35	0.10	0.18	0.43	0.35	0.28	0.35	0.14
Sequence G	0.22	0.22	0.22	0.15	0.85	0.33	0.22	0.29
Sequence H	0.17	0.35	0.15	0.65	0.77	0.42	0.35	0.28
Sequence I	0.17	0.50	0.15	0.25	0.48	0.31	0.25	0.17
Sequence J	0.15			0.95		0.55	0.55	0.57
Sequence K	0.78	0.78	0.80	2.13	0.80	1.06	0.80	0.60

A total of 1,562 variables were coded in the reliability test; this included 96 variables at the program level, 400 variables at the segment level, 322 sequence variables, and 744 character variables at the sequence level.

At the program level, a total of 96 variables were coded, not counting the special coding done within segments. The percentages of intercoder agreement for coding done at the segment level ranged from 87 to 99 agreement:

Coder

	B	C	D	E	F	G	H	I	J	K	L	M	N	O	P	Q	R	S
A	0.96	0.96	0.99	0.93	0.99	0.94	0.96	0.97	0.91	0.94	0.98	0.97	0.97	0.96	0.96	0.98	0.93	0.99
B		0.98	0.97	0.96	0.97	0.95	0.98	0.96	0.92	0.95	0.96	0.97	0.94	0.95	0.95	0.98	0.92	0.96
C			0.97	0.94	0.97	0.94	0.98	0.95	0.92	0.95	0.96	0.97	0.92	0.94	0.94	0.98	0.92	0.96
D				0.94	0.98	0.95	0.97	0.96	0.92	0.94	0.97	0.98	0.96	0.97	0.97	0.99	0.94	0.98
E					0.93	0.93	0.94	0.94	0.94	0.91	0.91	0.93	0.91	0.93	0.93	0.94	0.89	0.94
F						0.93	0.97	0.96	0.91	0.95	0.99	0.98	0.96	0.95	0.95	0.99	0.91	0.98
G							0.94	0.93	0.89	0.94	0.91	0.95	0.92	0.95	0.94	0.94	0.95	0.95
H								0.95	0.92	0.95	0.96	0.97	0.92	0.94	0.94	0.98	0.93	0.97
I									0.94	0.94	0.95	0.95	0.94	0.93	0.93	0.95	0.94	0.98
J										0.89	0.90	0.91	0.87	0.90	0.90	0.92	0.90	0.92
K											0.94	0.96	0.90	0.92	0.90	0.95	0.94	0.95
L												0.97	0.95	0.94	0.94	0.98	0.93	0.97
M													0.94	0.97	0.95	0.99	0.95	0.96
N														0.95	0.95	0.95	0.89	0.96
O															0.98	0.96	0.93	0.95
P																0.96	0.90	0.95
Q																	0.93	0.97
R																		0.94

Mean	0.94	
Median	0.95	
Mode	0.94	
St. Dev.	0.02	

Coding at the segment level involved a total of 400 coding decisions. Percentages of intercoder agreement for this coding phase ranged from 78 to 93:

Coder

	B	C	D	E	F	G	H	I	J	K	L	M	N	O	P	Q	R	S
A	0.93	0.89	0.89	0.89	0.93	0.89	0.87	0.83	0.89	0.86	0.84	0.86	0.91	0.89	0.86	0.91	0.82	0.85
B		0.88	0.91	0.89	0.93	0.90	0.87	0.82	0.90	0.86	0.84	0.87	0.93	0.90	0.87	0.92	0.82	0.84
C			0.88	0.88	0.88	0.86	0.90	0.86	0.87	0.87	0.85	0.88	0.88	0.88	0.85	0.87	0.81	0.83
D				0.88	0.89	0.89	0.87	0.85	0.88	0.87	0.88	0.89	0.89	0.88	0.84	0.91	0.80	0.87
E					0.88	0.86	0.85	0.82	0.88	0.84	0.83	0.87	0.89	0.86	0.83	0.89	0.79	0.85
F						0.89	0.90	0.82	0.89	0.86	0.87	0.86	0.92	0.89	0.85	0.92	0.84	0.84
G							0.84	0.83	0.87	0.85	0.83	0.85	0.88	0.85	0.83	0.90	0.79	0.85
H								0.84	0.86	0.90	0.85	0.89	0.86	0.87	0.83	0.87	0.84	0.81
I									0.81	0.83	0.79	0.83	0.82	0.85	0.78	0.85	0.79	0.84
J										0.86	0.83	0.85	0.91	0.89	0.83	0.90	0.79	0.82
K											0.84	0.90	0.87	0.88	0.82	0.87	0.80	0.81
L												0.83	0.85	0.83	0.78	0.84	0.80	0.82
M													0.89	0.87	0.84	0.87	0.81	0.83
N														0.89	0.83	0.90	0.83	0.84
O															0.83	0.90	0.84	0.84
P																0.86	0.78	0.83
Q																	0.81	0.86
R																		0.78

Mean	0.86	
Median	0.86	
Mode	0.84	
St. Dev.	0.03	

At the sequence level, coders made 322 coding decisions, excluding character coding decisions. Percentages of intercoder agreement at this level ranged between 86 and 95:

	B	C	D	E	F	G	H	I	J	K	L	M	N
A	0.94	0.94	0.93	0.95	0.89	0.95	0.91	0.94	0.92	0.93	0.92	0.93	0.93
B		0.93	0.94	0.92	0.89	0.94	0.92	0.94	0.92	0.91	0.91	0.92	0.93
C			0.93	0.93	0.92	0.94	0.92	0.94	0.91	0.91	0.91	0.94	0.91
D				0.91	0.89	0.93	0.92	0.94	0.93	0.90	0.91	0.93	0.91
E					0.88	0.93	0.91	0.91	0.91	0.92	0.90	0.92	0.91
F						0.91	0.90	0.91	0.89	0.90	0.86	0.91	0.89
G							0.92	0.94	0.92	0.94	0.91	0.93	0.95
H								0.93	0.93	0.91	0.89	0.95	0.93
I									0.93	0.92	0.91	0.94	0.91
J										0.95	0.89	0.95	0.91
K											0.89	0.93	0.93
L												0.90	0.89
M													0.94

Mean	0.92
Median	0.92
Mode	0.91
St. Dev.	0.02

Coding of characters at the sequence level involved 744 coding decisions. Percentages of intercoder agreement for this coding phase ranged between 85 and 95:

Coder

	B	C	D	E	F	G	H	I	J	K	L	M	N
A	0.84	0.94	0.93	0.93	0.94	0.95	0.90	0.93	0.93	0.92	0.95	0.92	0.94
B		0.86	0.87	0.85	0.87	0.87	0.85	0.85	0.85	0.87	0.87	0.86	0.86
C			0.93	0.93	0.95	0.93	0.90	0.93	0.91	0.93	0.94	0.91	0.94
D				0.91	0.94	0.94	0.94	0.94	0.92	0.94	0.93	0.93	0.95
E					0.93	0.92	0.91	0.93	0.90	0.90	0.94	0.90	0.93
F						0.94	0.92	0.95	0.92	0.94	0.94	0.91	0.94
G							0.93	0.92	0.94	0.92	0.95	0.92	0.94
H								0.93	0.91	0.91	0.93	0.92	0.92
I									0.90	0.92	0.94	0.93	0.95
J										0.91	0.94	0.93	0.91
K											0.93	0.92	0.93
L												0.91	0.94
M													0.92

Mean	0.92
Median	0.93
Mode	0.94
St. Dev.	0.03

Thus, at each level of analysis, our reliability tests show high levels of intercoder agreement.

RESULTS

For the 1996-1997 season, we analyzed 526 programs across 23 cable and network channels. This number is 6.5 percent larger than the number (494) of programs analyzed for the prior year and 34 percent larger than the number in the first year of the study (393). Since the number of programs in the sample, across the three seasons, has remained virtually constant, the increase in the number of reality programs indicates that reality fare constitutes a larger proportion of the television universe, a trend that began several years ago.[7]

Within the 526 programs were 2,389 segments; the ratio of segments to programs has remained about the same across the three years of the study. We will begin with general descriptive data of our sampled programs. These baseline data will then be followed by an analysis of how violence is portrayed across the seven reality program genres identified in our sample. Thus, the more contextualized analysis of violence portrayals in reality programming is offered in the examination of the different reality program genres.

Description of Sampled Programs

Reality programs are predominantly either one-hour or half-hour shows. One-hour shows again comprise 45 percent of the sample. This is the usual length of programs in some of the most popular reality genres such as talk shows and documentaries. Thirty-minute programs (44% of the sample) are concentrated among Entertainment News and-Review shows (e.g., *Entertainment Tonight*), Police Shows (e.g., *Cops*), Entertainment Non-News shows (e.g., *America's Funniest Home Videos*) and News and Public Affairs shows. Most of the remainder are two-hour shows (8%), mostly morning news shows such as *Good Morning America*. The longest program was a two-and-a-half-hour music awards ceremony.

Table 1 indexes a slight rise in most genres of reality programming across the three years of the study. However, large increases are apparent in Entertainment Non-News (this genre has tripled in size across the three years)[8] and Entertainment News and Review (44 more programs in the current year than in Year 1). However, in general both the number and proportions of programs in most reality-program genres are remarkably stable across the three years of the study.

---

[7] However, a portion of the large increase in the number of reality programs between 1994-1995 and 1995-1996 was likely an artifact, as we noted in last year's report, of heavy and preempted (and thus uncoded) coverage of the O.J. Simpson case in 1994-1995. See NTVS, 1997, p. 220. As Footnote 10, below, also notes, changes in inclusion rules for coding some categories of Entertainment Non News programs also accounts for a portion of the increase.

[8] Part of the increase in Entertainment Non-News was a coding decision to code, beginning with the second year, travelogue and fashion shows that were considered excluded categories in the first year Austin report but which were coded in the Santa Barbara report; that is, such shows are included in Year 2 and Year 3 University of Texas data.

Table 1: Reality Programs by Genre, 1994-95, 1995-96 and 1996-97:

Genre	1996-97	1995-1996	1994-1995
Talk Shows	21% (112)	24% (119)	27% (103)
News & Public Affairs	19% (98)	17% (86)	24% (91)
Documentaries	12% (65)	15% (74)	16% (62)
Entertainment News & Review	17% (90)	22% (106)	14% (56)
Entertainment Non-News	22% (115)	13% (66)	10% (41)
Tabloid News	6% (29)	6% (29)	5% (21)
Police	3% (17)	3% (14)	5% (19)
TOTAL	100% (526)	100% (494)	101% (393)

Reality programming is not evenly spread across channels. In general, the broadcast networks (represented here by their Los Angeles affiliates) and basic cable channels are the most frequent reality programmers: the four networks aired 157 reality shows during the constructed sample week, representing all seven of our reality genres. The 13 basic cable channels aired 202 programs, representing all genres except Police Shows and tabloid news. Together, the broadcast networks and basic cable account for two-thirds of all reality programming, virtually identical to the first two years. However, the single PBS station sampled airs more reality programs (58 in 1996-97, 60 in 1995-1995, 48 in the 1994-95 sample), most of them news and public affairs programs (n=32) or documentaries (n=15) or than any one of the four commercial network affiliates or cable stations or networks. Among the commercial networks, the NBC network owned-and-operated station, for the third year, broadcast more reality programs (52) than the CBS (42), ABC (38) or Fox (19) stations. As a group, network stations are the most diverse reality programmers, airing multiple programs representing each genre except documentaries. Independent stations are the primary vehicles for talk shows: Some 40 percent of all talk shows appear on the three independent stations analyzed, and almost half of all independent-station reality programming is talk shows. However, as a group, independent stations also broadcast at least one program in each of the other genres. Individual cable stations and networks show great variation. On basic cable, Lifetime and the Arts & Entertainment Network program the most reality programming, while most show little or none. However, the basic cable channels usually associated with music videos (MTV, VH-1) have moved more heavily into reality programming, airing 68 reality shows between them in 1996-1997 compared with 59 programs a year earlier and 24 programs in 1994-95. As was true in the past two years, child-oriented channels (Nickelodeon [No programs], Cartoon Network [0] Disney [2]) have little or no reality programming. Premium cable channels (HBO [9 programs], Cinemax [1], Showtime [1]) likewise have almost none; almost all premium-cable reality programs are documentaries, largely focusing on the making of current theatrical films. See Table 2.

Table 2: Genre by Channel Type, 1996-97, 1995-96 and 1994-95, in percents:[*]

Genre:	Network Stations	Independent Stations	Public TV	Basic Cable	Premium Cable
Talk Shows					
1996-97 (n=112)	29%	40%	3%	29%	--
1995-96 (n=119)	37	49	2	13	--
1994-95 (n=103)	38	49	--	13	--
News & Public Affairs					
1996-97 (n=98)	52	9	33	6	--
1995-96 (n=86)	39	7	38	16	--
1994-95 (n=91)	48	13	31	8	--
Documentaries					
1996-97 (n=65)	--	2	23	71	5
1995-96 (n=74)	5	4	31	53	7
1994-95 (n=59)	7	--	32	52	9
Entertainment News & Review					
1996-97 (n=90)	37	11	1	49	2
1995-96 (n=106)	31	5	3	59	2
1994-95 (n=56)	27	2	2	69	--
Entertainment Non-News					
1996-97 (n=115)	11	21	4	58	5
1995-96 (n=66)	8	14	--	79	--
1994-95 (n=37)	24	16	--	60	--
Tabloid News					
1996-97 (n=29)	66	34	--	--	--
1995-96 (n=29)	79	17	--	3	--
1994-95 (n=20)	60	40	--	--	--
Police Shows					
1996-97 (n=17)	53	6	--	41	--
1995-96 (n=14)	93	7	--	--	--
1994-95 (n=18)	83	17	--	--	--

---

[*]Percentages read horizontally.

Table 3: Genre by Time Block, 1995-96 and 1994-95, in percents:*

Genre:	6 a.m.-9 a.m.	9 a.m.-3 p.m.	3 p.m.-6 p.m.	6 p.m.-8 p.m.	8 p.m.-11 p.m.
Talk Shows					
1996-97 (n=112)	9%	58%	23%	3%	7%
1995-96 (n=119)	9	66	24	--	2
1994-95 (n=103)	4	65	30	1	--
News & Public Affairs					
1996-97 (n=98)	40	24	10	19	7
1995-96 (n=84)	38	16	8	23	16
1994-95 (n=91)	48	13	31	8	--
Documentaries					
1996-97 (n=65)	6	25	20	20	29
1995-96 (n=74)	5	31	22	15	27
1994-95 (n=59)	8	19	10	19	44
Entertainment News & Review					
1996-97 (n=90)	7	48	12	22	11
1995-96 (n=106)	9	48	26	12	6
1994-95 (n=56)	12	64	11	11	2
Entertainment Non-News					
1996-97 (n=115)	4	28	23	16	29
1995-96 (n=66)	3	41	15	18	23
1994-95 (n=37)	--	22	30	16	32
Tabloid News					
1996-97 (n=29)	--	14	14	69	3
1995-96 (n=29)	--	17	--	79	3
1994-95 (n=20)	--	--	10	90	--
Police Shows					
1996-97 (n=17)	--	6	65	--	29
1995-96 (n=14)	--	--	29	57	14
1994-95 (n=18)	--	--	22	61	17
ALL REALITY PROGRAMS					
1996-97 (n=526)	12	35	19	18	16
1995-96 (n=494)	12	40	19	17	12
1994-95 (n=393)	10	36	19	20	15

---

*Percentages read horizontally.

While there are virtually no variations by day on which reality shows appear (almost exactly one-seventh of the shows appear each day of the week), there are substantial variations by dayparts. News and public affairs shows are spread across the day (although three-fifths of the reality shows in the 6-9 a.m. block are News and public affairs shows) but few other genres are. Tabloid news shows are concentrated in the early evening. Talk Shows are concentrated during the day--9 a.m.-6 p.m., and they constitute more than a third of all reality programming in that time block In a change from years prior, Police Shows now appear in the 3 p.m.-6 p.m. block. Other genres spread across the broadcast day. See Table 3.

Many reality programs are *segmented*. For example, NBC's *Today* may move from a New York studio discussion of investment advice to a Detroit auto convention to a Los Angeles interview with a celebrity discussing her latest action-adventure film, complete with film clips. Increasingly-frequent network prime-time magazine programs likewise contain mini-documentaries. Each of these "stories" will have an internal unity that the overall program does not exhibit. To analyze all segments of a program as if the program were a unified whole strips segmented-television programs of their context.

How segmented *is* reality programming? More than half of all reality programs contain multiple segments. Clearly, there is substantial variation: virtually all News and Public Affairs, Tabloid News, and Entertainment News and Review programs are segmented, as are virtually all reality-based police programs. Two-hour morning news magazine shows may have a dozen or more segments. On the other hand, most talk shows and documentaries are unsegmented. To be able to discuss variables that "make sense" in some programs at the program level--that is, the program is not composed of separate segments but in other programs make sense only within specific segments, we choose here to describe these variables as segment-level variables, bearing in mind that where programs are unsegmented, these variables are in fact program-level variables.

Presence of Violence in Reality Programs

Our first, and most elementary, indicator of violence in reality programs is whether a program contains *any* violence, i.e., whether one or more violent sequences are coded. A program is considered violent if it contains one brief visual depiction of a threat of violence--if, for example, a police officer unholsters a handgun for one second--but the index also includes long, graphic sequences of violence as well. It should be remembered, too, that the sample excludes from analysis some genres which are likely to contain violence such as *bona fide* network and local news shows and sports programs, as well as programs that almost certainly do *not* depict violence such as instructional, religious, and game shows. Thus this relatively crude measure is presented only for baseline purposes. We discuss more contextualized depictions of reality violence below.

Sixty-one percent of our 526 sampled reality programs from 1996-1997 depict *no* visual violence, compared with 64 percent of 1995-1996 (n=494) programs and 62 percent of 1994-1995 programs (n=393). Thirty-nine percent of reality programs contain visual violence, compared with 36 percent last year and 39 percent in the first year.

An additional 10 percent of Year 3 reality programs, while not presenting visual violence, do present sequences featuring Talk About Violence, compared with 14 percent of Year 2 programs and 18 percent of Year 1 programs. Thus our overall index shows no meaningful, statistically significant change in the overall level of violence in

239

reality programming during the study years. Our Talk About Violence measures show a decline across the three years, but the year-to-year changes are within the statistical margins of error for the study. Overall, the stability in these indices appears to the researchers to be more notable than any changes.

Table 4: Violence in Reality Programs, 1996-97, 1995-96, and 1994-95:

	No Violence	Visual Violence	Talk About Violence
1996-1997 (n=526)	51.0%	39.2%	9.9%
1995-1996 (n=494)	49.4%	36.2%	14.4%
1994-1995 (n=393)	43.5%	38.7%	17.8%

There is a great deal of variation, among those genres which contain some violence, in the amount and types of violence they *do* contain. Table 5 shows that Police Shows and Tabloid news shows stand out from other genres in overall presence of violence For the third consecutive year, *every* police show in our sample contained visual violence, and 86 percent of Tabloid news shows present either visual (79%) or talk about (7%) violence sequences (93% of Year 2 and 100% of Year 1 Tabloid news shows contained either visual or talk about violence). As Table 5 indicates, in decreasing prevalence of violence, our genres array themselves this way: Police Shows, Tabloid News, Documentaries, Entertainment News and Review programs, News and Public Affairs, Entertainment Non-News programs and Talk Shows. Talk Shows are noteworthy because their violence, more than in any other reality genre, is in Talk About, rather than visual violence. Table 5 shows more *similarity* across the three years of study than difference, with two exceptions: Documentaries showed inconsistent levels of visual violence across the three years (although they were among the more violent genres in all three years, and Entertainment News and Review programs show monotonically increasing levels of visual violence across the study period. We examined how violence in reality programs varies by channel type. We should point out again that network television here includes all programming appearing on network affiliated stations, whether they are produced by the network or the station. We noted in the Year 2 report (NTVS, 1997, p. 226) that network- and locally-produced programs were slightly less violent by our overall prevalence index than were syndicated programs. For Year 3 programs, 53 percent of 291 network programs contained no violence (Year 2: 53%), while 48 percent of 223 syndicated shows (Year 2: 48%) contained no violence.[9] These minor differences may be explained by genre differences: all Police Shows and almost all Tabloid news shows, our most violent genres, are syndicated, not network, fare. In separate analyses of network vs. syndicated fare within each genre, no statistically significant differences emerge.

---

[9] Fifty percent of 16 locally produced programs contained no violence (Year 2: 65%). Year 3 differences between network, syndicated, and locally produced programs are not statistically significant (Chi-square [4d.f.]=5.42, p≤.247).

Table 6 indicates that there is some variation in the presence of violence on reality programming on different channels. Reality shows on public television (almost all are either News and Public Affairs or Documentary programs) are the least violent, although 27 percent do depict some visual violence. Independent stations are again noteworthy for their relatively low levels of visual violence and moderately high levels of Talk about Violence. This is one clear instance where station or channel type, type of violence and reality genre interact: just under half of Independent station programming in the 1996-97 season was talk shows, a genre comparatively high on Talk About Violence but low on visual violence; in the two prior seasons, almost two-thirds of all independent-station reality programming was of talk shows. Thus the Year 3 decline in Independent station Talk About Violence is likely attributable to the reduced proportion of Talk Shows in their reality programming. Premium cable shows marked variability in the presentation of violence across the three years, largely because reality programming is scarce on premium channels (11 programs in Year 3, 7 in Year 2, 5 in Year 1), so that the data are unstable.

There are important differences in the types and amounts of violence in reality programs across the broadcast day. See Table 7. Our Year 1 and Year 2 that daytime reality TV showed less violence than later programming, especially visual violence, remains true. Three quarters of 1996-1997 reality programs telecast before 3 p.m. contain no visual violence, and 60 percent of these programs contain neither Talk About nor Visual Violence. News and Public Affairs programs dominate the early (6 a.m.-9 a.m. block), and Talk Shows are the largest category of 3 p.m.-6 p.m. reality programming, followed by Entertainment News and Review shows. Almost half of reality programs air before 3 p.m. However, another fifth of all reality programs appear in the after-school 3 p.m.- 6 p.m. time block, and this year's data shows a marked increase in the prevalence of visual violence in this time period--in part owing to the migration of a number of Police programs from early prime time to late afternoon. And like late afternoon, the early prime time hours (6 p.m.-8 p.m.) are ones of particular concern because children and adolescents are more likely in the audience than in later prime time. For the second consecutive year, early prime time is the block in which reality programs show the greatest overall prevalence of violence and greatest degree of visual violence.

Table 5: Genre by Presence of Violence, 1996-97, 1995-96, and 1994-95, in percents:*

Genre:	1996-1997 (526 programs)			1995-1996 (494 programs)			1994-1995 (393 programs)		
	No Violence	Visual Violence	Talk About Violence	No Violence	Visual Violence	Talk About Violence	No Violence	Visual Violence	Talk About Violence
Talk Shows	63%	16%	21%	56%	15%	29%	55%	15%	30%
News & Public Affairs	58	29	13	50	37	13	52	26	22
Documentaries	26	66	8	46	53	1	19	73	8
Entertainment News & Review	57	42	1	59	31	10	64	21	14
Entertainment Non-News	59	33	7	56	35	9	49	40	11
Tabloid News	14	79	7	7	69	24	--	85	15
Police Shows	--	100	--	--	100	--	--	100	--

Table 6: Channel Type by Presence of Violence, 1996-97, 1994-95, and 1995-96 in %'s:*

Channel Type:	1996-1997 (526 programs)			1995-1996 (494 programs)			1994-1995 (393 programs)		
	No Violence	Visual Violence	Talk About Violence	No Violence	Visual Violence	Talk About Violence	No Violence	Visual Violence	Talk About Violence
Network Stations	41%	46%	13%	38%	47%	15%	40%	44%	16%
Independent Stations	61	24	15	48	23	29	42	25	33
Public TV	66	27	7	68	20	12	50	35	15
Basic Cable	51	44	5	54	39	8	49	38	13
Premium Cable	27	46	27	43	43	14	--	80	20

*Percentages read horizontally.**

Table 7: Daypart by Presence of Violence, 1996-97, 1995-96, and 1994-95 in %'s:*

Daypart:	1996-1997 (526 programs)		1995-1996 (494 programs)		1994-1995 (393 programs)	
	No Vio- Visual lence Violence	Talk About Violence	No Vio- Visual lence Violence	Talk About Violence	No Vio- Visual lence Violence	Talk About Violence
6 a.m. - 9 a.m.	60% 25%	14%	53% 37%	10%	47% 32%	21%
9 a.m. - 3 p.m	60 25	15	59 22	19	59 18	23
3 p.m. - 6 p.m.	43 50	7	53 38	9	38 38	24
6 p.m. - 8 p.m.	38 56	5	29 58	13	33 38	24
8 p.m. - 11 p.m.	47 48	5	35 58	7	29 61	10

*Percentages read horizontally.

Daypart differences are so great that it is not meaningful to present the percentage of violent shows that appear in each time block without noting the genre of program and the type of channel. See Table 3 and figures in the Appendix. In general, and as we have noted in the past two reports, reality genres vary in their times of appearance and also vary in the likelihood that they contain violence: News and Public Affairs, which are comparatively low in overall prevalence of violence, constitute the bulk of early-morning reality programming, but they are also spread across the broadcast day, although there are relatively few in prime time. Talk Shows, also comparatively low in visual and overall violence, are largely daytime programs (90 percent of 1996-1997 Talk Shows air before 6 p.m., and a third of 9 a.m.-3 p.m. reality shows are talk shows). Entertainment News and Review, Entertainment Non-News and Documentary programming, which in general contain intermediate levels of violence, are spread across the broadcast day after 9 a.m. (though the latter two constitute almost two-thirds of prime time reality programs). The two most violent genres, Tabloid News and Police programs, tend (or at least in the case of Police programs tended until this year) to be concentrated in early prime time.[10]

Genre differences are quite evident in violent scenes or sequences. It will be recalled that we select for further analysis only those scenes or sequences that contain either Visual Violence or Talk About Violence. Our 526 coded programs for Year 3 included 206 programs containing Visual Violence (VV) sequences (38%) and 52 programs (10%) containing Talk About Violence (TAV) sequences but no visual violence. Table 8 demonstrates that genres vary substantially by the proportion of violence that is in Talk About Violence (TAV) and Visual Violence (VV) scenes or *sequences* (n=1,578, or a mean of 6.1 violent sequences per violent program). Overall, 65 percent of Year 3 violent sequences are Visual Violence sequences (66% of Year 2 violent sequences were), and 35% are Talk About Violence sequences.[11] Genres in which most violence is in Visual sequences are Entertainment News and Review and Entertainment Non-News shows, Police Shows and Documentaries. Programs more balanced between Visual and Talk About violence are Tabloid News and News and Public Affairs. As is true at the program level of analysis, Talk Shows, when one considers sequences containing violence, feature primarily Talk About Violence.

Table 9 also arrays sequence data to examine differences between genres. Essentially, it answers the question, for 1996-1997 programs, what is the likelihood, if one tunes in a program in a particular genre, that one will find violent scenes or sequences, and how many sequences would one on average see? The last two columns, showing the average numbers of Visual Violence and Talk About Violence sequences per program, are consistent with other data we have presented over all three years, showing that Police programs in particular are heavily laden with violent sequences,

---

[10] We would note that the shift we find in Police programs, which are syndicated shows, out of the 6 p.m.-8 p.m. daypart and into the 3 p.m.-6 p.m. block, is in our Los Angeles-based sample. This may not have occurred in the rest of the country.

[11] A coding change between the first and second years means that beginning with Year 2 data, sequences are on average longer, and our number of coded sequences proportionately somewhat lower, in the second and third years.

followed by Tabloid News programs and Documentaries,[12] Entertainment Non-News and Entertainment News and Review programs, News and Public Affairs, and Talk Shows. We will discuss the comparison of program-level and sequence violence further when we turn to individual genres.

Table 8: Violent *Sequence* Type by Genre, 1996-97, 1995-96, and 1994-95:*

	Visual Violence	**Talk About Violence**
Talk Shows		
1996-97	19%	81%
1995-96	29	71
1994-95	21	79
News & Public Affairs		
1996-97	55%	45%
1995-96	54	46
1994-95	35	65
Documentaries		
1996-97	70%	30%
1995-96	84	16
1994-95	58	42
Entertainment News & Review		
1996-97	90%	10%
1995-96	76	24
1994-95	79	21
Entertainment Non-News		
1996-97	77%	23%
1995-96	72	28
1994-95	46	54
Tabloid News		
1996-97	68%	32%
1995-96	59	41
1994-95	66	34
Police Shows		
1996-97	77%	23%
1995-96	81	19
1994-95	79	21

*Percentages read horizontally.

[12] We order Tabloid News before Documentaries although the average number of violent scenes for the Documentaries is higher because all Tabloid News shows are half-hour programs while the modal documentary is an hour-long program.

Table 9: Violent Sequences by Genre, 1996-1997 (n=526 programs; 258 violent programs; 1,018 Visual Violence sequences, 560 Talk About Violence sequences.) Cell entries for programs are N's; cell entries for Average number of violent sequences are means.

| | | | Average No. of Violent Sequences in: | | | |
| | | | *Violent* Programs | | *All* Programs | |
Genre:	Total Programs	Violent Programs*	VV	TAV	VV	TAV
Talk Shows	112	18 + 23	1.0	4.5	0.4	1.7
News & Public Affairs	90	28 +13	2.1	1.7	0.9	0.7
Documentaries	65	43 + 5	5.6	2.5	4.1	1.9
Entertainment News & Review	90	38 + 1	3.5	0.4	1.5	0.2
Entertainment Non-News	115	39 + 8	4.8	1.4	2.0	0.6
Tabloid News	29	23 + 2	4.3	2.1	3.8	1.8
Police Shows	17	17 + 0	8.6	2.5	8.6	2.5

*The first entry is programs containing any Visual Violence (VV) sequences; the second entry is for programs containing no VV sequences but containing one or more Talk About Violence (TAV) sequences. Thus, for example, among the 29 Tabloid News programs in the sample are 23 programs containing Visual Violence sequences and 2 containing no visual violence but with Talk About Violence.

Contextual Factors in Violent Portrayals

We now describe *what* reality violence depicts and describes--the nature of violent acts, the means by which violence is accomplished, and the extensiveness of the violence, as indexed in several ways. In addition, we discuss other contextual features in a section, below, on specific genres of reality programming.

First, 60 percent of 1996-1997 Visual Violence sequences involve actual acts of violence, down a bit from the 65 percent in Year 2; compared with 21 percent which portray credible threats and 18 percent which show consequences of violence. By comparison, and quite similar to Year 2 data, 73 percent of Talk About Violence sequences concern acts, while about a sixth discuss threats and a ninth discuss consequences; in other words, and consistent with the two earlier years, Talk About Violence sequences are more likely to deal with violent acts than are their visual counterparts. There are again some important genre differences in Year 3 in Visual sequences, as there were in the first two years. In 1996-1997, a third of Police show visual depictions are in the form of credible threats--higher than any other genre. These depictions most frequently are scenes in which police officers draw guns. By comparison, Police Shows visually depict violent *acts* (56% of sequences) proportionately less often than other genres, except for News and Public Affairs (53%). News and Public Affairs, Documentaries and Tabloid News are more likely than other genres to feature consequences of violence. Interesting genre differences in Talk About Violence concerning acts vs. consequences vs. threats are that Police Shows and Entertainment Non-News shows disproportionately feature threats, and Documentaries, consequences of violent acts.

Second (see Figure 6 in the Appendix), many means of violence characterize reality programming, and the 1996-1997 data generally parallel findings from the prior two years, with one major exception: shooting (50% of means in 1996-97 sequences, 39% in the prior year) has replaced hitting and punching (35% in 1996-97, 42% in 1995-96) has the major means of violence. After shooting and "strong-arm" violence, in descending order of frequency in visual sequences, reality "violence" means war acts or acts of mass violence (13%); cutting or slashing (9%); abducting or kidnapping (8%); stalking or frightening (7%); strangling or choking (5%); sexual assault (2%); or poisoning (1%).[13] Talk About Violence, as has been true in previous years, generally parallels Visual Violence in the rank orderings of means of committing violence, with several qualifications: it less frequently involves shootings (about half as often as in visual sequences, ranking shootings second to strong-arm violence) and war/mass violence (Talk About Violence sequences are half likely than Visual sequences to concern war) and is far more likely to concern sexual assaults (11% of sequences vs. 2% of visual sequences). As was true in Years 1 and 2, war and mass violence are largely the province of Documentaries (73% of all Visual war sequences and 61% of war-related Talk About sequences are in documentaries), Entertainment Non-News (10% and 17%, respectively) and News and Public Affairs (5% and 11%, respectively). Police Shows stand out for their high proportions of gun-related violence (73% of their Visual Violence sequences involve shootings, up from 47% in 1995-96).

Figure 7 in the Appendix presents data on weapons used in violence. Consistent with our findings that shootings have escalated in Visual Violence sequences, guns (50% of VV sequences vs. 42% in 1995-96) have replaced "natural means," i.e., use of the body rather than a weapon, as the most frequent means of violence (35% of VV sequences vs. 41% in 1995-96). In Talk About Violence sequences, "natural means" (39% of 1996-97 TAV sequences, 52% in 1995-96) are more frequently used than are guns (26% in 1996-97, 30% in 1995-96). Again in the 1996-1997 season, war weapons are prevalent in Visual sequences (11%) but rare in Talk-About sequences (3%), again because war sequences are predominantly visual ones.

Our first measure of the extent of the impact of violence in sequences is the extent of injury, to the point of death, in a sequence. If more than one person is killed or injured, the most extensive injury is coded. As Table 10 indicates, for all years, the distribution of extent is bimodal at either no injury or death. Thirty-four percent of 1995-1996 Talk About Violence sequences lead to deaths and 26 percent of visual sequences do. There are few genre differences in this measure of extent.

---

[13] A sequence may involve more than one means of violence.

Table 10: Extent of Injury Visual Violence and Talk About Violence Sequences: 1996-97 VV n=1995-96 VV n=806, 1994-95 VV n=607; 1995-96 TAV n=433, 1994-95 TAV n=590; excluded are sequences in which extent could not be ascertained (317 in 1996-97, 238 in 1996-96, 282 in 1994-95).

	Visual Sequence			TAV Sequence		
	96-97	95-96	94-95	96-97	95-96	94-95
None*	35%	23%	33%	30%	18%	26%
Minor injury	9	17	17	8	8	14
Injury, extent indeterminate	22	23	11	20	25	8
Moderate injury	4	6	6	5	7	8
Severe injury	4	4	5	3	4	4
Suicide	2	--	1	2	1	3
All other deaths	24	26	27	32	37	37
	100%	99%	100%	100%	100%	100%

---

* Includes credible threats not involving actual violence and unsuccessful attempts at violence such as firing a gun and missing the target.

A second index of extensiveness is the number of individuals harmed. We exclude violent sequences in which no one was harmed and/or the number of individuals harmed could not be determined. About 60 percent of all sequences across all genres involve harm to a single individual and another 20 percent involve harm to two people. In general, sequences in entertainment-oriented programs tend to describe harm to one or two individuals or small groups, and news-oriented programs to substantially larger numbers, owing to their coverage of mass violence. When data are truncated to avoid skewing distributions (when more than 100 persons are harmed, the sequence is coded as having harmed 100), the mean number harmed in the various genres ranges downward from News and Public Affairs (12.2 per VV sequence, 3.2 per TAV sequence) to Documentaries (8.2 VV, 4.0 TAV), Tabloid News (7.3 VV, 6.9 TAV); Police Shows (5.1 VV, 1.9 TAV); Entertainment Non-News (2.7 TAV, 3.0 TAV), Entertainment News & Reviews (2.3 VV, 1.2 TAV), and Talk Shows (2.0 VV, 2.5 TAV). By genre, the rank-orderings and magnitudes are fairly consistent across the three years, with the exception of Police Shows, in last place in Years 1 and 2 and in fourth place this year. This was likely due to one very violent "outlier" program in the current year. The big genre differences, though, are between News and Public Affairs and Documentaries, on the one hand, where multiperson violence is frequent due to their coverage of large-scale conflicts, and other genres, where they are rare. In general, Visual Violence sequences involve more persons hurt or killed (mean: 5.6), than Talk About Violence sequences (mean 2.9).

Two other indicators measure the extent to which violence leads to harm and pain which has effects on victims, and on others beyond the immediate victim.

The first of these indexes whether a victim is shown as suffering any harm or pain, and, if so, whether this harm or pain has effects that last beyond that sequence, as when, for example, a person wounded in one sequence is shown crippled or in pain later in a program. If the harm does not persist beyond the sequence, i.e., the victim reappears in a later sequence as a "whole person," this indicates no lasting harm. See Table 11. The table indicates that in only about half of the instances of Visual Violence (43% in Year 3, down from 54% in Year 2), and in only slightly more cases of Talk About Violence (56% in Year 3, 55% in Year 2) are harm and pain likely to persist after violence.

Table 11: Presence & Persistence of Harm/Pain in Visual Violence and Talk About Violence Segments, by Genre, 1996-97 (VV n=348, TAV n=295) **and 1995-96** (VV n=283, TAV n=263):*

Genre:	Visual Segments			Talk About Violence Segments		
	No Harm or Pain	Harm Within	Harm Persists	No Harm or Pain	Harm Within	Harm Persists
Talk Shows						
1996-97	53%	43%	5%	31%	53%	16%
1995-96	46	41	13	46	33	21
News & Public Affairs						
1996-97	61	34	5	47	36	17
1995-96	50	44	6	47	42	11
Documentaries						
1996-97	49	42	9	40	42	18
1995-96	35	52	13	24	60	16
Entertainment News & Review 1996-97	79	18	4	62	33	5
1995-96	56	39	5	51	39	10
Entertainment Non-News 1996-97	60	30	10	58	25	17
1995-96	53	28	19	48	16	36
Tabloid News						
1996-97	45	37	18	42	37	22
1995-96	69	19	12	65	16	19
Police Shows						
1996-97	45	47	8	27	63	10
1995-96	35	43	22	29	43	29
ALL REALITY PROGRAMS						
1996-97	58	34	9	44	40	16
1995-96	46	41	13	45	37	18

*Percentages read horizontally.

One way of reading Table 11 is as evidence of "sanitized violence"--violence that leads neither to harm and pain, nor to enduring consequences to victims. The genre best characterizing this interpretation is Entertainment News and Review programs, and as we note elsewhere, many violent sequences in this genre are brief, decontextualized clips from theatrical films. At the other extreme, violence seems to "hurt most" in Police Shows, and, in the current year, Tabloid News, marking a significant reversal in this genre from the prior two years. In every genre and across both years, Talk About Violence segments are likely to involve more evidence of harm and pain than are their visual counterparts.

A related index assesses whether depicted effects of violence go beyond the immediate participants and have effects on others--families, friends and wider communities or the society. This is not the mode for reality programming, but our 1996-1997 data do suggest some improvement over the prior year. See Table 12. Just a quarter of Year 2 visual segments suggest an impact beyond the violent incident, and about a third of Year 2 of Talk About Violence segments do. In Year 3, however, a third of Visual Violence segments and just over half of Talk About Violence segments suggests the social effects go beyond the immediate participants, and this holds true (though in most cases, not statistically significantly so) for Visual Violence in every genre and for Talk About Violence in five of seven genres. While there is but one consistent genre differences (Entertainment News and Review shows again emerge as the genre least likely to see radiating social effects of violence, in both VV and TAV segments), there is a difference in the form of presentation: in every genre, "social impact" is more something that is talked about than is present in visual presentations. The single exception is 1996-1997 Tabloid News.

Another important context variable is the degree to which violence is rewarded or punished; consistent with our Santa Barbara colleagues, our definitions of reward, and especially punishment, tend to be fairly expansive, including not only material rewards or punishments but, in the case of punishment, for example, any expression by a perpetrator of regret or any expression--oral or nonverbal--of opprobrium by another character. Our 1996-1997 data are consistent in that on average, violence in reality programs is neither rewarded nor punished. It was rewarded in 11 percent of 1996-1997 visually violent reality programs and segments (8% in 1995-96, 9% in 1994-95) and punished in 31 percent (25% in 1995-96, 33% in 1994-95). Consistent with prior years, in Talk About Violence programs and segments, violence is about equally likely to be rewarded (14% in 1996-97, 7% in 1995-96, 4% in 1994-95), compared with Visual Violence, and, in Years 2 and 3, more likely to be punished (41% in 1996-97, 40% in 1995-96, 33% in 1994-95). Consistent and significant genre differences will be reported below.

Just 17 of 268 (6%) violent reality programs in 1996-1997 carried any sort of advisory concerning the presence of violence, down from 12 percent one year ago. Of these, two used oral advisories, seven employed written advisories, and 10 carried both. Police programs were most likely to employ advisories-seven of 17 violent programs did so, three as written advisories, two as oral, and three as both. Four of 47 (8.5%) Entertainment Non-News violent programs carried advisories, two of them both oral and written, two written. Five of 48 (10%) violent documentaries listed program advisories, one written and four oral and written. One violent Talk Show of 41 (2%) displayed a written advisory, and *no* violent Entertainment News and Review (n=39), News and Public Affairs (n=41), or Tabloid news show (n=25) displayed a program advisory.

Table 12: Violence Impact Beyond Participants, by Genre, 1996-97 and 1995-96, in percents (1996-97 VV n=348, TAV n=295; 1995-96 VV n=281, TAV n=261):[*]

	Visual Segments		TAV Segments	
Genre:	No Impact	Impact Beyond	No Impact	Impact Beyond
Talk Shows				
1996-97	68%	32%	57%	43%
1995-96	76	24	64	36
News & Public Affairs				
1996-97	50	50	34	66
1995-96	76	24	67	33
Documentaries				
1996-97	49	51	33	67
1995-96	66	34	59	41
Entertainment News & Review 1996-97	84	16	76	24
1995-96	85	15	77	23
Entertainment Non-News				
1996-97	70	30	55	45
1995-96	76	24	48	52
Tabloid News				
1996-97	57	43	63	37
1995-96	79	21	74	26
Police Shows				
1996-97	68	32	57	43
1995-96	76	24	52	48
ALL REALITY PROGRAMS				
1996-97	65	35	49	51
1995-96	74	26	65	35

---

[*]Percentages read horizontally.

We also looked at one other important context variable, whether segments depicting or talking about violence furnished any information that would help those watching the programs and segments avoid violence or diminish its impacts. In particular, we coded whether segments discussed *techniques* for coping with or avoiding violence or whether they gave concrete information about hotlines, helplines or other ways of seeking help. Relatively few programs or program segments do: six

251

percent of Year 1 violent segments provided such information, 11 percent of both Year 2 and Year 3 segments do so: fifteen percent of 1996-97 Talk About Violence segments discuss such alternatives (up a statistically insignificant one percentage point from the prior year), but just eight percent of 1996-97 Visual Violence segments do, again up one point from the prior year.

As noted in the UC-Santa Barbara report, the addition of humor to a violent sequence is a significant contextual variable. As their reports have consistently noted, reality programs are among those least likely to couple humor with violence. In Year 1, three percent of both VV and TAV sequences presented violence in a humorous context; in Year 2, eight percent of VV sequences and four percent of TAV sequences did, and in Year 3, five percent of VV and two percent of TAV sequences present humorous violence. As in prior years, most (77% in Year 3) of the humorous visual violence sequences appear in the "entertainment" categories, Entertainment Non-News (25, or 51% of humorous VV sequences, accounting for 11% of all VV sequences in the genre) and Entertainment News and Review (n=13, 27% of all VV sequences, 10% of the genre's VV sequences). Otherwise, humorous violence is rare in reality television.

Additional Context Features in Reality Program Visual Violence

We examined, in 1,018 sequences, four contextual features of violence depictions: whether or not the depiction was a reenactment or recreation; whether violence occurred on- or off-screen; the degree of intensity of depicted violence; and depiction of the graphicness of the consequences of violence.

Reenactment-Recreation: some 22 percent of 1996-97 Visual Violence sequences involved reenactment of a violent event (16% in 1995-96, 27% in 1994-1995). Almost all of these occur in three genres, the Police show (49% of its violent sequences are reenactments), and its cousin, the non-news reality entertainment program, which includes such "police-like" shows as *Rescue 911* and shows about occult and paranormal phenomena (e.g., *Sightings, Unsolved Mysteries*) (32%) and Documentaries (24%). Reenactments and recreations were used in six percent of News and Public Affairs violent sequences (5 of 81) and in one of 107 Tabloid News VV sequences.

On- or Off-Screen Depictions: off-screen depiction of visual violence, noted in the overall report as a moderating or militating contextual factor, is comparatively infrequent in reality-program visual violence, employed in nine percent of 1996-1997 sequences, compared with 9.5 percent of 1995-1996 and only four percent of 1994-1995 sequences; in each year, then, the large majority of violence appears on-screen, and again in Year 3, there are no significant genre differences in this measure.

Intensity of Visual Violent Acts: visually violent sequences were coded as depicting mildly (46% in Year 3, 44% in Year 2, 49% in Year 1), moderately (35% in Year 3, 34% in Year 2, 40% in Year 1) or extremely intense violence (19% in Year 3, 23% in Year 2, 11% in Year 1. The data are fairly stable across years, although Year 2 and Year 3 show somewhat more intense depictions than Year 1. There are few substantial variations from these average percentages by genre, although in Year 3 data, Police Shows are ten percentage points less likely to depict mild violence (33%) than any other genre (the modal Police visual sequence is Moderate), and Tabloid News shows are 11 percentage points *more* likely than any other genre to show extremely intense violence (33%).

Graphicness of Consequences of Violence: Here we note the degree of blood and gore or injury occasioned by violent events. In 1996-97, 67% of violent sequences showed *no* consequences (60% in 1995-96, 59% in 1994-95). Another 24 percent (32% in Year 2, 33% in Year 1) show somewhat graphic consequences, and 9 percent (9% in Year 2, 7% in Year 1) show very graphic consequences. Three genres stand out in not portraying consequences of violence: as was true in Years 1 and 2, Police Shows rarely show any consequences of violence (76% in Year 3, 71% in Year 2, 75% in Year 1 do not); as we have earlier noted, this is due in part to the nature of violence on Police Shows: A third of it constitutes threats rather than harmful acts, much of the remainder involves "natural means" of grabbing, hitting and restraining); nonetheless, 72% of Police show visual violence involves shootings and/or the display of guns. Likewise, Entertainment News and Review shows present few consequences of violence (83% in 1996-97, 68% in 1995-96), and as we noted earlier, this likely is because many of its visually violent sequences are brief clips of current theatrical films, a genre in which "sanitized" violence is prevalent. Finally, Tabloid News shows present few consequences of violence (70% do not in 1995-96). The "realistic" genres stand out for *showing* somewhat or very graphic consequences--News and Public Affairs (30% in 1997-97, down sharply from 62% in 1995-96), Documentaries (41%), and Tabloid News (43%, up from 30% in 1995-96).

Context Features in Reality Program Talk About Violence

We considered two characteristics of talk about violence to be important contextual features. First, and somewhat parallel to our measure of the graphicness of visual violence, was the *graphicness* of the discussion of violence. Just as visual violence may vary in its graphicness, so too may talk, from the abstract to the concrete. Vividness of detail might particularly be related to the possibility that violent descriptions might instill fear. In 1996-1997, 55% of 552 TAV sequences furnished concrete or graphic details of a violent incident (53% in 1995-1996, but only 38% in 1994-95) while 45% did not (47% in Year 2, 62% in Year 1). In 1996-97, as in the year prior, Entertainment Non-News shows (e.g., *Unsolved Mysteries, Rescue 911*) (71% in Year 3, 68% in Year 2) were the most likely to talk using concrete details. While Talk Shows had employed the most concrete details in 1994-95, in Years 2 and 3, they were about average for all genres--but because the average had moved to a more graphic point: in 1994-95, 49 percent of Talk Show sequences provided graphic details; in 1995-96, 51 percent did, and in 1996-97, 58 percent did.

We also again analyzed the nature of description of violence from the standpoint of the speaker--whether the description was *first person*, i.e., describing his or her own involvement in it, *second person*, describing violence one has witnessed or in which intimates of the speaker are involved, and/or *third person* accounts, describing violence not witnessed and which occurred to unknown others (the usual mode of journalistic reporting). We speculate that where the testimony is first- or second-person, emotional intensity and the potential arousal of fear are greater, and the likelihood of desensitization is perhaps lessened. A sequence can involve more than one sort of description, and in 1996-97, about one in six did. Across all reality genres, 34 percent of Talk About Violence accounts were first person (35% in 1995-96, 30% in 1994-95),

29% were second person (18% in 1995-96, 30% in 1994-95), and 52% percent were third-person accounts (48% in 1995-96, 30% in 1994-95). Unsurprisingly, Talk Shows were again highest in First-person accounts (53%; 61% in Year 2); they were again also highest in using multi-person perspectives (i.e., combinations of first-, second-, and third-person accounts. Documentaries (46%) and Entertainment News and Review shows replaced Police Shows (27% in Year 3, 33% in Year 2) as highest on second-person witness and relative accounts (33%). Highest on third-person accounts were Tabloid News (76% third-person accounts), Documentaries (68%), Police Shows (63%) and Entertainment News and Reviews (60%). These data again suggest three "types" of "reality talk" genre--a "news" type in which third-person accounts dominate, a "reality-entertainment" type (Police and Entertainment Non-News shows) featuring all three voices, and a "personal" type--the Talk Show. (cf. NTVS, 1997, p. 234).

Characters Involved in Violence

In the 526 reality programs coded in the 1996-1997 television season, 5,174 characters were found to be involved in violence. In Year 2's 494 programs, 6,087 characters were involved in violent sequences,[14] and in Year 1's 393 programs, 4,089 characters dealt with violence. Characters involved in violence only, not all characters in all programs, are coded.

As we have found consistently, almost seven-eighths of the characters involved in violence in reality programs are identifiable humans with virtually all the remainder crowds or groups of indistinguishable individuals; a few characters each year were mostly human-like super creatures such as are found in movie clips shown on Entertainment News and Review shows.

The ratio of males to females also did not change across years, with men outnumbering women three to one. Age patterns also remained unchanged. Each year, characters involved in violence on reality programs were overwhelmingly younger adults 21-44 and this year the same holds, with 77% of the characters in that age range.

Of the characters involved in reality-program violence in all years, a third were neither perpetrators nor victims, but are instead those indirectly involved in the violence, including family members, friends, witnesses, attorneys and the like; program hosts and commentators are also coded here. An additional 15 percent of Year 3 characters, 12 percent of Year 2 characters and nine percent of Year 1 characters were both perpetrators and victims, such as fist-fighters. Slightly more of the "pure" perpetrators and victims were perpetrators (27% in 1996-97, 29% in 1995-96) than victims (26% in each year). Table 13 shows what the perpetrators and victims typically look like. As was observed last year, men are three times as likely to be *characters* in violent sequences as are women, and women are considerably more likely to be the target of violence than the instigators of violence. Young children and older people are unlikely to be characters, and, again, when they are, they are far more likely to be victims than

---

[14] One program, a three-hour war documentary which aired on a basic cable channel, was excluded from character analyses for Year 2 as an outlier; see NTVS, 1997, p. 235, footnote 15.

Table 13: Characters involved in violence, by Gender, Age and Ethnicity, 1996-97 and 1995-96. Excluded are nonhuman characters, crowds and characters for which a trait could not be ascertained. Cell entries are percentages, read across rows, except for "Total" column, which expresses percentages within the demographic category.

		Both Victim & Perpetrator	Victim Only	Perpe-trator Only	Neither	Total / (n=)
Gender						
Female	1996-97	9%	36%	17%	39%	16% (690)
	1995-96	9	39	16	36	25% (939)
Male	1996-97	21	22	31	26	84% (3,711)
	1995-96	10	23	5	35	75% (2,751)
Age						
0-5	1996-97	9%	57%	15%	17%	1% (46)
	1995-96	5	62	16	17	2% (82)
6-12	1996-97	2	54	22	21	2% (85)
	1995-96	3	49	17	31	4% (153)
13-20	1996-97	30	34	19	17	4% (152)
	1995-96	8	35	27	29	9% (403)
21-44	1996-97	21	23	30	27	77% (2,784)
	1995-96	15	23	27	35%	70% (3,090)
45-64	1996-97	6	20	22	51	14% (489)
	1995-96	4	26	18	52	14% (602)
65+	1996-97	5	51	9	35	2% (57)
	1995-96	5	54	11	29	1% (79)
Race						
Asian	1996-97	20	23	33	24	4% (150)
	1995-96	26	28	23	23	7% (310)
Black	1996-97	15	33	31	21	15% (584)
	1995-96	10	23	24	43	14% (628)
Hispanic	1996-97	19	25	34	21	7% (276)
	1995-96	10	26	23	41	10% (448)
White	1996-97	19	24	27	29	74% (2,966)
	1995-96	13	26	26	35	68% (3,100)

Table 14: Gender of Perpetators and Victims in Visual Violence and Talk About Violence, 1995-1996 Reality Programs, 1996-97. Characters who are neither perpetrators nor victims are excluded; characters who were both perpetrators and victims are enumerated in each column.

Genre	Visual Violence				Talk About Violence				Total
	Perpetrators		Victims		Perpetrators		Victims		
	Male	Female	Male	Female	Male	Female	Male	Female	% Female
Police n=855	95%	5%	64%	36%	88%	12%	69%	31%	12%
Entertainment Non-News n=842	87	13	82	18	78	22	49	51	20%
Entertainment News & Review n=533	83	17	91	8	94	6	93	7	8%
News & Public Affairs n=393	93	7	71	29	86	14	43	57	27%
Tabloid News n=481	81	19	78	22	85	15	51	49	23%
Documentaries n=1,447	95	5	89	11	92	8	32	64	14%
Talk Shows n=701	85	15	73	27	60	40	31	69	41%
Total	**91%**	**9%**	**74%**	**26%**	**77%**	**23%**	**41%**	**59%**	**24%**
N. characters	**1836**	**177**	**1660**	**578**	**447**	**132**	**280**	**411**	**5521**

perpetrators. Only adults aged 21-44 are more likely to be perpetrators than victims. All these findings are consistent across all three years.

Our findings relative to ethnicity are very similar to those for Years 1 and 2; we noted in Year 2 that Asian-American representation had doubled from Year 1; in Year 3, it declines to Year 1 levels. Ethnic groups, in their overall representation as characters in violent sequences, come close to their representation in the U.S. population (again, whites are slightly underrepresented). Of great interest in Table 12 is that no ethnic group is strongly disproportionately represented either as perpetrators or victims; however, as in both prior years, the table masks some key differences: white perpetrators are much more likely to be "officials," largely police and military officers, while Hispanic and particularly African-American perpetrators are far less likely to have official status; that is, they are more likely to be criminals.

As noted above, the world of reality TV violence is predominantly male. The strong tendency of perpetrators in visual violence sequences to be male that was noted in Years 1 and 2 remained unchanged. Nine of 10 are male. Still, women do stand out in certain types of violence, genres, and roles. See Table 14. Mirroring the two prior years, women are substantially more likely to be victims in Talk About violence sequences than in Visual Violence sequences, and this is true for all but one genre (Police Shows in 1996-1997) for both Years 3 and 2. As was found in both earlier years, women continue to appear in proportionately large numbers in talk shows. In these programs, they make appearances as both perpetrators and victims, but especially as victims, and in both visual and talk sequences, but especially in talk sequences. In contrast, Police Shows continue to be populated primarily by men, as are Entertainment News and Review shows, the latter more markedly so in the third year than in earlier years.

VIOLENCE IN REALITY GENRES

The analyses above suggest that genre is a particularly powerful contextual variable for reality programs. Consequently, further analyses of how violence is portrayed on reality shows are offered here for the seven reality program genres identified in our sample.

Police Shows

Police Shows constitute just three percent of the television reality-programs universe, but in all three years, Police Shows are the most violent reality programs. Each year, every police show we analyzed contained at least one sequence of visual violence. On a number of our measures, police-show violence emerges as among the most intense violence in reality television as well. Tuning into a 30-minute police program in the past year, for example, would have led a viewer to see an average of 8.6 visually violent sequences, more than double the number in any other reality genre.

More than any other genre, Police Shows feature guns, both in visual and talk violence. Three-fourths of cop-show visual violence sequences show guns, higher than any other reality genre. Police-show visual violence is more likely than other genres to depict not only credible threats, but both threats and actual acts of violence. And, as noted above, police programs are less likely than the average reality show to depict violence as leading to harm and pain. At the same time, they are more likely to show violence as rewarded and punished.

The past season saw a time-block shift for police programs in our sample from the early evening (6-8 p.m.) to the late afternoon (3-6 p.m.), although we suspect that this trend may be peculiar to our Los Angeles-based sample; children and adolescents constitute a significant portion of the audience in both time blocks.

Contrary to the past two years, in which just one of 111 violent Police-show segments presented an alternative to, or mode of preventing or coping with violence (e.g., hotlines, helplines, techniques for avoiding violence) eight of 22 TAV segments and 6 of 40 VV segments did in the past year.

Entertainment Non-News

Virtually tied with Talk Shows as the largest genre within reality programs, Entertainment Non-News is a catchall category rather than a true genre. It represents a range of reality shows including medical-emergency shows (*Emergency Call, Rescue 911*), many of which resemble the police programs as well in the reality and intensity of violent depiction. It also includes programs focusing on the paranormal, many of them using entertainment-program techniques to heighten emotional intensity (*Sightings, Unsolved Mysteries*). And like Police Shows, this genre is relatively high in reenactments and recreations. However, the category also includes cinema-verité shows (MTV's *Real World*), comedy-verité (*America's Funniest Home Videos*) and variety-and-award shows which rarely have violent content. Thirty-three percent of the programs contained visual violence, a proportion that has declined slightly each year (35% in Year 2, 40% in Year 1). Talk About Violence, without visual violence, occurs in seven percent of the programs (9% in Year 2, 11% in Year 1).

Although visual violence predominates in this genre, when violence is talked about, it is overwhelmingly graphic (71% of Talk About Violence sequences), and it is, for the second straight year, the most likely of all genres to present violence in a humorous context: half of all reality-program violent-humor sequences were in this genre.

We find 17 instances of 138 program segments presenting alternatives to violence in this genre, compared with 17 of 61 in Year 2 and two of 51 in Year 1.

Entertainment News and Review

We again find that this genre differs from all other reality genres in its characteristic mode of showing violence. Visual Violence in Entertainment News and Review shows tends to come in the form of short clips--from theatrical films and entertainment TV programs. While the overall *level* of violence in this genre is generally lower than the average reality show (57% of 1996-97 programs have no visual or talk about violence), the prevalence of visual violence in programs has consistently increased across years (21% in Year 1, 31% in Year 2, 42% in Year 3). This should be a matter of concern.

This genre in all three years was *lowest* among reality genres in sequences displaying the consequences or aftermath of violence (as opposed to acts or credible threats). Guns appear in 50 percent of visual sequences, (38% in Year 2, 49% in Year 1), more than the reality-program average. Other indicators that decontextualized film clips pervade violence presentations in this genre: ninety percent of all its sequences are Visual Violence sequences, as opposed to TAV sequences; more than half its violent segments present fictional and fantasy violence; and it is the second most likely to couple humor to violence (17% of sequences vs. 8% overall for reality programs). Finally (see Table 14), violence in this genre is far and away the most "masculinized" of any genre, particularly in this past year.

Seven of 84 segments in the genre present alternatives to violence, compared with four of 101 segments in 1995-1996 and two of 47 segments in 1994-95.

Documentaries

Documentaries, which account for an eighth of all reality programs, are spread fairly evenly across the broadcast day after 9 a.m. and are found disproportionately on basic cable channels. Among all reality genres, they show the greatest year-by-year variation, especially on violence measures. For example, in Year 1, 73 percent of documentaries contained some visual violence; in Year 2, 53 percent did, and in Year 3, 66 percent did-- an average year-to-year variation of 16.5 percentage points, compared with an average for all other reality genres of 6.2 percentage points. In some respects, we should be unsurprised to find the greatest variation in this genre, because the amount, type and context of violence in documentaries is somewhat dependent on the documentarian's choice of subject matter. Documentaries, too, are more likely than programs in other genres to be produced independently as freestanding programs, rather than as series.

While "documentary" is clearly recognized by broadcasters and filmmakers as a true genre, the 65 documentaries in the 1996-1997 sample represent a hybrid genre between "real" reality and entertainment-reality programming. Some resemble news shows (e.g. *POV*) and many are war-related historical programs (*Great Escapes of World War I*), while others are more entertainment-based (*The Making of Donnie Brasco, Selena*). This dichotomy leads to the paradox that while many documentaries were nonviolent, when violence was presented, it tended to be extensive, to involve larger-than-average numbers of victims, and to present violence grimly and relatively realistically, focusing more than other genres on long-term consequences of violence and effects of violence on victims' friends, families and communities. They are usually above the reality-program averages for both the rewarding and punishment of violence.

Seven of 98 violent documentary segments (4 of 85 in Year 2, six of 70 in Year 1) offered alternatives to violence.

News and Public Affairs

Our 98 News and Public Affairs programs in the 1996-1997 sample (19% of all reality programs), again do not include regularly scheduled network, national or local newscasts or news "drop-ins" in morning news shows; they do include the morning programs themselves, news magazines such as ABC's *20/20* and interview programs such as *Meet the Press.*

Some 58 percent of all News and Public Affairs programs contain no violence, and almost 71 percent contain no visual violence. In the first and third years of the study, News and Public Affairs programs ranked below the reality-show averages for visual violence, and in all three years was second only to Talk Shows in the proportion of violence presented in Talk About Violence, rather than Visual Violence, sequences.

Visual Violence in news programs tends, as it does in documentaries, to involve more victims--largely because these two genres focus more than other reality genres on large-scale conflicts such as war--and to paint violence more realistically in terms of harm and pain, and in terms of spillover effects on friends, families and communities. More than any other genre, too, News and Public Affairs depicts violence in terms of consequences, rather than acts or threats.

News and Public Affairs programs presented 9 instances of alternatives or correctives to violence in 97 Year 3 segments (10 of 79 in Year 2, 11 of 77 in Year 1).

Tabloid News

For the third consecutive year, Tabloid News (29 programs, 6% of all reality shows) emerged as second only to Police Shows as a violent genre. In 1996-1997, 79 percent of Tabloid shows contained visual violence, and another seven percent contained one or more TAV sequences. On average, a viewer turning into a 30-minute Tabloid News program this past year would have seen almost four Visual Violence sequences and almost two Talk About Violence sequences.

Tabloid News, however, focuses less than other news shows on war-related issues, and the number of persons harmed tends to be smaller (7.2 per Visual Violence sequence, compared with 12.2 per News and Public Affairs visual sequences).

In 1996-1997, however, there were some signs that suggested improvement in the presentation of violence on tabloid news. First, and unlike in prior years, there was just one instance of humorous violence among 109 VV sequences, and none in 52 TAV sequences; in the two prior years, in was closer to the entertainment-reality genres. Second, in both VV and TAV sequences, it was significantly more likely to show the consequences of violence beyond the participants than in Year 2, and it presented visual violence significantly less graphically than in the prior two years. Finally, the genre declined significantly, and was below News and Public Affairs programs and the reality-program average, in featuring guns in visual sequences. The fact remains, however, that the genre is on average a violent one.

Two of 92 Tabloid news segments in 1996-1997 (3 of 85 1995-96, none of 56 in 1994-95) presented alternatives to violence. Suggesting how to avoid or prevent violence, or to cope with violence's aftermath, has not been the genre's strong suit.

Talk Shows

Some 21% of all reality programs in 1996-1997 were Talk Shows (down from 24% in 1995-96 and 27% in 1994-95), the genre that has consistently been lowest in both overall prevalence of violence and especially the prevalence of visual violence. Some 63 percent of Year 3 Talk Shows contained no violence (56% in Year 2, 55% in Year 1) and 84 percent contain no visual violence (85% in both prior years). A viewer tuning into a 1996-1997 Talk Show would on average see less than one-half a visually violent sequence, and 1.7 TAV sequences.

Moreover, in visual sequences in Talk Shows (and in 1996-97 just 19% of its violent sequences were visual sequences, a proportion again less than half of any other reality genre), the focus tends to be on presentation of consequences of off-screen violence; nonetheless both in Visual and in Talk About Violence, across a number of indicators, the presentation tends to be intense and graphic, though the *form* of violence depicted and discussed differs markedly from other genres: it is more likely to involve "natural means" rather than guns or weapons, to involve only one or two victims per sequence. In Year 3, again on a variety of indicators, most especially in TAV sequences, Talk Show violence is up-close-and-personal: violence hurts people--both victims and their families and friends, and the community at large.

Our Year 3 data are consistent with prior years, too, in painting Talk Shows as the most "feminized" of the reality genres, in that women are disproportionately presented as victims of, and to a lesser extent, as perpetrators of violence. The genre also is the one most likely to present sexual assault as a form of violence.

On our "alternatives to violence" measure, Talk Shows, as in Year 2, show both the highest absolute levels of providing assistance; 17 of 64 Talk Show segments in Year 3 (19 of 76 in Year 2, but just 4 of 58 in Year 1) presented help or alternatives.

SUMMARY, CONCLUSIONS AND RECOMMENDATIONS

Reality programming, we have already suggested, appears to be a growing segment of the television environment. "Reality shows," however, are very diverse, and the ways they present and contextualize violence are oftentimes sufficiently different from fictional, entertainment programming to warrant separate consideration of them, as the National Television Violence Study recognized from its inception. We think that three years of research have validated that proposition. We also believe that this research has amply supported the idea of the variety of "reality shows," particularly in varying genres within the overall reality rubric.

We begin our summary by again noting that the 1996-1997 data are in most cases quite consistent with data from the past two years, that three years of research, in which 1,413 programs, 683 of them with violent content, point to firm generalizations about reality program violence. At the same time, three years of data also allow us to see any trends that may have occurred from the fall of 1994 to the spring of 1997.

As a genre of television programming, reality programming is less violent than television programming overall. However, both in considering reality programming, and most especially in examining *violence* in reality programming, there are a number of contextual considerations that must be addressed, among them where these programs appear in the broadcast universe, when they appear, and some special considerations that reality programming demands attention to.

We again find, as we noted in our first-year report, "Violence is a feature of every genre of televised reality programming." In the 1996-1997 season, 61 percent of reality programs contained no visually depicted violence at all, virtually the same as in the two prior years. An additional 10 percent of programs show discussions of violence without any visual depictions down a statistically insignificant four percentage points from Year 2, but down eight percentage points from the first year. As in prior years, as an overall genre, reality programs are on average less violent than television at large, but in general, they share--and have for all three seasons--the following characteristics with television programming: violence is infrequently either rewarded or punished, although it is more frequently shown as being punished than rewarded; reality programming relatively rarely shows very graphic violence, although our separate analysis of Talk About Violence suggests that violent talk provides concrete details of violence more often than not; and reality programs rarely provide viewers alternatives to violence or suggest ways of coping with or avoiding violence.

More specifically, we note the following descriptions of reality programs:

A. *Where:* In sheer prevalence, reality programs tend to be concentrated on network stations and, to an increasing extent across the study period, on basic cable; public television programs proportionately more reality fare but in most television markets constitutes but a single channel. Premium cable focuses almost exclusively on entertainment, not reality, programming. Consistently for three years, we have found that public television reality programs contain the least violence and network-affiliated stations the most. A finding in Year 2 that network-produced programs (for this analysis, broadcast and cable networks were combined) were somewhat less violent than syndicated reality material, did not replicate in Year 3.

B. *When:* Reality shows are more a daytime than a nighttime phenomenon. We have consistently found over three years, however, that prime-time reality programs are more violent than daytime shows, and, in fact, in Years 2 and 3, early prime-time programs appear slightly more violent than 8-11 p.m. reality shows. Of concern in Year 3 is a significant increase in levels of visual violence in the late afternoon (3-6 p.m.), a time when children and adolescents are an important segment of the audience.

C. *Genre Considerations:* We have argued, and now have three years of data to support the notion that "reality programs" as a genre merit special consideration for both formal and discursive reasons. Reality programs, first, tend to be segmented (just over half in each year are) to a degree not found in entertainment programming, requiring a different form of analysis. Further, we now have compelling evidence to support our notion that examining not just visual depictions of violence but also the nature and structure of *Talk About Violence* provides a richer context in understanding violence in reality programs. More to the point, we have consistent evidence that "reality" as a genre itself is too broad. Both conceptually, and now empirically, we argue that to understand violence in "reality" television requires subdividing the category into genres that are on many contextual dimensions distinctive. Police Shows are clearly the most violent reality programs, and Talk Shows the least violent. Tabloid News programs are more likely to feature violence than other News and Public Affairs programs, and "entertainment-reality" genres represent something of a hybrid between the entertainment television analyzed by our Santa Barbara colleagues and "real reality" programs.

We find ourselves making the same recommendations to television and cable programmers and producers as we have in the two prior years, for the consistency in our data render them pertinent.

1. *Program advisories and ratings*

Findings from the NTVS Study

Just six percent of violent non-fictional reality programs in Year 3 were preceded by advisories, compared with 11 percent in Year 2 and 12 percent in Year 1.

Recommendation

Programs with substantial violent content should be preceded by oral and written advisories outlining the nature of the violent content.

While we hope that consumers and parents will use the broadcasters' and cablecasters' voluntary violence ratings, we would also encourage the industry to employ concrete and reasonably specific written and oral advisories, in addition to the small program "V" logos and age ratings, in programs which contain particularly violent content.

2. *Scheduling of Violent Reality Programming*

Findings from the NTVS Study

In all three seasons, the prevalence of violence in reality programming was greatest in evening programming, but in Year 3, violence increased in the 3-6 p.m. block, when substantial numbers of young people are watching.

Recommendation

Programs with substantial violent content should be scheduled late in the broadcast day.

Violent reality programs, especially Police programs and kindred non-news entertainment reality shows, should be scheduled in later-evening time blocks. Where network-affiliated stations are unable to move programs into late prime time, they should consider moving such fare to late-night time blocks. Our 1997-1998 data indicate that visual violence has declined in late prime time and increased in the late afternoon. We again strenuously urge the nation's programmers to put their most violent fare later in the evening.

3. *Alternatives to Violence*

Findings from the NTVS Study

Only six percent of Year 3 violent reality programs and segments suggest alternatives to violence or ways of avoiding violence or coping with its aftermath, a fraction comparable with the two prior seasons.

Recommendation

Producers and programmers should find ways to suggest ways of avoiding violence or coping with its effects.

Program creators, when dealing with violence as a topic, should share, where appropriate, information to help audiences gain more information about avoiding violence, suggesting alternatives to violent means, or coping with the aftermath of violence, through, for example, hotlines and helplines.

REFERENCES

Davison, W.P. (1983). The third-person effect in communication. *Public Opinion Quarterly, 47,* 1-15.

Ghanem, S. and Evatt, D., (1995, August). The paradox of public concern about crime: An interim report. Paper presented to the Association for Education in Journalism and Mass Communication, Washington, DC.

National Television Violence Study (1998). *National Television Violence Study, Vol. 2.* Thousand Oaks, CA: Sage.

National Television Violence Study (1997). *National Television Violence Study, Vol. 1.* Thousand Oaks, CA: Sage.

Oliver, M.B, 1994. Portrayals of crime, race, and aggression in "reality-based" police shows: A content analysis. *Journal of Broadcasting & Electronic Media 38:*179-192.

----- and Armstrong, G. B, 1995. Predictors of viewing and enjoyment of reality-based and fictional crime shows. *Journalism Quarterly 72,* 559-570.

Tulloch, M.I. (1995). Evaluating aggression: School students' responses to television portrayals of institutionalized violence. *Journal of Youth and Adolescence, 24,* 95-116.

Tulloch, M.I. & Tulloch, J.C. (1992). Attitudes to domestic violence: School students' responses to a television drama, *Australian Journal of Marriage & Family 13,* 62-69.

APPENDIX 1

Reality Shows in the 1996-1997 Sample

Shows in the present sample which were *not* in the 1995-96 sample are in ***boldface***.

<u>GENRE</u>	<u>FREQUENCY</u>
<u>Police Shows</u>	
America's Most Wanted	4
Cops	3
Real Stories of the Highway Patrol	4
Top Cops	4
Bounty Hunters	**1**
World's Scariest Police Shootout	**1**
<u>Entertainment Non-News Shows</u>	
America's Funniest Home Videos	14
Court TV	1
People's Court	7
Real World	8
Rescue 911	10
Road Rules	4
Unsolved Mysteries	6
America Undercover	**3**
Attack of the Bradys	**1**
Barry Manilow	**1**
Beatles Video Collection	**1**
Before they were Stars	**1**
Best of the Midnight Special	**1**
Breakfast with the Arts	**1**
Buzz Kill	**2**
CMN Champions Telethon	**1**
Comic Relief's 10th Anniversary	**1**
Disney's Beauty and the Beast	**1**
Donna's Day	**1**
Extremists	**2**
Fire Rescue	**1**
Gameworks Premiere Party	**1**
George Carlin	**1**
Great Performances	**2**
Hard Rock Live	**1**
Hispanic Heritage Awards	**1**
INXS Rocks the Rockies	**1**
John Denver: The Wildlife Concert	**1**
John Lennon: Live in New York	**1**
John Tesh: the Avalon Concert	**1**

GENRE	FREQUENCY

Entertainment Non-News Shows

Judge Judy	**5**
Love at First Sight	**1**
Making It! Minority Success Stories	**1**
Matthew Perry Interview	**1**
Michael Jackson	**1**
MTV Movie Awards	**1**
MTV Video Music Awards	**1**
1996 Life Beat Concert	**1**
1997 Preview Saturday	**1**
Paul McCartney	**1**
Real TV	**6**
Rodman World Tour	**1**
Straight Dope	**2**
Tonight's Show 19th Anniversary	**1**
Travels with Chuck Henry	**1**
TV's Bloopers	**5**
Unexplained	**2**
Unplugged	**1**
Unusual Occupations	**1**
U2 Mini Concert	**1**
Vanessa Williams	**1**
Voice and Harmony	**1**
World's Funniest Outtakes	**1**

Entertainment News and Review Shows

Day and Date	2
Entertainment Tonight	7
Fashionably Loud	1
Fashion TV	3
Flix News	1
Healthy Kids	2
Inside the NFL	2
MTV News Unfiltered	1
MTV Sports	5
NBA Inside Stuff	1
NBA Showtime	2
Our Home	10
Regis and Kathie Lee	4
Screen Scene	6
Siskel and Ebert	1
Unfiltered	1
Visiting with Huell Howser	1
Week in Rock	3

Access Hollywood	**6**
American Sportswomen	**1**
Behind Closed Doors	**1**

GENRE	FREQUENCY

Entertainment News and Review Shows

Caryl and Marilyn	5
Crook and Chase	2
The Dish	1
Everyday Living	3
House of Style	1
Inside the NBA	2
NBA Tipoff	1
NFL Youth Special	1
One to One	2
Real Life	1
RuPaul	2
Scoop	4
Slam-n-jam Wrap-Up	1
Soul of VH-1	1
Summer Movie Showcase	1
TV.COM	1
Visit L.A.	1
Wide World of Sports	1

News and Public Affairs

Bob Navarro's Journal	1
CBS This Morning	10
Dateline	3
Face the Nation	2
Firing Line	1
Frontline	1
48 Hours	1
Good Day LA	5
Good Morning America	6
Investigative Reports	2
Lead Story	2
Life and Times	8
Main Floor	1
McLaughlin Group	1
Meet the Press	1
Morning News	5
News Hour with Jim Lehrer	10
Nightly Business Report	5
Pacesetters	1
Primetime Live	1
Real Business	2
Rights and Wrongs	1
60 Minutes	1
Today	6
Tony Brown's Journal	1
To the Contrary	1
20/20	1

GENRE	FREQUENCY

News and Public Affairs

Wall Street Journal	1
Wall Street Week	1
Washington Week in Review	1
After Breakfast	**5**
Fox News Sunday	**1**
John McLaughlin's One on One	**1**
Midday Sunday	**2**
Newscope	**3**
Sunday Morning	**1**
Think Tank	**1**
This Week with David Brinkley	**1**

Tabloid News Shows

American Journal	5
EXTRA	10
Hard Copy	9
Inside Edition	5

Documentaries

American Justice	5
America's Castles	2
Ancient Mysteries	3
Biography	12
California Gold	2
National Geographic	2
Nova	1
20th Century	1
Voyages	1
Wildlife Mysteries	1
Alchemy in Light	**1**
America in Perspective	**1**
American Experience	**2**
Bill T. Jones	**1**
Chicano	**1**
Entrepreneurial Revolution	**1**
Faces of Culture	**1**
Football America	**1**
Great Escapes of WWI	**1**
Great Railway Stories	**1**
Irish in America	**1**
Intimate Portrait	**4**
Las Vegas: House of Cards	**1**
Making of Donnie Brasco	**1**
Making of 101 Dalmatians	**1**
Making of Drop Zone	**1**

GENRE	FREQUENCY

Documentaries

Making of Private Parts	1
Making of Richie Rich	1
Making of Star Wars	1
Mysteries of the Bible	2
The Origins of the Ghost	1
POV	1
Rogers and Hammerstein	1
Selena	1
Taking Care of Business	1
Taste of Africa	1
A Very Jefferson Reunion	1
Waging Peace	1
Whitney Houston Video Collection	1

Talk Shows

American Baby	1
BET Talk	4
David Frost	1
Geraldo	3
Gordon Elliott	5
In Person with Maureen O'Boyle	5
Jenny Jones	10
Leeza	6
Maury Povich	5
Montel Williams	6
Oprah Winfrey	5
Richard Bey	2
Ricki Lake	9
Rosie O'Donnell	5
Sally Jesse Raphael	12
Teen Summit	5
What Every Baby Knows	5

Ancestors	1
Archives	5
Here's Donny	1
Home and Family	5
Kids These Days	6
Pat Bullard	1
Spilled Milk	1

APPENDIX 2:

TABLES AND FIGURES

Table A: Profile of Reality-Program Violence Across Genres

Figure 1:   Reality Shows by Genre

Figure 2:   Program Genre by Channel Type

Figure 3:   Program Genre by Daypart

Figure 4:   Genre and Type of Violence

Figure 5:   Type of Channel and Type of Violence

Figure 6:   Means of Violence in Visual and Talk About Violence Sequences

Figure 7:   Weapons in Visual and Talk About Violence Sequences

Figure 8:   Type of Violence by Genre by Daypart (6-9 a.m.)

Figure 9:   Type of Violence by Genre by Daypart (9 a.m.-3 p.m.)

Figure 10:   Type of Violence by Genre by Daypart (3-6 p.m.)

Figure 11:   Type of Violence by Genre by Daypart (6-8 p.m.)

Figure 12:   Type of Violence by Genre by Daypart (8-11 p.m.)

Table A:
Profile of Reality Program Violence Across Genres
1996-97 n=526 programs, 1995-96 n=494 programs,
1994-95 n=393 programs

	Year	Overall %	Police Shows	Ent'mnt Non-News	Ent'mnt News and Review	Documentary	News and Public Affairs	Tabloid News	Talk Shows
% of Programs with some visual violence	1996-97	39%	100	33	42	66	29	79	16
	1995-96	36%	100	35	31	53	37	69	15
	1994-95	38%	100	46	21	73	26	86	15
% of Programs with some talk about violence	1996-97	10%	0	7	1	8	13	7	21
	1995-96	14%	0	9	10	1	13	24	29
	1994-95	18%	0	7	14	8	22	14	30

Among Programs which contain violence
Violence in Visual sequences:
% of sequences...

	Year	Overall %	Police Shows	Ent'mnt Non-News	Ent'mnt News and Review	Documentary	News and Public Affairs	Tabloid News	Talk Shows
Depicting acts	1996-97	67%	61	75	67	65	59	69	76
	1995-96	73%	66	68	81	74	63	69	80
	1994-95	61%	54	57	70	63	52	79	53
Depicting credible threats	1996-97	36%	56	38	47	30	39	10	26
	1995-96	32%	57	37	30	29	21	14	41
	1994-95	34%	65	26	45	23	14	18	21
Showing no harm and pain	1996-97	44%	32	41	70	34	65	36	64
	1995-96	41%	37	28	49	35	41	68	44
	1994-95	37%	33	38	45	33	29	44	50
In which violence occurs off screen	1996-97	9%	6	12	7	7	8	11	12
	1995-96	10%	7	19	5	8	12	9	20
	1994-95	3%	2	13	0	1	5	2	3
In which a gun is used	1996-97	43%	72	39	50	34	52	27	26
	1995-96	40%	67	55	38	37	38	26	26
	1994-95	43%	70	50	49	30	25	44	21
In which perpetrators are rewarded	1996-97	11%	15	17	8	13	14	4	0
	1995-96	8%	8	3	12	17	3	0	8
	1994-95	9%	20	3	0	12	11	5	0
In which perpetrators are punished	1996-97	35%	55	22	24	49	30	37	48
	1995-96	25%	38	23	24	35	15	26	46
	1994-95	33%	64	32	7	25	43	26	30
In which violence is extremely intense	1996-97	19%	33	22	9	19	13	33	10
	1995-96	23%	27	16	26	21	15	25	36
	1994-95	10%	11	10	4	10	12	12	21
In which violence is very graphic	1996-97	9%	6	11	1	12	12	10	10
	1995-96	9%	6	7	7	10	12	3	15
	1994-95	7%	3	3	1	11	12	12	6

Table A:
Profile of Reality Program Violence Across Genres
1996-97 n=526 programs, 1995-96 n=494 programs,
1994-95 n=393 programs

	Year	Overall %	Police Shows	Ent'mnt Non-News	Ent'mnt News and Review	Documentary	News and Public Affairs	Tabloid News	Talk Shows

Violence in Talk about violence sequences:
   % of sequences...

	Year	Overall %	Police Shows	Ent'mnt Non-News	Ent'mnt News and Review	Documentary	News and Public Affairs	Tabloid News	Talk Shows
Discussing acts	1996-97	78%	72	66	80	67	84	77	88
	1995-96	78%	76	87	67	81	62	65	89
	1994-95	65%	47	53	88	63	61	62	80
Discussing credible threats	1996-97	22%	30	38	20	24	14	19	16
	1995-96	21%	14	13	22	18	29	22	20
	1994-95	28%	42	27	17	29	28	43	18
Involving no harm and pain	1996-97	29%	21	54	77	20	39	24	31
	1995-96	40%	37	12	41	13	45	70	48
	1994-95	54%	50	54	59	35	60	59	65
In which a gun is used	1996-97	26%	49	25	53	30	15	34	16
	1995-96	27%	43	27	47	34	24	9	23
	1994-95	24%	35	26	42	14	33	46	16
In which perpetrators are rewarded	1996-97	14%	17	15	14	20	17	5	9
	1995-96	7%	5	4	13	19	0	0	8
	1994-95	6%	14	0	0	15	6	7	0
In which perpetrators are punished	1996-97	46%	53	29	38	53	41	56	51
	1995-96	40%	48	29	58	46	41	26	38
	1994-95	40%	86	23	6	46	40	48	31
In which talk is graphic, concrete	1996-97	55%	56	71	40	50	44	56	58
	1995-96	53%	48	71	44	63	53	43	51
	1994-95	38%	34	48	30	32	28	35	49
Involves first person testimony	1996-97	34%	20	31	20	18	28	28	53
	1995-96	40%	24	39	28	22	36	18	61
	1994-95	31%	36	38	22	20	21	32	47
Involves second person testimony	1996-97	29%	27	23	40	46	35	12	23
	1995-96	20%	33	18	20	18	14	20	23
	1994-95	27%	25	33	9	22	32	29	26
Involves third person testimony	1996-97	52%	63	50	60	53	48	76	45
	1995-96	53%	48	46	59	68	58	75	38
	1994-95	42%	39	29	70	55	47	38	26

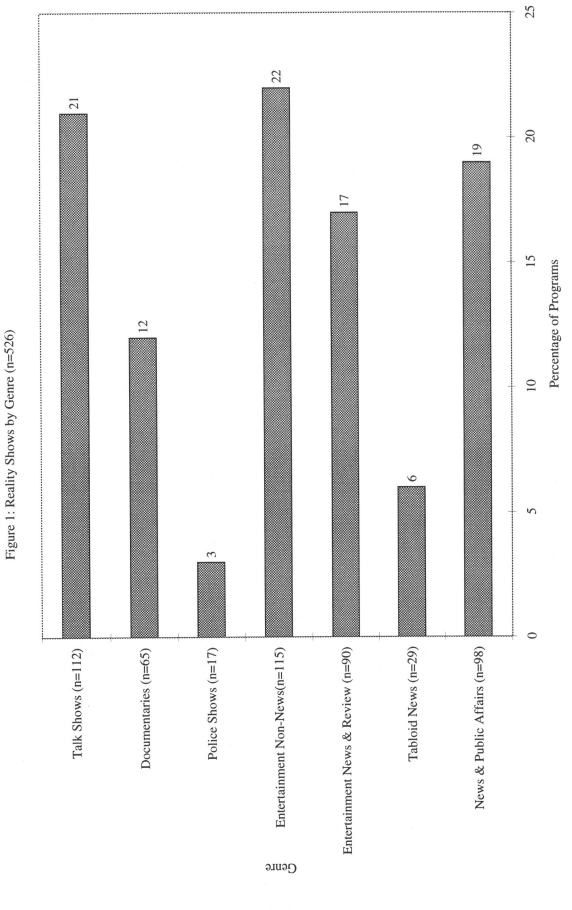

Figure 1: Reality Shows by Genre (n=526)

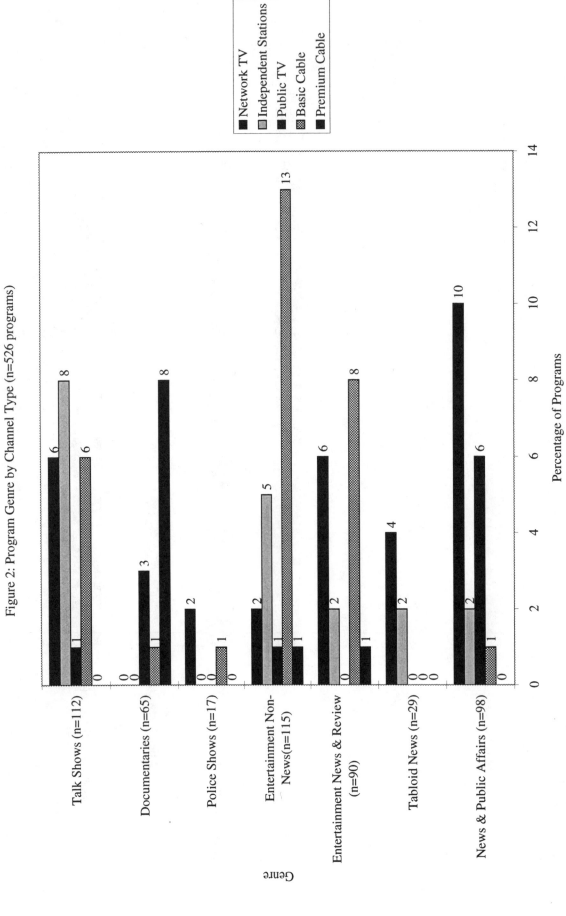

Figure 2: Program Genre by Channel Type (n=526 programs)

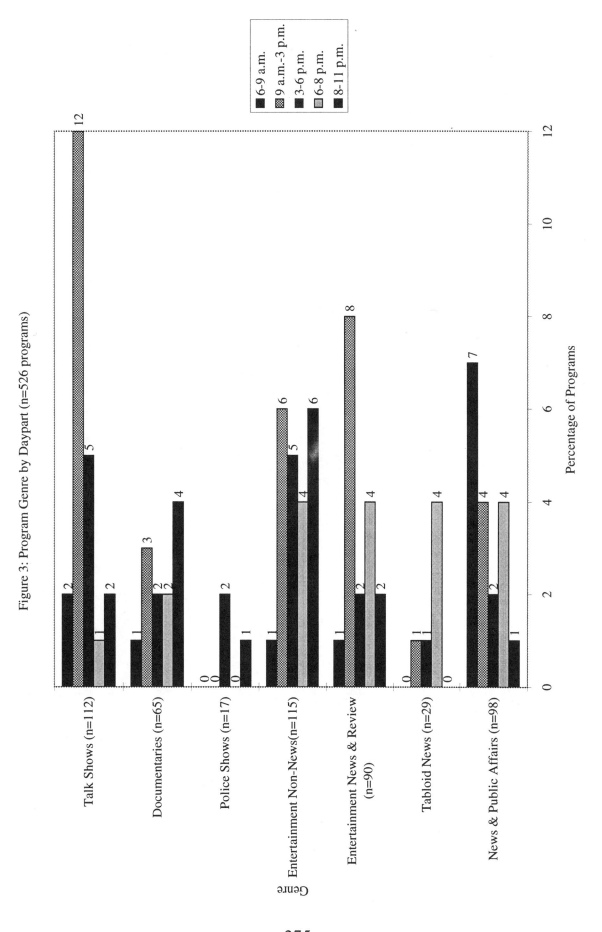

Figure 3: Program Genre by Daypart (n=526 programs)

275

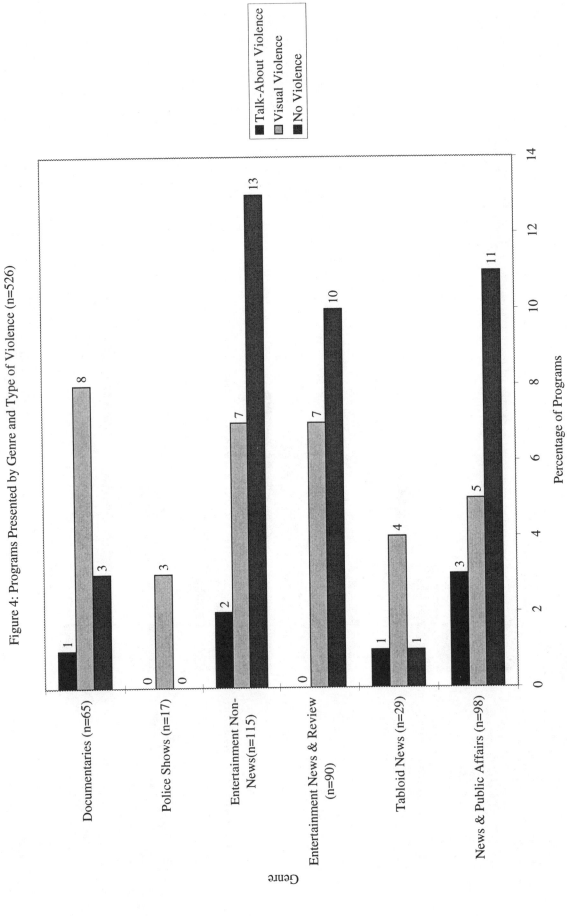

Figure 4: Programs Presented by Genre and Type of Violence (n=526)

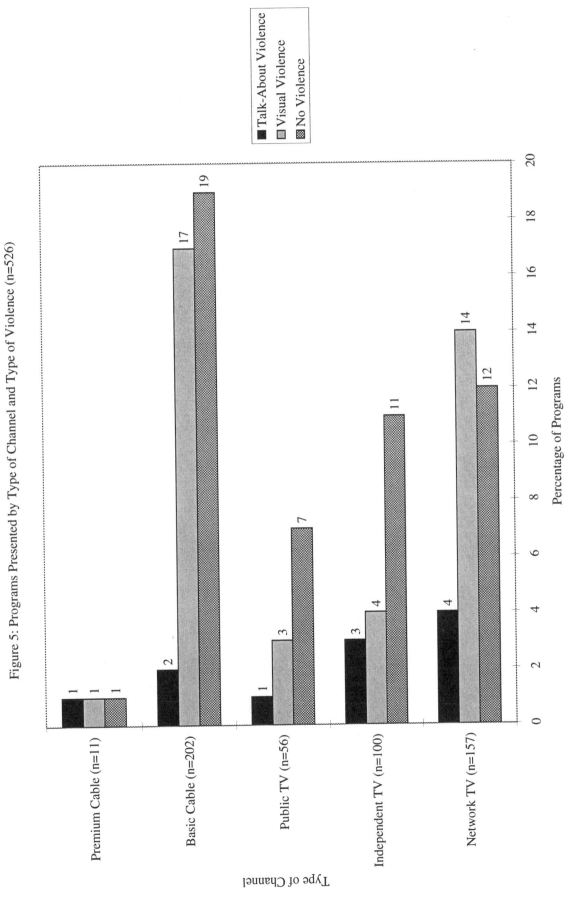

Figure 5: Programs Presented by Type of Channel and Type of Violence (n=526)

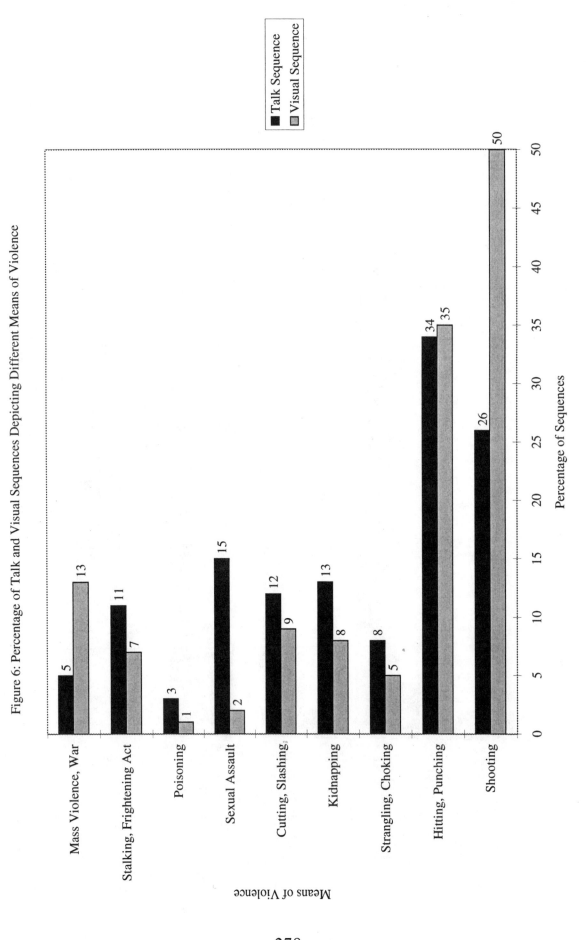

Figure 6: Percentage of Talk and Visual Sequences Depicting Different Means of Violence

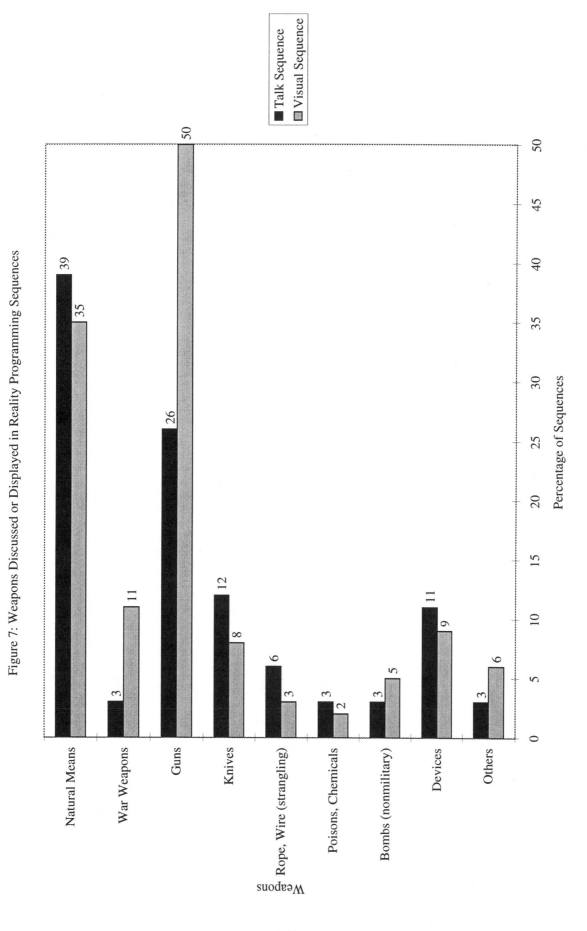

Figure 7: Weapons Discussed or Displayed in Reality Programming Sequences

279

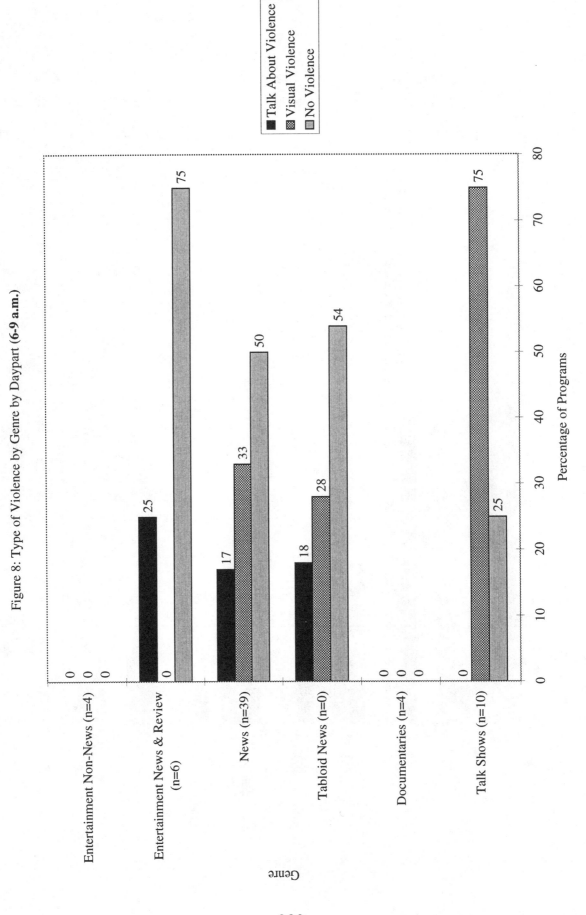

Figure 8: Type of Violence by Genre by Daypart (6-9 a.m.)

280

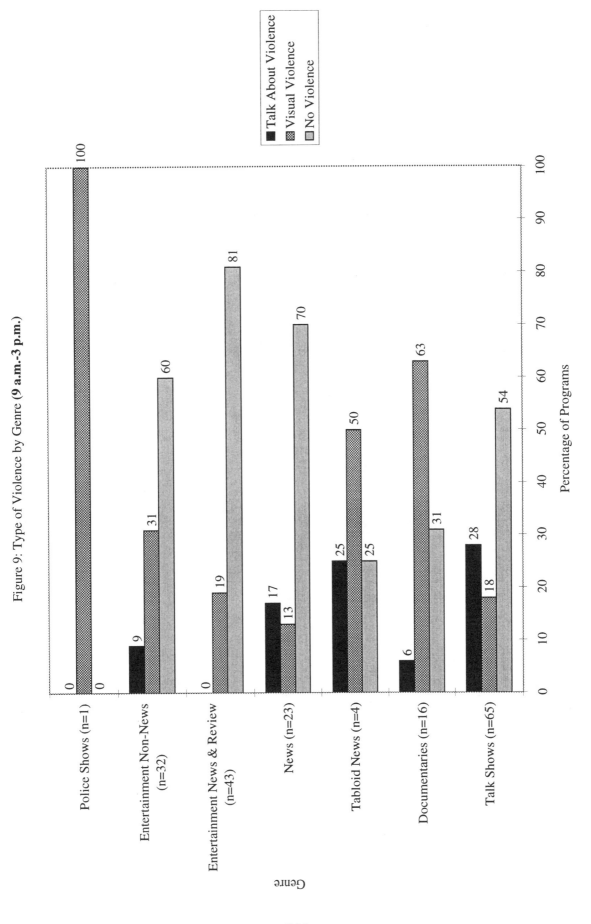

Figure 9: Type of Violence by Genre (**9 a.m.-3 p.m.**)

Genre

Percentage of Programs

Talk About Violence
Visual Violence
No Violence

281

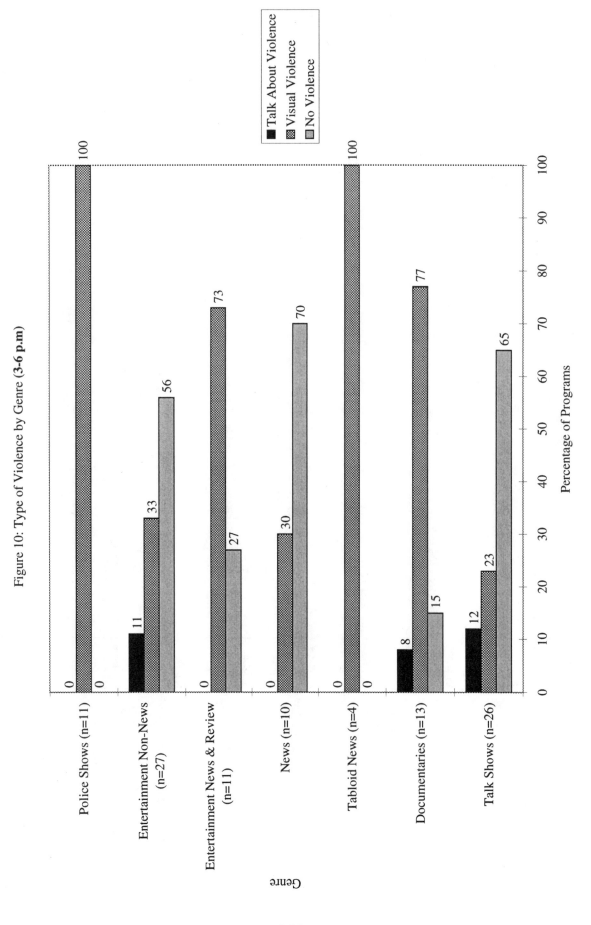

Figure 10: Type of Violence by Genre (**3-6 p.m**)

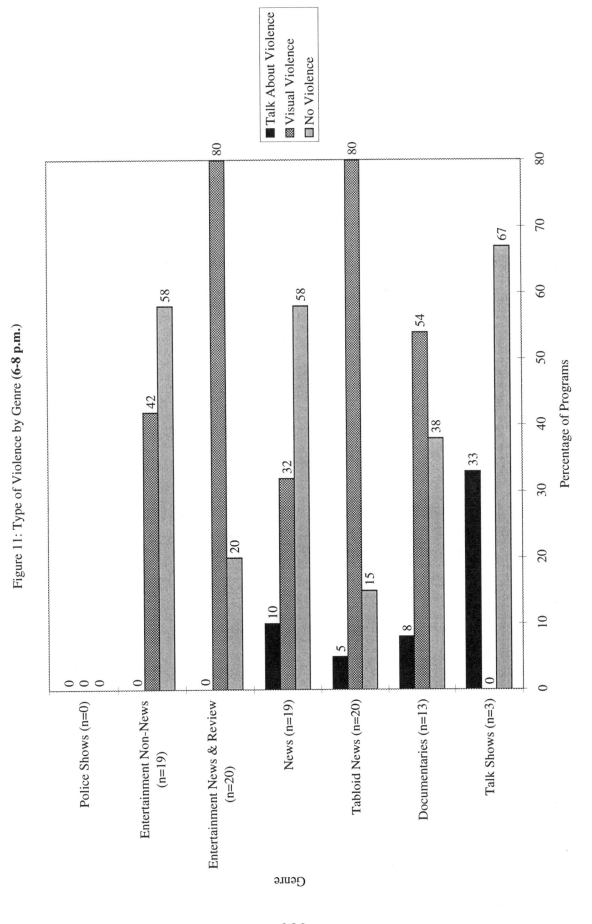

Figure 11: Type of Violence by Genre (**6-8 p.m.**)

283

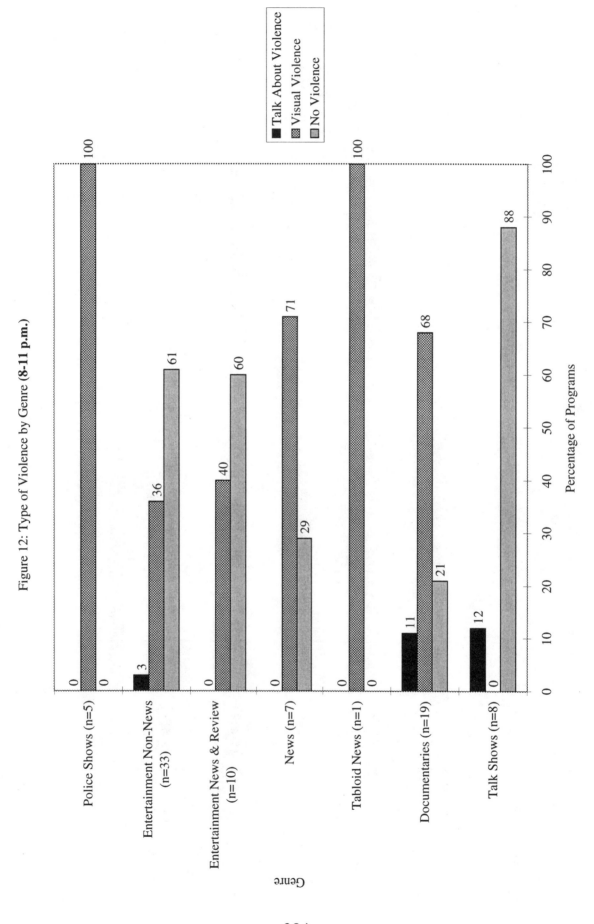

Figure 12: Type of Violence by Genre (**8-11 p.m.**)

PART III

RATINGS AND ADVISORIES
FOR TELEVISION PROGRAMMING:
UNIVERSITY OF WISCONSIN-MADISON STUDY

Dr. Joanne Cantor
Amy Nathanson

SUMMARY

The third year of research on ratings and advisories explored how often, at what times, and on what channels the different types of ratings and advisories appeared in the composite week of television. As in previous years, the analyses involved advisories, Motion Picture Association of America (MPAA) ratings, and the content codes developed by the premium channels HBO, Showtime, and Cinemax. In addition, this report includes the first systematic analysis of a random sample of programming that included the new TV Parental Guidelines, which were implemented beginning on January 1, 1997.

The content analysis showed that most networks and cable channels were quick to apply the TV Parental Guidelines to the programs for which they were intended (all programming except news and sports). By March, the guidelines were being applied to about two-thirds of such programs. Only two channels did not use the new ratings system at all, Black Entertainment Television (BET) and the PBS affiliate station (KCET). The new ratings were presented mostly in written, on-screen form. Oral announcement of the rating occurred only 2% of the time.

TVG was the most frequently used rating, with TVPG a close second. The TVMA rating was used for only one program in the sample (0.1% of eligible programs). The distribution of rating levels varied dramatically by program genre and by channel. Although many critics of the early application of the ratings system had observed that the rating of TVPG was being applied to a majority of programs, this criticism was not valid for the sample overall, and only one major network affiliate used this rating on a majority of its programs. Of the rated programs on the NBC affiliate, 67% were rated TVPG. In fact, all of the rated programs on NBC's prime-time schedule in the sample were rated TVPG.

Our analyses of children's programs (those designated as TVY or TVY7) showed that a significantly higher proportion of TVY7 programs than of TVY programs contained violence. However, the distributions of the TVG, TVPG, and TV14 ratings were almost identical for programs with violence and programs without violence. These results suggest that the TV Parental Guidelines as originally designed provided no guidance as to the presence of violence in programming intended for general audiences.

The use of advisories, MPAA ratings, and content codes did not change much over the three-year content analysis period. Advisories are used on a small proportion of programs and are rarely descriptive of the content to be expected. MPAA ratings and content codes are used heavily by the premium channels. New to the Year 3 sample was the use of advisory-type messages to recommend shows rather than warn against them.

INTRODUCTION

The third year of research at the University of Wisconsin focussed on how ratings and advisories are being used on television. This analysis is especially interesting because it is the first systematic content analysis of the use of the new television ratings, the TV Parental Guidelines, which were implemented beginning on January 1, 1997. This research also explores trends in the use of other types of ratings and advisories over the three years of the National Television Violence Study.

When content coders at the University of California at Santa Barbara and at the University of Texas at Austin screened programs, they noted the presence of advisories, MPAA ratings, content codes, and TV Parental Guidelines. The coders also indicated whether these messages were communicated orally, in written form, or both orally and in writing. For ratings and content codes, they noted the level or code that was presented. For advisories, they transcribed the text verbatim.

Chapter 1

THE USE OF "TV PARENTAL GUIDELINES" IN THE COMPOSITE WEEK OF TELEVISION

The Telecommunications Act of 1996 mandated that within two years of passage, most new televisions be manufactured with a "V-chip," to permit parents to block their children's exposure to content they consider harmful (Telecommunications Act, 1996). The V-chip works by reading a code imbedded in the transmission of the program. The Act included the provision that television programming that contains sexual, violent, or other indecent material be rated or labeled in a form that would be readable by the V-chip. It directed the Federal Communications Commission (FCC) to prescribe guidelines and recommended procedures for rating programs, but only if video program distributors had not established an acceptable ratings system within one year of passage of the Act. Shortly after the Act's passage, entertainment industry executives agreed to develop a ratings system that would be implemented in early 1997. The new system, named the "TV Parental Guidelines," was unveiled on December 19, 1996, and began being implemented on January 1, 1997.

The new system was in many ways similar to the Motion Picture Association of America's (MPAA) decades-old movie rating system. Like the MPAA ratings, the TV Parental Guidelines gave general ratings that indicated the appropriateness of programs for different age groups. Programs not specifically designed for children were given one of four ratings: TVG, General Audience, TVPG, Parental Guidance Suggested, TV14, Parents Strongly Cautioned, and TVMA, Mature Audiences Only. A separate, two-level ratings system was also included for programs that were considered to be designed for children: TVY, All Children and TVY7, Directed to Older Children.

As a result of broad-based criticism from parents and pressure from major child advocacy groups and influential members of the United States Senate and House of Representatives, the television industry agreed to amend its ratings system in July of 1997 (Farhi, 1997). The revised ratings system adds content letters to denote the presence of coarse language, sex, violence, and sexual dialog in a program. The revised system began being implemented on October 1, 1997 on all major networks except NBC and Black Entertainment Television (BET).

Sampling for the composite week of television for the Year 3 NTVS Report began on October 5, 1996 and ended on June 6, 1997. Therefore, a portion of the sample (36%

of the programs in the sample) was selected before the TV Parental Guidelines were in use. The analyses of these ratings were by necessity restricted to the programs sampled in the January-June period. The entire sample was collected before the revised system went into effect. The analyses presented here, therefore, report how the original system was used during its first five months of implementation.

Implementation of the New Ratings System

The first question we asked about the new television ratings was how quickly and widely they were implemented beginning in January 1997. The ratings system was intended to apply to all programming with the exception of news and sports. Whereas news and sports programs occurred in the composite week of television, they are considered "not in sample" for the purposes of the content analysis. The analyses reported below exclude news and sports programs from the calculations.

Our first analysis looked at the proportion of programs that received TV Parental Guidelines ratings month by month during the composite week of television. Figure 1 shows the results of this analysis. The data reveal that compliance with the new ratings system began swiftly. Already in January, 44% of the programs for which the ratings were intended received the new ratings, and the proportion climbed to 56% in February. By March, the percentage of programs rated had reached the mid sixties in terms of percentage, and remained in that range over the course of the period studied. Most (98%) of the guidelines were presented in written form without any accompanying voice-over announcement of the rating.

Figure 1
Percent of Programs Receiving TV Parental Guidelines
Over the Period Studied (October 5, 1996 through June 6, 1997)

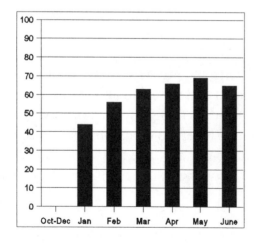

Note. The bars indicate the percent of programs aired (excluding news and sports) with TV Parental Guidelines. n's are as follows: Oct-Dec=985; Jan=475; Feb=314; Mar=399; Apr=202; May=321; Jun=43.

In order to interpret this percentage compliance, it is instructive to look at the extent to which the different television channels adopted the new guidelines. Because Figure 1 showed that compliance had leveled off by March, this analysis looked at the proportion of programs that were given ratings during the sampling period of March 1 to June 6. Figure 2 presents these findings. In this figure, the solid bars indicate the percentage of programs that received TV Parental Guidelines, and the shaded areas indicate the percent of programs not receiving TV Parental Guidelines but bearing another form of rating or advisory (that is, an MPAA rating, a content code, or an advisory). As can be seen from the figure, adoption of the Guidelines varied dramatically by channel. Compliance was high among the broadcast network affiliates, with ABC, Fox, and NBC at or approaching 90%. CBS gave TV Parental Guidelines to 66% of its eligible programs and gave alternative ratings or advisories to an additional 2%.

Figure 2
Percent of Programs Receiving TV Parental Guidelines
(or Any Other Rating) Across All Channels (March 1-June 6, 1997)

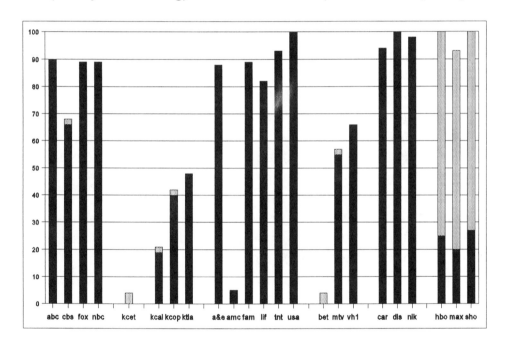

Note: The solid bars indicate the percent of programs (excluding news and sports) with TV Parental Guidelines. The shaded area indicates the percent of programs with any other rating. n's are as follows: ABC=31; CBS=58; Fox=73; NBC=36; KCET=57; KCAL=52; KCOP=43; KTLA=48; A&E=32; AMC=19; FAM=26; LIF=17; TNT=28; USA=36; BET=26; MTV=64; VH1=62; CAR=86; DIS=44; NIK=85; HBO=12; MAX=15; SHO=15.

291

Further analyses revealed that CBS's lower percentage was predominantly due to its low level of compliance with regard to programs in the "reality" category. One reason for this may have been the ambiguity of the definition of the exempt "news" category. Our content analysis definition limited the news category to bona fide news programs and breaking news. Among CBS's unrated programs were *CBS This Morning* and *Face the Nation*, which the network may have considered news but which fell into our reality show category of "news and public affairs." However, CBS's sample of unrated shows also contained several unrated nonnews reality shows, such as *Real Stories of the Highway Patrol*. When reality programs were excluded from the analysis, the CBS affiliate's compliance rate became 90% -- a level comparable to the other three networks.

KCET, the public broadcast station in the sample, did not use the TV Parental Guidelines at all. This finding is consistent with public statements made by PBS that it would not adopt the new ratings system because it considered it inadequate (Hall, 1997). KCET assigned other forms of ratings and advisories to 4% of its programs.

The three independent broadcast stations in the sample varied in their level of use of the TV Parental Guidelines, from 19% for KCAL to 48% for KTLA. The general entertainment cable channels used the TV Parental Guidelines heavily, with the exception of American Movie Classics (AMC), which applied these ratings to only 5% of its programs. The remaining five channels in this category assigned these ratings to most of their programs, ranging from 82% for Lifetime (LIF) to 100% for the USA Network. One possible explanation for the lower levels of compliance by AMC and the independent broadcast stations is that they are airing more syndicated programs and older movies, which may take more time to rate than current productions.

Black Entertainment Television (BET) did not adopt the TV Parental Guidelines at all, although 4% of their programs had advisories. This finding is consistent with the channel's public statements, in which they indicated that they would not adopt the ratings (Hall, 1997). The other two music-oriented cable channels used the Guidelines with a majority of their programs, MTV using them for 55% of programs and VH1 using them for 66%.

The three child-oriented cable channels used the TV Parental Guidelines on almost all of their programs, with percentages ranging from 94% for the Cartoon Network to 100% for the Disney Channel.

Finally, the three premium channels were not heavy users of the TV Parental Guidelines, with utilization ranging from 20% for Cinemax to 27% for Showtime.

However, as Figure 2 shows, almost all programs on these channels received some type of rating or advisory, ranging from 93% for Cinemax to 100% for both HBO and Showtime.

Distribution of Rating Levels

The next set of analyses dealt with the frequency with which the various levels of the TV Parental Guidelines were assigned to programs. Figure 3 displays the distribution frequency of the various rating levels across the sample of programs that received TV Parental Guidelines (N=1018). As can be seen from the figure, almost a third (32%) of all rated programs received a rating of TVG. Close behind that was the TVPG rating, with 29%. Twenty-three percent of the programs were rated TVY, and 11% were rated TVY7. The TV14 rating was used sparingly, with only 6% of the rated programs being assigned that rating. The TVMA rating was virtually nonexistent: Only one program in the entire sample, or 0.1%, received that rating. The program was a George Carlin Comedy Special on HBO. Because only one program received the TVMA rating, that rating will be excluded from most of the remaining analyses in this section.

Figure 3
Distribution of Rating Levels
Across Programs Receiving TV Parental Guidelines (N=1018)

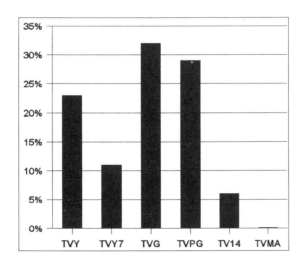

Distribution of rating levels within genres. The next set of analyses explored the distribution of the TV Parental Guidelines across the various genres of programs in the sample. As can be seen from Figure 4, of the 147 programs in the Drama Series genre that received ratings, the most frequent rating was TVPG (46%). In addition 29% received a TVG and 24% received a TV14. Only 2 drama series (1.4%) received a TVY7. These were *Degrassi Jr. High* on Showtime and *Spellbinder* on Disney.

Figure 4
Distribution of TV Parental Guidelines for Drama Series (n=147)

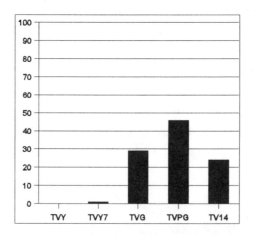

Figure 5 presents the distribution of ratings over the 151 programs in the Comedy Series genre. The majority of rated programs in this category received a TVG rating (62%). The next most frequent rating in this category was TVPG (33%). A few programs in this genre were rated TVY7 (3%) or TV14 (1%). The TV14 comedy programs were *Married with Children* on Fox and *Ellen* on ABC.

Figure 5
Distribution of TV Parental Guidelines for Comedy Series (n=151)

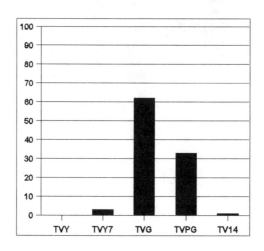

Figure 6 represents the very different distribution of Parental Guidelines over the 427 programs in the Children's Series genre. As would be expected, most of these programs (54%) received the TVY rating, and the frequency of occurrence of each rating declined as the level of the rating became more restrictive. Twenty-three percent of the rated children's series received a TVY7, and 20% received a TVG. Very few programs of this type were rated TVPG (2%) or TV14 (1%). The TV14 programs that were classified in the Children's Series genre were all episodes of *Beavis and Butthead* (MTV). This program is perhaps placed in the Children's genre because of its animated format. However, although it may have many child viewers, there are very few people who would consider this program to be designed for children.

Figure 6
Distribution of TV Parental Guidelines for Children's Series (n=427)

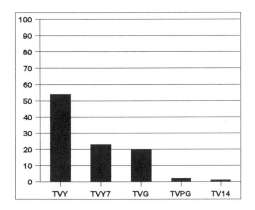

Figure 7 shows the distribution of the TV Parental Guidelines for the 67 Movies that were assigned these ratings. As the figure shows, TVPG was the most frequently used rating for movies (45%), followed by TVG (34%). Eighteen percent of these movies were rated TV14, and only one movie was rated TVY (*Educating Mom* on ABC). No movies were rated TVY7.

Figure 7
Distribution of TV Parental Guidelines for Movies (n=67)

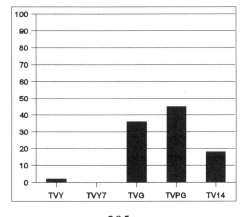

As Figure 8 shows, for the 173 Reality-Based programs that received TV Parental Guidelines, the most frequent rating was TVPG (53%). TVG was the next most frequent rating for this genre (42%). A few of these programs were rated TV14 (5%). These programs were individual episodes of the following series: *Jenny Jones* (KCOP), *The Oprah Winfrey Show* (ABC), *Leeza* (NBC), *Sally Jesse Raphael* (KTLA), and *Gordon Elliott* (CBS), and programs with the following titles: *Love at First Sight* (Cinemax), *Rodman World Tour* (MTV), and *World's Scariest Police Shootouts* (Fox). Only two of the programs in the Reality genre (1%) were rated TVY7. These programs were *NFL Youth Special* and *NBA Inside Stuff*, both on NBC.

Figure 8
Distribution of TV Parental Guidelines for Reality-Based Programs (n=173)

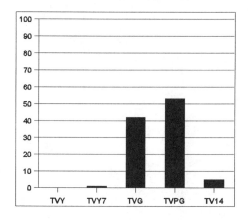

Figure 9 shows the distribution of TV Parental Guidelines for the 52 music video programs that received these ratings. Almost all of these programs (90%) were rated TVPG, while 10% were rated TVG.

Figure 9
Distribution of TV Parental Guidelines for Music Video Programs (n=52)

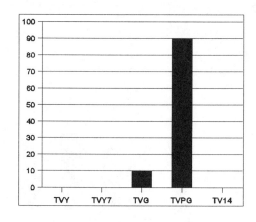

Distribution of rating levels within channels. The next set of analyses dealt with the distribution of the TV Parental Guidelines ratings within channels, grouped by channel type. Figure 10 displays the data for the four commercial broadcast affiliates in the sample. As can be seen from the figure, the distribution of ratings was different for the different channels. For example, of the 45 programs receiving TV Parental Guidelines on ABC, the most frequently used rating was TVPG (44%), followed by TVG (29%), with TV14 (13%), TVY (9%), and TVY7 (4%) being used relatively little. In contrast, the 44 rated programs on CBS were evenly split between TVPG and TV14 (both at 43%) with the lower three ratings used rarely (TVY: 2%, TVY7: 2%, and TVG: 9%). Fox was the only channel in this category that used the TVG rating more than any other in the shows it rated (n=95). Fifty percent of the programs rated on Fox received a TVG, and TVPG was used on 21% of rated programs. The remaining ratings were distributed as follows: TVY, 15%, TVY7, 10%, and TV14, 5%. NBC was the only commercial broadcast affiliate that assigned more than half of its rated programs (n=49) to one category. Two-thirds (67%) of these programs were rated TVPG, while 22% were rated TV14. No programs on the NBC affiliate were rated TVY, 6% were rated TVY7, and 4% were rated TVG.

Figure 10
Distribution of TV Parental Guidelines on Commercial Broadcast Network Channels

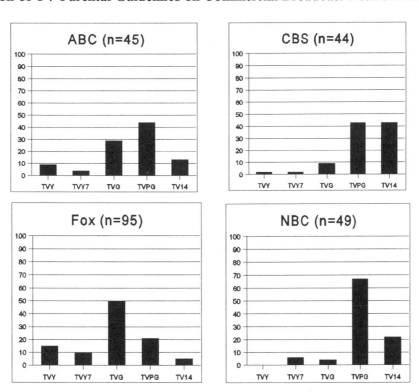

Note.   n's indicate the number of programs that received TV Parental Guidelines
in the sample.

Because the networks themselves have much more control of their prime-time schedules than of the entire schedules of their affiliates, we redid these analyses using only the programs that occurred during prime-time. This analysis provided stronger evidence of NBC's overreliance on the TVPG rating. Although all four major networks used the TVPG rating on at least half of the prime-time programs that appeared in the January to June random sample, NBC used the TVPG rating on all (100%) of its prime-time shows (n=14). CBS used it for 50% of its programs (n=10); ABC used it for 62% (n=16), and Fox used it for 70% (n=13). Figure 11 shows these distributions.

Figure 11
Distribution of TV Parental Guidelines during Prime Time
on Commercial Broadcast Networks

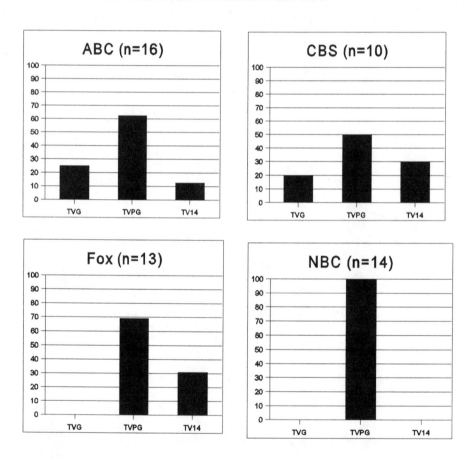

Note. n's indicate the number of programs that received TV Parental Guidelines in the prime-time sample.

Based on the data available in the Year 3 analyses, it is unclear what the lack of variability in NBC's ratings is attributable to. One possible explanation is that in the view of the programs' producers, all of these programs contained "infrequent coarse language, limited violence, and/or some suggestive sexual dialog and situations," as the definition of the TVPG rating suggested, and that none of these programs had less nor more controversial content than that definition implies. Another possible explanation is that these ratings were based on considerations other than the programs' contents.

Figure 12 shows the distribution of TV Parental Guidelines across the independent broadcast channels. As the figure shows, these three channels were somewhat similar in their use of these ratings, with the exception that KCAL had no programs rated TV14, and KCOP had no programs rated TVY.

Figure 12
Distribution of TV Parental Guidelines on Independent Broadcast Channels

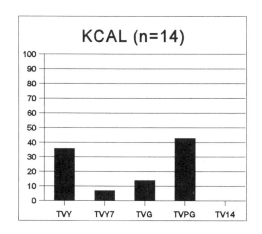
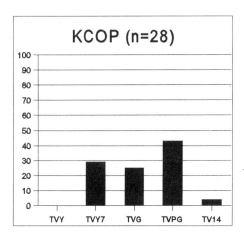

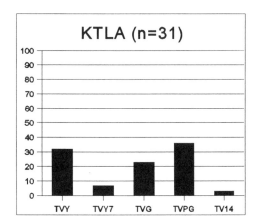

Note. n's indicate the number of programs that received TV Parental Guidelines in the sample.

Figure 13 shows the distribution of TV Parental Guidelines within general entertainment cable channels. In general, TVG and TVPG were used most frequently on these channels. A&E and the Family Channel rated more than 60% of their programs TVG.

Figure 13
Distribution of TV Parental Guidelines on General Entertainment Cable Channels

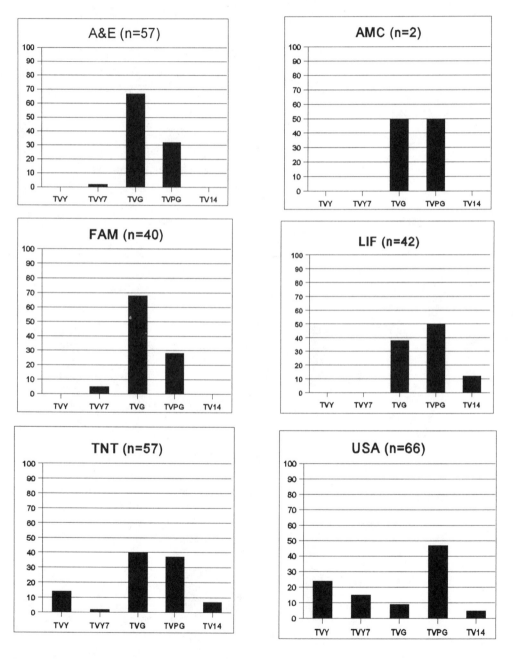

Note. n's indicate the number of programs that received TV Parental Guidelines in the sample.

Figure 14 shows the distribution of these ratings on the music cable channels. TVPG was the dominant rating on these channels. As indicated earlier, BET did not use these guidelines.

Figure 14
Distribution of TV Parental Guidelines on Music Cable Channels

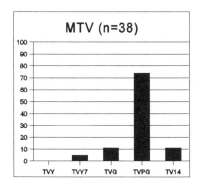
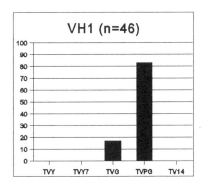

Note. n's indicate the number of programs that received TV Parental Guidelines in the sample.

Figure 15 shows the use of the TV Parental Guidelines on the children's cable channels. It is interesting to note that although Disney and Nickelodeon rated most of their programs TVY, the Cartoon Network almost completely avoided this rating, and used TVG for the majority of its programs.

Figure 15
Distribution of TV Parental Guidelines on Children's Cable Channels

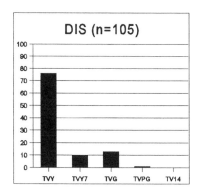
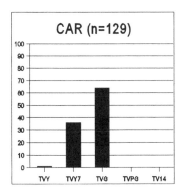
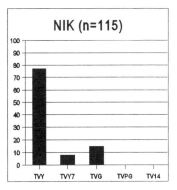

Note. n's indicate the number of programs that received TVParental Guidelines in the sample.

The Use of TV Parental Guidelines in Programs With vs. Without Violence

As we did in previous years, we next explored the degree to which the ratings distinguished between programs that contained violence and those that did not. For these purposes, we divided the sample of programs into two groups, those that the coders at Santa Barbara or at Austin had identified as containing any violence according to the content analysis criteria, and those that had not been identified as containing violence.

Figure 16 looks at programs rated TYY or TVY7 -- those identified by their rating as being designed for children. It shows the distribution of the ratings of TVY and TVY7 across programs containing vs. not containing violence. As the figure shows, of the 101 nonviolent programs designed for children, 83% were rated TVY and 17% were rated TVY7. In contrast, of the 240 programs for children that contained violence, 62% were rated TVY and 38% were rated TVY7. A chi square analysis computed on these frequencies showed that the distributions were significantly different ($X^2_{(1)}$=15.11, $p<.001$). In other words, as would be expected, a higher proportion of violent than of nonviolent programs received the TVY7 rating. Looking at the same data another way, 64% of programs rated TVY contained violence, while 84% of those rated TVY7 did so. These data suggest that the presence of violence had an impact on the rating of children's programs.

Figure 16
Distribution of TVY and TVY7
in Violent (n=240) and Nonviolent
Programs (n=101)

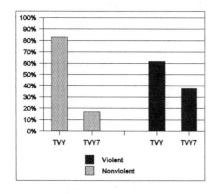

Figure 17
Distribution of TVG, TVPG, and TV14
in Violent (n=405) and Nonviolent
Programs (n=271)

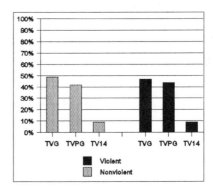

Figure 17 displays the data for programs not specifically designed for children. It shows the distribution of TVG, TVPG, and TV14 ratings across programs with vs. without violence. As the figure shows, these ratings were distributed almost identically among nonviolent and violent programs (nonviolent: TVG, 49%; TVPG, 42%; TV14, 9%; violent: TVG: 47%, TVPG, 44%; TV14, 9%). A chi square analysis showed that the difference between these distributions was trivial ($X^2_{(2)}=0.23$, $p=.893$). Looked at another way, the same data reveal that the proportion of programs with violence was virtually the same for all three ratings. Fifty-nine percent of programs rated TVG, 61% of those rated TVPG, and 60% of those rated TV14 contained violence.

These analyses suggest that the presence of violence was a criterion for the choice between the ratings of TVY and TVY7 for children's programs, but that it was not a predominant factor in determining which of the four general-audience ratings a program received. The import of these analyses is not to suggest that the programs were rated erroneously. The present analyses do not permit that determination. What it does suggest is that other elements in these programs, such as sex and coarse language, play enough of a role in a program's rating that the TV Parental Guidelines as originally implemented provided no guidance as to the presence or absence of violence.

Distribution of TV Parental Guidelines Across Dayparts

To determine how programs with the various TV Parental Guidelines were distributed throughout the day, days were divided into dayparts consistent with the analyses being conducted at the other sites. Programs were placed into dayparts as a function of the time a program began. The dayparts were as follows:

1. 6-9 am, Early Morning
2. 9 am - 3 pm, Daytime
3. 3-6 pm, Late Afternoon
4. 6-8 pm, Early Evening
5. 8-11 pm, Prime Time

Figure 18 shows the distribution of the various ratings, as well as programs that did not receive TV Parental Guidelines, over the course of the day. As can be seen from the figure, programs rated TVY were most prevalent in the early morning, and their availability diminished as the day wore on. The proportion of programs that were rated TVY ranged as follows over the five dayparts (1: 24%, 2: 13%, 3: 14%, 4: 10%, 5: 2%). The proportion of programs rated TVY7 varied little over the course of the day and was always less than 10% of available programs (1: 6%, 2: 9%, 3: 5%, 4: 4%, 5: 4%). The proportion of programs rated TVG also varied little over the course of the day, with their percentage remaining in the high teens until prime time, at which time it rose to the mid-twenties (1: 17%, 2: 18%, 3: 17%, 4: 18%, 5: 24%).

The proportion of programs rated TVPG rose steadily over the course of the day, from 5% in the early morning period to 29% during prime time (1: 5%, 2: 14%, 3: 21%, 4: 24%, 5: 29%). The TV14 rating was relatively infrequent, but its use peaked twice during the day, once during the daytime period and again during prime time (1: 0.3%, 2: 6%, 3: 0.3%, 4: 1%, 5: 7%). The only TVMA program in the sample was aired during prime time.

Figure 18
Distribution of TV Parental Guidelines Across Dayparts

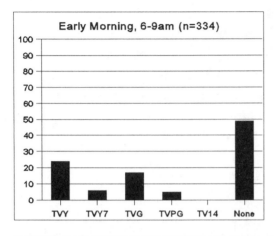

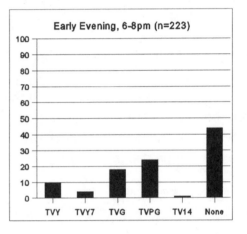

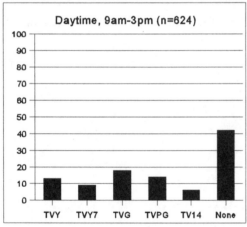

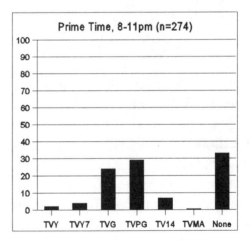

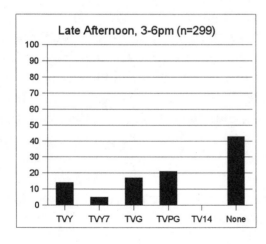

Chapter 2

USE OF ADVISORIES, RATINGS, AND CONTENT CODES IN THE COMPOSITE WEEK OF TELEVISION

Use of Advisories in the Sample

Presence of Oral and Written Advisories

Of the 2750 programs that were coded and part of the usable sample, 116 (4%) were presented with an oral advisory and 138 (5%) were presented with a written advisory. Of the 23 channels examined, three had no advisories, either written or oral. These channels were American Movie Classics (AMC), VH1, and the Cartoon Network (CAR). In Year 2, nine channels had no advisories; in Year 1, eight had no advisories. In the current sample, there were 10 programs that featured an oral advisory and no written advisory, and thirty-two advisories were presented visually only but not orally. Finally, 106 advisories were presented in both oral and written form. As in previous years, the analyses reported here involved written advisories. Figure 19 shows the distribution of written advisories over the various channels. Similar to both Year 1 and Year 2, Showtime used advisories the most, this year contributing 43% of the advisories in the sample.

Figure 19
Number of Programs and Advisories by Channel
in the Composite Week of Programming

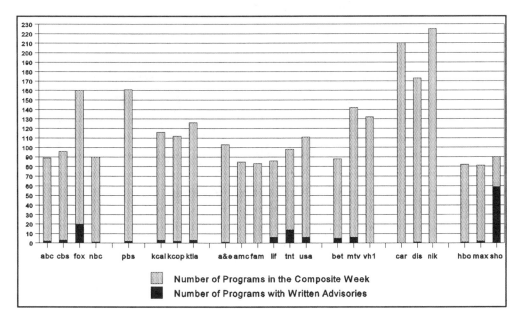

305

When we looked only at the 1688 programs that were coded as containing violence, we found that 123 or 7% of these were shown with written advisories, a slightly higher percent than for programming overall.

Text of Advisories

Two coders at the Madison site independently categorized the text of the advisories on the series of variables that follows. Reliability was computed as Cohen's Kappa.

Whose discretion is advocated? The advisories were first coded according to whether or not discretion was advised, and further, according to whose discretion was being advocated. Advisories were coded as advocating "parental" discretion (e.g., "parental discretion advised"), "viewer" discretion, (e.g., "viewer discretion advised"), "discretion" without a specific target (e.g., "discretion advised"), as presenting a "warning" or other admonition, but no mention of discretion (e.g., "warning: this program contains ..."), or as including no reference to discretion or warnings (Kappa = 1.00).

Figure 20 shows the distribution of these categories in the sample. As can be seen from the figure, more than half of the advisories (53%) advocated viewer discretion, while 11% urged parental discretion. In the previous two years, a higher proportion of the advisories advocated viewer discretion (Year 1: 63%; Year 2: 64%). This change seems to be due to an increase in the "none of the above" category, which comprised 30% in Year 3, up from 14% in Year 1 and 9% in Year 2. Further analyses will show that the increase in the "other" category is due primarily to the use of advisories to recommend programs.

Figure 20
Percent of Advisories Advocating
Discretion (n=138)

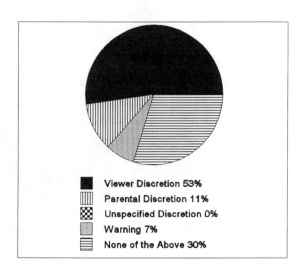

Unsuitable for which viewers? Independent of the presence of "discretion" or "warnings," the advisories were coded for whether they indicated that the program might be inappropriate for specific viewer categories. Advisories were coded as indicating that the content might be inappropriate for children, (e.g., "portions of the following may not be suitable for younger audiences") or for unspecified viewers, not including children (e.g., "the following movie may be too intense for some viewers"), or as not indicating any inappropriate viewer categories (Kappa = 1.00).

As can be seen from Figure 21, only 6% of advisories suggested that the material was unsuitable for children, and 1% said they were unsuitable for others.

Figure 21
Percent of Advisories with Specific Content (n=138)

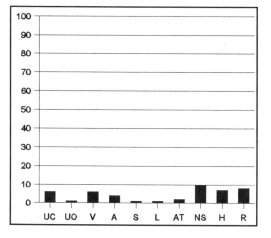

UC = Unsuitable for Children 6%
UO = Unsuitable for Others 1%
V = Violence Mentioned 6%
A = Action Mentioned 4%
L = Language Mentioned 1%
S = Sex Mentioned 1%
AT = Adult Themes Mentioned 2%
NS = Nonspecific Subject Matter 10%
H = Humor Involved 7%
R = Program Recommended 8%

Content mentioned. Six variables indicated whether or not the advisory mentioned the following content: violence, action, language, sex or nudity, adult themes, or unspecified inappropriate content. (Kappa = 1.00). The "action" category is new to the Year 3 analysis.

As can be seen from Figure 21, violence and action were mentioned in advisories more than the other categories of content, but violence was mentioned in only 6% of advisories and action in only 4%.

Humor. Another variable indicated whether or not the advisory seemed to be presented in a "tongue in cheek" fashion, rather than in a serious mode. (Kappa = .93). For example, the following advisory aired on BET: "Caution: Images on screen will appear funkier than they normally are" for *Rap City*. As can be seen from Figure 21, 7% of the advisories were coded as containing humor.

Program recommendation. A new category was added in Year 3 to indicate whether an advisory recommended viewing the program or highlighted a program's positive features. (Kappa = 1.00). For example the advisory, "the following program has been recommended for viewing by the American Federation of Teachers and the National Education Association" appeared before *Adventures in Wonderland* on Disney, and "Family fun for all Fox kids" appeared before *Life with Louie* on Fox. Figure 21 shows that 8% of advisories recommended viewing the program rather than advising against it.

Use of MPAA Ratings and Content Codes in the Sample

MPAA Ratings

Because MPAA ratings are used only for movies, the following analyses involved only those programs that were classified as movies. Of the 455 movies in the sample, 261 or 57% were shown without an MPAA rating, and 192 were designated as G, PG, PG-13, R, or "not rated." Practically all of these designations (182) were given in both oral and written form. Consistent with both Years 1 and 2, we found that the MPAA ratings were mostly used on the premium channels Cinemax, HBO, and Showtime. Also consistent with the previous two years, KTLA was the only other channel that used the MPAA ratings. Specifically, KTLA broadcast one movie with an R rating and another movie with a PG-13 rating. Figure 22 shows the use of the MPAA ratings on the three premium channels.

Figure 22
Percent of Movies on Premium Channels with MPAA Ratings

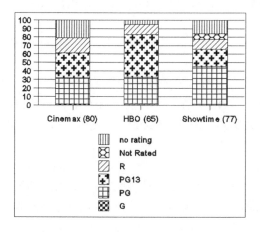

Note. Numbers in parentheses show total number of movies on each channel.

Combing these channels, 86% of movies were shown with an MPAA rating. Most movies were rated PG (36%) or PG-13 (32%). Less than one percent of movies were rated G and 14% were rated R. Two percent were labeled "not rated" and 14% had no rating designation. As in the two previous years, no movies were rated X or NC-17 in the sample.

Although MPAA ratings are rarely used on nonpremium channels because the movies are usually edited for television, it is interesting to compare the distribution of MPAA ratings on premium channels with the original MPAA ratings of movies shown on other channels. For all movies in the sample on nonpremium channels, we explored whether they had been given an MPAA when originally released, by looking up the title in the Motion Picture Rating Directory. Of the 100 movies in this category for which an original MPAA rating was found, the distribution of ratings was as follows: G, 18%; PG, 31%; PG-13, 19%; R, 32%, a different pattern than for the Premium Channels. Figure 23 compares the distribution of MPAA ratings for premium and nonpremium channels. As can be seen from the figure, the distribution of movies across the four ratings is much more even within nonpremium channels, reflecting an increased availability of movies rated both G and R.

Figure 23
Distribution of MPAA-rated Movies
on Premium and Nonpremium Channels

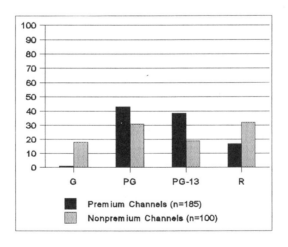

Note: For nonpremium channels, MPAA ratings refer
to a movie's rating when it was released.

Content Codes

Content codes are independent of any MPAA designation, and are assigned to a movie by the channel carrying it. The codes involve notations for violence, language, nudity, adult content, and rape. As in previous years, we found that the content codes were used almost exclusively by the three premium channels, with the exception again being KTLA, which showed one movie that received a V for Violence, an SL for Strong Language, and an AC for Adult Content. This movie was the same one that received an R rating on that channel.

Figure 24 shows the percentage of movies broadcast on the three premium channels that used the content codes for violence. Forty-nine percent of the premium movies had these codes. Specifically, 28% received a V for Violence, 19% received an MV for Mild Violence, and 2% received a GV for Graphic Violence.

Figure 24
Percent of Movies on Premium Channels with Violence Codes

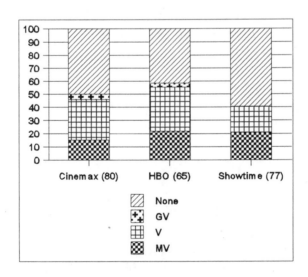

Note. Numbers in parentheses show total number of movies
on each channel.

We also looked at the use of violence codes in the sample of movies that had been content analyzed as containing violence. Of the 224 movies on the premium channels, 198 or 88% contained violence according to the content analysis definition. Two movies that received a V: Violence (both shown on Cinemax) and one movie that received an MV: Mild Violence (shown on HBO) failed to meet the criteria for violence as defined by the content analysis. Among the movies that had been content analyzed as containing violence, 106 or 54% were shown with a violence code, a slight increase over the 49% of all movies using these codes.

Figure 25 shows the percentage of movies that had the other content codes, for the three premium channels separately. Combining the three premium channels, the language codes were used the most frequently, with 68% of the movies on these channels featuring the code AL: Adult Language. The AC: Adult Content code was also heavily used, with 50% of movies using this label. Fewer than 1% of the movies used the SC: Strong Sexual Content, or the GL: Graphic Language labels. Only one movie used the RP: Rape notation. Nudity notations were used on 20% of movies, with 12% carrying the BN: Brief Nudity label and 8% carrying the N: Nudity label.

Figure 25
Percent of Movies on Premium Channels with
Other Content Codes

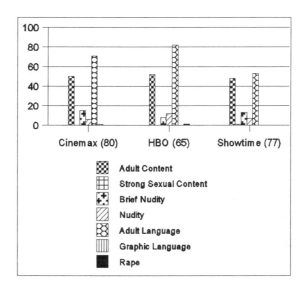

Note. Numbers in parentheses show total number of movies on each channel.

As in Year 2, Showtime presented almost all of the content codes both visually and orally. In contrast, all of the content codes on HBO and all except one of the content codes on Cinemax were shown visually only.

311

Relationship Between MPAA Ratings and Content Codes

As we did in the Year 2 report, we looked at the degree to which the various MPAA ratings corresponded with the distribution of content codes in the movies that received both types of notations. As indicated above, these movies occurred almost exclusively on the premium channels, HBO, Cinemax, and Showtime. As in previous years, we limited these analyses to movies that were released after 1983, because the PG-13 rating did not exist until 1984.

None of the G-rated movies had codes for violence, language, adult content, or nudity. This suggests that the MPAA committee of parents agreed with the premium channel personnel that the G-rated movies in the sample did not contain controversial content. However, only 1% of the movies on premium channels were designated as G-rated.

Figures 26, 27, and 28 show the distribution of "adult content," "nudity," "violence," and "language" codes in post-1983 movies rated PG, PG-13, and R, respectively, in the sample. The figures show that the proportion of movies with these contents generally increases as the rating becomes more restrictive.

<table>
<tr>
<td align="center">

Figure 26
Percent of PG Rated Movies
Having Each Content Code
--Post 1983 Sample (n=58)

</td>
<td align="center">

Figure 27
Percent of PG-13 Rated Movies
Having Each Content Code
--Post 1983 Sample (n=72)

</td>
</tr>
<tr>
<td>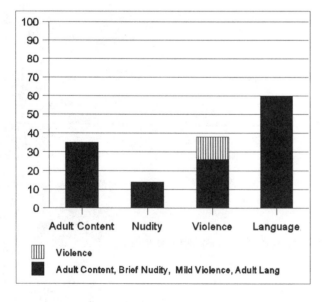</td>
<td>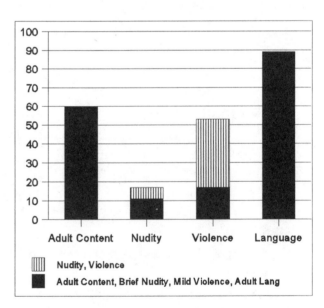</td>
</tr>
</table>

312

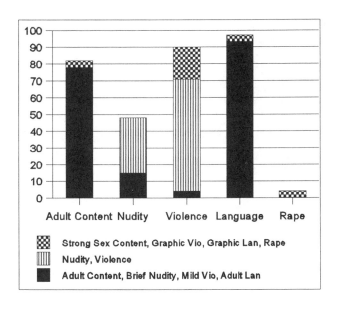

Figure 28
Percent of R Rated Movies
Having Each Content Code
--Post 1983 Sample (n=27)

Another set of analyses explored the different combinations of content codes that appeared in movies rated PG, PG-13 and R in the sample. As we had done in Year 2, we determined the frequency with which the various MPAA ratings were associated with language, violence, and sex, alone or in various combinations. For simplicity's sake we again combined the "adult content" and "nudity" codes into a single category suggesting sexual content. We then determined for each MPAA rating, what percentage of the post-1983 movies in the sample was aired with each of these three types of content codes, alone and in all possible combinations thereof.

Figures 29, 30, and 31 show these data for the PG, PG-13, and R ratings, respectively. As Figure 29 shows, the PG rating is not very informative because the rating reflects a diversity of content possibilities that are almost equally probable: language and violence, 22%; sex only, 21%; language only, 19%; and language and sex, 16%. Figure 30 shows that the PG-13 rating is only slightly more informative, with the bulk of the films comprising three categories: language and sex, 38%; language and violence, 26%; language, sex, and violence, 18%.

Figure 29
Distribution of Language, Sex, & Violence
Codes in Post-1983 PG Rated Movies (n=58)

Figure 30
Distribution of Language, Sex, &Violence
Codes in Post-1983 PG-13 Rated Movies (n=72)

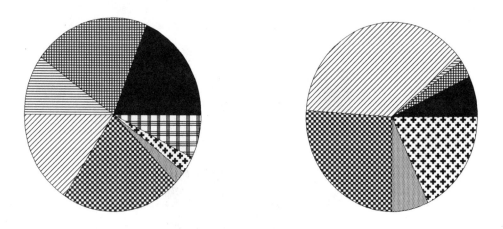

Figure 31
Distribution of Language, Sex, & Violence Codes in
Post-1983 R Rated Movies (n=27)

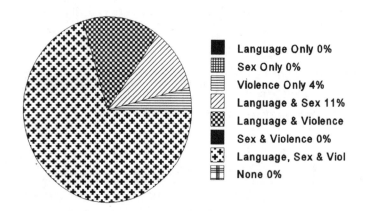

■ Language Only 0%
▦ Sex Only 0%
▤ Violence Only 4%
▨ Language & Sex 11%
▦ Language & Violence
■ Sex & Violence 0%
✚ Language, Sex & Viol
▦ None 0%

Figure 31 shows that the R rating is the most informative, as it was in Year 2, because the majority of films with these ratings (70%) have all three types of content, language, sex, and violence.

Scheduling of Advisories, Ratings, and Codes

To determine how programs with advisories were distributed throughout the day, days were divided into the same dayparts that were used in the analysis of the TV Parental Guidelines.

Figure 32 shows the percent of programs aired with advisories by daypart. Interestingly, the proportion of programs aired with advisories increased over the course of the day, but then dropped during the early evening period. As the figure shows, the prime time daypart featured the highest proportion of programs with advisories.

Figure 32
Percent of Programs Aired with Advisories by Daypart

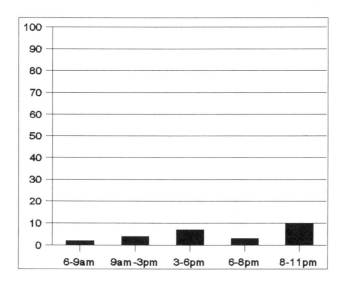

(n=492) (n=1000) (n=495) (n=329) (n=423)

Figure 33 shows the use of MPAA ratings on premium channels by daypart. As the figure shows, no G-rated movies in the sample were aired on premium channels after 3 p.m. R-rated movies were shown only in the prime time and early morning hours.

Figure 33
Percent of Movies on Premium Channels with MPAA Ratings by Daypart

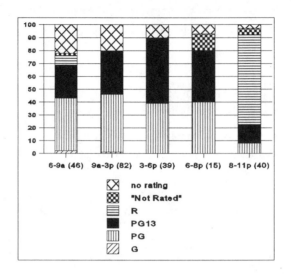

Note. Numbers in parentheses show total number of movies in each daypart.

Figure 34 shows the use of content codes on premium channels by daypart. For the most part, the frequency with which these codes were used tended to increase over the course of the day, with the heaviest use during the prime time hours.

Figure 34
Percent of Movies with Content Codes on Premium Channels
by Daypart

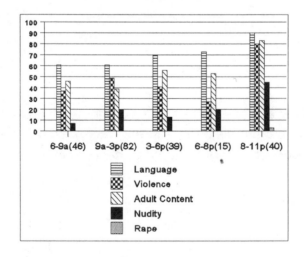

Note. Numbers in parentheses show total number of movies in each daypart.

Chapter 3

DISCUSSION OF FINDINGS AND IMPLICATIONS

Findings of the Content Analysis

The Use of the TV Parental Guidelines

Adoption of the new system. The content analysis of the portion of the composite week of television that was sampled beginning January 1, 1997 revealed that most networks and cable channels were quick to implement the new ratings system and to apply it to the programs it was intended for. Already in the first month of the new system's implementation, 44% of programs (excluding news and sports) were rated, and by March, the utilization had leveled off to about two-thirds of such programs. With the exception of the two channels that made public statements indicating that they would not use the new ratings system, Black Entertainment Television (BET) and the PBS affiliate station (KCET), all stations complied to some extent. Aside from the two channels that rejected the system, only American Movie Classics (AMC) used the ratings on fewer than ten percent of its eligible programs during the period of March 1 through June 6. The new ratings were presented almost exclusively in written, on-screen form, without voice-over accompaniment.

By March of 1997, all four broadcast affiliates were using the new ratings on two-thirds or more of their programs, with three out of the four networks nearing 90% compliance. Most of the general entertainment cable channels (the exception being AMC) were using the new ratings on 80% or more of their programs, and the three children's channels were showing 90% or more compliance. The two music channels that used the new system rated more than half of their programs, while the three independent broadcast stations ranged from 18% to 48% compliance.

The three premium channels used the new ratings system on only about one fourth of their eligible programs. However, more than 90% of their programming displayed some type of program rating or advisory.

Distribution of rating levels. The analysis of the use of the six different rating levels revealed that with the exception of TVMA, which was used only once in the entire sample, the remaining five ratings were used to distinguish between programs considered to be appropriate for various age levels. Overall, TVG was the most frequently used rating, followed closely by TVPG. TV14 was used relatively rarely (6% of rated programs).

As would be expected, different program genres showed different distributions of the possible ratings. For example, TVY was the most frequently used rating for Children's Series and TVG was the most frequently used rating for Comedy Series. TVPG was the most frequently used guideline for Drama Series, Movies, Reality-Based Programs, and Music Video Programs.

Although many critics of the early application of the ratings system had observed that the rating of TVPG was being applied to a majority of programs (Aversa, 1997), this criticism was not valid for the sample overall, and only one major network channel, that of the NBC affiliate, used this rating on a majority of its programs. On that channel, 67% of rated programs were rated TVPG. Moreover, all prime-time programs in the sample that NBC rated received the TVPG rating.

Finally, the three Children's Cable Channels differed in their use of the guidelines. Both Disney and Nickelodeon gave three-fourths of their programs the TVY rating. In contrast, the Cartoon Network almost completely avoided TVY, and gave a TVG to almost two-thirds of its programs.

Distinguishing violent from nonviolent programs. Because a good deal of the pressure for program ratings and the V-chip was based on the belief that parents would need to be informed regarding the presence of violence in programs, our analyses explored the extent to which the TV Parental Guidelines distinguished between programs that our content analysis identified as containing violence and those identified as not containing violence. Our analyses of the TVY and TVY7 ratings showed that a significantly higher proportion of violent than nonviolent programs were designated TVY7, indicating that they were for older children. However, the distributions of TVG, TVPG, and TV14 ratings were almost identical for programs with violence and programs without violence. These results suggest that the TV Parental Guidelines as originally designed did not provide guidance as to the presence of violence in programming intended for general audiences.

Use of Advisories, MPAA Ratings, and Content Codes in the Sample of Programs

The analysis for Year 3 revealed that the use of program advisories has changed little over the three-year period of the National Television Violence Study. Approximately 5% of programs overall and 7% of programs with violence contained advisories. Throughout the three-year period of the study, one channel, Showtime, contributed almost half of the advisories in the sample. The content of advisories remained relatively constant as well, with "viewer discretion advised" being the most frequent advisory. Advisories rarely gave specific information about the reason that discretion was advised.

One emerging trend in advisories over the past year is the use of advisories that do not urge caution, but rather encourage viewing. Year 3 was the first year this type of advisory emerged in the sample. Some of these advisories designate programs as educational, in compliance with the FCC's new processing guideline that stations air three hours per week of educational/informative children's television programs (Federal Communications Commission Report and Order, 1996). Others simply promote the program.

The use of MPAA Ratings and content codes remained relatively constant over the three years of the study. These labels were used heavily and almost exclusively by the three premium channels. Again, premium channels were showing predominantly PG and PG-13 rated movies, with very few movies rated G (fewer than 1 percent in Year 3). A new analysis showed that movies that were originally rated G or R are more frequent on nonpremium channels, however. Again in Year 3, AL: Adult Language and AC: Adult Content were the most frequent content codes.

In the Year 3 analysis, we found that movies rated PG, PG-13, and R were better differentiated than in past years in their use of codes designating controversial content. However, as in previous years, the PG rating, and to a lesser extent, the PG-13 rating, encompassed a wide diversity of content combinations, allowing very little predictive information about a movie's contents.

In general, the scheduling of ratings and advisories suggested that content became more controversial as the day wore on, with the most controversial content occurring during the evening hours.

Implications

The findings suggest that the television industry in general deserves credit for swiftly implementing the new TV Parental Guidelines. Within two months of implementation of the system, a majority of channels were using it on a majority of the programs that the system was designed for. Only two channels refused to use the system at all, KCET, the PBS affiliate, and BET. Moreover, now that the ratings system has been revised to incorporate content indicators, PBS has agreed to implement the system and is now doing so (Lowry, 1997).

319

Although the use of the system has been generally widespread, it is unfortunate that most of the TV Parental Guidelines are being communicated visually only, without sound. Accompanying sound would make these guidelines much more accessible and much more likely to be noticed. The addition of sound would no doubt be appreciated by parents, who often do not pay visual attention to the screen during the first few seconds of a program, but who may listen for cues indicating whether or not to turn off the set or change channels.

Television programmers also deserve some credit for making distinctions between programs by using most of the available rating levels. With the exception of TVMA, all ratings were used with some frequency. Programmers should be encouraged to use the TVMA rating when appropriate. As well, stations that have lumped most of their offerings into one category should make sure that they are not overlooking important distinctions.

The fact that the ratings of TVG, TVPG, and TV14 did not differentiate between programs with vs. without violence suggests that the amended ratings system, which indicates the reasons for a program's rating, will represent a significant improvement of the system for viewers who are especially interested in avoiding violent programs. It is particularly unfortunate that NBC, the broadcast network that used the TVPG rating the most, is the one network that has refused to add content letters to that system.

The findings reported in these analyses reflect merely the beginning of a new phase of information availability about television program content. Research on the use of the amended system is clearly needed, as well as research that shows trends over the years in the utilization of ratings. In addition, national surveys will be needed to determine how parents are reacting to the amended system, how well they understand it, and how helpful they find it.

Finally, we will need to explore how the new ratings system affects children's interest in programs. Research in the Year 1 and Year 2 reports showed that age-based ratings that encourage parental restrictions, like the MPAA ratings and the phrase "parental discretion advised," attract many children to content they otherwise would be less interested in. It will be important to determine whether the TV Parental Guidelines in their original form, as well as in their amended form, have a similar magnetic effect or whether they indeed are helpful in shielding children from harmful content.

References

Aversa, J. (1997, July 24). TV Industry wants more ratings. <u>Washington Post</u>.

Farhi, P. (1997, July 10). TV ratings agreement reached. <u>Washington Post</u>, p. F1.

Federal Communications Commission (1996). <u>Report and Order</u> (FCC 96-335). August 8, 1996.

Hall, J. (1997, March 31). PBS, BET dig in against TV ratings. <u>Los Angeles Times</u>, p. F1.

Lowry, B. (1997, July 12). PBS agrees to use enhanced ratings. <u>Los Angeles Times</u>.

Telecommunications Act of 1996, Pub. LA. No. 104-104, 110 Stet. 56 (1996).

PART IV

TESTING THE EFFECTIVENESS OF PUBLIC SERVICE ANNOUNCEMENTS THAT DEPICT IMMEDIATE PHYSICAL CONSEQUENCES OF HANDGUN VIOLENCE: UNIVERSITY OF NORTH CAROLINA-CHAPEL HILL STUDY

Jay M. Bernhardt
Dr. Jane Brown
Shelley Golden

SUMMARY

In Year 1, the research team at the University of North Carolina at Chapel Hill (UNC) conducted seven studies to evaluate anti-violence public service announcements (PSAs) and educational programs (Biocca et al., 1997b). The studies tested the effects of 15 randomly selected PSAs with convenience samples of training school students (aged 12 - 19) and eighth-grade middle school students from suburban North Carolina.

Each study used different methodology and measures, including in-depth interviews, focus groups, pretest/posttest self-reported measures, and posttest only self-reported surveys. Participants from both audiences rated PSAs with a narrative format (i.e., dramatic story with a plot and fictional characters) significantly higher on interest and arousal measures than PSAs with testimonials or "talking heads" (Biocca et al., 1997b). Narrative PSAs that portrayed a violent encounter received the highest interest and arousal ratings of all PSAs tested. These PSAs, however, had no significant effect on attitudes toward violence measured by pretest/posttest change scores on a Huesmann Aggression Scale (Huesmann, Guerra, Miller, & Zelli, 1994).

In Year 2, we content analyzed 100 anti-violence PSAs that had been collected and aired in 1994 or 1995 (Biocca, Brown, Makris, Bernhardt, & Gaddy, 1997a). Among PSAs with narrative format, more than three-quarters were found to feature at least one violent act that occurred with no negative consequence, physical or otherwise. Gerbner (1995) suggested that PSAs of this type might contain a "hidden message" to viewers that violence is acceptable and unlikely to have negative consequences. Such a message may reinforce societal violence and contribute to negative effects that may result from watching violent television programs.

In the third and final year reported here, we sought to answer the following question: Are public service announcements that depict negative physical consequences of using handguns more effective among adolescents than public service announcements that depict no physical consequence of using handguns?

We evaluated new anti-violence PSAs that we created at UNC based on Year 1 and 2 findings, the violence prevention literature, and behavioral theory. Each PSA has a unique ending that depicts one of two possible physical consequences to the perpetrator of handgun violence (paralysis, death) or one comparison condition (no consequence).

Our findings suggest that observing death as a consequence of handgun violence is more effective at influencing expected outcomes than observing paralysis, which is more effective than observing no consequence of handgun violence in anti-violence PSAs. These findings are consistent with social cognitive theory that states that expected outcomes can be influenced by observing someone modeling a behavior that results in a negative consequence (Bandura, 1986).

Chapter 1

INTRODUCTION

Handgun violence in the United States is a public health crisis that takes a disproportionate toll on young people. In 1993, homicide was the third leading cause of death for adolescents between 5 and 14 years of age in the United States, and the second leading cause of death for teens and young adults between 15 and 24 years old (National Center for Health Statistics, 1996). The homicide rate among young males in the United States is 20 times higher than the rate in other industrialized countries (Roper, 1991).

Although overall homicide rates have recently dropped slightly, (Federal Bureau of Investigation, 1997), handgun violence among young people has increased dramatically over the last decade. Between 1985 and 1993, the rate of firearm-related homicides among youth aged 15 to 19 more than tripled and the rate of arrests for weapon offenses among adolescents under 18 more than doubled (Ash, Kellermann, Fuqua-Whitley, & Johnson, 1996). In 1991, 53% of people arrested for murder were between 15 and 24 years of age (Maguire, Pastore, & Flanagan, 1993), and almost half of the estimated 6.4 million non-fatal crimes of violence in 1991 were committed by offenders in that same age group (US Department of Justice, 1992). A recent national survey found that one fifth of the students had carried a weapon during the 30 days preceding the survey and 7.6% had carried a gun (Centers for Disease Control and Prevention, 1996). Clearly, adolescents are both victims and perpetrators of interpersonal violence.

Youth violence is not only a problem in urban areas; suburban and rural areas also have high rates of violence and victimization. Although rates are higher in the inner city, one study found that 17% of suburban youth had been assaulted in the last year, 27% knew someone who was assaulted with a weapon, and 26% knew someone who was shot (Gladstein, Slater, Rusonis & Heald, 1992). Another study found that 59% of suburban students had heard gunshots in their neighborhood (Campbell & Schwartz, 1996).

Weapon use is a significant cause of violence-related mortality, and carrying the most deadly weapon, firearms, is at an all time high among teenagers (Blumstein, 1995). In 1992, almost one quarter of males aged 12-21 reported carrying a weapon in the last month, and among those who had carried weapons, one quarter of the 12-14 year old males and one fifth of the 15-17 year old males reported carrying a firearm (Adams, Schoenborn, Moss, Warren & Kann, 1995).

Decades of research suggest that handgun violence is caused by an interaction among several complex factors: an individual's psychosocial development; biological, neurological and hormonal differences; and various social processes (National Research Council, 1993). Whether and/or how these factors contribute to handgun violence varies by individuals and situations.

Recently, many programs and interventions have been implemented to address those causes that are preventable and/or subject to change. Popular interventions include school-based curricula, community-based programs, and efforts to reduce handgun availability (Tolan & Guerra, 1994). Unfortunately, few of the violence prevention programs that have been evaluated have been found to be effective (Zuckerman, 1996). The National Research Council (1993) concluded that successful violence prevention programs should be theoretically informed and should use interventions that specifically target attitudes and beliefs toward the desirability and appropriateness of handgun violence.

Health communication campaigns

The need for innovative, well-evaluated interventions designed to reduce handgun violence is clear. One possibility is more extensive use of the mass media as a part of interventions, and in particular, more effective use of public service announcements (PSAs). PSAs are commercial-length videos shown during television program breaks that deliver messages intended to raise awareness, change attitudes and beliefs, and/or change behaviors. Independent organizations (e.g., the Ad Council) under the direction of government agencies or private, not-for-profit organizations (e.g., Mothers Against Drunken Driving) often create them. Networks, affiliates, and local stations usually broadcast PSAs at no cost during commercial breaks in television programs along with other paid commercial advertising.

Public service announcements

PSAs have been used to motivate and mobilize Americans since 1917, when silent film star Mary Pickford appeared on posters used to prepare the nation for war (Gladstone, 1996). PSAs are now one of the primary ways that television is used to promote health and prevent disease through social marketing campaigns (Atkin & Arkin, 1990), and have been used for crime reduction (e.g., "Take a bite out of crime"), drunk-driving prevention (e.g., "Friends don't let friends drive drunk"), and illegal drug use prevention (e.g., "Just say no").

A number of public health experts cite media based interventions when calling for more research on the use of anti-violence information campaigns. Zwerling, et al. (1993, p.55) included "the development and marketing of public service announcements for the electronic media…" among their list of recommendations for reducing firearm injuries. Zuckerman (1996) concluded that "violence prevention efforts seem more sure of success if they (use) … the proven power of television, videotapes, and film to change attitudes towards guns and violence" (p. 397). Moreover, health communication campaigns using mass media have been used to address other injury-related public health problems. For example, televised PSAs on the issue of alcohol-impaired driving are credited with introducing the concept of "designated drivers" and with reducing the occurrence of alcohol-related automobile crashes (National Center for Health Statistics, 1996).

Televised PSAs may also be a particularly good way to deliver anti-violence messages to adolescents. Bandura (1986) indicates that as dependence upon media for creating one's perception of social reality increases, social impact of media messages also increases. Since children spend more time watching television than they do in school (Singer, Singer & Zuckerman, 1990), television may therefore be a particularly effective way of modeling behaviors for adolescents. Moreover, anti-violence interventions aimed at children not yet engaged in serious violence may reduce the need for later rehabilitation (National Committee for Injury Prevention and Control, 1989).

Unfortunately, lack of resources and methodological challenges (Flay & Cook, 1989), combined with a belief among campaign planners that evaluation is not necessary have limited evaluation of PSA campaigns. Of those that have been evaluated, however, some have been found to be effective (Knight, Kemp, Biocca & Brown, in press). The national "Take a bite out of crime" PSA campaign, for example, was found to have produced statistically significant increases in awareness, knowledge, attitudes, and behaviors (O'Keefe, 1985).

Study Objectives

The research conducted at UNC has explored ways in which television can be used to help *reduce* violence among adolescents. Year 1 research revealed that anti-violence PSAs with at least one violent scene elicited the highest levels of interest and arousal from different adolescent audiences, but there were no significant effects on attitudes toward violence (Biocca et al., 1997b). Content analysis of 100 PSAs in Year 2 revealed that among anti-violence PSAs with at least one scene of violence, very few depicted immediate physical consequences to the perpetrator (Biocca et al., 1997a). We hypothesized that anti-violence PSAs would be more effective if they demonstrated immediate physical consequences of violent behavior (Biocca et al., 1997a).

Based on findings from Years 1 and 2, the violence prevention literature, and behavioral science theory, we created "prototype" anti-violence PSAs. The PSAs feature portrayals of two possible immediate physical consequences to the perpetrator of handgun violence (paralysis, death) and one comparison condition (no physical consequence to the perpetrator). The effectiveness with which each of these three versions changed young adolescents' attitudes toward handguns was tested in a randomized, controlled experiment with pretest and posttest measures.

Chapter 2

THEORETICAL PERSPECTIVES

Many theories have been used to explain the causes of physical violence and to predict the effects of violence-prevention interventions among youth. The most frequently used is Social Cognitive Theory (Bandura, 1986). This theory explains the causes of handgun violence using a triadic-reciprocal model that includes environment, behavior, and cognitions. Unlike unidirectional theories, this model recognizes that violence is influenced by both biological and environmental factors (Hoffman, Ireland, & Widom, 1994).

Social Cognitive Theory of Violence

Social Cognitive Theory suggests that most human behavior is learned through modeling; observing the behavioral outcomes that others experience can alter the observer's behavior just as much as if the observer had directly experienced the outcome. When someone observes others performing a behavior, he or she creates rules of the behavior, and uses those rules as a guide for future action (Bandura, 1986). Observing new or novel behaviors can teach cognitive skills and new behavior patterns; watching known behaviors can strengthen or weaken inhibitions to performing those behaviors (Bandura, 1986). "As a general rule, seeing certain courses of behavior succeed for others increases the tendency of observers to behave in similar ways, whereas seeing behavior punished decreases the likelihood that they will use similar means" (Bandura, 1986, p. 283).

Bandura (1986) cites many examples of human and animal research that support the positive and negative effects of vicarious consequences. In one school-based study (Benton, 1967), for example, teachers punished children who acted aggressively while other students witnessed the punishment. Those children who had observed the punishment restrained their aggressive behavior to the same degree as those who had been punished themselves. Therefore, there was a similar restraining effect for those who were directly punished and for those who experienced the consequence vicariously.

Outcome expectations

One of the two primary constructs of Social Cognitive Theory is outcome expectations. Outcome expectations are a person's perception of the likely consequences that will occur as the result of his or her performance of a specific behavior. Outcome expectations are thought to predict behavior through their influence on motivation. People are more motivated to perform behaviors that they expect will be rewarded, and are less motivated to perform behaviors that they expect will be punished (Bandura, 1986).

Violence prevention theory

These aspects of social cognitive theory can be used to guide design of anti-violence interventions. Several studies of adolescent aggression and violent behavior have found that outcome expectations are significantly associated with violent behavior (Hoffman et al., 1994; Perry, Perry, & Rasmussen, 1986). Research using Social Cognitive Theory has found that one may learn to be more violent by observing violent behavior that is rewarded or that has no negative consequences (Bandura, 1986). Social Cognitive Theory also suggests that one may learn to be *less* violent by observing violent behavior that is punished or that does have negative consequences. In other words, people may learn that violence doesn't pay by observing handgun violence resulting in negative consequences for the person behaving violently. Applied to televised PSAs, this theory suggests that portrayals of negative consequences of handgun violence may be powerful anti-violence messages.

Consequence severity

Many studies have found that increasing the severity of an observed consequence leads to increases in behavioral restraints (Bandura, 1986). Furthermore, when the modeled behavior offers some intrinsic rewards to the person performing it, observing weak consequences has little effect, observing moderate consequences may be partially restraining, and observing severe consequences can substantially reduce the prohibited behavior. The challenge of applying Social Cognitive Theory to anti-violence PSAs is determining what adolescents consider to be the most severe negative consequence of using a handgun.

Although death is the most final of all physical consequences, many adolescents may not perceive it as the most severe. Research from the Year 1 and 2 studies suggests that adolescents perceive paralysis to be a more salient and severe consequence of violence than death. Year 1 participants reported the highest levels of emotional arousal in reaction to narrative PSAs that showed pain or paralysis as the consequence of violence; moderate levels of emotional arousal in reaction to death as the consequence of violence; and low levels of emotional arousal in reaction to PSAs that did not show any consequences (Biocca et al., 1997a).

The research designs used in Years 1 and 2 did not allow determination of the relative effects of observing paralysis and death as consequences of handgun violence on attitudes towards violence. The primary goal of the Year 3 study, therefore, was to determine which observed immediate physical consequence of committing handgun violence (paralysis, death, or no consequence) is most effective at changing handgun-related beliefs among adolescent PSA viewers.

Observer Characteristics

Social Cognitive Theory suggests that an individual's attributes can influence observational learning (Bandura, 1986). For example, it is possible that an individual's previous experience with violence may influence the processing and effects of observing an anti-violence message. Adolescents who have never committed or been victims of violence before may perceive messages differently from those that have frequently committed violence and/or used weapons against others.

Experience with violence

Two important observer characteristics that may affect message effects are experience with fighting and weapons. For example, adolescents who have started fights may differ in their perceptions of anti-violence messages from those who have been in fights that they have not started. Similarly, adolescents who have used a firearm may differ in their message processing from those that have carried but not used a firearm, and each of these groups may differ from adolescents who have never carried a firearm. These audience characteristics were used in Year 2 research to group adolescents into seven segments (Aggressors, Defenders, Combatants, Fist Fighters, Carriers, Observers, Avoiders). Adolescents in each of these segments differed significantly in their backgrounds and experiences. We predicted that each segment requires different anti-violence messages (Biocca et al., 1997a), and that each audience segment will be differently affected by specific anti-violence messages.

Exposure to violence

Exposure to violence, both in real life and on television, may also influence anti-violence message effects. For example, adolescents who have seen someone use a gun may perceive the PSA characters or messages differently from those who never have. Similarly, adolescents who watch a lot of violent television may vary in their perceptions from those who watch little or no television violence. High exposure to television violence can teach adolescents to be more violent, desensitize adolescents to portrayals of violence, and can cultivate a belief among adolescents that the world is a very violent place (Wilson et al., 1997).

Intervention Model

Figure 1 depicts the intervention model for this study. The model is based on Social Cognitive Theory and explains the observational learning of anti-violence public service announcements. Adolescent participants who observe anti-violence PSAs that show immediate physical consequences of handgun violence should learn to expect negative outcomes of similar handgun violence. There also may be differences in message effects associated with different individual characteristics.

Figure 1. Observation learning of anti-violence PSAs

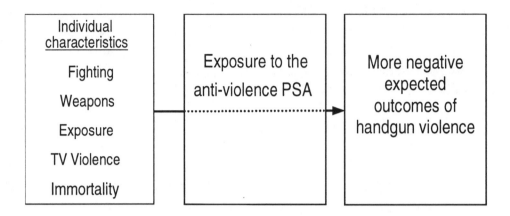

Chapter 3

PSA DEVELOPMENT

The anti-violence PSAs were created based on formative research from Years 1 and 2, the violence prevention literature, and theories of communication and behavioral science. This chapter presents the background and development of the PSAs for this study, and explains their content.

Background

One PSA in the Year 1 studies, *Et Tu Brutus* (Turner, 1994) scored considerably higher than any other PSA on self-reported, posttest measures of arousal, pleasure, and in some cases, the dominance felt by members of the middle school and training school audiences (Biocca et al., 1997b). It was also the best remembered PSA. Research also indicated, however, that the PSA was severely flawed. Its subtle and artistic ending confused many participants.

Et Tu Brutus is from a series of PSAs produced by Home Box Office, and features a dramatic chase in which a man with a gun (whose face is not visible) chases another man down the street, shooting at him as they run. The scene climaxes in an alley when the hooded man corners the other man and points his weapon. The man with the gun removes his hood to reveal that he is identical to the man he had chased. As he shoots, he asks, "Remember me? Remember me?" and a narrator's voice adds, "Stop. You're only killing yourself."

Although the PSA implied that the consequence of the violence was the death of the victim, most viewers did not realize that the victim and perpetrator were supposed to be the same person. Several study participants from the Training School believed that the victim must have done something to the perpetrator and, therefore, deserved to be shot (Biocca et al., 1997b). Gerbner (1995, p. 297) notes that despite "splendid artistry of the production… the complex roots of violence - its motivation, circumstances, and justification - remain unexamined (in *Et Tu Brutus* and other HBO PSAs)."

PSA Content

Because of its strong effects, the composition, characters, plot, and setting of the prototype PSAs tested here were based on *Et Tu Brutus*. The ending of the PSA was replaced with three different endings that feature portrayals of different immediate physical consequences of handgun violence. In these endings: (1) the perpetrator is paralyzed, (2) the perpetrator is killed, or (3) no consequence to the perpetrator is shown (comparison condition). By varying only the consequence, all other PSA factors (e.g., characters, setting, pacing, and score) are held constant.

333

Based on the principles of observational learning in Social Cognitive Theory, the PSAs seek to change expected outcomes of handgun violence by modeling handgun violence and portraying a (negative) consequence. The PSA portrays a dramatic chase where the perpetrator pursues the victim into an alley. After the chase starts, the PSA "flashes back" to show an altercation between the two characters on the steps of their school, and one of the characters getting a handgun from a friend. In the two PSAs with consequences, the perpetrator trips and drops his gun, which discharges upon impact with the ground. In one PSA, the perpetrator is shot in the back and later appears paralyzed in a wheelchair. In another PSA, the perpetrator is shot in the chest and killed. Both PSAs end with the slogan "GUNS HURT YOU."

In the comparison condition PSA, the perpetrator chases the victim into an alley and aims the gun at him but does not trip or drop his gun. The screen fades to black and the slogan ("GUNS HURT YOU") appears. This ending was selected for the comparison condition because it is consistent with the majority of existing narrative anti-violence PSAs and with regular violent television. A content analysis of existing anti-violence PSAs conducted in Year 2 revealed that among narrative PSAs with a violent encounter, 75% showed no consequence to the perpetrator of the violent behavior and 50% showed death or injury to a victim (Biocca et al., 1997a). Similarly, 75% of all violent scenes in regular television programming portray no immediate punishments for violence and 44% depict no injury to the victim (Wilson et al., 1997). Figure 2 contains a graphical portrayal of the PSA content.

Richard Simpson, professor in the UNC-CH School of Journalism and Mass Communication, coordinated the production of the PSAs with the assistance of undergraduate students in his video production class. Local adolescent actors were hired to play the parts and audio and video professionals shot the PSAs on Beta video.

Figure 2. Content of the three PSAs

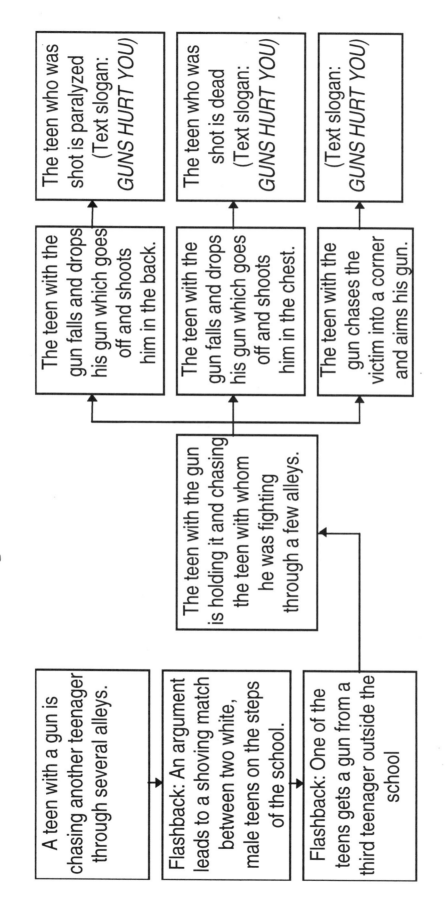

Chapter 4

METHODS

This project was designed to determine which of two immediate physical consequences of handgun violence in anti-violence PSAs had a greater effect on cognitive outcomes among adolescents. It also was designed to determine the relationship between individual characteristics and message effects of the anti-violence PSAs. These research questions were addressed using a randomized, three-group, pretest/posttest/follow-up experimental design. See Figure 3 for a graphical depiction of the study design. Each component from the figure is explained below.

Study participants

This study was conducted with middle school students ($N=92$) from two after-school programs located in suburban North Carolina. The programs are affiliated with the North Carolina "Support Our Student" program (SOS). SOS is under the authority of the Department of Youth Services in the NC Department of Human Resources and has programs held at middle schools in 63 counties. Data from the two sites were combined prior to analysis.

All SOS students who were from the two selected locations, understood English, were present on the say the study was implemented, and could complete a self-report survey were eligible to participate in the study. Those students who met these criteria were given a consent form and an explanation of the study to take home to a parent or legal guardian and to return within one week. The parental consent form and cover letter explained the study in its entirety. The student assent form described the study as assessing youth television preferences and perceptions.

Students who did not meet the eligibility criteria, did not receive parental consent, or did not provide individual assent, were given other activities to do while the study was implemented. Of those eligible students who were present and had obtained parental consent, 84% participated and completed pretest and posttest measures. All participants at each location were randomized to three groups after baseline data collection, stratifying by race and gender. One group watched the PSA that showed no consequence to the perpetrator of handgun violence ($n=32$), another watched the PSA that showed death as the consequence ($n=31$), and the third group watched the PSA that showed paralysis as the consequence ($n=29$). The North Carolina SOS program and each SOS site received a donation of approximately five dollars per student participant when the study was completed.

Figure 3. Study Design

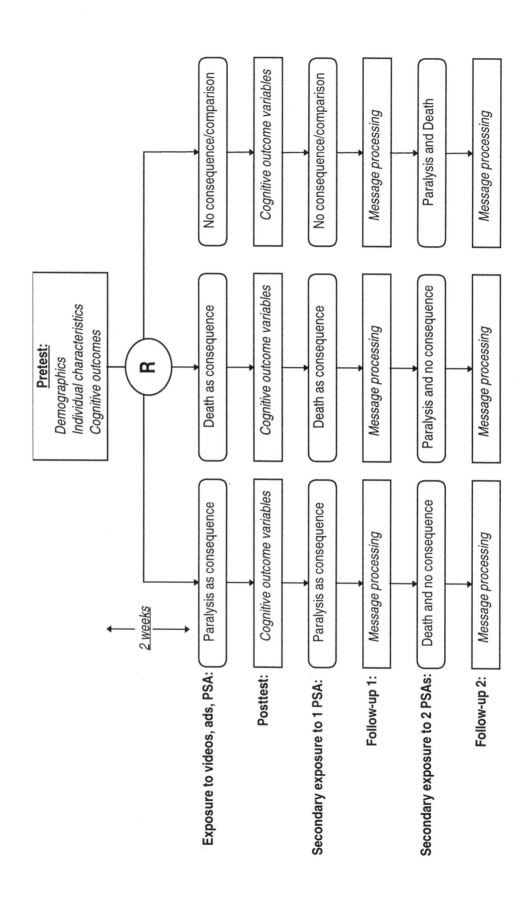

Procedure

Theater testing

It would have been ideal to evaluate the effectiveness of the PSAs in a natural setting because PSAs are shown on television within regular programming, but it was prohibitively expensive and methodologically unfeasible to air the PSAs on television and evaluate their effects on adolescents. Therefore, the PSAs were evaluated using a controlled experimental design that simulated natural PSA exposure using a procedure called "theater testing" (Atkin & Freimuth, 1989).

In each experimental condition, a prototype PSA was embedded twice, along with commercial advertisements, within about 14 minutes of regular television programming (four music videos) to create about 20 minutes of total television footage (the "stimulus tape"). There were two groups of commercial interruptions and the PSA was placed in the middle of each commercial break.

The music videos and other commercials were used to mask the intent of the testing situation as is recommended (Atkin & Freimuth, 1989). The videos were selected from among those in regular rotation on television at the time of the study and were held constant across each experimental group. The selected music videos and commercials contained absolutely no violent scenes or lyrics.

Showing the 30-second PSA only twice was a conservative test of PSA exposure effects. Other experimental studies of PSA effects have included more PSA exposures (Flora & Maibach, 1990; Reeves, Newhagen, Maibach, et al., 1991; Siska, Jason, Murdoch, Yang, & Donovan, 1992), and two PSA exposures are recommended in the literature (Atkin & Freimuth, 1989).

Pretest

After collecting parental consent forms, assent forms were distributed and collected at each site and pretest measures were distributed. All pretest measures were read aloud by a trained research assistant and completed individually by each participant using paper and pencil. At pretest, each participant completed measures of individual characteristics (described below). Study measures were mixed with measures on television preferences and perceptions to help disguise the topic of the study.

Randomization

All participating students were randomly assigned to one of three groups at each participating school stratifying by race and gender. Randomization was done at an individual level, regardless of grade or class, between pretest data collection and implementation of the experiment.

Experiment

After completing the pretest surveys, participants assembled with their randomly assigned groups in classrooms and were given instructions by a trained research assistant. The chairs in each classroom were spread out to maximize the distance between them. As is consistent with other studies using theater testing (e.g., Hensley & Ducal, 1976), the researcher explained to the participants that they needed to remain silent and that the purpose of the research was to learn about *their* individual feelings, so they shouldn't share their thoughts or answers with each other. These instructions minimized, but did not completely eliminate, potential group level effects.

To reduce social desirability answer bias, the researchers told the participants that the study was about their preferences and perceptions of television programs and commercials. After all instructions were presented, the group was shown the stimulus tape from video on a large television monitor in the front of the classroom.

Posttest

After watching the stimulus tape, each participant again completed measures of cognitive outcome variables (described below). Questions about the music videos and the other commercials were included to serve as foils. All questions were read aloud by a trained research assistant.

Secondary exposure and follow-up measures

After completing the posttest the participants were shown another video that featured all three experimental PSAs. First they were shown the same PSA that was already shown to their group, and they were asked to complete measures that assessed their processing of the messages. They were then shown the other two PSAs and were asked to complete more measures about their message processing. The teachers read a letter from the researchers aloud at a subsequent meeting to debrief the participants on the research topic.

Study Variables and Measures

Cognitive outcome variables

Expected outcome of committing handgun violence were assessed at pretest and posttest using questions that were adapted from existing measures of these constructs (Crick & Dodge, 1996; Perry et al., 1986). These scales are appropriate for participants as young as 9 years old and were found to have a Cronbach alpha of .65 and .74 respectively (Crick & Dodge, 1996).

The newly written items were designed to closely mirror the portrayed content in the PSAs. Each question was answered with choices on a 4-point Likert scale: Definitely no, Probably no, Probably yes, Definitely yes. Several different items were asked to assess each construct. For example, outcome expectations for handgun violence were assessed with multiple items including: "If *you* **use** a handgun, will you get physically hurt?" and, "If a teenager **uses** a handgun, will he get physically hurt?"

Individual characteristics

Survey questions were administered at pretest on the following: fighting experiences, firearm carrying and usage, exposure to violence.

Fighting and weapon experiences were assessed using "Yes/No" survey questions similar to those used in Year 2 research (Louis Harris & Associates, 1995). One question about involvement in fights asked, "[In the last 30 days] have you **been in** a physical fight with someone your own age?" Another question asked, "Have you **started** a physical fight with someone your own age?" Weapon use was assessed by asking, "Have you been in a physical fight where someone **used** a weapon like a gun or a knife?" Carrying and use of knives, handguns, and other weapons also were assessed.

Exposure to real-life and television violence was measured using modified "Yes/No" survey questions from Year 2 research (Louis Harris & Associates, 1995). A series of questions about witnessing violence included items such as: "[In the last 30 days] have you seen someone carrying a gun?" "Have you seen people fist fighting?" and "Have you been threatened by someone with a gun?"

Finally, perception of perceived risk of handgun violence was measured using an item adapted from the ASAP study (Wallerstein & Sanchez-Merki, 1994). This item used 4-point Likert scale responses (Definitely no, Probably no, Probably yes, Definitely yes) and asked, "Do you think that teenagers **like you** are at the greatest risk of getting hurt from handgun violence?"

PSA perception variables

Following the first post-hoc exposure of the same PSA, the first follow-up survey assessed the following individual perceptions about the PSA messages and characters: perceived outcome of the handgun violence (i.e., degree of success or failure), perceived severity of the consequence, perceived similarity of the model to oneself, perceived ability of the model, and perceived personal relevance of the PSA. Following the second post-hoc exposure to the other two PSAs, the second follow-up survey assessed the following: relative severity of the PSA consequences (i.e., which PSA had the most severe consequences), and relative strength of the PSA failure.

All of the follow-up survey questions about participant PSA perceptions used

4-point Likert response choices of "Definitely no, Probably no, Probably yes, Definitely yes." The item to measure perceived outcome of the observed handgun violence was worded: "Did the teenager with the gun succeed in doing what he wanted to do?" Perceived severity of the portrayed consequence was assessed by adapting an existing Likert-scale item used to assess the severity of criminal consequences (Horan & Kaplan, 1983). The item was worded: "Did the teenager with the gun get hurt very badly?"

Perceived similarity to model was assessed using several items that asked the participant to rate the degree of similarity between the perpetrator and the victim in the PSA and himself or herself. Questions included, "Could you imagine yourself as the teenager with the gun?" and "Could you imagine yourself as the teenager being chased?"

Perceived ability of the model (perpetrator) was assessed using a single item that asked each participant to rate the perpetrator's ability to perform the handgun violence. The item was worded, "Did the teenager with the gun know how to use guns?"

Perceived realism of the modeled behavior was assessed by adapting existing measures of perceived relevance and issue involvement. One item was worded, "Do you and your friends ever act like they did in this commercial?"

Relative PSA perceptions were assessed by asking the participants questions about the PSAs and having them answer the questions by choosing one of the three PSAs they saw. Relative outcome was assessed with several items including, "Which commercial worked out **best** for the teenager with the gun?" and "Which commercial worked out **best** for the teenager being chased?"

Relative severity of the consequences across PSAs was assessed using several items including, "Which commercial showed the **most** serious injury to the teenager with the gun?" and "Which commercial showed the **most** serious injury to the teenager being chased?"

Foils

In order to help mask the nature of the study, all study measures were mixed with foils on television preferences and recall and attitude toward the music videos and the commercials.

Table 1. Study Measures and Administration Time

Type	Construct	Pretest	Posttest	Follow-up
Individual Chars.	Exposure to real-life violence	X		
	Fighting experience	X		
	Weapon experience	X		
	Demographics	X		
	Perceived risk	X		
Cognitive Outcome	Outcome expectations		X	
	Free recall		X	
Message Processing	Perceived outcome of behavior			X
	Perceived severity of consequence			X
	Perceived ability of model			X
	Character identification			X
	Perceived realism			X
PSA Comparisons	Best outcome			X
	Worst outcome			X
	Most serious injury			X
	Perceived effectiveness			X

Chapter 5

RESULTS AND DISCUSSION

Background

Participants (*N*=92) ranged in age from 11 to 15 (*M*=12.7, *SD*=1.12) and were distributed relatively evenly across sixth, seventh, and eighth grades (37%, 29%, 35%). There were more males (61%) than females and more African Americans (84%) than whites (15%).

The participants reported watching 3.7 hours of television each day on average, and slightly more on Fridays and slightly less on Sundays. Nearly two-thirds (65%) reported that "real life" is more violent than "TV," 28% said both are equally violent, and only 7% thought TV is more violent. When asked whether they thought that teens like themselves are at the highest risk of handgun violence, 47% reported "kind of yes" and 40% reported "definitely yes."

Violence exposure and experience

The participants had high exposure to violence in the 30 days prior to the survey (See Table 2). For example, 87% reported witnessing a physical fight, 37% saw someone carrying a gun, 18% saw someone shooting a gun, and 69% heard gunshots in the neighborhood. In addition, many participants reported first-hand experience with violence in the 30 days prior to the survey including being in a physical fight (58%), starting a physical fight (26%), and carrying a handgun (4%). The participants' exposures and experiences exceed national averages for older adolescents (grades 9-12) for fighting but were lower for gun carrying. Nationally, 7.6% of older adolescents had carried a gun in the last 30 days and 38.7% had engaging in a physical fight in the last 12 months (CDC, 1996).

Table 2. Violence exposure and experience in the last 30 days (*n*=92)

Saw physical fighting	87%
Saw someone carrying a knife	42%
Saw someone carrying a gun	37%
Saw someone shooting a gun	18%
Heard gunshots in neighborhood	69%
Been in a physical fight	58%
Started a physical fight	26%
Been in a fight with a weapon	9%
Carried a knife	8%
Carried a gun	4%

Group Equivalence

The experimental groups were checked using 2-tailed Pearson Chi Square tests to determine equivalency. No significant differences were found for grade level (X^2=4.40, df=4, p=.36), race (X^2=2.47, df=4, p=.65), sex (X^2=2.47, df=2, p=.29), or age (X^2=7.08, df=8, p=.53).

Recall

A free-recall question was asked at posttest to assess if the participants paid attention to the PSA when it was shown mixed with the music videos and other commercials, and if they remembered it. Overall, nearly all the participants (94%) recalled seeing the PSA. Most listed the PSA by writing the slogan "guns hurt you" or simply "guns." All of the participants in the group with death as the consequence recalled seeing the PSA compared to 93% in the paralysis as consequence group and 93% in the comparison group. It was the first or second commercial remembered for nearly two thirds (64%) of the participants, and three quarters of those who recalled seeing it said that they remembered "a lot" of it.

Outcome expectations

An Analysis of Variance (ANOVA) was used to test the main effects of the PSAs on outcome expectations. The ANOVA for expecting that "using handguns will result in a serious injury" was significant: $F(2,89)$=3.728, p<.03. A post-hoc test of Least Significant Differences (LSD) found significant differences between the no consequence PSA and the PSA with death as a consequence (p<.02) and between the no consequence PSA and the paralysis PSA (p<.05). (See Figure 4) The four-point scale used to measure this construct ranged from 1 ("definitely no") to 4 ("definitely yes") that a serious injury would result from using handguns. The mean levels of this measure were 3.44 for the no consequence group, 3.87 for the death as consequence group, and 3.79 for the paralysis as consequence group.

Other measures of expected outcomes of handgun use were found to have similar relationships (death > paralysis > no consequence) but they were not statistically significant. Several possible interactions were examined including race and sex, but no statistically significant interaction effects were found.

These data suggest that observing death as a consequence of handgun violence is more effective at influencing expected outcomes than observing paralysis, which is more effective than observing no consequence of handgun violence in anti-violence PSAs. These findings are consistent with social cognitive theory that states that expected outcomes can be influenced by observing someone modeling a behavior that results in a negative consequence (Bandura, 1986).

Figure 4. Serious injury as expected outcome of handgun use.

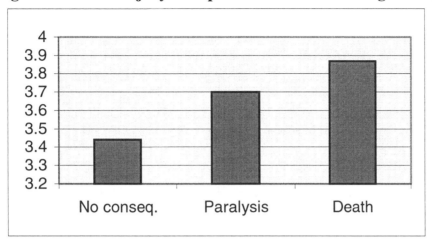

n=92, F=3.728, p<.02

On the other hand, these findings contradict one expectation based on qualitative interviews conducted in Year 1. Participants who observed different existing anti-violence PSAs were more emotionally affected by PSAs that showed pain or paralysis than by those that showed death as a consequence of violent behavior (Biocca et al., 1997b). While we conclude that depicting death as a consequence of handgun violence can be effective at influencing outcome expectations when compared to no consequence, we are reluctant to dismiss paralysis as a potentially effective consequence. The relatively weaker effect of paralysis may be due to its very brief depiction in the PSA (less than 3 seconds). When exploring this issue, however, it is important to recognize the possible stigmatizing effect of portrayals of paralysis as a negative consequence on those living with similar disabilities (Wang, 1992).

Message processing

ANOVA was used to test for differences in PSA message processing among the PSA experimental groups (*n*=48). All measures for these variables used four-point response choices ranging from 1 ("definitely no") to 4 ("definitely yes"). All the differences but one were not statistically significant. Many were in a similar trend as the main effects on outcome expectations. For example, participants who saw the PSA with death as the consequence perceived that the injury to the "teenager with the gun" was more severe (*M*=3.84) compared to those who saw paralysis as the consequence (*M*=3.57) and those in the comparison group (*M*=3.67).

The ANOVA for perceived realism (whether the participant believes that behaviors like those portrayed really happen) of the PSA depiction was significant: $F(2,43)=3.447$, *p*<.05. (See Figure 5) The mean levels of this measure were 3.40 for the no consequence group, 2.53 for the death as consequence group, and 3.00 for the paralysis as consequence group. In other words, the PSA with no consequence was considered the most realistic, the PSA with paralysis as a consequence was considered less realistic, and the PSA with death as a consequence was considered the least realistic.

The perception among the participants that observing someone dying as the result of handgun use is not so realistic as seeing someone remain unscathed may reflect the lack of depictions of negative consequences to violence on television. When a violent scene is shown, three quarters of television programs (Wilson et al., 1997) and three quarters of PSAs (Biocca et al., 1997a) do not show any negative consequences to the perpetrator of the violence.

Another possible explanation for perceiving the PSAs with consequences to be less realistic than the no consequence PSA is the fact that the negative consequences occurred as the result of an accident: the perpetrator tripped over a trash can and dropped the gun, which discharged and wounded the perpetrator. Although participants may have perceived this exchange to be unrealistic, the PSA with death as a consequence still was more effective than the no consequence PSA. We believe that if PSAs that show negative consequences can be made so viewers perceive them as more realistic, their effects on outcome expectations will be even stronger.

Figure 5. Perceived realism of PSA ($n=47$, $F=3.447$, $p<.05$)

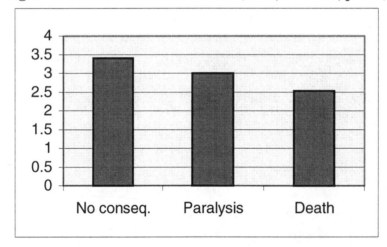

PSA comparisons

After completing all posttest measures, participants were shown all three PSAs and were asked several survey questions to compare different aspects of the PSAs. Chi square tests were conducted to determine if differences were statistically significant ($n=48$). Unless otherwise reported, all of the following relationships were statistically significant ($p<.001$).

As a manipulation check on the comparison group PSA contents, we asked the participants which PSA showed the *best* outcome (i.e. no consequence) for the teenager with the gun. Nearly all of the participants (94%) selected the PSA that showed no consequence, compared to only 4% who selected the PSA with paralysis and 2% who selected the PSA with death. Therefore, the participants clearly perceived the comparison PSA to have no negative consequence to the perpetrator.

Participants were asked which PSA showed the *worst* consequence for the perpetrator. More than three quarters (77%) selected the PSA that showed death as the consequence, 21% selected the PSA that showed paralysis, and 2% selected the comparison/no consequence PSA. (See Figure 6)

Figure 6. Worst consequence for the perpetrator (*n*=48)

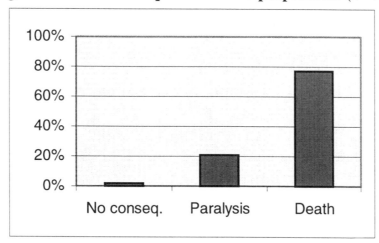

Similar results were found with respect to the participants' perceptions of most serious injury. More than three quarters (80%) selected the PSA that showed death as the consequence, 18% selected the PSA that showed paralysis, and 2% selected the comparison/no consequence PSA. (See Figure 7)

Figure 7. Most serious injury to the perpetrator (*n*=48)

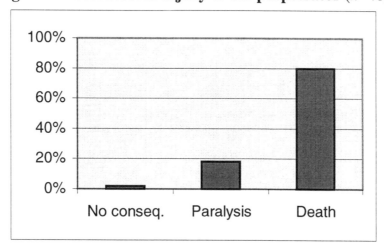

These findings help explain the expected outcomes results. The participants perceived death to be a worse consequence of handgun violence, and a more serious injury, than paralysis, which helps explain why participants in the death as consequence group had more negative expected outcomes than participants in the paralysis or comparison groups.

Finally, the participants were asked to select the *least* and *most* effective PSAs for teenagers like themselves. For *least* effective, nearly three quarters of the participants (73%) picked the no consequence PSA, 16% picked the PSA with death as the consequence, and 11% picked the PSA with paralysis. For *most* effective, more than half of the participants (56%) selected the PSA with death as the consequence, one quarter (26%) selected the no consequence PSA, and 18% selected the paralysis PSA. See Figure 8 for a comparison of PSAs selected to be most effective.

Figure 8. Most effective PSA (*n*=43, p<.01)

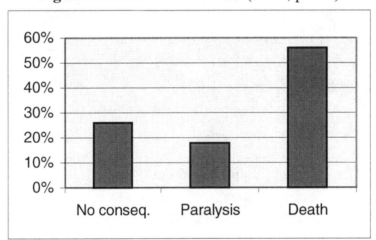

Chapter 6

FINAL RECOMMENDATIONS

In three years of research, we have explored whether or not television can and/or should be used to deliver effective violence prevention messages. We have focused our research on the most common and overt strategy of violence prevention on television: anti-violence public service announcements. In the course of this research, we have accomplished the following:

- Content analysis of cable-television-industry produced PSAs to determine their format, sources, messages, style, and depictions of violence.

- Quantitative and qualitative quasi-experiments with different groups of adolescents to evaluate the effectiveness of these PSAs.

- Secondary data analysis to determine meaningful ways of segmenting adolescents for developing and implementing anti-violence mass media campaigns.

- Development, production, and evaluation of anti-violence PSAs to determine the most effective physical consequence to depict for reducing handgun violence among adolescents.

The results *from **three years of research**,* in conjunction with other studies and the scientific literature on violence, violence prevention, and health communication, lead us to offer the following final recommendations.

Making PSAs more effective

Current violence prevention efforts using televised anti-violence public service announcements are not likely to be effective at changing attitudes towards violence or reducing violent behavior among adolescents. Most existing anti-violence PSAs rely too heavily on celebrity endorsements, have messages that are difficult for adolescents to understand, and/or depict interpersonal violence without punishment or negative consequences.

The following recommendations are intended to assist the television industry and violence prevention organizations to create more effective anti-violence public service announcements.

Target Audience Composition

Findings from the NTVS Study:

Adolescents are not a homogeneous audience with respect to violent attitudes, behavior, and prevention.

Recommendation:

Know your audience, in terms of experience with, and exposure to fighting and weapons.

Consider targeting non-adolescent audiences as well.

In Year 2, we conducted a secondary analysis of a national representative sample of more than 2,000 adolescents aged 11-20 (Biocca et al., 1997a). We found that adolescents are not a homogeneous audience with respect to violent attitudes, behavior, and prevention. The findings indicated that experience with, and exposure to fighting and weapons may be effective variables on which to segment adolescents.

Our analysis revealed seven mutually exclusive segments that we named: Aggressors (started fights and carried weapons), Combatants (started fights), Defenders (been in fights and carried weapons), Fist Fighters (been in fights), Carriers (carried weapons), Observers (seen fights with weapons), Avoiders (never seen fights). These groups significantly differed on a number of attributes, including basic demographic characteristics, family configuration and support, the safety of their neighborhoods, and the extent to which they adopt violence-enabling beliefs and behaviors (Biocca et al., 1997a). Other variables that may be meaningful for audience segmentation include gender, racial or ethnic group, and/or geographic location.

These findings leads us to recommend that careful attention be paid to potential PSA audiences. Audience segments should be considered when developing and pretesting anti-violence mass media campaigns and when selecting delivery channels. In addition, audiences other than adolescents themselves must be targeted to create significant reductions in interpersonal violence among adolescents. For example, parents could be targeted with messages to reduce child abuse. Families and communities could be targeted with messages promoting cohesion. Citizens could be targeted with messages to encourage support of policies that restrict handgun access to adolescents and that promote economic opportunities for low-income communities. Changes made by different audience at different levels can have a stronger effect on reducing interpersonal violence among adolescents and in general.

Public Service Announcement Format

Findings from the NTVS Study:

Half of all existing anti-violence PSAs featured a celebrity endorsement.
Celebrity endorsement PSAs scored lower on interest and memory measures
among adolescents than PSAs with narrative format did.

Recommendation:

Create anti-violence PSAs with narrative format.
Celebrity endorsement PSAs should only be used when the goal is to raise
awareness, not to change knowledge, attitudes or behavior.

Content analyses of existing anti-violence PSAs in Year 2 revealed that half of all
PSAs featured a celebrity endorsement (Biocca et al., 1997a). Quasi-experiments in Year
1 found that celebrity endorsement PSAs scored lower on interest and memory measures
among adolescents than PSAs with a narrative format did (Biocca et al., 1997b).
Although they may be easier and less expensive to produce, we recommend that celebrity
endorsement PSAs only be used when the goal of the campaign is to raise awareness, as
opposed to changing knowledge, attitudes, or behavior. Narrative PSAs that feature a
dramatic scene being modeled will be more effective for campaigns that seek higher-
order individual changes. If celebrities are to be used at all, spokespeople must be
selected who are credible and likeable to the targeted audience segment. In addition,
public service announcements with celebrity actors will be more effective when the actor
performs a dramatic scene than when he or she sits on a stool and reads a cue card.

Writing Public Service Announcement Messages

Findings from the NTVS Study:

Many existing anti-violence PSAs contain messages that are unclear and confusing
to adolescents.
PSAs that depict a negative consequence of handgun use can lead to more negative
expected outcomes of handgun use among adolescents than PSAs that
depict no consequence of handgun use.
PSAs that depict death as an immediate physical consequence of handgun violence
may have greater impact than PSAs that depict paralysis as an immediate
physical consequence.

Recommendation:

Anti-violence public service announcements that model violent scenes should depict
punishments and negative consequences of the violent behavior.

In Year 1 we found that even the most interesting and memorable PSAs often contained confusing or mixed messages (Biocca et al., 1997b). Effective anti-violence PSAs need to present their messages in a clear way that is accessible and understandable to the target audience. Narrative PSAs that model their messages are likely to be more effective that those that present them only verbally or in writing.

Depicting violent scenes in anti-violence PSAs can increase interest and arousal among adolescent viewers, however, the context and consequences of the depicted violence are extremely important (Biocca et al., 1997a). Like violence that appears in television programs, modeled violence in PSAs that goes unpunished or that has no negative consequences may actually *increase* violence among viewers.

Anti-violence public service announcements that model violent scenes should depict punishments and negative consequences of the violent behavior. The depicted consequence can be *physical*, as in the Year 3 PSAs, *emotional*, such as depictions of suffering among victims or their families, *criminal*, such as depictions of perpetrators being arrested and jailed, or *social*, such as depictions of loss of social capital or respect from peers after acting violently.

In Year 3, we found that PSAs that depict a negative consequence of handgun use can lead to more negative expected outcomes of handgun use among adolescents than PSAs that depict no consequence of handgun use. Furthermore, a PSA that depicted death as an immediate physical consequence of handgun violence had greater impact than a PSA that depicted paralysis as an immediate physical consequence.

While we conclude that death may be an effective consequence to show to adolescents, we are not yet ready to dismiss paralysis as a potentially powerful consequence because in-depth interviews from Year 1 revealed that consequences that feature pain or suffering (such as paralysis) elicited strong emotional responses from adolescents. We recommend that the pain, suffering, and physical limitation aspects of injury be emphasized if paralysis is to be used as a physical consequence. PSA developers, however, must also be sensitive to potential stigma caused by portraying people with disabilities in a negative light.

In addition, PSA depictions should be made as realistic as possible. In Year 3, the PSA that depicted death as a consequence had the greatest effect despite the fact that the participants considered it to be less realistic than the other two PSAs. When pursuing realism, however, the PSA creator must remember that showing consequences may not ever be seen as realistic when compared to all the unpunished acts of violence that appear in regular television programs and other anti-violence PSAs.

Taking Credit

Findings from the NTVS Study:

Most existing anti-violence PSAs have tags, or corporate logos of the producing television network, that appear for an average of 18% of the total PSA time.

Recommendation:

Keep corporate logo and tag length to a minimum.

Content analysis in Year 2 revealed that most existing anti-violence PSAs have tags, or corporate logos of the producing television network, that appear for considerable lengths of time (Biocca et al., 1997a). The average tag length was 18% of the total PSA time and the range was from 0 to 50% of the total PSA time. Organizations and networks that produce anti-violence PSAs should refrain from including tags that detract from or shorten the message. Taking credit for important and quality messages is acceptable and warranted but airing excessively long tags begs the question of whether the PSA is designed to reduce violence or increase corporate or organizational public relations.

Television and Violence Prevention

Creating effective PSAs is only part of the solution. Currently, effective televised anti-violence public service announcements risk being drowned out by the vast majority of television programs and commercials that contain violent messages and scenes. Realistically, if television is to be used to significantly reduce violence in society, effective PSAs need to be created and aired with great frequency *and* effective anti-violence themes and messages need to be incorporated within regular television programming.

REFERENCES

Adams, P.F., Schoenborn, C.A., Moss, A.J., Warren, C.W. & Kann, L. (1995). Health risk behaviors among our nation's youth: United States, 1992. National Center for Health Statistics. Vital Health Stat 10 (192).

Ash, P., Kellermann, A.L., Fuqua-Whitley, D. & Johnson, A. (1996). Gun acquisition and use by juvenile offenders. JAMA, 275, 22, 1754-1758.

Atkin, C., & Arkin, E. (1990). Issues and initiatives in communicating health information to the public. In C. Atkin & L. Wallack (Eds.), Mass Communication and Public Health: Complexities and Conflicts. Newbury Park, CA: Sage Publications.

Atkin, C. K., & Freimuth, V. (1989). Formative evaluation research in campaign design. In R. Rice & C. Atkin (Eds.), Public Communication Campaigns. Newbury Park, CA: Sage Publications.

Bandura, A. (1986). Social Foundations of Thought and Action: A Social Cognitive Theory. Englewood Cliffs, NJ: Prentice Hall.

Benton, A. (1967). Effects of the timing of negative response consequences on the observable learning of resistance to temptation in children. Dissertation Abstracts, 27, 2153-2154.

Biocca, F., Brown, J. D., Makris, G., Bernhardt, J. M., & Gaddy, G. (1997a). Improving anti-violence public service announcements through systematic analysis and design, National Television Violence Study Volume 2. Thousand Oaks, CA: Sage Publications.

Biocca, F., Brown, J. D., Shen, F., Bernhardt, J. M., Batista, L., Kemp, K., Makris, G., West, M., Lee, J., Straker, H., Hsiao, H., & Carbone, E. (1997b). Assessment of television's anti-violence messages, National Television Violence Study Volume 1. Thousand Oaks, CA: Sage Publications.

Blumstein, A. (1995). Youth violence, guns and the illicit-drug industry. Journal of Criminal Law and Criminology, 86, 10-36.

Campbell, C. & Schwarz, D.F. (1996). Prevalence and impact of exposure to interpersonal violence among suburban and urban middle school students. Pediatrics, 98, 3, 396-402.

Centers for Disease Control and Prevention (1996). Youth Risk Behavior Surveillance – United States, 1995. MMWR, 45, (No. SS-4).

Crick, N. R., & Dodge, K. A. (1996). Social information-processing mechanisms in reactive and proactive aggression. Child Development, 67(3), 993-1002.

Federal Bureau of Investigation (1997). Uniform Crime Report 1996 Crime Statistics. URL: http://www.fbi.gov/pressrel/ucr/ucr.htm

Flay, B., & Cook, T. (1989). Three models for summative evaluation of prevention campaigns with a mass media component. In R. Rice & C. Atkin (Eds.), Public Communication Campaigns. Newbury Park, CA: Sage Publications.

Flora, J. A., & Maibach, E. W. (1990). Cognitive responses to AISA information: The effects of issue involvement and message appeal. Communication Research, 17(6), 759-774.

Gerbner, G. (1995). The hidden message in anti-violence public service announcements. Harvard Educational Review, 65, 292-298.

Gladstein, J., Slater Rusonis, E.J. & Heald, F.P. (1992). A comparison of inner-city and upper-middle class youths' exposure to violence. Journal of Adolescent Health, 13, 275-280.

Gladstone, B. (1996). Public service announcements: More complex than in past. All Things Considered (April 16, 1996 ed.): WUNC-National Public Radio.

Hensley, V., & Ducal, S. (1976). Some perceptual determinants of perceived similarity, liking, and correctness. Journal of Personality and Social Psychology, 34(2), 159-168.

Hoffman, J. P., Ireland, T. O., & Widom, C. S. (1994). Traditional socialization theories of violence: A critical examination. In J. Archer (Ed.), Male Violence (pp. 1-22). New York: Routledge.

Horan, H. D., & Kaplan, M. F. (1983). Criminal intent and consequence severity: Effects of moral reasoning on punishment. Personality and Social Psychology Bulletin, 9(4), 628-645.

Huesmann, L., Guerra, N., Miller, L., & Zelli, A. (1994). The normative beliefs about aggression scale (NOBAGS). Chicago, IL: University of Illinois at Chicago.

Knight, M., Kemp, K., Brown, J. D., & Biocca, F., (in press). Stop the violence: Lessons from anti-violence campaigns using mass media. In J. Hamilton (Ed.), Television Violence and Public Policy. Ann Arbor, MI: University of Michigan Press.

Louis Harris, & Associates. (1995). Teens Attitudes (Survey Instrument).

Maddux, J. E. (1995). Self-efficacy theory: An introduction. In M. JE (Ed.), Self-Efficacy, Adaption, and Adjustment: Theory, Research, and Application. New York, NY: Plenum Press.

Maguire, K., Pastore, A. L., & Flanagan, J. T. (1993). Sourcebook of criminal justice statistics 1992. Washington, DC: US Department of Justice, Bureau of Justice Statistics, USGPO.

National Center for Health Statistics. (1996). Advance report of final mortality statistics, 1993. Monthly Vital Statistics Report, 44(7), supplement.

National Committee for Injury Prevention and Control (1989). Injury Prevention: Meeting the Challenge. (Education Development Center, Inc.) New York, NY: Oxford University Press.

National Research Council. (1993). Understanding and Preventing Violence. (Vol. 1). Washington, DC: National Academy Press.

O'Keefe, G. J. (1985). "Taking a bite out of crime" The impact of a public information campaign. Communication Research, 12(2), 147-178.

Perry, D., Perry, L., & Rasmussen, P. (1986). Cognitive social learning mediators of aggression. Child Development, 57, 700-711.

Reeves, B., Newhagen, J., Maibach, E., et al. (1991). Negative and positive television message: Effects of message type and context on attention and memory. American Behavioral Scientist, 34(6), 679-694.

Roper, W. L. (1991). The Prevention of minority youth violence must begin despite risks and imperfect understanding. Public Health Reports, 106, 229-231.

Singer, D.G., Singer, J.L. & Zuckerman, D.M. (1990). Use TV to your child's advantage. Reston, VA: Acropolis Books.

Siska, M., Jason, J., Murdoch, P., Yang, W. S., & Donovan, R. J. (1992). Recall of AIDS public service announcements and their impact on the ranking of AIDS as a national problem. American Journal of Public Health, 82(7), 1029-1032.

Tolan, P., & Guerra, N. (1994). What works in reducing adolescent violence: an empirical review of the literature. Boulder, CO: Center for the Study and Prevention of Violence.

Turner, M. (1994). Et Tu Brutus. New York, NY: Home Box Office.

US Census (1990). World wide web site: http://www.census.gov/

US Department of Justice. (1992). Criminal victimization in the United States 1991 (NCJ-139563). Washington, DC: Bureau of Justice Statistics, US Department of Justice.

Wallerstein, N. & Sanchez-Merki, V. (1994). Freirian praxis in health education: Research results from an adolescent prevention program. Health Education Research, 9, 1, 105-118.

Wang, C. (1992). Culture, meaning, and disability: Injury prevention campaigns and the production of stigma. Social Science and Medicine, 35, 9, 1093-1102.

Wilson, B. J., Kunkel, D., Linz, D., & Potter, J. (1997). Violence in television programming overall, National Television Violence Study Volume 1. Thousand Oaks, CA: Sage Publications.

Zuckerman, D.M. (1996). Media violence, gun control, and public policy. American Journal of Orthopsychiatry, 66,3:378-389.

Zwerling, C., McMillan, D., Cook, P.J., Gunderson, P., Johnson, N., Kellerman, A.L., Lee, R.K., Loftin, C., Merchant, J.A. & Teret, S. (1993). Firearm injuries: Public Health Recommendations. Public Health Reports, 9, 3, 52-55.

Index

A&E, 26, 29, 49, 50, 57, 100, 141, 175
   advisories, 206
   Parental Guidelines, 206, 300
   reality programming, 236
ABC, 26, 29, 49, 50, 57, 259
   advisories, 198
   Parental Guidelines, 198, 291, 296, 297, 298
Adams, P. F., 326
Advisories, 197, 287, 288, 291, 318-319
   humorous, 307
   oral, 250, 305
   program recommendations, 308, 319
   reality-based programs, 250-251, 263
   scheduling, 315-316
   text, 306-308
   written, 250, 305, 306
   See also specific channels/networks
Aggression. *See* Learning of aggression, violent portrayals and
Alfert, E., 15
Alioto, J. T., 16
AMC, 26, 29, 49, 50, 57, 100, 141, 175
   no advisories, 305
   Parental Guidelines compliance, 207, 292, 317
Anti-violence public service announcements (PSAs), 343-349
   content, 335
   corporate logos/tags, 353
   development, 333-335
   format, 351
   handgun violence, 326-327
   making more effective, 349-353
   message processing, 345-346
   narrative format, 325
   observational learning, 331-332, 334

   target audience composition, 350
   testing effectiveness of, 336-342
   writing, 351-352
   See also Social cognitive theory of violence
Anti-violence themes, 34-35, 62-63, 99, 108, 120, 164-165, 168, 178-179
   children's programming, 103
   comedy series, 101
   drama series, 99, 101
   movies, 102
   music videos, 103-104
   prevalence of programming, 62
   reality programming, 101-102
Applefield, J. M., 183
Arkin, E., 327
Armstrong, G. B., 226
Ash, P., 326
Atkin, C., 17, 327
Atkin, C. K., 338
Aversa, J., 318

Bandura, A., 14, 17, 325, 328, 329, 330, 331, 345
Baron, R. A., 18
Baron, R. S., 18
Batista, L., 325, 328, 333, 345, 351, 352
Benton, A., 329
Berger, A. A., 18
Berkowitz, L., 15, 16, 18, 129, 132
Berndt, E. G., 14
Berndt, T. J., 14
Bernhardt, J. M., 325, 328, 330, 331, 333, 334, 345, 350, 351, 352, 353
Berry, M., 129, 130, 131, 132, 135
BET, 26, 29, 49, 50, 57, 100, 103, 141, 175
   advisories, 208, 307
   noncompliance with parental guidelines, 287, 289, 292, 301, 317, 319

Biocca, F., 325, 328, 330, 331, 333, 334, 345, 350, 351, 352, 353
Blumenthal, E., 10, 12, 22, 30, 111, 128, 129, 130, 131, 132, 135
Blumstein, A., 326
Broadcast networks, commercial, 26, 56-57, 59, 169, 175
   animated programs, 85
   anti-violence themed programs, 99, 101, 171
   consequences of violence, 92, 93, 96, 171
   graphicness of violence, 82, 171
   guns, 171
   high-risk programming for older children/adolescents, 150-151, 157
   high-risk programming for young children, 141, 142, 143, 144, 155
   high-risk time of day, 143, 144, 152-153
   humor and violence, 98, 171
   justified violence, 171
   lethal violence, 171
   live action programs, 85
   perpetrators, 65, 171
   presence of violence, 107, 171
   prevalence of violence, 59, 115-116, 124, 125, 126, 170
   prime-time programming, 105
   prime-time versus non-prime-time hours, 106
   rate of violence, 62, 171
   realism of violence, 84, 171
   reality-based programs, 223, 236, 237, 242, 262, 274
   saturation of violence, 61
   talk about violence, 277
   targets, 71
   unpunished violence, 171
   violent interaction frequency, 59, 63, 171
   visual violence, 277

See also specific commercial broadcast networks/affiliates
Brown, D., 17
Brown, J. D., 325, 328, 330, 331, 333, 334, 345, 350, 351, 352, 353
Bryant, J., 14, 17, 18

Cable, basic, 26, 59, 169, 175
  animated programs, 85
  anti-violence themed programs, 101-102, 103-104, 171
  consequences of violence, 92, 93, 96, 171
  graphicness of violence, 82, 171
  guns, 171
  high-risk programming for older children/adolescents, 150-151, 156, 157, 163
  high-risk programming for young children, 141, 142, 143, 144, 155, 156, 162
  high-risk time of day, 143, 144, 145, 151, 152-153
  humor and violence, 98, 171
  justified violence, 171
  lethal violence, 171
  live action programs, 85
  Parental Guidelines compliance, 317
  perpetrators, 65, 171
  presence of violence, 171
  prevalence of violence, 115-116, 124, 126, 170, 171
  prime-time versus non-prime-time hours, 106
  rate of violence, 62, 107, 171
  realism of violence, 84, 171
  reality-based programs, 223, 236, 237, 242, 262, 274
  saturation of violence, 61
  talk about violence, 277
  targets, 71
  unpunished violence, 171
  visual violence, 277
  See also specific basic cable channels
Cable, premium, 26, 59, 169, 175
  animated programs, 85

anti-violence themed programs, 102
  consequences of violence, 92, 93, 94, 95, 96-97, 171
  graphicness of violence, 81, 82, 109, 171
  guns, 171
  high-risk programming for older children/adolescents, 150-151, 156, 157, 163
  high-risk programming for young children, 141, 142, 143, 144, 155
  high-risk time of day, 143, 144, 150, 152-153
  humor and violence, 98, 171
  justified violence, 171
  lethal violence, 171
  live action programs, 85
  perpetrators, 65, 69, 171
  presence of violence, 171
  prevalence of violence, 58, 115-116, 124, 170-171, 241
  prime-time programming, 105
  prime-time versus non-prime-time hours, 106
  rate of violence, 62, 107, 171
  realism of violence, 84, 171
  reality-based programs, 223, 237, 241, 242, 274
  saturation of violence, 61, 107
  talk about violence, 277
  targets, 70, 71, 72, 74
  unpunished violence, 171
  violent interaction frequency, 63
  visual violence, 277
  See also specific premium cable channels
Campbell, C., 326
Cantor, J. R., 14
Carbone, E., 325, 328, 333, 345, 351, 352
Carlson, M., 15
Cartoon Network, 26, 29, 49, 50, 57, 100, 141, 142, 162, 175, 236
  no advisories, 305
  Parental Guidelines, 210, 292, 301, 318

Cartoons, 7, 138, 162, 163, 176, 183-184. *See also* Children's shows
CBS, 26, 29, 49, 50, 57, 99, 100
  advisories, 199
  Parental Guidelines, 199, 291, 292, 296, 297, 298
Carveth, R. A., 17
Center for Communication and Social Policy, University of California, Santa Barbara, 2
Centers for Disease Control and Prevention, 326, 343
Channel(s):
  consequences of violence, 91, 92, 93, 95, 96-97
  distribution of rating levels, 297-301
  graphicness of violence, 81, 82
  high-risk for young children, 141-145
  humor and violence, 97-98
  means of violence/presence of weapons, 77
  perpetrators, 65, 66, 68, 69
  presence of violence, 107, 169-172
  prevalence of violence, 58-59
  rate of violence, 62, 107-108
  realism of violence, 84
  reality-based programs, 237, 241, 242
  saturation of violence, 61, 107
  targets, 70-72, 74
  See also specific channel types; specific channels
Children's shows, 60
  animated, 85, 86, 138
  anti-violence themed, 100, 103
  consequences of violence, 91, 92, 93, 94, 95, 96, 109, 172-173, 174
  extent of violence, 79
  graphicness of violence, 82, 173, 174
  guns, 173, 174
  high-risk portrayals, 136, 137, 138, 147, 155, 156, 157, 162, 175-176
  high-risk time of day, 139, 140, 148-149

humor and violence, 97, 98, 109, 172, 174
live action, 86
means of violence/weapons, 77, 78
Parental Guidelines, 287, 295, 318
perpetrators, 66, 68, 69
prevalence of violence, 116, 117
punishment patterns, 89
rate of violence, 62, 107
realism of violence, 84-85, 109, 173, 174
saturation of violence, 61
targets, 71, 73, 74-75
Cinemax, 26, 29, 49, 50, 57, 100, 102, 236, 287, 312
advisories, 217
content codes, 311
MPAA ratings, 217, 308
Parental Guidelines, 217, 292, 293, 296
violence codes, 217
Cline, V. B., 16
Collins, W. A., 132, 133
Comedy programs, 60
animated, 86
anti-violence themed, 100, 101
consequences of violence, 91, 92, 93, 94, 95
extent of violence, 79
graphicness of violence, 82, 172, 174
guns, 172, 174
high-risk portrayals, 136, 137, 146, 147, 155, 157
high-risk time of day, 139, 140, 148-149
humor and violence, 97, 98, 109, 172, 174
live action, 86
means of violence/weapons, 77, 78
Parental Guidelines, 294, 318
perpetrators, 66, 68
presence of violence, 107
prevalence of violence, 60, 116, 117, 126
punishment patterns, 89
rate of violence, 62, 108

realism of violence, 84, 172, 174
reasons for violence, 76
saturation of violence, 61, 107
targets, 71, 72, 73, 74
violent interaction frequency, 63
Comisky, P., 14
Comstock, G., 12, 17, 129, 132, 183
Content codes, 287, 288, 291, 310-311, 319
AC, 310, 311, 312, 313, 319
AL, 311, 319
BN, 311
GL, 311
language, 312, 313
MPAA ratings and, 312-314
N, 311, 312, 313
RP, 311
SC, 311
SL, 310
See also Violence codes
Contextual variables, television programming, 11, 19-20
assessing change, 119-123
consequences of violence, 12, 17-18, 33, 63, 90-97, 109, 119, 122, 126
extent/graphicness of violence, 12, 15-16, 32, 34, 63-64, 78-82, 108-109, 119, 122, 126
humor and violence, 12, 18, 34, 63, 97-98, 109, 119, 122, 127
justification for violence, 13, 15, 32, 76, 108
nature of perpetrator, 12, 14, 36, 63, 64-69, 108, 119, 122, 126, 127
nature of target, 12, 14, 36, 63, 70-75, 108, 119, 122, 126, 127
presence of weapons, 12, 15, 32, 63, 76-78, 108, 119, 122, 126
realism of violence, 12, 16-17, 35, 63, 83-84, 109, 119, 122, 126
reason for violence, 12, 14-15, 32, 63, 75-76, 108, 119, 122, 126

sexual violence, 98
violence rewarded/punished, 12, 17, 34, 35-36, 37, 63, 87-90, 109, 119, 122, 126
See also Anti-violence themes
Cook, P. J., 327
Cook, T., 328
Courrier, S., 16
Crick, N. R., 339
Croft, R. G., 16

Danielson, W., 25
Data quality, checking, 38-42
Davidson, L. A., 16
Davison, L., 16
Davison, W. P., 228
Desensitization effect, 2, 10, 11, 16, 18-19, 20, 166, 182
Disney Channel, 26, 29, 49, 50, 57, 100, 103, 141, 142, 162, 175, 236
advisories, 218
Parental Guidelines, 218, 292, 301, 318
program recommendations, 308
Documentaries, 236, 244, 268-269, 273
advisories, 250
channel type, 237, 241, 242, 274
consequences of violence, 247, 259
extensive violence, 259
graphicness of consequences, 253
impact beyond participants, 250, 251, 259
individuals harmed, 248, 259
presence/persistence of harm/pain, 249
prevalence of violence, 240, 242
punishing violence, 259
realistic violence, 259
reenactments/recreations, 252
rewarding violence, 259
second-person accounts, 254
talk about violence, 245, 246, 276, 281-284
third-person accounts, 254
time of day, 238, 243, 275, 281-284

361

visual violence, 244, 245, 246, 276, 281-284
war/mass violence, 247
Dodge, K. A., 339
Donnerstein, E., 10, 12, 16, 18, 22, 30, 111, 128, 129, 130, 131, 132, 135
Donovan, R. J., 338
Dorr, A., 132
Dramas, 60
anti-violence themed, 99, 101, 101
consequences of violence, 92, 93, 95, 97, 172, 174
extent of violence, 79
graphicness of violence, 82
guns, 172, 174
high-risk time of day, 139, 140, 147, 148-149
high-risk portrayals, 136, 137, 138, 146, 147, 155, 156, 157, 163, 176
humor and violence, 97, 98
means of violence/weapons, 77, 78, 108
Parental Guidelines, 294, 318
perpetrators, 66, 68
presence of violence, 107, 172, 174
prevalence of violence, 59, 116, 117
punishment patterns, 88-89, 90, 172, 174
rate of violence, 62
realism of violence, 84, 172, 174
saturation of violence, 61
targets, 71, 72, 73
Ducal, S., 339

Ellis, G. T., 183
Entertainment news and review shows, 223, 224, 235, 236, 266-267, 273
channel type, 237, 242, 274
fictional/fantasy violence, 258
graphicness of consequences, 253
guns, 258
humor and violence, 252, 259

impact beyond participants, 250, 251
individuals harmed, 248
men in, 257, 259
presence/persistence of harm/pain, 249
prevalence of violence, 240, 242
sanitized violence, 150
second-person accounts, 254
talk about violence, 245, 246, 258, 272, 280
third-person accounts, 254
time of day, 238, 241, 243, 244, 275, 280-284
visual violence, 244, 245, 246, 258, 271, 276, 281-284
Entertainment non-news shows, 235, 236, 265-266, 273
advisories, 250
channel type, 237, 242, 274
graphicness, 253, 258
humor and violence, 252, 258
impact beyond participants, 250, 251
individuals harmed, 248
presence/persistence of harm/pain, 249
prevalence of violence, 240, 242
reenactments/recreations, 252, 258
talk about violence, 245, 246, 258, 272, 276, 281, 282, 284
threats, 247
time of day, 238, 243, 244, 275, 281-284
visual violence, 244, 245, 246, 258, 271, 276, 281, 282, 283, 284
war/mass violence, 247
Eron, L. D., 16
Evatt, D., 226
Extensive/graphic television violence, 13, 15-16

Family Channel, 26, 29, 49, 50, 57, 100, 141, 175, 209
advisories, 209
Parental Guidelines, 209, 300
Farhi, P., 289

Federal Bureau of Investigation, 326
Federal Communications Commission, 289, 319
Feshbach, N. D., 14
Feshbach, S. 16
Flanagan, J. T., 326
Flavell, J. H., 132
Flay, B., 328
Flora, J. A., 338
Fox, 26, 29, 49, 50, 57
advisories, 200
Parental Guidelines, 200, 291, 296, 297, 298
program recommendations, 308
reality-based programs, 236
Fredriksen, S., 14
Freimuth, V., 338
Friedrich, L. K., 183
Fuqua-Whitley, D., 326

Gaddy, G., 325, 328, 330, 331, 334, 350, 351, 352, 353
Gaer, E. P., 14
Geen, R. G., 15, 16, 17
Genre. See Program genre(s)
Gerbner, G., 130, 325, 333
Ghanem, S., 226
Gladstein, J., 326
Gladstone, B., 327
Glamorized television violence, 7
Goransen, R. E., 18
Gray, T., 10, 12, 22, 30, 111, 128, 130
Greenberg, B. S., 18
Gross, L., 130
Guerra, N., 325, 327
Gunderson, P., 327
Gunter, B., 12, 14, 17, 18

Hall, J., 292
HBO, 26, 29, 49, 50, 57, 219, 236, 287, 293, 312
advisories, 219
MPAA ratings, 219, 308
violence codes, 219
Heald, F. P., 326
Hearold, S., 129
Hensley, V., 339

High-risk violent interactions
    (older children/adolescents),
    132, 145-146, 162-163, 175
by channel, 150-153, 163
by genre, 146-149, 163
change in, 156-157
examples, 159-161
High-risk violent interactions
    (under age 7), 132, 134, 136,
    142, 162, 163, 175, 183-184
by channel type, 141-145, 162
by genre, 136-140, 162
change in, 154-156, 162
examples, 158-159
See also Learning of
    aggression, violent
    portrayals and
Hoffman, J. P., 329, 330
Hoffner, C., 14, 16
Horan, H. D., 341
Hoyt, J. L., 15
Hsiao, H., 325, 328, 333, 345, 351,
    352
Huesmann, L., 325
Huesmann, L. R., 16, 129, 132

Independent broadcast networks,
    26, 57, 59, 169, 175
animated programs, 85
anti-violence themed programs,
    101, 171
consequences of violence, 92,
    93, 96, 171
graphicness of violence, 82, 171
guns, 171
high-risk programming for
    older children/adolescents,
    150-151
high-risk programming for
    young children, 141, 142,
    143, 144
high-risk time of day, 143, 144,
    145, 150
humor and violence, 97, 98
justified violence, 171
lethal violence, 171
live action programs, 85
Parental Guidelines, 292
perpetrators, 65, 69, 171
presence of violence, 171

prevalence of violence,
    115-116, 124, 170, 171
prime-time programming, 105
prime-time versus
    non-prime-time hours, 106
rate of violence, 62, 107, 171
realism of violence, 84, 171
reality-based programs, 236,
    237, 242, 274
saturation of violence, 61, 107
talk about violence, 241, 277
targets, 70-71, 74
unpunished violence, 171
visual violence, 277
*See also specific independent
    networks*
Ireland, T. O., 329, 330

Jason, J., 338
Jo, E., 15
Johnson, A., 326
Johnson, N., 327
Justified television violence, 13,
    15, 32, 76, 108

KABC, 25
    reality-based programs, 236
Kann, L., 326
Kaplan, M. F., 341
KCAL, 26, 29, 49, 50, 57
    advisories, 205
    Parental Guidelines, 205, 292,
        299
KCBS, 25
    reality-based programs, 236
KCET, 26
    advisories, 202
    noncompliance with parental
        guidelines, 287, 292, 317,
        319
KCOP, 26, 29, 49, 50, 57, 100, 101
    advisories, 204
    Parental Guidelines, 204, 296,
        299
Kellerman, A. L., 326, 327
Kemp, K., 325, 328, 333, 345, 351,
    352
Klijn, M., 25
KNBC, 25, 287, 318

reality-based programs, 236
Knight, M., 328
KTLA, 26, 29, 49, 50, 57, 100, 310
    advisories, 203
    MPAA ratings, 203
    Parental Guidelines, 203, 292,
        296
    violence codes, 203
KTTV, 25
Kunkel, D., 10, 12, 22, 30, 111,
    128, 129, 130, 131, 132, 135,
    331, 334, 346

LaSorsa, D., 25
Lazarus, R. S., 15, 16, 17
Learning of aggression, violent
    portrayals and, 2, 10, 11, 12,
    16, 17, 18, 20, 166, 182
attractive perpetrator, 130, 131,
    135, 138, 161
definitional issues, 129-131
justified violence, 130, 131,
    136, 138, 161
realistic violence, 130
violence rewarded/sanctioned,
    130, 132, 138, 161
violence showing no pain/harm,
    130, 132, 136, 138, 161
Lee, J., 325, 328, 333, 345, 351,
    352
Lee, R. K., 327
Lefkowitz, M. M., 16
Leyens, J. P., 15
Lifetime channel, 26, 29, 49, 50,
    57, 100, 141, 175
    advisories, 211
    Parental Guidelines, 211, 292
    reality programming, 236
Linz, D., 10, 12, 16, 22, 30, 111,
    128, 129, 130, 131, 132, 135,
    331, 334, 346
Liss, M. B., 14
Loftin, C., 327
Lopez, R., 25
Louis Harris & Associates, 340
Lowry, B., 319

Maguire, K., 326
Maibach, E. W., 338

Makris, G., 325, 328, 330, 331, 333, 334, 345, 350, 351, 352, 353
Marcus-Newhall, A., 15
McMillan, D., 327
Means of violence, 32, 247, 278-279. *See also* Weapons
Mean world syndrome, 11
Mediascope, 2
Merchant, J. A., 327
Miller, L., 325
Miller, N., 15
Mordkoff, A. M., 16
Moss, A. J., 326
Movies, 60
    animated, 86
    anti-violence themed, 100, 102
    consequences of violence, 92, 93, 94, 95, 97, 173, 174
    extent of violence, 79
    graphicness of violence, 82, 109, 173, 174
    high-risk portrayals, 136, 137, 138, 146, 147, 155, 156, 157, 163, 176
    high-risk time of day, 139, 140, 147, 148-149
    humor and violence, 98
    live action, 86
    means of violence/weapons, 78
    Parental Guidelines, 295, 318
    perpetrators, 66, 68
    presence of violence, 107
    prevalence of violence, 59, 116, 117, 173, 174
    punishment patterns, 89
    rate of violence, 62
    realism of violence, 84, 173, 174
    saturation of violence, 61, 107
    targets, 71, 72, 73
    violent interaction frequency, 63
MPAA ratings, 196, 287, 288, 289, 291, 308-309, 319
    content codes and, 312-314
    G, 196, 308, 309, 312, 319
    PG, 196, 308, 309, 312, 313, 319
    PG-13, 196, 308, 309, 312, 313, 319

R, 196, 308, 309, 312, 313, 314, 319
MTV, 26, 29, 49, 50, 57, 100, 101, 141, 175
    advisories, 212
    Parental Guidelines, 212, 292, 295, 296
    reality programming, 236, 258
Mueller, C., 18
Mullin, C. R., 16
Murdoch, P., 338
Murray, J. P., 128
Music videos, 60
    animated, 86
    anti-violence themed, 100, 103-104
    consequences of violence, 91, 92, 94, 95
    extent of violence, 79
    graphicness of violence, 82
    high-risk portrayals, 136, 137, 138, 146, 147, 155, 157
    high-risk time of day, 139, 140, 148-149
    humor and violence, 97, 98, 173, 174
    live-action, 86
    means of violence/weapons, 77, 78
    Parental Guidelines, 296, 318
    perpetrators, 66, 68, 69, 173, 174
    prevalence of violence, 116, 117, 126, 173, 174
    punishment patterns, 89, 90
    rate of violence, 62
    realism of violence, 84, 173, 174
    reasons for violence, 76
    saturation of violence, 61, 107
    targets, 71, 72, 73, 74, 75
Mussen, P., 183

National Cable Television Association (NCTA), 1, 8, 23, 56, 196
National Center for Health Statistics, 326, 328
National Committee for Injury Prevention and Control, 328

National Research Council, 326, 327
National Television Violence Study:
    coding and reliability, 37-46
    content measures, 30-37
    goals, 8
    1998, 224, 225
    1997, 224, 225, 240, 254
    number of hours of television programming examined, 7
    number of violent interactions analyzed, 7
    sample of programs, 25-29
National Television Violence Study, multi-year methods
    assessment, 52
    composite weeks of programming, 47
    data quality checking, 51
    reliability, 51-55
    sample exclusions, 47, 50
    sampling periods, 47, 48
    total program count/error rate, 47, 49
NBC, 26, 29, 49, 50, 57, 201, 239
    advisories, 201
    Parental Guidelines, 201, 289, 291, 296, 297, 298, 299, 320
Network Television Association, 12
Newhagen, J., 338
News and public affairs programs, 223, 224, 226, 235, 236, 244, 262, 267-268, 273
    channel type, 237, 241, 242, 274
    consequences of violence, 247, 260
    graphicness of consequences, 253
    impact beyond participants, 250, 251, 260
    individuals harmed, 248, 260
    presence/persistence of harm/pain, 249
    prevalence of violence, 240, 242
    realism of violence, 260
    reenactments/recreations, 252
    talk about violence, 245, 246, 259, 272, 276, 280-281, 283
    time of day, 238, 239, 241, 243, 244, 275, 280-284
    violent acts, 247

visual and talk about violence,
244
visual violence, 245, 246,
259-260, 271, 276, 280,
281-284
war/mass violence, 247, 260
Nickelodeon, 26, 29, 49, 50, 57,
141, 142, 162, 175, 236
advisories, 213
Parental Guidelines, 213, 301,
318
Nomikos, M. S., 17

Ogles, R. M., 16
O'Keefe, G. J., 328
Olivarez, A., 25
Oliver, M. B., 226
Opton, E. M., Jr., 17

Paik, H., 12, 17, 129, 132, 183
Parental Guidelines, TV, 287, 288
adoption, 317
distinguishing violent versus
nonviolent programs, 318
distribution of ratings levels,
293-301, 317-318
implementation, 290-293
programs with versus without
violence, 302-303
ratings levels within channels,
297-301
ratings levels within genres,
294-296
time of day, 303-304
TV14, 196, 287, 289, 293, 294,
295, 296, 297, 299, 302,
303, 318, 320
TVG, 196, 287, 289, 293, 294,
295, 296, 297, 300, 301,
302, 303, 317, 318, 320
TVMA, 181, 196, 287, 289,
293, 304, 320
TVPG, 196, 287, 289, 293, 294,
295, 296, 297, 299, 300,
301, 302, 303, 318, 320
TVY, 179, 196, 287, 289, 293,
295, 297, 299, 301, 302,
303, 318

TVY7, 179, 180, 196, 287, 289,
293, 294, 295, 296, 297,
302, 303, 318
See also V-chip
Parke, 15
Pastore, A. L., 326
PBS, 29, 49, 50, 57, 100, 292. See
also Public broadcast network
Penrod, S., 16
Perpetrators of violence, 69, 108
age, 66-67, 118, 119
apparent ethnicity, 67, 118, 119
attractive, 13, 14
character type, 64-66, 118, 119
good/bad, 68-69, 118, 119
hero status, 68, 118, 119
nature of perpetrator, 12, 14,
36, 63, 64-69
sex, 66, 118, 119
See also specific
channels/networks; specific
program genres
Perry, D., 330, 339
Perry, L., 330, 339
Piaget, J., 132
Police shows, 223, 225, 235, 236,
262, 265, 273
advisories, 250
channel type, 237, 274
graphicness of consequences,
253
gun-related violence, 247, 257
impact beyond participants,
250, 251
individuals harmed, 248
intensity of violence, 252
men in, 257
presence/persistence of
harm/pain, 249, 250
prevalence of violence, 240
reenactments/recreations, 252
second-person accounts, 254
talk about violence, 245, 272
third-person accounts, 254
threats, 247, 257
time of day, 238, 239, 241, 244,
275, 281-282, 284
violence rewarded, 257
violence punished, 257
violent acts, 247, 257

visual violence, 244, 245, 257,
271, 276, 281-282, 284
Potter, J., 10, 12, 22, 30, 111, 128,
129, 130, 131, 132, 135, 331,
334, 346
Potter, W. J., 131
Powers, P. C., 15, 132
Practical significance, 57
Prime time, 104
Prime-time programming:
analysis, 104-106
analysis of change in, 123-126
change in contextual variables,
124-125, 127
change in prevalence of
violence, 123-124, 127
Processing television content:
developmental differences, 19
Program genre(s), 172-174,
257-261
animated versus live action, 86
consequences of violence, 91,
92, 93, 94-95, 96-97
excluded, 25
extent of violence, 79-80
graphicness of violence, 81-82
humor and violence, 97-98
means of violence/presence of
weapons, 77-78
Parental Guidelines
distribution, 294-296
perpetrators, 65, 66, 68, 69
presence of violence, 107
prevalence of violence, 59-60
punishment patterns, 88-90
rate of violence, 62, 107-108
realism of violence, 84
reality-based programs, 242,
244, 262, 273-276
reasons for violence, 76
saturation of violence, 61
targets, 71, 72, 73, 74-75
See also specific genres
Programs:
animated, 85
live-action, 85
sample, 25-29
selection, 26, 28
time of day, 25
See also National Television
Violence Study; National

Television Violence Study,
multi-year methods
assessment
Public broadcast network, 26, 59,
169, 175
consequences of violence, 91,
92, 93, 95, 96
graphicness of violence, 81, 82
high-risk programming for
young children, 141, 142,
143, 144
high-risk time of day, 143, 144
humor and violence, 97, 98
means of violence/weapons, 77
perpetrators, 65, 67, 69
presence of violence, 107, 171
prevalence of violence, 59,
115-116, 170
rate of violence, 62, 108
realism of violence, 84
reality-based programs, 223,
236, 237, 241, 242, 262, 274
saturation of violence, 61, 107
talk about violence, 277
targets, 71, 72
violent interaction frequency, 63
visual violence, 277
See also PBS
Public service announcements
(PSAs), 327
health communication
campaigns, 327
"take a bite out of crime," 328
See also Anti-violence public
service announcements
(PSAs)

Rakosky, J. J., 17
Randall, B., 12
Rankin, N. O., 17
Rasmussen, P., 330, 339
Ratings. See Content codes; MPAA
ratings; Parental Guidelines,
TV; V-chip; Violence codes
Rawlings, E., 15
Realistic television violence, 13,
16-17, 261-262
Reality-based programs, 60,
224-226
advisories, 263

anti-violence themed, 100,
101-102, 263
channel types, 223, 237, 262
characters involved in violence,
254-257
consequences of violence, 92,
93, 94, 95
diversity, 173, 174
extent of violence, 79, 80
graphicness of violence, 82,
261-262
guns, 173, 174
high-risk portrayals, 136, 137,
146, 147, 155, 157
high-risk time of day, 139, 140,
148-149
humor and violence, 97, 98,
173, 174, 252
impact beyond participants,
250, 251
live action, 86
means of violence/weapons, 77,
78, 108
Parental Guidelines, 296, 318
perpetrators, 66, 68, 173, 174
presence of violence, 107,
239-246
presence/persistence of
harm/pain, 249
prevalence of violence, 60, 116,
117, 126, 173, 174
punishment patterns, 89, 90, 261
rate of violence, 62, 108
realism of violence, 84, 173,
174
reasons for violence, 76
recommendations, 263-264
saturation of violence, 61, 107
targets, 71, 73, 74, 75
time of day, 223, 238, 241, 262,
263
violent interaction frequency, 63
See also specific types of
reality-based programs;
Reality programming; Talk
about violence; Visual
violence
Reality-based programs, measuring
violence in:
definition of violence, 226
levels of analysis, 226-229

methods, 230
reliability, 230-235
sampling, 229
See also Reality-based programs
Recommendations on television
violence:
for academic community,
184-186
for parents, 182-184
for public policy-makers,
180-182
for television industry, 177-180
Reeves, B., 338
Reinhardt, L. C., 14
Reliability testing, 38-40
coder performance fatigue, 42
reliability coefficients, 43-46
results, 41-42
Reno, J., 128
Roe, K., 14
Roper, W. L., 326
Ross, D., 17
Ross, S. A., 17

Sanchez-Merki, V., 340
Sander, I., 18
Sanders, G. S., 18
Sanitization effect, 7
Sanitized violence, 250
Schmutte, G. T., 18
Schoenborn, C. A., 326
Schwarz, D. F., 326
Sekyra, F., 183
Self-defense, violence and, 14
Sexual violence, 98
Shen, F., 325, 328, 333, 345, 351,
352
Showtime, 26, 29, 49, 50, 57, 236,
287, 312
advisories, 220, 305, 318
content codes, 311
MPAA ratings, 220, 308
Parental Guidelines, 220, 292,
293
violence codes, 220
Siegler, R. S., 132
Singer, D. G., 328
Singer, J. L., 328
Siska, M., 338
Slater Rusonis, E. J., 326

Smith, R., 183
Smith, S., 10, 12, 22, 30, 111, 128, 129, 130, 131, 132, 135
Social cognitive theory, 329
Social cognitive theory of violence, 329
  consequence severity, 330
  experience with violence, 331, 343
  exposure to violence, 331, 343
  outcome expectations, 329, 344-345
  observational learning, 331, 334
  See also Anti-violence public service announcements (PSAs)
Speisman, J. C., 16
Speisman, M., 16
Statistical significance, 57
Stein, A. H., 183
Steuer, F. B., 183
Stonner, D., 15
Straker, H., 325, 328, 333, 345, 351, 352

Tabloid news shows, 223, 225, 236, 244, 262, 268, 273
  channel type, 237, 242, 274
  depicting consequences of violence, 247
  depicting individuals harmed, 248
  graphicness of consequences, 253
  guns, 260
  impact beyond participants, 250, 251, 260
  intensity of violence, 252-253
  presence/persistence of harm/pain, 249, 250
  prevalence of violence, 240, 242
  reenactments/recreations, 252
  talk about violence, 245, 246, 260, 272, 276, 280-281, 283
  third-person accounts, 254
  time of day, 238, 239, 243, 244, 275, 280-284
  visual and talk about violence, 244

  visual violence, 245, 246, 260, 271, 276, 280-284
Talk about violence, 223, 226, 227, 228, 229, 230, 231, 239, 240, 242, 243, 244, 247, 262
  extent of injury, 248
  graphicness, 253
  impact beyond participants, 250, 251
  individuals harmed, 248
  point of view, 253-254
  presence/persistence of harm/pain, 249
  See also specific types of reality-based programs
Talk shows, 223, 224, 236, 262, 269, 273
  advisories, 250-251
  channel type, 236, 237, 242, 274
  consequences of off-screen violence, 260-261
  depicting individuals harmed, 248
  first-person accounts, 254
  graphicness, 253, 261
  impact beyond participants, 250, 251, 261
  multi-person perspectives, 254
  presence/persistence of harm/pain, 249
  prevalence of violence, 240, 242
  sexual assault, 261
  talk about violence, 244, 245, 246, 261, 272, 281-284
  time of day, 238, 239, 241, 243, 244, 275, 280-284
  visual violence, 245, 246, 260, 261, 271, 280-282
  women in, 257, 261
Tannenbaum, P. H., 14
Targets of violence, 74-75, 108
  age, 72, 118, 119
  apparent ethnicity, 72-73, 118, 119
  attractive, 13, 14
  character type, 70-71, 118, 119
  good/bad, 73-74, 118
  hero status, 73, 118
  nature of target, 12, 14, 36, 63, 70-75
  sex, 72, 118, 119

  See also specific channels/networks; specific program genres
Taylor, S. P., 18
Telecommunications Act of 1996, 289
Television violence:
  changes, 166-169
  definition, 20-21, 23, 30, 58, 114
  extent, 165
  fear of victimization, 2, 10, 11, 12, 17, 20, 166, 182
  graphic, 166
  guns, 166
  motivation, 165
  presence, 58-63
  prevalence, 58-60, 63, 126, 164
  punished, 13, 17
  rate, 62
  rewarded, 13, 17
  sanitized, 165
  saturation, 60-61
  social problem, 7
  trivialization, 166
  unpunished, 165
  See also specific channel types and genres; Television violence, assessing change in; Television violence, measuring
Television violence, assessing change in:
  contextual variables, 119-122, 126-127
  overall prevalence, 114-115
  perpetrators, 118-119
  prevalence by channel, 115-116, 126
  prevalence by genre, 116-117, 126
  prevalence levels, 114-117
  prime-time analysis, 123-126
  targets, 118-119
  thresholds for, 110-114
Television violence, measuring 20-23
  coding of content, 22, 23
  measures, 22
  reliability, 23
  sample, 22-23

sampling, 23
violent incidents, 21
See also Units of analysis
Tell, P. M., 16
Teret, S., 327
Thomas, M. H., 16
TNT, 26, 29, 49, 50, 57, 100, 141, 175
   advisories, 214
   Parental Guidelines, 214
Tolan, P., 327
Tulloch, J. C., 227
Tulloch, M. I., 227
Turner, M., 333

U.S. Department of Justice 326
Unitizing, 38-40, 41
Units of analysis, 21-22, 23, 30-32, 131-132
   PAT level, 21, 23, 30, 31, 56
   program level, 21, 23, 30, 31-32, 56
   scene level, 21, 23, 30, 31, 56
Unjustified television violence, 13, 15, 32
USA, 26, 29, 49, 50, 57, 100, 141, 175, 215
   advisories, 215
   Parental Guidelines, 215, 292

V-chip, 289, 318
   rating system, 179-180, 181

See also Parental Guidelines, TV
VH-1, 26, 29, 49, 50, 57, 100, 104, 141, 175, 216
   no advisories, 305
   Parental Guidelines, 216, 292
   reality programming, 236
Violence codes, 196, 312
   GV, 179, 180, 196, 310
   MV, 196, 310, 311
   V, 196, 310, 311
Violence Index, Gerbner's, 130
Violent depictions:
   accidents, 59
   behavioral acts, 20, 30, 58, 59, 63, 107, 114, 115, 246, 247
   credible threats, 20, 30, 58, 59, 107, 114, 115, 246, 247
   harmful consequences of unseen violence, 20, 30, 58, 59, 107, 114, 115, 246, 247
Visual violence, 227, 228, 229, 230, 231, 239, 241, 242, 243, 244, 247
   extent of injury, 248
   graphicness of consequences, 253
   impact beyond participants, 250, 251
   individuals harmed, 248
   intensity of acts, 252-253
   on/off-screen depictions, 252
   presence/persistence of harm/pain, 249
   reenactment-recreation, 252

See also specific types of reality-based programs

Walder, L. O., 16
Wallerstein, N., 340
Wang, C., 345
Warren, C. W., 326
Wartella, E., 25
Weapons:
   guns, 166, 171, 172, 173, 174, 247, 279
   presence, 13, 15, 76-78, 108, 279
   See also Means of violence
Weapons effect, 15
West, M., 325, 328, 333, 345, 351, 352
Whitney, C., 25
Widom, C. S., 329, 330
Wilson, B., 10, 12, 22, 30, 111, 128, 129, 130, 131, 132, 135
Wilson, B. J., 12, 331, 334, 346
Windhausen, J., 128
Wotring, C. E., 18

Yang, W. S., 338

Zelli, A., 325
Zillmann, D., 14, 18
Zuckerman, D. M., 327, 328
Zwerling, C., 327